The
GREAT GAME
in the
BUDDHIST
HIMALAYAS

PHUNCHOK STOBDAN

The
GREAT GAME
in the
BUDDHIST
HIMALAYAS

INDIA *and* CHINA'S
QUEST *for* STRATEGIC
DOMINANCE

VINTAGE
An imprint of Penguin Random House

VINTAGE

USA | Canada | UK | Ireland | Australia
New Zealand | India | South Africa | China

Vintage is part of the Penguin Random House group of companies
whose addresses can be found at global.penguinrandomhouse.com

Published by Penguin Random House India Pvt. Ltd
7th Floor, Infinity Tower C, DLF Cyber City,
Gurgaon 122 002, Haryana, India

First published in Vintage by Penguin Random House India 2019

10 9 8 7 6 5 4 3 2

This book is a work of non-fiction. The views and opinions expressed in the
book are those of the author only and do not reflect or represent the views and
opinions held by any other person.

This book is based on a variety of sources including published materials and
those collected through interactions of the author with persons named in the
book. It reflects the author's own understanding and conception of such
materials and/or can be verified by research.

The objective of this book is not to hurt any sentiments or be biased in favour
of or against any particular person, region, caste, society, gender, creed, nation
or religion.

ISBN 9780670091393

Typeset in Adobe Garamond Pro by Manipal Digital Systems, Manipal
Printed at Replika Press Pvt. Ltd, India

www.penguin.co.in

Contents

Acknowledgements

This book is an attempt to provide an overview of the political and strategic process at work in the Buddhist Himalayas. While trying to understand the various intricate issues in the region, an attempt has been made to trace the Tibetan factors that impinge on India. The book is mostly about identifying critical points that are important for evolving a sound Indian policy towards this strategic Himalayan region.

The book does not in any sense purport to be an academic endeavour on Buddhist, Tibetan or Himalayan studies but merely a narrative as well as an analytical account—a result of my own self-education and understanding gathered through extensive interactions with wide sections of people all over the Himalayas, including in Nepal and Bhutan. The book contains aspects that are critical for enhancing India's further understanding of the complexities of the Buddhist Himalayas.

While writing the book, I have largely relied on official sources and vernacular media reporting. Some of the points identified as well as analysed are a result of my participation in various conferences, seminars and discussion held in the region over the years. Some of the impressions I have gathered are based on personal visits to various places in Sikkim, Bhutan, Himachal Pradesh, Arunachal Pradesh, Nepal and West Bengal.

Being a native of the Himalayan region has definitely helped in writing this book. The facts and opinions expressed here are my own and do not necessarily reflect the views or position of the government. Assumptions made within the analysis are also not reflective of the position held by the departments and institutions where I have served in the past.

Let me first thank Swati Chopra, my editor at Penguin Random House India, whose excitement over the subject was a driving force for writing this book. I would not have indulged in writing such a manuscript but for her insistence. She has been instrumental in my being able to share my views and perspective on an issue of critical importance to Himalayan and Indian security. I am grateful to Shreya Chakravertty for the time she spent in copy-editing and minutely going through the manuscript. I appreciate her guidance.

I wish to thank everyone who gave me valuable inputs for understanding the issues, especially Dr M.S. Pratiba for helping me collect material and translate articles from Chinese into English. I must also thank my daughter Shumzin Wangmo for helping me arrange meetings with various organizations and experts in Delhi and other cities.

I must also express gratitude to my siblings, my wife, Rigzin Yangdol, and my daughters, Nansel Odbum and Shumzin Wangmo, for their constant love and support. And finally, I must also acknowledge the encouragement and affections extended to me by my former colleagues at the IDSA, especially Ms Prabha Murthy, Ms Shabonti Roy Dadwal, Dr Uttam Sinha, Dr Rajiv Nayan and Dr Ashok Behuria.

Preface

The Himalayas has been a theatre of competition by proxy between India and China for over half a century now. The two countries have been locked in a long-standing unresolved border dispute in this extensive mountain range that stretches from Ladakh to Arunachal Pradesh. It has witnessed dramatic military stand-offs that have not turned bloody since November 1962. This aside, China's meddling with Himalayan river flows, especially the diversion of the Brahmaputra and Sutlej waters for hydroelectric dam construction, has frequently chafed India. India's concerns also include China's increasing footprint in Nepal—long regarded as part of the former's sphere of influence.

The military dimension of the Himalayas, especially China's systematic building of infrastructure, means for reconnaissance and surveillance and operational capabilities, has remained a part of India's security discourse for decades. The US Department of Defense has occasionally been cautioned about China's increasing troop build-up along the Indian border in addition to it establishing 'naval logistic hubs' in Pakistan.

Very little is known about the pattern of other shadowy wars that are non-military in nature, launched by both sides in the Himalayas; these are not easily discernible but have an equally powerful impact on the shaky balance of Himalayan security.

China has been standing by Pakistan to destabilize the Kashmir Valley through proxy sponsorship of terrorist activities and by consistently blocking the listing of Pakistan-based terrorists in the United Nations (UN) list. In the eastern Himalayas, China has been playing the religion card to claim the Tawang region from India. The Chinese have also openly supported various insurgent groups, including the United Liberation Front of Assam (ULFA).

In the central Himalayas, China supported the Maoist insurgency during the civil war in Nepal during 1996–2006. It continues to influence the people of Nepal to undercut their natural affinity with India.

While China also faces problems both in its Xinjiang province and the Tibet Autonomous Region, so far no direct Indian involvement has been observed in either. India has been engaged in a shadow-boxing game by holding on to its 'Tibet card' for almost six decades. In 2016, New Delhi tried to add the Xinjiang card to its arsenal by issuing a visa to an Uyghur activist to attend the Eleventh Inter-ethnic/Interfaith Leadership Conference organized by Dharamshala. For the moment, though, China seems to be in firm control of both Tibet and Xinjiang, and there are no visible signs of it facing any major challenges on either of these fronts. Of course, one cannot predict what will happen in the longer run.

According to conventional wisdom, the Indian Himalayan region at least is peaceful, and this freedom of religion and democracy has ensured stability on our side of the mountain range. But, sadly, this is no longer the case. The Indian Himalayan belt from Tawang to Ladakh has been subject to a string of incendiary events which are threatening to pitchfork the region into crisis.

The Indian Buddhist Himalayan complexity is fast changing and could be a source of considerable concern for India's security. In part, this seems to be arising from an excessive Tibetan influence ('Tibetanization') in the Himalayas via a gradual taking over of Indian institutions by Tibetan lamas in the Buddhist Himalayas. Worryingly, more powerful lamas are seen setting up their parallel sectarian networks and infrastructure from Ladakh to Arunachal Pradesh. They have also brought along their cultural and sectarian affiliations, differences and discords (intrinsic to Tibetan politics) that could potentially destabilize the Indian Himalayas.

The long-term presence of Tibetan refugees in India and the future of the institution of the Dalai Lama have created a sense of uncertainty. The Dalai Lama has already indicated that he would possibly take his next rebirth in India. Even for the main stakeholder, the US, to play Tibet politics, requires controlling the Tibetan leader's next reincarnation. This would mean the Tibetan issue will continue to create a situation to make the Himalayan region a bigger geopolitical tinderbox. In the process, India's own Buddhist institutions are speedily undermined to the detriment of India's interest. This is where China would try to win both the Tibetan and the Buddhist Himalayan game.

The Buddhist Himalayas will continue to remain a contested geo-cultural landscape between the competing narratives of India and China. However, in the current scenario, India's interests in the Buddhist Himalayas remain even more compromised than during the colonial period, when British strategists were able to play the Himalayan game more perceptively.

The British could understand the dynamic interplay between the Tibetans vis-à-vis Himalayan Buddhism, especially the devotional power of various sectarian groups within Lamaism, to achieve the results they desired. They created 'buffer zones' and an 'Inner and Outer' defence line for protecting its Himalayan frontiers.

However, in the current situation, India seems to lacks sufficient wherewithal to understand the critical interplay between Buddhism and the Himalayas, and this has weighed heavily on the minds of the Dalai Lama and his government-in-exile. Of late, the 'Tibet card' is being redefined, albeit on the grounds of Buddhist diplomacy.

The geopolitics of the Himalayas has become more obscured ever since the mantle of India's Tibet–China policy has fallen into the hands of the Americans. The Tibet issue has already overshadowed the Himalayan identity, which has served to further blur the Indian frontier outlook. In contrast, the Chinese may have been thinking about playing the reverse strategic depth policy by leveraging the critical interplay between Buddhism and the Himalayas.

In the post-1950s period, China never viewed the Himalayan ranges as a barrier, but rather a bridge to create additional spheres of influence.

Gone are the days when India exercised a complete stronghold over the Himalayan region. If the developments so far have proven anything, China has gradually and successfully expanded its influence in Nepal.

Beijing has even been setting its gaze on Bhutan through various diplomatic means, not completely without success. The Bhutanese public perception about China certainly seems to have undergone a substantive change over the years.

China also has its eye on other parts of the Himalayas which are equally fertile places for Chinese influence to grow because of their proximity to Tibetan culture.

There are already direct and visible pointers of the Chinese beginning to harness Tibetan resources for steering the Himalayan game in their favour. In fact, the entire belt has witnessed an intense process of Tibetanization, from the point of view of cultural as well as political mobilization. Most Indian monasteries have already fallen under the control of Tibetan lamas.[1]

The Central Tibetan Schools Administration (CTSA)[2] under the Ministry of Human Resource Development runs sixty-seven schools across India for the education of Tibetan children living in India. In the name of preserving and promoting Tibetan culture, they are teaching the entire history of Tibet rather than emphasizing Indian history and literature. The Tibetan Children's Villages are following the same pattern.

Most of the issues are seemingly steered by a Tibet-oriented agenda, be it sectarian, linguistic or political. For example, the agenda of getting the Bhoti (Tibetan) language included in Schedule VIII of the Indian Constitution was initially set by Dharamshala through its proxies from the Himalayan region. The move is gaining momentum and being embedded in the agenda of local political parties. In fact, the Dalai Lama and other Tibetan institutions have become rallying platforms for the Himalayan people to assert their cultural causes.

The other critical points include a subtle insertion of Tibetan sectarian history, culture and religion in the curriculum of government schools. This has been achieved successfully in Ladakh. Similarly, in 2017, Arunachal Pradesh chief minister Pema Khandu also talked about popularizing and teaching Bhoti to people, especially in schools. And here, it is difficult to imagine why the further intensification of Tibetan culture and language in the area will not be leveraged by China.

Clearly, then, the Tibetan presence in the Himalayan region cannot be dismissed as a mere political incident. It is the result of a brilliant strategy and flawless execution of China's strategy. In fact, despite all the rumblings, they seem quite at ease with the silent movement launched by the Tibetan lamas with their easy-going demeanour. It is rather both low in intensity and cost but high in geopolitical returns. Beijing will find it essential to reflect these in its policy thinking in the future.

In fact, the 2017 Doklam crisis brought into focus what will be one of the most difficult issues in the Himalayas in future—the tensions rising from conflicting territorial claims by both India and China in the Himalayan region over history, culture and trade.

All these events are unfolding at a time when the Western romance with Tibetan Buddhism is gradually fading even as India is forced to watch the ensuing developments askance. More seriously, India's ability to deal with the Buddhist Himalayas vis-à-vis China only through the prism of military power is unlikely to be sufficient. India particularly seems to have failed to grasp the dynamic interplay between sectarian affiliation and power politics—between the Tibetan plateau and the political landscape in the Indian Himalayas. It is a case of missing the woods for the trees. Clearly, understanding the Tibetan polity in India requires much more than bureaucratic bean-counting.

This book tries to deal with the complexities of the Buddhist Himalayas—the interplay between religion and politics, the sectarian divides, the historical turning/rift points, and the Himalayan linkages with Tibet—from a geopolitical perspective only. It tries to take into consideration the overriding power of the conflicting cultural interests that are linked to the geopolitical interests of both China and India. At the same time, the book suggests how Buddhism could become a potential source for recultivating awareness towards an India–China congruity in the current context.

1

A Profile of Himalayan Buddhism

The Himalayas and Buddhism are almost synonymous, for the Buddha himself was born in the foothills of the Himalayas. There are references to Buddhist missionaries who were sent to the region by Emperor Ashoka. The early Indian Buddhist sutras probably came to the Himalayas in the second century, when Buddhism was spreading into China and Central Asia.

The fourth and fifth centuries onwards, the Mahayana tradition was introduced by Acharya Vasubandhu and others in places like Nepal. There was further transmission during the Amshuvanna period (AD 576–620), in addition to the Mahasanghika Buddhist missionaries who made their presence felt thereafter.

However, the real impact came when the famous logician Acharya Santarakshita (AD 705–62), a product of the Nalanda monastery, passed through the Great Himalayas. He also visited Tibet in the year 743.

It was later in the eighth century that the legendary Indian Tantric guru Padmasambhava profoundly sowed the seeds of the Indian Vajrayana form of Buddhism in the Himalayas. Padmasambhava ('lotus-born') is popularly thought to have been born in Oddiyana (modern-day Swat Valley in Khyber Pakhtunkhwa), then a hub of northern Buddhism. However, another legend has it that Oddiyana referred to ancient Odisha or Odra, Odivisa, Utkala and Kalinga.[1] Most historiographers suggest that it was Odisha which actually gave birth to the Tantrayana form of Buddhism in the first century AD and continued to flourish up to the seventh and eighth centuries.

Nyingma, Kagyu, Gelug, Sakya

Historian Bimalendu Mohanty[2] says that the Tantrayana form of Buddhism that developed in Odisha included the Buddhakapalatantra propounded by Saraha, the Hevajratantra propounded by Kambalapada and Padmavajra, the Samputatilaka propounded by Luipa, and the Sahajayana propounded by King Indrabhuti's sister Laxmikara.

It is said that Padmasambhava was an adopted son of Indrabhuti, the king of Sambala (Sambalpur), who had synergized all these forms of Tantrayana Buddhism into the Vajrayana. Indrabhuti's sister Laxmikara is said to have founded the Sahajayana. Padmasambhava married Princess Mandarava of Jahore (Keonjhar), who helped the former attain Mahasiddhi in the Sahajayana.

The type of Tantrayana Padmasambhava practised was esoteric and wrathful. The Mahayana Buddhists give a primordial status to Padmasambhava, even considering him to be the Second Buddha.

Padmasambhava's cult practice was termed Nyingmapa ('the oldest one'), which is actually the mother of all other esoteric traditions that developed later. Padmasambhava went to Tibet at the invitation of his brother-in-law, Shantirakshita, who had gone there earlier. Padmasambhava established the first Tantric centre, or 'Samye', in Tibet after subduing evil spirits as well as the local Bonpo (animistic) followers. He spent a long period in the Himalayas where he performed several miraculous acts and revealed sacred treasures. In fact, the religious histories of the Himalayan regions (Bhutan, Sikkim, Ladakh, Nepal and Monyul) are associated with his legendary acts and Tantric miracles. Padmasambhava's legacy remains the religious foundation of the people of the entire Himalayan range.

His twenty-five major disciples worked to disseminate Padmasambhava's tradition. Later, the Nyingma school faced persecution in Tibet but continued to thrive in the Himalayas.

In Nepal, Padmasambhava is known as Oddiyana Acharya, and elsewhere in the Himalayas he is known as Guru Rinpoche.

Later, more Vajrayana Tantric teachings of Indian Mahamudra were introduced in the upper Himalayan regions by two Buddhist masters, Marpa (1012–97) and Milarepa (1052–1123). They traced their practices to the teachings of Bengali saints Tilopa (988–1089) and Naropa (1016–1100).

Their teaching lineages came to be known as Kagyu (oral transmission), which took deep roots in the region. In fact, the sacredness of many places and mountains in the Himalayas are associated with Marpa and Milarepa.

The Kagyu lineage was further developed by their disciples into four major and eight minor tradition holders and spread all over the Himalayan belt. Among the main schools of the Kagyu lineage were Karma Kagyu, Drukpa Kagyu and Drikung Kagyu. Their approaches differ slightly from one another but they follow the main teachings of the Indian adepts Tilopa and Naropa. Each of these Kagyu sects has its own spiritual leaders. The Gyalwang Karmapa is the head of the Karma Kagyu school, Gyalwang Drukpa is the head of Drukpa Kagyu, and Kyabgon Chetsang Rinpoche is the head of Drikung Kagyu.

By the eleventh century, other Indian masters such as Atisha Dipamkara of Vikramashila also reached Tibet and introduced a more refined version of Buddhism. Atisha emphasized monastic values and 'mind training' as per the sutras. His famous treatise *Bodhipathapradeepa* (Lamp for the Path to Enlightenment) became popular in Tibet for it strongly prohibited monks from practising Tantra.[3] Later, his disciple Dromton established the Kadampa sect in Tibet which followed Atisha's teachings of Lojong (mind training) and Lamrim (stages of path). The Kadampa tradition continued for 300 years until a Tibetan master, Tsong Khapa (1357–1419) from Amdo (Qinghai), established the Gelugpa sect in the fourteenth century.

Tsong Khapa probably synergized the key teachings of Kadampa with the Sakya Tantric teachings. He emphasized monasticism, celibacy, scholarship and adherence to Vinaya (monastic discipline). Tsong Khapa's philosophical elucidation of 'the Stages of the Path' (Lam Rim Chenmo) is key to the Gelug tradition.

The Gelugpa sect grew phenomenally in Tibet after three monasteries—Ganden (1409), Drepung (1416) and Sera (1419)—were set up as great centres of learning.[4]

From the seventeenth century, the Gelugpa sect became more popular after Gushi Khan of Qusot Mongol helped the Fifth Dalai Lama establish the Ganden Phodrang Tibetan regime in 1642. Later, the Qing rulers also promoted the Dalai Lama as the political and religious head of Tibet. Thereafter, both the Dalai Lama and the Panchen Lama remained valued intermediaries or tools for the Qing Empire's expansion from 1720 until 1912.

The Qing rulers expanded the geographical reach of the Gelugpa not only within Tibet but also in Mongolia, Buryatia, Manchuria, China proper, Yunnan and northern Burma. Thus, Gelug history is largely based on the history of the Qing Empire's expansion.

However, the Gelug authority that spread from Tibet in the north (perhaps due to political reasons) had historically failed to exert influence on the people of the Himalayan region, with the exception of some pockets where it was established by the use of political and military force during the Mongol–Manchu rule of Tibet.

Padmasambhava's Buddhist teachings that laid emphasis on mantra rituals and exorcism continued to be the mainstay of the Himalayan religious tradition. Apart from Nyingma, the Kagyu tradition of Vajrayana Buddhism comprising the Karma Kagyu, Drukpa Kagyu and Drikung Kagyu schools has been traditionally patronized and followed by the rulers of Monyul, Bhutan, Sikkim, Nepal and Ladakh.

A sprinkling of members of the Sakya (grey earth) order is present in the Himalayan belt. It was founded in 1073 by a member of the aristocratic Khon family and was based on the teachings of the great Virupa. The Sakyas were known for great scholarship. They thrived on trade as they were also patronized by local rulers in Tibet. The great Sakya Pandita, known for his expertise in magic rituals, was invited to the Mongol court in the twelfth century.

The Sakyas maintained their lineage by birth, and the dynastic leaders were used as respected intermediaries by the Mongols.

After Sakya Pandita died in 1251, his son Dogon Chogyal Phagpa became the overlord of Tibet. In 1253, Kublai Khan invited Sakya Pandita's nephew to become the religious patron of the Yuan Dynasty.

The Sakya sect is non-controversial and enjoys legitimacy among the Tibetan Buddhist schools as one of them. The head of the Sakya order, Sakya Trizin, is considered second only to the Dalai Lama in the Tibetan spiritual hierarchy. The sect still maintains a familial lineage, and the headship is chosen not by reincarnation but by inheritance from father to son or from uncle to nephew.

The last Sakya head, Ngawang Kunga, served as the Forty-first Sakya Trizin, becoming the longest reigning head. He lived in

Dehradun and New York. The current Forty-second Sakya Trizin, Ratna Vajra Rinpoche, also known as Kyabgon Gongma Trizin Rinpoche, lives in the United Sates.

Nepal and Sikkim

The outline of the Himalayan landscape revolves around the legend of the original Nyingmapa tradition established by Guru Padmasambhava and its subsequent offshoot Kagyu lineages. For example, in Nepal, Nyingmapa monasteries are scattered throughout the northern belt—such as Humla, Mugu, Dolpo, Mustang, Manang, Gorkha, Rasuwa, Dolakha, Solukhumbu, Sankhuwasabha and Taplejung.[5]

Similarly, different variants of the Kagyu order have an overwhelming presence in the Himalayan region. The Drikung Kagyu monastery is located at Halali near Humla. The Sakyas and Kagyus have a dominant influence in the adjoining areas of Manang and Mustang. The Drukpa Kagyus are dominant in Gorkha, Rasuwa and Sindhupakhowk. Similarly, the Karma Kagyus also have a significant presence in Nepal.

It was only after the flight of the Fourteenth Dalai Lama from Tibet that the Tibetan Gelugpa lamas moved into this part of the Himalayas. They are largely concentrated in the Kathmandu Valley, especially around the Swayambhu and Bodhnath stupas. According to Min Bahadur Shakya, Tibetan forms of Buddhism are rapidly growing in Nepal with considerable financial support from outside, perhaps China and overseas Chinese citizens.

At the same time, the Newar form of Buddhism, which is the last representative of Indian Vajrayana Buddhism, has undergone a rapid decline. Newar Vajrayana Buddhism traces its lineage from the Siddha tradition of Nalanda and Vikramashila.[6] In fact, the Bahas and Bahis are in 'ruins and in a dreadful state of dilapidation', whereas the rare Buddhist manuscripts and texts have been smuggled out from the Himalayan regions.

Legend has it that the ethnic Lepchas of Sikkim (who have a close affinity with the Khasis of Meghalaya) were influenced by the teachings of Padmasambhava in the eighth century. Later, in the twelfth century, a prince from eastern Tibet came to settle in Sikkim, or Denzong (valley of rice) as it was originally known. He set up the Khye Bumsa Dynasty in Chumbi Valley. In the thirteenth century, the Khye Bumsa family inherited the kingdom of the Lepcha king Thekong Tek as well.

In the seventeenth century, persecution of the Nyingmapa sect in Tibet led to many followers of the Padmasambhava tradition to flee Tibet and seek refuge in places like Sikkim and Bhutan. After Lhastsum Chempo Rimpoche escaped persecution at the hands of the Gelug sect in Tibet, Sikkim became a hub of the Nyingmapa order.

In 1642, a descendant of Khye Bumsa, Phuntsog Namgyal, established the first Chogyal theocracy in Yuksam, and his rule extended from Chumbi Valley in the north to Ha Dzong in Bhutan, the Arun River in Nepal and the Jalpaiguri area in Bengal.

The Kagyu order has its own history in Sikkim. The Rumtek monastery (*rum theg dgon pa*), for example, was originally built in Sikkim on the direction of Changchub Dorjee, the Twelfth Karmapa Lama, in the mid-1700s.[7] He had to come to India and Nepal due to the sectarian strife in Tibet.[8]

Rumtek became a major seat of the Karma Kagyu lineage after Ranjung Rigpe Dorjee, the Sixteenth Karmapa, took refuge in Sikkim in 1959. He received the support of Sikkim's royal family and the general public to rebuild the Rumtek monastery which was lying in ruins. Currently, Rumtek is the largest Karma Kagyu monastery in India.

More than 200 monasteries or gonpas belonging to the Nyingma and Kagyu orders are scattered all over Sikkim. Some of them are related to travels in the region by Ugyen Rinpoche, as Padmasambhava is known here.[9] In north Sikkim, the Chawang Ani monastery located near Phensang was built during the reign of Chogyal Tshudphud Namgyal. Tsemo Rinchenthang is another old monastery built in 1651. The Phensang monastery was built in 1721 during Jigme Pawo's time. Other known Nyingma monasteries in north Sikkim include Palden Phuntshog Phodrang, Thonglung, Tingbung Rigdzn Tharling gonpa, Ringyim or Rigon Rigdzin Tharling gonpa, Phodrang gonpa, Lingtem gonpa, Lachen and Lachung.

In east Sikkim, the famous Enchey monastery was built during the reign of Thutob Namgyal (1874–1914). Sanga Chelling, built in 1697, is the second-oldest Nyingma gonpa in Sikkim. The Sinon monastery was built in 1716. Other major Nyingma sites include Rhenock, Khatok and Sang. In west Sikkim, the Dubdi monastery near Yuksom was built in 1700 during the time of Chakdor Namgyal. Khechopri, Melli and Tashiding are important Nyingma monasteries in west Sikkim.

The Pemayangtse monastery in Gyalshing is a major centre of the Nyingma school. All Nyingma monasteries in Sikkim are subordinate to it.

Similarly, in south Sikkim, the Namchi monastery was built during the reign of Chogyal Gurmed Namgyal (1717–33), and the Kwezing monastery was built at the time of Chogyal Thutob Namgyal (1874–1914). Other Nyingma monasteries in the south include the Ralong gonpa, Bermoik gonpa, Dalling gonpa, Yangyang, Simik and Hee Gyathang monasteries.

Sikkim's Buddhist landscape therefore reflects the religious tradition set up by Guru Padmasambhava, or Ugyen Rinpoche as they call him. Besides, the Karma Kagyus have gained a stronghold in Sikkim which makes the entry of non-Kagyu sects rather difficult. In fact, this could be one of the reasons the sect is in a constant state of flux.

Bhutan

Bhutan historically formed a part of Lho-Mon (southern Monyul). Until the seventeenth century, several aspects of Tantric mysticism and the politics of reincarnation shrouded Bhutanese linkages with Tibet.

In 1616, a monk, Ngawang Namgyal (1594–1651), a hereditary prince of the traditional Drukpa seat of the Ralung monastery in Tibet, fled to present-day Bhutanese territory. Ngawang Namgyal wanted to establish an independent state of his own on the basis of Drukpa lineage.

Upon reaching Monyul (present-day Tawang), he built his first *dzong* (fortress) at Simtokha in 1627. In 1629, Ngawang Namgyal had to face a military attack from the Tibetan king Karma Tenkyong. In 1634, Shabdrung triumphed in the second Tibetan invasion called the Battle of Five Lamas. Finally, in 1637, Ngawang Namgyal was able to establish Druk Gyalkhap or Druk-Yul (Nation of the Thunder Dragon) as an independent state.[10]

In 1639, Karma Tenkyong made another attempt to invade Bhutan, but in vain. This was followed by a joint Mongol–Tibetan invasion in 1643. It was the period when Gushi Khan, who patronized the Fifth Dalai Lama as Tibet's political head, launched a series of military campaigns against the rulers of Sikkim, Bhutan, Monyul and Nepal. The objective was to undermine the hold of the Nyingmapa and Kagyu orders in the Himalayan region and replace them with the Tibetan Gelug order.

A series of Tibetan–Mongol attacks against Bhutan continued till 1647. In 1714, the Tibetan troops of Lajang Khan attacked Bhutan from the Tawang side and destroyed many Nyingmapa and Kagyu religious establishments. Some of the old monasteries including the Ugyenling monastery were completely wiped out by the troops of Mongol general Sokpo Jomkhar. In the ensuing sectarian war, the Tibetan–Mongol army failed in Bhutan but succeeded in establishing the Gelug institution in the Mon-Tawang area.

Gradually, Ngawang Namgyal assumed the status of a god-king in Bhutan, equivalent to the Dalai Lama of Tibet. He came to be known as Shabdrung (*zhabs-drung* means 'before the feet of') or 'Dharma Raja' of the 'land of the peaceful dragon'.[11]

Drukpa Kagyu became the state religion of Bhutan, and Shabdrung ran the state through the *choe-sidnyiden* or dual governance system

Shabdrung Ngawang Namgyal (1594–1651), the founder of Bhutan

wherein a regent, Desid (Deb Raja), headed temporal affairs while religious affairs were supervised by the Je Khenpo (Dharma Raja).

The most learned members of the clergy occupied the post of regent. However, soon after the demise of the First Shabdrung (1651), the Deb Raja and Dharma Raja duo manipulated the successive Shabdrung incarnates and their rise to power for over 250 years. The institution of Shabdrung lasted until the British India government installed the present-day monarchy of Ugyen Wangchuk in Bhutan in 1907.[12]

The entire landscape of Bhutan is that of the Nyingma and Drukpa Kagyu traditions. The country has endless monasteries, with Taktsang, Kyichu Lhakhang and Rinpung Dzong in Paro Valley among the major ones.

The Cheri monastery near Thimphu was built in 1642 by Ngawang Namgyal. The Tango monastery in Thimphu was built in the thirteenth century. Many of the ancient monasteries are in Bumthang. The Kurjey Lhakhang monastery is one of the oldest ones directly associated with Padmasambhava's visit to the area.

The Tamshing Lhakhang monastery is where sacred masked dances and the Tshechu festival are held annually. Other important monasteries include Punakha Dzong which is a major remnant of the Drukpa period of Ngawang Namgyal and Terton Pema Lingpa. Lhuentse Dzong was originally built by Kuenga Wangpo and is dedicated to Padmasambhava.

Jambay Lhakhang in Jakar is said to have been built by the Tibetan king Songtsen Gampo. The Gangteng monastery is an important Nyingmapa monastery established in 1613 by the grandson of the great Bhutanese 'treasure finder', Terchen Pema Lingpa (1450–1521). The present Druk King Wangchuk Dynasty family traces its origin to the descendants of Pema Lingpa.

Monyul (Tawang)

Monyul, or the land of the Mon people, has a history dating back to 500 BC. By AD 600, it had come under the control of adjoining rulers. The ethnic Mons are today scattered all over the Indian Himalayas, Bhutan, Tibet and the Yunnan province of China. They don't consider themselves Tibetans as they speak a separate Tibeto-Burman dialect. The closest affinity the Indian Monpas have is with the eastern Bhutanese

Sharchokpa, or *shar phyogs pa.* There are several sub-Monpa tribes which speak their own dialects.[13]

The Monpas earlier practised animistic Bon rituals. But according to legend, Guru Padmasambhava arrived in Monyul in the eighth century while passing through Nepal. He was believed to have vanquished the evil mountain god Dsa-mun through his spiritual power.

The entire area is believed to be imbued with esoteric significance, for Padmasambhava also visited the mystic site where Karpotsang gonpa was built later. It was here that he revealed the sacredness of places such as Shou, Taksang, Domzang and Ugyenling. He is also said to have unveiled the sacredness of the exoteric realm of Le-go-shi (the 'four entrances to rightful endeavour') comprising Tsang Valley, Nye Valley, Lho Valley and Kongbu Valley.[14]

Much of the history of Monyul—what now constitutes the area east of Bhutan and west of Kemeng, called Shar-Mon and populated by Drukpas, Mons and Thongi (Shardukpens)—was interlinked. The Shardukpens formed a single cultural unit and were associated with Padmasambhava's revelations. This area was also linked to the Kagyu lineage founded by Marpa but traced to Bengali saints Tilopa (988–1089) and Naropa (1016–1100).

Some of the earliest Buddhist shrines, such as Domzang, Garam (Jangda), Kyimre (Jang) and Banga-janga, were founded by Gyalwang Karmapa Rangjung Dorjee in the late twelfth century. The famous Karpotsang gonpa was founded by Tertun Ranalingpa, a disciple of the Karmapa.

In an interesting development, the official website of *the* Karmapa (https://kagyuoffice.org/karmapa) flashed a headline in December 2016: After 400 years the Gyalwang Karmapa Returns to Arunachal Pradesh.[15] The Karmapa made a historic journey to Arunachal Pradesh in November–December 2016 where he said he was happy to revive the 900-year-old connection of the Karmapas with the area. The article said, '[H]is first incarnation, Dusum Khyenpa (1110–93) visited and founded monasteries here, and the relationship continued with the third and fourth Karmapas while the last visit was made by the ninth Karmapa, Wangchuk Dorje (1556–1603).' The Karmapa was warmly received by the Monpas, and he visited over twenty monasteries during his four-day visit.[16]

The lineages of the Nyingmapas and Karma Kagyus probably provided inspiration for the Drukpa Kagyu doctrine by Tsangpa Yeshey Dorjee (1161–1211) in the eastern Himalayas. Tsangpa Yeshey Dorjee's disciples, LoRespa and Gompo Dorjee, propagated two streams of Drukpa lineages which are now followed by the whole of Bhutan and Ladakh.

In fact, most of the ancient monasteries in Tawang, such as Ugyenling, Sangyling and Tsogyeling, were associated with either Nyingma master Ugyen Zangpo and Karmapa Rangjung Dorjee or Drukpa masters LoRespa and Gompo Dorjee. It is difficult to distinguish which lineages they carried because they were all destroyed by the invading Tibetan–Mongol army sent by the Fifth Dalai Lama and Gushi Khan in the seventeenth century.

Several details of Buddhist sectarian growth in Monyul are found in the 'Blue Annals' (Debter Sgonpo) completed in 1476, written by Lotsawa Zhunnu-pel.

The Tawang area lying south of the Sela Pass was also called Tso-sum (three areas).[17] For the Monpas, the place was critical because of its location to repel the Tibetan threat. This too was a stronghold of Kagyu followers, like other areas in the southern Himalayas.

But things changed when the Tibetans from the north sought to exert control over Lho Mon through numerous relentless military campaigns across the Himalayas in the seventeenth century. Since then, the Mon area was separated from the Shar-Mon of east Bhutan. T.S. Murty notes that Gelug missionary lamas had arrived here for proselytization in the sixteenth century.[18]

Tibetans argue that 'Monyul' is a Tibetan term and Lho Mon (southern Mon) includes Sikkim and Bhutan as well. Tibetan records included places inhabited by the Mons such as in Dakpa, Panchen and Lhekpo in the north and Nyima Tso Sum, Hoi Dhing Jan Dhak, Sangye Dzong, Numa Dhing, Pema Chogyue and Rong Nang in the east.[19] These practically covered the entire area from Bom-La in the north to the plains of Assam in the south.

Much of Monyul's later history is shrouded in religious mystery, but the Tibetans claim their links with the area from their first king, Ngytri Tsenpo (127 BC). More specifically, the Tibetan king Songtsen Gampo had built a temple, 'Zen Sa Lhek Po', in Monyul to tame numerous, supposedly supine female demons, Sermo-Gangyul-Dang-Nal-Wa or Semo-Gangyul, as the place was known for them.

Another legend goes that Tibetan king Tri Ralpachen exiled his brother, Prince Tsangma, to Lho Mon in the eighth century, where his successors ruled over the region. However, most of the areas around Dirang and Tawang were under the influence of the Karma Kagyu sect, apart from settlements in the region affiliated to the Nyingmapa sect such as in Pelingpa, Bodongpa and Brokpa.

Incorporation into Tibet

Monyul's history changed when the Tibetans successfully took control of it through military conquest at the time of the Fifth Dalai Lama, Ngawang Lobsang Gyatso (1617–1682).

Since the seventeenth century, Tawang (which literally means 'place chosen by horse') became the most mythical site in Monyul when a monastery was built to establish a Tibetan theological centre in the southern Himalayas.

Since then, the Ganden Phodrang government of Tibet under Qing patronage ruled Monyul through a Council Shi Drel comprising four members including the abbot. The council enjoyed both spiritual and temporal authority and exercised full administrative powers, collected taxes and maintained law and order through a network of monasteries that included Tak Lung gonpa, Sak Thing gonpa, Dor Lap gonpa, Tsu Gon Gya Gon and many others.

Some writers have alluded to a Tibetan disciple of the First Dalai Lama who arrived in Monyul in the fifteenth century.[20] Gelug missionaries had built monasteries here at the time of the Second Dalai Lama.

But in the seventeenth century, the Fifth Dalai Lama, Ngawang Lobsang Gyatso, backed by the Mongol and Qing Empires, was able to expand his celestial outreach here, outside the sphere of Sino-Tibetan power.

The story goes that when a Monpa, Lama Lodre Gyatso, who was a priest at the Tashilhunpo monastery in Lhasa, learnt about the attack of Lho-Mon by Drukpas of Bhutan, he rushed to seek help from Tibet's theocratic establishment.[21]

The Fifth Dalai Lama ordered Lodre Gyatso to quickly set up a branch of the Drepung monastery in Lho-Mon. Gyatso then returned to Merak, only to face stiff resistance from the Drukpas, who opposed the spread of the Gelug sect. By that time, the Drukpas had acquired greater power under Ngawang Namgyal, who established the Drukpa nation (Bhutan) in 1616.[22]

The Drukpas forced Lodre Gyatso to shift to Tso-sum (the place where Tawang is located). Tso-sum was then predominantly a bastion of the Nyingmapa and Karmapa sects, and had several famous monasteries including Gangardung gonpa of Karmapa and Thechpa gonpa of Nyingmapa.

The two home-grown sects foiled Gelug invasions but were later defeated by military troops sent by Ganden Phodrang headed by Mongol general Sokpo Jomkhar in 1647.

The Monpas built several dzongs to protect themselves against enemies; the famous ones include Thembang Dzong, Tsona Dzong, Senge Dzong, Dirang Dzong and Taklung Dzong.

Sokpo Jomkhar also waged similar wars against Bhutan (1643) within the context of the Tibetan struggle to establish Gelug supremacy. Some of the oldest monasteries of Nyingmapa and Karmapa in Tso-sum such as Ugyenling, Sangyling and Tsogyeling, were completely destroyed by the Tibetan–Mongol troops.

Lodre Gyatso was able to fulfil the wishes of the Fifth Dalai Lama and completed the construction of the Tawang gonpa in 1681. It was named Galdan Namgye Lhatse (paradise-celestial-divine)—'celestial paradise of the divine site chosen by horse'.

Lodre Gyatso then rushed to Lhasa to invite the Dalai Lama for the consecration ceremony. Due to his advanced age, the Dalai Lama probably failed to accept the invitation but promised to visit Tawang at a later time.

The Ganden Phodrang immediately brought Tawang under the monastic fold of the Drepung monastery in Lhasa. A senior monk and two monastic officials from Drepung were deputed as abbot and *niertsang* (attendants) to manage spiritual affairs, whereas the *dzongpen* (governor) of Tsona Dzong was ordered to take Tawang under judicial control.[23] According to the edict issued by the Fifth Dalai Lama in 1680, Monyul was administratively divided into thirty-two *tsho*s and *ding*s (territorial units).

With this, the Tibetans (under the administrative control of the Khushut Mongols and the Qing Dynasty) finally brought Monyul under the theocratic control of the Tibetan Gelug, with Tawang as its centre.[24] As a result, the local sects ceased to grow while many monasteries such as Ugyenling were brought under the control of the Tawang establishment.

Mystery of the Sixth Dalai Lama

The Tibetan move didn't stop there. More powerful esoteric modus operandi prevailed. Following the death of the Fifth Dalai Lama in 1682, the secular political head of Tibet, the tripa, Sanggye Gyatso, found out that the Fifth Dalai Lama may have been reborn in the Mon-Dawang area. The boy was Sange Tenzin, born in 1683 in a Monpa family in Ugyenling. He was brought to Sona and the news was kept secret; not even his parents were aware of it.

Although Sanggye Gyatso was aware of the demise of the Fifth Dalai Lama, the Qusot Mongol Khan and Emperor Kangxi of the Qing Dynasty doubted whether the Fifth Dalai Lama had actually died.

Somehow, Tripa Sanggye Gyatso was able to convince the Qing emperor that the Fifth Dalai Lama had died several years earlier and had been reincarnated already. Sanggye Gyatso informed him that the reincarnation was fifteen years old and should be recognized by the emperor. It is said that Emperor Kangxi first doubted Sanggye Gyatso's main contentions, but later agreed to go by his advice on the matter. The tripa also produced a letter of 'power transfer' which he received from the Fifth Dalai Lama before he had passed away. Since the letter was signed by the Fifth Dalai Lama, Kangxi couldn't refuse and conferred the title of 'prince' on Sanggye Gyatso along with a golden seal of authority.[25]

The Monpa boy was brought from Sona to Nanggarze in 1697, where he was tonsured by the Fifth Panchen Lama, who gave him a religious name: Tsangyang Gyatso. In the same year, he was anointed on the golden throne in Potala Palace as the Sixth Dalai Lama, Tsangyang Gyatso (1683–1706).

The enthronement was witnessed by the entire Tibetan clergy. The Qusot Mongol Khan, representatives of Emperor Kangxi headed by Sanggye Ngawang Quidain, presented gifts to the Sixth Dalai Lama at the ceremony.

It was significant for two reasons: a) for the first time, a layperson supervised the selection process of the Dalai Lama, and b), for the first time, the Qing emperor was formally involved in the authentication of the Dalai Lama.

The Mon-born Dalai Lama, Tsangyang Gyatso, turned out to be unusually talented. He was a poet, writer, singer and a lover of wine and women. He composed lyrics which became popular and were recited by people. He lived a short and desolate life.

In 1702, Lhazang Khan took over as the Khan of the Qusot Mongols. Lhazang was the grandson of Gushi Khan who had given the title of 'Dalai' to the Fifth Dalai Lama in 1641.

Soon, differences erupted between Tripa Sanggye Gyatso and Qusot Lhazang Khan. The conflict probably revolved around the authenticity of the Sixth Dalai Lama, whether he was actually a reincarnation of the Fifth Dalai Lama, and the fact that the search and acknowledgement of the reincarnate was confirmed only by the tripa and a layman against religious norms. The rift between the two widened and the tripa was captured and killed.

Tsangyang Gyatso was forced to renounce his monastic vows and return to life as a layman. However, the monastic community continued to consider him the true Dalai Lama despite his unusual behaviour. Qusot Lhazang Khan informed the Qing emperor, Kangxi, that Tsangyang Gyatso was an impostor. Kangxi ordered Lhazang Khan to assume power and asked him to send Tsangyang Gyatso to Beijing under guard.

Legend has it that Qusot Lhazang Khan plotted to take away the Monpa-born Dalai Lama from Potala Palace to Beijing in 1706.[26] An angry mob of lamas attacked the escorts, rescued the Dalai Lama and took him to the Summer Palace at Drepung. The Dalai Lama allowed himself to be taken to the imperial court but died on the way, near Gonggar Nur Lake in Qinghai (Amdo). He was only twenty-four. Rumour had it that he was killed, but the official version was that he died from illness. According to another story, he escaped and lived incognito thereafter in Qinghai, Gansu and Mongolia for a long period of time, and died in Alashan in Inner Mongolia. Another version says that he managed to escape from Tibet back to India and spent many years in Bihar. Possibly, he died near Rajgir.

The Monpa-born Dalai Lama's life became a mystery—indicative of the fact that even a Dalai Lama could become a pawn in the power struggle between clerical and temporal elite interest groups.

In 1686, Qusot Lhazang Khan found a monk from Kham, Ngawang Yeshe Gyatso, to be anointed as the 'true' Sixth Dalai Lama. The move was vehemently opposed by the lamas and other Mongol rulers in Qinghai. Chinese sources suggest that Emperor Kangxi went by Qusot Lhazang Khan's selection and granted a golden seal of authority to Ngawang Yeshe Gyatso.

But the problem didn't end there. The news immediately emerged that the Sixth Dalai Lama, Tsangyang Gyatso, had escaped from Lhazang Khan's custody and had been living in Lithang in Kham. Since the majority of Tibetans and Mongols of Qinghai had not recognized Yeshe Gyatso, the focus was on Lithang to look for the reincarnation of Gyatso.

The reason the theory of his being reborn in Lithang seemed probable was a prophecy. When he was taken away from Lhasa in 1706, Tsangyang Gyatso wrote the following words to his lady friend who lived in Shol: [27]

> White crane
> Lend me your wings
> I will not fly far
> From Lithang, I shall return.

True to this prophetic song, a boy called Galsang Gyatso was found in Lithang as the true reincarnation of Tsangyang Gyatso in 1708. Chinese scholar Chen Qingying also cites a verse from Gyatso's love songs;

> I borrow white crane's wings to fly in the sky
> I will not go very far and will return from Litang.

Another prophecy left by Tsangyang Gyatso said he would be reincarnated in a region south-west of Xining. Chen Qingying quotes another record of a monk at Lithang monastery who claimed to be possessed by the Oracle, Neqoin (Nechung), which told him that

Tsangyang Gyatso would be reincarnated in Lithang. Yet another story goes that the father of Galsang Gyatso was an attendant of the Sixth Dalai Lama and was close to the lamas of all the three major monasteries in Lhasa. Hence, it was not accidental that Tsangyang Gyatso was reborn in Lithang.

Whatever the truth might be, the reincarnated boy, Galsang Gyatso, was immediately whisked away from Lithang to the Tar monastery in Qinghai by Mongol leaders opposed to Qusot Lhazang Khan.

Internecine conflict broke out among various Mongol tribes over the Dalai Lama and their struggle to gain control over Tibet proper. Finally, according to Chen Qingying, Emperor Kangxi on 20 May 1720 dispatched his fourteenth prince to the Tar monastery, and in Amdo granted 'a golden seal of authority and golden sheets of confirmation along with abundant gifts to Galsang Gyatso'.[28]

In turn, Galsang Gyatso bowed before the Manchu prince and promised to visit Beijing to thank the emperor personally.[29]

Chinese sources quote that the imperial court granted Galsang Gyatso the seal and sheets as the Sixth Dalai Lama and hence the successor of the Fifth Dalai Lama.

With this decision, the titles given to the previous two candidates, (1) Mon-born Tsangyang Gyatso, found by Tripa Sanggye Gyatso, and (2) Yeshe Gyatso, found by Qusot Lhazang Khan, were both nullified. However, the Tibetan monastic community continued to regard Tsangyang Gyatso as the Sixth Dalai Lama, and Galsang Gyatso, born in Lithang, as the Seventh Dalai Lama.

All in all, the life of the Sixth Dalai Lama (born in Tawang) became controversial owing to his own personal behaviour and the way he was manipulated in a power struggle. However, many Tibetans felt that Tsangyang Gyatso was a great Tantric practitioner—his sexual energy found expression in one of his erotic verses.[30]

> Never have I slept without a sweetheart
> Nor have I spent a single drop of sperm.

In the short span of his life, the Sixth Dalai Lama wrote sixty poems. Some of his sensuous love poems are popular among the Tibetans and Chinese till today.

The Qing Dynasty had recognized the Tawang-born Sixth Dalai Lama in 1706; it also endorsed the enthronement of the Lithang-born Galsang Gyatso as the real Sixth Dalai Lama in 1720.

Beijing modified its position later. The Chinese author Chen Qingying writes that sixty years later, when the Sixth Panchen Erdeni came to Chende to congratulate Emperor Qinglong on his seventieth birthday in 1780, the emperor accepted Gyiangbai Gyamco (Tibetan: Jamphel Gyatso) (1758–1804) as the Eighth Dalai Lama. By implication, Galsang Gyamco naturally became the Seventh Dalai Lama in the records of the Qing Dynasty.[31] In turn, the Chinese had possibly endorsed (rectified in their records) the Monpa Tsangyang Gyatso as the Sixth Dalai Lama.

No wonder, then, that the Chinese embassy in New Delhi released a news report quoting the Chinese news agency Xinhua that the Tibetan government in April 2017 had opened a museum in Lhasa to commemorate the Sixth Dalai Lama. The museum had collections of publications, books, calligraphy, poems and records of the legendary Tsangyang Gyatso.[32] It said that 100 pieces of calligraphy and fifty poems from fans of Tsangyang Gyatso were displayed by way of contests. It also added, 'Gyatso wrote more than 60 poems in Tibetan that have been passed down for generations. He was also regarded as a victim of a political struggle, deposed by the Qing emperor, with his end remaining a mystery.' The museum was opened against the backdrop of the Fourteenth Dalai Lama's controversial visit to Tawang in April 2017.

The fact that the Sixth Dalai Lama was born in 1683 in a Monpa family in Ugyenling (Tawang) is a point of argument still pushed by both the Tibetans and Chinese today. To strengthen their point of view, Tibetans also cite numerous other Monpa figures who played an important role in Tibetan Gelug history, such as Merak Lodre Gyatso, a strong Gelug advocate, Sholkhang Dhondup Phuntsog, who served as minister in the Thirteenth Dalai Lama's cabinet, Dhak Tulku, who held the position of Ganden Tri, head of the Gelug sect in Ganden. While making these arguments, little or no mention is made about the Mongolian Sokpo Jomkhar's military invasion of Lho-Mon in the seventeenth century.

But the crucial aspect and one of the implications of Tibetan control was the virtual dissipation of the indigenous Himalayan Nyingma and Karma Kagyu sects. The Kagyupas were virtually extinguished; however, the Nyingma lamas till today continue to perform their Tantric rituals and practices such as warding off demons, sacred astrology, etc.

The loss of their sectarian stronghold paved the way for the Tibetan–Manchu–Mongol troika, a *cho-yon* (priest–patron)[33] relationship stitched around the Gelug order to gain full political control over the lower tracts of the Himalayas.

In the seventeenth century, the Tibetans had even secured brief control over parts of the Assamese plains. They couldn't overlook the area's significance for fending off threats posed to central Tibet from the southern Monpas and Drukpas who professed the Nyingma and Kagyu orders. The economic importance of Lho Mon was another factor. In his book *Hidden Treasures and Secret Lives,* historian Michale Aris[34] discusses the importance of establishing Tibetan control over Tawang: 'Not only did it provide the only direct corridor to the Indian plains lying completely within Tibetan territory, but the whole region was extraordinarily rich in natural products unobtainable on the Tibetan plateau. . . . Apart from the trans-Himalayan trade through the corridor which the government could carefully control to its advantage, the whole area was easily exploited for those natural products which lay in such heavy demand in Tibet.'

Writer Tsewang Dorji contends that the foundational facts of Monyul are 'unflinchingly' linked to Tibetan history—the key to understanding the narrative of Tawang rather than relying on 'numerous flimsy narratives made by Chinese, Indian and western scholars'.[35]

Ladakh

Buddhism arrived in Ladakh directly from northern India as early as the second century, at the same time as it was diffusing into Afghanistan, Central Asia and China. But it was after Padmasambhava travelled from north-west India to Ladakh and the rest of the Himalayan region that the Tantric version of Buddhism took root in Ladakh.

Evidence of Padmasambhava's journey can still be found in archaeological and historical inscriptions, including caves in Ladakh. The Takhtok monastery is one of them, where the Nyingmapa tradition founded by him is a living reality. For the Tibetans believe Padmasambhava travelled to Ladakh from Oddiyana (Afghanistan) and then to Kashmir, where his knowledge and skills earned him the name Sthira-mati, 'the intelligent youth'.[36]

On the historical part, Ladakh has scant information. It is said that in the ninth and tenth centuries, a breakaway prince of Tibet, Sklde Nyimagon, fled from Lhasa to Ngari in western Tibet. Prior to that, Ladakh was inhabited by Dardic people—called Brokpa in Ladakh.

Nyimagon settled in Maryul (the original name of Ladakh) and married the daughter of a local chieftain of the Thi Dynasty, Tashitsen. He had three sons: Paldegon, Tashigon and Detsugon.[37] The first, Paldegon, ruled over Maryul (Ladakh), Tashigon ruled the area around Mount Sangpo (Zanskar and Spiti), and Detsugon controlled the region of Guge, with Mount Kailash as its capital. The three regions are popularly known as *stod-mnga-ri-skor-gsum*, meaning water, mountains and grasslands.

In the middle of the sixteenth century, a local chieftain, Bhagan of Basgo, overthrew the earlier king of Ladakh and established his own dynasty called the Namgyal Dynasty, which survived until the Dogra ruler conquered Ladakh in 1834.

Kings Tashi Namgyal (1555–75) and Tsewang Namgyal (AD 1575–95) were able to consolidate Ladakh and extend the kingdom up to the border of Nepal. After Tsewang Namgyal died, his eldest son, Jamyang Namgyal, took the reins of the Namgyal Dynasty in 1595 and remained in power until he died in 1616. Jamyang Namgyal was married to a Muslim princess, Gyal Khatun, daughter of Baltistan's ruler, Ali Sher Khan Anchan.

Jamyang Namgyal and Gyal Khatun gave birth to Singge Namgyal, the 'Lion King', in 1570; his reign marked the greatest historical turn for Ladakh. He was enthroned soon after the death of Jamyang Namgyal in 1616.

The greatest king of Ladakh

Singge Namgyal proved to be the greatest king Ladakh had ever seen. After consolidating the western Himalayas into one political unit, he laid the foundation for the establishment of the Ladakh kingdom based on the Drukpa Kagyu lineage.

No doubt Singge Namgyal was an astute military commander. Even prior to his ascendancy to the throne, he was able to capture the strategic town of Rudok (now in Tibet) in 1614. The very next year, he conquered Spurangs (Burang) near the Nepal border. Following his father's death, he pursued a policy of vigorous expansion until he took complete control of the kingdom of Ngari—Guge (western Tibet)—by 1619. He annexed the kingdom of Guge in 1630. Singge was immensely disliked by the Tibetans, who called him *rdud-rgyal* or the 'evil king' of Ladakh.

By the end of the seventeenth century, Singge had expanded the kingdom of Ladakh to cover the widest territory in its history. By the time he died, his kingdom extended to the border of Nepal in the east, Baltistan in the west, Karakoram in the north, and Spiti–Zanskar in the south.

Singge Namgyal died in 1642 in Hanle, on his return from a battlefield in Tibet where he had fought against the invading Tibetan–Mongol army.

Courtesy of Chemrey gonpa, Ladakh

Gyalpo Singge Namgyal, king of Ladakh (1570–1642)

He pursued a far-sighted policy for the expansion of trade with neighbouring Tibet, Nepal, the Spiti–Kangra Valley and Punjab in the east and south. He paid greater attention to expanding Ladakh's trade with Kashmir to the west and Sinkiang (Hor-yul) to join the fabled Silk Road to the north.

He ushered in a new era of cultural and religious activities in his kingdom. Despite being born to a Muslim mother, he was a devout Buddhist. Like the Shabdrung Ngawang Namgyal of Bhutan, he was a devotee of the Ralung lineage of the Drukpa school. As a mark of respect, he offered legal rights over a series of monasteries near Mount Kailash to Bhutan's Shabdrung Ngawang Namgyal. These included Darchen, Kangri, Diraphu, Zuphu, Rizong, Chaskip, Yarigon-phu, Yazer, Somgu and Shara—located either at the foot of Mount Kailash or near Gartok.

The two rulers became closer to each other because of their shared faith. Ladakh's Namgyal Dynasty and Bhutan's spiritual leader, Kunkhyen Pema Karpo or the Fourth Gyalwang Drukpa, not only established a priest–patron relationship but also maintained a strategic tie to counter Tibetan expansionism in the Himalayas. A prince, Standzin (1570–1642) of Ladakh, in fact, rose to become the governor of Wangdi Phodrang in Bhutan and won the battle of Punakha against the invading Tibetan army. The Ladakh–Bhutan axis prompted the Fifth Dalai Lama to stage a brutal attack on Ladakh in 1684.

Respa

Singge Namgyal was an astute political thinker who wanted to carve out a kingdom to protect the autonomy of the Himalayan region vis-à-vis Tibetan hegemony. Probably in early 1620, he invited the famous Drukpa lama, Stagsang Respa Ngawang Gyatso, 'Tiger Lama', to Ladakh to become his preceptor and adviser. Ngawang Gyatso was born in 1574 in Tibet's Gyantse region and was a disciple of prominent Drukpa teacher Lhatsewa Ngawang Zangpo. Ngawang Gyatso set out on several trips across China and Central Asia. He visited Ladakh and Kailash and then returned to Tibet.

It is believed that Ngawang Gyatso spent a number of years meditating in Tsari, a sacred place near Namcha Bawa at the great bend of the Brahmaputra. While meditating in the Stagsang Valley, he met the Sixth Shamarpa Chokyi Wangchuk (1584–1630) who praised Ngawang Gyatso for his ability to subdue demon elements and gave him the nickname 'Stagsang Respa'. Ngawang Gyatso had written of a vision in Stagsang Valley according to which he would be charged with the well-being of Ladakh by a king whose name began with 'Singge'.

Later, in 1612, he set out on a trip to northern India to visit places associated with Naropa and Tilopa. He visited Jalandhar, Kashmir, Ladakh and Swat to follow the trail of the famous Tibetan Tantric scholar Orgyenpa Rinchen Pel (1230–93), whose travel record was widely known.[38]

Stagsang Respa, on his way to Afghanistan, passed through the Sutlej Valley to reach Punjab and Kashmir. He reportedly paused to meditate at Nagarkot temple in Kangra, which is said to be the abode of Vajravarahi. On his way back, Stagsang Respa spent a year in Zanskar hosted by a local ruler, Tsering Pelde. While there, King Jamyang Namgyal of Ladakh invited him to establish the Drukpa tradition in his kingdom. Stagsang Respa declined the offer but spent time in Gya village in Ladakh with Drungpa Sherab Zangpo, who was also a disciple of Lhatsewa.

In 1615, Stagsang Respa again headed to the Swat Valley but was kidnapped on the way and sold into slavery. Other Buddhist travellers saved him. A fellow traveller, Buddhanata, gave Respa the name 'Shymbo-natha'. Stagsang Respa also encountered a Buddhist yogini from Oddiyana named Pelanata who helped him join a party of traders to reach Swat.

In the Swat Valley, Stagsang Respa found only the remains of Buddhist monuments as most of the places had long been converted to Islam. He returned to Tibet via Kashmir and Ladakh in 1620.

Stagsang Respa became famous for his voyage to Oddiyana, and gradually people began popularly calling him 'Orgyenpa' (native of Oddiyana). A monument of Stagsang wearing Pathani headgear was built in Hemis and can still be seen by visitors.

Stagsang Respa wrote his travel account, and was presented to the Tsang king Karma Puntsok Namgyel (1597–1632). The king advised Respa to return to Ladakh, where he spent the rest of his life serving King Singge Namgyal. Together with Singge Namgyal, Stagsang Respa was able to lay a strong foundation for the Drukpa tradition in Ladakh.

They built major monasteries, palaces and shrines including the Hemis monastery and the Hanle monastery in 1630.

Singge was also responsible for the renovation of the Golden temple of the Tabo monastery in the Spiti Valley. The Chemrey monastery was built in 1642 in Singge Namgyal's memory following his death.

While Singge Namgyal aggressively promoted Buddhism, he also allowed the Muslim community to practise their own religion without disturbance. They were mainly Shia Baltis who came along with Singge's mother, and Kashmiri Muslim traders and artisans who were allowed to settle in Ladakh during the time of Jamyang Namgyal. It seems that Singge encouraged intensive confluence between Buddhists and Muslims in many areas of social life.

There is not enough research being done to ascertain whether Muslims were part of the ruling class. They did work as craftsmen, artisans, entertainers, soldiers and servants. The two communities

Shambu Nath, the founder and preceptor of the Hemis monastery, had studied in Swat Valley and returned to Ladakh wearing Pathani headgear in the 1620s.

acknowledged and respected each other's rights in all aspects of social and religious life.

The active partnership between Singge Namgyal and Stagsang Respa is still remembered. One wonders whether Singge Namgyal had other considerations than just religion in patronizing Stagsang Respa. He probably found in Stagsang qualities such as geographical knowledge and exposure to the outside world, especially an understanding of the affairs of Afghanistan, Kashmir, Punjab, China and Tibet.

In 2016, I thought of instituting the annual Ladakh Spalnyam celebration. The idea was to commemorate the 400th anniversary of the 'Lion King' Gyalpo Singge Namgyal (1570–1642), the 'Tiger Lama' Stagsang Respa (1574–1651) and Spon Namkha Spalgon—three great architects of historical Ladakh.

Battle for Ladakh

Like the Bhutanese ruler, Singge Namgyal despised the hegemonic tendency of the Tibetan Ganden Phodrang government headed by the Fifth Dalai Lama at the time. As previously explained, it was operating under the control of China's Qing Dynasty and its goal was to bring all Himalayan states into the Gelugpa fold.

Following Singge's death, his son Deldan Namgyal (1642–94) had to seek the help of Mughal emperor Aurangzeb to repel the invading Tibetan army of the Fifth Dalai Lama.

The Tibet–Ladakh–Mughal War of 1679 was fought between the Gelug Tibetan government and the Drukpa kingdom of Ladakh. The Tibetan Ganden Phodrang government under the Fifth Dalai Lama dispatched a military mission in 1679 under the command of a Zungar Mongol commander, Galdan Boshugtu Khan,[39] also known as Galdan Tsewang, who was a lama of the Tashilhunpo monastery in Lhasa. The aim of the war was to subjugate Drukpa rule and impose the Gelug order in Ladakh.

Galdan Tsewang first defeated the Ladakhi army, led by Sakya Gyatso, at Khanmar, and subsequently, other areas fell to it. However, the Ladakh king Deldan was able to hold on to the fortresses of Basgo and Tingmosgang for at least three years until he sought military intervention from the Mughal Empire. It is said that

Deldan was able to enlist Mughal support by promising to build a mosque in Leh.[40]

Aurangzeb extended complete military support to Ladakh to repel successive Tibeto-Mongol onslaughts. The support was extended through the Mughal army under Fidai Khan, the son of the Mughal viceroy of Kashmir, Ibrahim Khan. The Ladakh–Mughal army defeated the Dalai Lama's troops in the plains of Chargyal, near Nimoo village located 25 kilometres west of Leh.

It was rumoured that the Mughal Empire's assistance was based on the condition that the Ladakh king, along with his subjects, convert to Islam. But the fact remained that such a situation never prevailed in the ensuing period.

It is said that the Tibetan rulers always despised the sectarian affiliation between Ladakh and Bhutan. The kings of Ladakh and Bhutan followed the same Drukpa Kagyu tradition of the Ralung lineage. Their relationship extended beyond the sectarian bond to protecting the Himalayas from falling under the Tibet–China hegemony.

In their attempt to establish Gelug supremacy, the Tibetans used maximum brute force against Ladakh and Bhutan. It is said that at critical times Ladakh and Bhutan formed strategic ties to counter Tibetan expansionism. Prince Standzin (1570–1642) of Ladakh in fact rose to become the governor of Wangdi Phodrang in Bhutan and won the battle of Punakha against the invading Tibetan army.

It is said that the Ladakh–Bhutan axis prompted the Fifth Dalai Lama to once again stage a brutal attack on Ladakh in 1684 with the help of reinforcements from the Zungar Mongols. By then, the Mughals withdrew support to the Ladakh king after being paid off by the Fifth Dalai Lama.[41]

Deldan's son Delek Namgyal had no option but to seek an alliance with Bhutan. While Shabdrung Ngawang Namgyal was preoccupied due to an invasion by Tibet, he sent his representative Choje Mukzinpa to Ladakh.[42]

The Tibetans defeated Ladakh in 1684 and wrested away half its territory, including what is called western Tibet—covering Rudok, Guge, Kailash and Burang up to the Nepal border junction—which used to be integral parts of the Ladakh kingdom during the reign of Singge Namgyal.

Subsequently, Tibet compelled the ruler of Ladakh to sign the treaty of Tingmosgang[43] in 1684 after snatching a substantial part of eastern Ladakh (Guge and Purang)—almost half of its territory.

It is said that the Tibetan government in Lhasa and the Deva-Jung (the Grand Lama authority of Lhasa) had sought the help of the Sixth Drukchen Rinpoche Mipham Wangpo (1641–1717)—a Drukpa lama whose previous incarnation was the patron lama of the king of Ladakh to broker the 1684 peace treaty. According to Ladakhi scholar Dr Smanla,[44] the role of Mipham Wangpo in the peace treaty remained dubious and controversial. Wangpo probably negotiated the deal in Lhasa's favour as a result Deva-Jung authorized the Drukpa Lama to rule the entire Ngari-khor-sum region of eastern Ladakh comprising the Guge kingdom located near Mount Kailash. Consequently, Ladakh, through the treaty of 1684, was stripped of nearly half its territory. However, the Ladakh king retained his rights to collect the revenue of a few villages of Menser at the foot of Mount Kailash on the bank of Mansarovar lake.

But for the Mughal and Bhutanese military and political support, the whole of Ladakh would have been snatched by the Fifth Dalai Lama's government and by implication it would have been a part of China today.

The loss of territory to Tibet weakened Ladakh's economy and political independence and led to its fall to the Dogra maharaja Gulab Singh (1792–1857). By 1834, the Dogra general Zorawar Singh militarily subjugated Ladakh and dethroned the king, Tshespal Namgyal, and exiled him to Stok. It seems the Dogras wanted to recapture the lost territory of Ladakh from the Tibetans, but Zorawar Singh was killed by the Tibetan army at the mouth of the Sutlej.

However, as a result of the Ladakh–Tibet war, the affinity between Ladakh and Bhutan got stronger, which is evidenced in the several religious estates that were offered by the rulers of Ladakh to the Bhutanese in Menser, Zanskar and Ladakh proper. The Stakna monastery or 'Tiger's Nose', located 35 kilometres from the capital, Leh, established by Choje Mukzinpa, became the main seat of the southern Drukpa Kagyu tradition in Ladakh. The Stakna monastery retains all the artefacts and religious texts relating to Ladakh–Bhutan ties, including the ones gifted by Shabdrung Ngawang Namgyal.

Since the 1684 settlement, Ladakh's boundary has been confined to the existing territorial limits. But the entire context of the ongoing territorial dispute between India and China has its origin in the Tibetan invasion of Ladakh and the snatching of Drukpa monastic land and property by the Tibetan Gelug army. For example, the Chinese People's Liberation Army (PLA) continues to claim areas in Demchok (owned by the Hemis monastery) based on the assertion made by Tibet since the Fifth Dalai Lama in the seventeenth century. It is an irony that the forces that have seized hold of Indian territory in Ladakh are being viewed by India as a forfend against the threat to its interest—a strategic and historical paradox indeed.

Hemis gonpa and its sacred treasure

The Hemis monastery (*dgon-pa*) is now over 350 years old and follows an unbroken tradition dating back to the reign of Gyalpo Singge Namgyal (1570–1642) and his preceptor–founder Lama Stagsang Respa (1574–1651).

The duo built numerous monasteries, palaces and monuments including sculptures and paintings which continue to function as living museums of Ladakh's glorious past. The two great leaders had also patronized some of the best and brightest minds of the era—including poets, musicians, artists, philosophers and architects. Undoubtedly, the two were the architects of historical Ladakh and the period of the duo was considered as the golden age of Ladakh.

It is said that the Hemis monastery existed before the eleventh century and was linked to Naropa, the saint who founded the Kagyu sect. In the course of history, Hemis suffered, especially during the invasion of Ladakh by the Tibetan–Mongol ruler in the early seventeenth century.

A gonpa is a religious establishment, a place of worship. It caters to the religious and spiritual needs of the people, besides being a centre for education and learning. Families would send one of their sons to the monastery to lead a monastic life and follow the righteous path—a lifelong commitment to work for *dhamma*. Gonpas were supported by their *chin-dag* (patron). The king, nobles and individual households and communities affiliated to the monastery sustained its functioning.

Most Drukpa monasteries were supported by nearby villages but their followers would also come from far-flung villages. The Hemis monastery, for instance, is supported by many villages in all parts of Ladakh. They provide services to the monastery in the form of donation and work and by sponsoring rituals. The monks in turn provide religious services to village households. Each family has a household altar, the *chokang* (*mchod khang*), in which the monk performs monthly or annual rituals for the family. The chokang is a sacred space where offerings are made to the Three Jewels of Buddhism.

Apart from religious activities, the Hemis monastery also pursues agriculture and cultural, social and welfare activities.

The three large Drukpa Kagyu gonpas in hierarchical order in Ladakh are: Hemis gonpa, Chemrey gonpa and Hanle gonpa.

Hemis is the main seat where the central authority—the abbot—is based. But other gonpas also manage a large number of medium- and village-level monasteries including *lhakhang*s and chapels that are found in every Buddhist village in Ladakh. The village lhakhangs are attached to medium-level monasteries and they in turn are linked with a major monastery. A total of over 200 medium and small gonpas/lhakhangs are attached to the Hemis monastery.

The Hemis gonpa is the main headquarters where the central authority of the *chagzod* is based. The Chemrey gonpa has its own chagzod who supervises the administrative control of the monastery and its estate property.

A traditional administrative structure of management and governance which is more than three centuries old runs the affairs of the Drukpa estate. These customary guidelines were developed indigenously in the eighteenth century by Dadmokarpo, or Rgyalsras Rinpoche, who was a prince of Ladakh and later became the head of the Hemis monastery.

Three important drafts define the codes of governance written on the silk brocade clothes:

- Goshen Marpo, the red silk brocade fabric, and the *ye-ghon cha-yig* (rule enforcement catalogue) contains rules for monks who have taken ordination.
- Goshen Serpo, the yellow silk brocade fabric, contains the monastery's land-estate records, detailing the revenue from its land leased to *shaspa*s or tenants.

- Goshen Karpo, the white silk brocade fabric, contains the draft organizational structure of the Hemis monastery and guidelines for the administrative staff and their charter of duties.

The organizational structure of the Hemis monastery is rather extensive and hierarchical. It is embedded in monastic guidelines. A great deal of religious and non-religious duties and activities of the monastery's officials can be discerned from the Goshen Karpo code. The monastic order is also based on hierarchy and seniority. The importance of hierarchy is maintained through the seating arrangement of the monks during the assembly (*tshogs*).

Chief abbot/guardian

Lama Stagsang Respa is the chief abbot of the Hemis monastery. He was the founder and royal preceptor of the erstwhile kingdom of Ladakh. Stagsang Respa is an incarnate lama or Rinpoche who is chosen through the process of reincarnation. These accounts show that he holds the sole proprietorship of Hemis. He holds the chief administrative position and is responsible for managing the monastery and its extensive operations through his administrative staff.

However, currently, in the absence of the monastery's chief abbot Stagsang Rinpoche, the role of guardian is performed by His Holiness the Twelfth Gyalwang Drukpa, the supreme head of the Drukpa Kagyu school of Buddhism.

Chagzod (chief supervisor/administrator)

The chagzod holds the next administrative position. He is responsible for the entire administration of the gonpa. He is nominated by the chief guardian through seniority of position in the hierarchy or otherwise. The chagzod is mandated to manage all monastic affairs impartially and incorruptibly. The chagzod's mandate may last for life or until the synod releases him from his duty. The abbot can recommend the extension, acceptance or resignation of the chagzod's term of office.

Appointment procedures

Except for the chief guardian, all other positions are filled from the ordained monk gelong through seniority of position and qualifications. They are eligible for the various offices and administrative services. Usually, the officers are appointed for a period of three years. All senior monks acquire a wide experience of the main offices and monastic affairs.

The monastery's organization is well organized into two separate streams: one involved in religious matters and the other in financial administration.

Hemis is famous for its annual festival, Tse-chu, celebrated in honour of Guru Padmasambhava in June every year. The festival was instituted in the eighteenth century by Rgyalsras Rinpoche. Every year, the portrait of Dadmokarpo is put on display at the festival for all to admire and worship.

The festivities take place for two days and include highly choreographed ritual mask dances called *cham* performed by monks, which is a part of the Tantric tradition. The cham is directed by the *cham-pon* (ritual orchestra master). The dances are performed in the monastery's courtyard by a select group of resident lamas of the Hemis and Chemrey gonpas. They also make ritual offerings to wrathful tutelary deities (*yi dams*) or protectors (*srung ma*) of the monastery and the faith. The cham-pon performs a ritual dance during the annual ritual cake.

Drukpa lineage in Hemis

Currently, apart from the His Holiness Gyalwang Drukpa, the Hemis gonpa is also the abode of other Drukpa lineage masters such as the Gyalwa Dokhampa, Thugsey Rinpoche and many others.

Hemis is the main headquarters of all the Drukpa Kagyu gonpas where the central authority of the abbot or *the-tse* (seal of authority) is located. The seal is held by Stagsang Rinpoche. All sacred treasure chambers or stores are sealed once the annual stocks are taken. And once the chamber locks are sealed, the chagzod takes charge of their keys. Many of the chambers remain sealed by the abbot and cannot be opened until he returns.

Traditionally, the Hemis chagzod held administrative control of the Drukpa monasteries and their estates in Ladakh. Lately, the Chemrey gonpa has started appointing its own chagzod. But the Hanle gonpa still comes under the jurisdiction of the Hemis chagzod.

The monasteries affiliated to the Hemis gonpa are organized along geographical lines. A *kamsang* (zonal branch) controls several small village-level gonpas, chapels, lhakhangs, etc. Monks of specific regions cater to the households or chin-dags of those areas. The kamsangs take up the largest part of the monastery. The Hemis has five kamsangs spread over Ladakh which are responsible for running the smaller gonpas.

Each kamsang sends one senior representative to the central administration for duties for a specific period. They are in turn appointed as *nyerpa*s (managers) by the chagzod for revenue duties. In this way, the Hemis chagzod has five assistants or subordinates to perform administrative responsibilities.

The monastic administrative ranks include:

- Rinpoche (chief abbot/guardian)
- Chagzod (chief supervisor)
- Du-gner (guardian of treasures)
- Nyerpa (manager)
- Nyer-chung (assistant manager)
- Ngo-tsap (representative)
- Mgron-gner (chapel in-charge)
- Dge-bsko (disciplinarian/dean)

The Goshen Karpo draft envisages a wide range of administrative powers for the chagzod. He has control of the monastery's judicial and financial power. The chagzod holds the keys to the monastery's treasury and *zod-khang* (treasure chambers) including the *dzod-nag* (black chambers) where precious objects and belongings are kept. He is assisted by the *du-gner* (property/treasure in-charge or guardian of treasures) who is in charge of all the artefacts in the chapels, prayer halls, libraries, lhakhangs, etc. They keep track of the monastery's property.

Nyerpas (managers) deal with monastic affairs, which include some of the heaviest work in the monastery. The main nyerpa is in charge of finances, including supervising vast external purchases of provisions and other day-to-day needs. The junior nyerpa or nyer-chung (assistant manager) plays the role of butler and manages the main kitchen, bakery, buttery, pantry and other food-related work within the monastery complex. He also keeps account of daily purchases and expenditure incurred for the monastery's activities.

Nyerpas appointed for various kamsangs are also responsible for collecting annual taxes from the monastery's shaspas. They submit annual financial and tax collection reports to the chagzod. The records of income and expenses are kept by the chagzod as per the provision envisaged in the draft Goshen Karpo.

The chagzod has judicial power and represents a kind of court to which parties turn to in order to resolve all kinds of civil disputes. The chagzod and the du-gner also control estate matters and related legal issues. They discuss all disagreements and disputes on property matters. However, in case of a serious dispute, the matter is put before the abbot.

The chagzod in consultation with assistants makes lower appointments of monks to perform duties at smaller branches and sub-branches of the Hemis gonpa. The chagzod also appoints *ngo-tsaps* (representatives) who perform special tasks related to the monastery.

The monastery often constitutes a special committee for development and construction activities which would comprise several members including laypersons who can oversee the projects.

There are minor positions of responsibility in the monastery including that of cook, *gonyer* (doorkeeper), *chapri* (water-bearer), chapel caretaker, maker of offerings/cakes for altars and rituals, collector of offerings from worshippers.

The monastery also has full-fledged kitchen pantries, butlers, attendant staff, tea servers, worker monks and laymen or hired help that are responsible for providing meals for the community, in addition to skilled workers, artisans, craftsmen and painters.

The gonpa economy

Goshen Serpo consists of land records and revenues earned from rented and leased lands that belong to the gonpa, including land annually and permanently leased to shaspas. The land records are now synchronized with the government's revenue records.

The monastery owns large landholdings that include both agricultural and non-agricultural land. Many of these include fertile irrigated lands in villages that came into the possession of the gonpa through donations from rulers, patrons and village families over generations. The lands belonging to the monastery are widely scattered all over Ladakh.

As per monastery records, the Hemis gonpa owns 30,000–40,000 kanals of land. In measurement 1 kanal is equivalent to 0.125 acre. It is believed that Hemis owns almost 40 to 45 per cent of Ladakh's irrigated land.

In fact, the role of the Hemis monastery in the economy of Ladakh is extremely significant. The lands held by the gonpa are let out to farmers for crop cultivation or as pasture. The dwellers and leaseholders work and earn their living on the gonpa's land either as shaspa tenants or as agricultural labourers. The tenants pay some percentage of the produce to the monastery.

Traditionally, earned income consisted of revenues from leased lands and interest accruing from loans rendered to families. The loans taken in the form of wheat, barley, etc. for a specific period were repaid by dwellers with generally one-fifth extra as interest in addition to the borrowed quantity. Of course, the practice of farmers taking loans from the monastery has declined over the years.

The gonpa has a combination of instituted income accumulated from specific ritual sponsorships, offerings, donations, rites and ceremonies, and sponsorships from the chin-dag. Donations and offerings could be in the form of wheat, barley, barley flour, butter, wool and hides. These items are further sold or auctioned in villages to add to the monastery's economy.

Besides, the gonpa lets out spaces, land and building for commercial activities and for various enterprises so that the minor revenue earned from them can be utilized for the development, repairs and upkeep of the monastery.

Since Ladakh opened up to tourists in 1974, monasteries also earn revenue from tourist fees, which generate useful income in cash. This income is utilized for the maintenance of monasteries, monuments and stupas, as well as for supporting religious activities including the conduct and performance of important monastic rituals.

The idea of earning extra income is not for profit but in the interest of securing the monastery financially. The idea is to keep it in good condition and pass it on to the next generation. However, maintaining a monastery is not an easy task, especially given the increasing cost of maintenance and wages, the declining number of monks joining the monastery and the hurdles created by modern state laws as well as the challenges posed by the contemporary economic reality.

No doubt monastic life today conflicts with the modern-day free-market system and laws.

Lama Stagsang Respa

Lama Stagsang Respa and the Hemis monastery form an important node of Himalayan geopolitics—something that has been overlooked in India either due to political myopia or deliberate policy neglect.

Until India's independence, Hemis was headed by Ngawang Jampal, the Fifth Stagsang Respa, who passed away in the late 1940s. The present Sixth Stagsang Respa, Nawang Stanzin, was born in central Tibet in 1941 and was brought to be enthroned at the Hemis in 1945. It is said that he returned to Tibet in the 1950s at the insistence of his parents and did not come back even after the 1959 political crisis in Lhasa.

No one knows the truth behind his not returning to Ladakh. There are several controversies surrounding it that cannot be explained due to political sensitivity, but Stagsang Respa was the chief lama of Ladakh until Jawaharlal Nehru started to patronize Gelug Lama Kushok Bakula as the leader of Buddhism in Ladakh in the early 1950s. The present Stagsang Rinpoche is eighty years old and is unlikely to return to Hemis.

It is useful to mention here that the First Stagsang Respa, Ngawang Gyatso (1574–1651), was considered the reincarnation of the great Indian mahasiddha Savrai Shawaripa who was among the eighty-four mahasiddhas in India.[45] Respa spent a number of years in Afghanistan and Kashmir before he became the preceptor for the king of Ladakh, Singge Namgyal, in the 1620s. He built Ladakh's biggest Hemis monastery as well as the Hanle monastery and established the Drukpa Kagyu order on behalf of the king. Stagsang Lama was also popularly known as Shambunath or Ugyenpa in Ladakh.

The present Stagsang Respa has a Sinified name: LADA awang Dan Zeng. He lives in Lhasa and at some stage held the position of vice president of the Chinese Buddhists Association, Tibet branch. It shows his credibility within the Chinese establishment.

At the persistent invitation of the people of Ladakh, Lama Stagsang Respa was allowed to visit Ladakh for a short while in the late 1980s. Thereafter, he has never visited despite repeated appeals made by officials of the Hemis and Chemrey monasteries.

Stagsang Respa remains the tallest spiritual leader for over 75 per cent of Ladakh's population, which consists of followers of his Drukpa Kagyu sect. The fact that Stagsang Respa, who is also the legal owner/keeper of the Hemis monastery and the revenue lands it owns, is a Chinese citizen makes the case more complicated. The next birth of Stagsang Respa should be found within India for it would signify somewhat the revival of Himalayan Buddhism in the country.

In Stagsang Respa's absence, the Hemis and other Drukpa monasteries are well managed by a team under the supervision of the Gyalwang Drukpa.[46] To a great extent, the status of Hemis and its functioning, both administratively and in terms of monastic discipline, have improved greatly. However, the vacuum left by Stagsang Respa in Ladakh's religious space has been filled by other non-Drukpa lamas.

Conclusion

The actual mapping of Buddhism in the Himalayas is a complex process, but in general it comprises two major streams of practice.

In the southern/lower (Tarai) Himalayas and the Kathmandu Valley in Nepal, the Newar form of Vajrayana Buddhism based on the Siddha tradition of Nalanda and Vikramashila has been popularly practised by the Sakyas and Vajracharyas. This tradition is gradually being allowed to die and efforts are not being made to sustain the Indian Buddhist tradition in the Himalayas.

In the northern/higher Himalayas, the original Nyingmapa tradition established by Guru Padmasambhava and its subsequent offshoot—the Kagyu lineage—are still kept alive by Sherpas, Manangis, Limbus, Bhutias, Lepchas, Drukpas, Monpas, Karjapas and Ladakhpas.

Of course, most of the sacred mountain caves and seats of masters such as Marpa, Milarepa and Gampopa are found in the upper reaches of the Himalayas. Many of the Kagyu monasteries earlier located in central or southern Tibet have been relocated to the southern Himalayas since the 1960s.[47]

Apart from Karma Kagyu, with its centre in Rumtek (Sikkim), Drikung Kagyu, headed by Drikung Kyabgon, has founded its branch, Jangchub Ling, in Sahastradhara in Dehradun.

The principle seat of the Drukpa Kagyu, Druk Thubten Sangag Choeling, was established by Thukse Rinpoche and Drukchen Rinpoche in Darjeeling.

The Palpung monastery, headed by the Twelfth Tai Situpa Rinpoche, has its new centre, Sherabling, in Bir, Himachal Pradesh. Nyingmapa too has several new centres in India; among the main ones is the Namdoling monastery in Coorg, Karnataka.

Unfortunately, Western scholars studying Tibetan Buddhism have tended to lump together the entire Buddhist landscape in one semantic category of 'Tibetan Buddhism'. This lack of distinction and identification has served to confuse rather than clarify the issues, with phenomenal geopolitical implications.

2

India's Himalayan Frontiers

In the early twentieth century, the British set the physical limits of India's Himalayan boundaries. The task must have been quite a challenging one in terms of comprehending what's 'ours' and what's not. It required metaphorically accepting 'what's yours will be yours, and what's not yours will never be yours, no matter how much you want it to be'.

Clearly, the key challenge for the British would have been to make a distinction between the subtle, emotional and the tangible, physical boundaries. A failure to consider this coexisting reality had policy implications and was the reason why the British had to try several formulations such as Inner and Outer Tibet, buffers and frontiers, autonomy versus independence, and suzerainty verses sovereignty, et al.

It is rather difficult to discern the actual cultural mapping of the Buddhist Himalayas, but the British seem to have followed the spatial patterns of Buddhist taxonomic distinctness revolving around two distinct faultlines.

The first is the Himalayan version, primarily dominated by Indian Tantrayana Buddhism, based on the Siddha tradition of Nalanda and Vikramashila, and the thoughts and traditions set by Indian saints such as Padmasambhava, Naropa, Tilopa, Marpa and others. The Nyingmapa tradition established by Guru Padmasambhava and its subsequent offshoots in the Kagyu lineages still hold the Himalayas together and are kept alive by Sherpas, Manangis, Limbus, Bhutias, Lepchas, Drukpas, Monpas, Karjapas, Ladakhpas and others.

The second is the Tibetan version within the Tibetan plateau dominated by the Gelug order, which has evolved more dynamically since the seventeenth century. Unlike the Siddha tradition in the Himalayas, the Gelug tradition, both in its temporal and spiritual functions, has been embedded into the Mongol and Manchu imperial systems.

While setting boundaries, the British probably relied on the context—the central factor of the environment determining the pattern of behaviours, attitudes and perceptions. In that sense, Indian frontiers have evolved over a long period of acculturation that included social mobility and economic interdependency. Clearly, the Himalayas, apart from being Sanskritized and Indianized, have been relatively Anglicized, at least when it comes to language. This is in contrast to the Tibetans, who have come under a greater degree of cultural contact with the Chinese for centuries.

British protectorates

By the end of the nineteenth century, the British Empire had effectively brought the Himalayas under its influence. Although Nepal and Bhutan remained ostensibly independent, they became British protectorates— Nepal in 1815 and Bhutan in 1866. Sikkim too became a British protectorate in 1890.

Nepal

Without going into the merit of history, the Gurkhas of Nepal, after the Anglo-Nepalese War of 1814–16, remained under British influence. The treaty of Segauli (1816) settled the border between Nepal and British India. Through the treaty, the British gained a tract of the Himalayas, including Simla, which later became the summer capital of British India.

For economic reasons, Nepal maintained a friendly relationship with China and Tibet, but despite its occasional attempt at leaning towards China, the rulers in Kathmandu maintained a pro-British policy. Britain helped Nepal in its conflict against Tibet in 1792. It also stood with Nepal in the Nepalese–Tibetan War of 1855–56 that was fought over a trade and boundary dispute in the Kuti area. The matter was resolved after the Tibetans agreed to pay an annual subsidy of 10,000 rupees to the durbar of Nepal following the signing of the Thapathali treaty.

Later, Britain supplied modern arms to Nepal against the potentially growing Russian influence in Tibet. It agreed to assist Nepal with arms provided it allowed the recruitment of Gurkhas in the British army.

After the de facto alliance with British India in 1860, the Nepal regime allowed the recruitment of Nepalese in the Gurkha units of the British army. British India guided Nepal's foreign policy in exchange of the former guaranteeing the latter's defence.

Sikkim

The Himalayan kingdom of Sikkim had been ruled by the Namgyal–Chogyal Dynasty from 1642. It came under British India's influence in the middle of the nineteenth century. Since the seventeenth century, it had been a hub for the Nyingmapa Tantric order following important Nyingma lamas fleeing persecution in Tibet at the hands of the Gelug sect.

In the early nineteenth century, the British helped Sikkim defeat Nepali troops in the Gurkha war of 1814. Sikkim regained some of its lost territories from Nepal after the 1817 Titaliya treaty signed between British India and Sikkim.

In 1835, the area of Darjeeling, part of Sikkim, was taken on lease by British India for a fee of Rs 3000 per annum. The British developed the hill areas of Darjeeling for tea plantation and for promoting trade ties with Tibet through the Chumbi Valley.

Owing to some political and juridical differences, the British made a punitive attack on Sikkim. Darjeeling was later annexed to British India in 1853, and Sikkim's theocratic Chogyal chief became a titular ruler under the directive of the British governor. Claude White became the first political officer in 1889. In 1890, Sikkim became a British protectorate.[1]

The British later encouraged the large-scale migration of Nepali-speaking people to Sikkim, a move which was kept in check by the pro-Tibetan ethnic Bhutias. A treaty to check the Tibetan presence in Sikkim came into effect in 1867. Finally, the Tibetans were driven out of Lingthu in 1888. The subsequent Anglo-Chinese Convention signed in Calcutta on 17 March 1890 fixed the Sikkim–Tibet boundary. With the Government of India creating a political agency in Gangtok, the

Tibetan hegemony over Sikkim came to an end. In 1949, a dewan was appointed by the Indian government as the state's chief administrative officer, whereas Chogyal remained the symbolic ruler of Sikkim until it joined the Indian Union in 1975.

Bhutan

British India's political interaction with Bhutan can be traced back to 1772, when there was a conflict between the princely state of Cooch Behar and the Deb Raja of Bhutan.

The British interest in Bhutan grew further with the East India Company's desire to promote trade with Tibet. Another reason to gain control over Bhutan was to counter Russian expansion.

British India and Bhutan fought a war between 1864 and 1865 over territories in the lower Himalayan Duar. As per the treaty of Sinchula signed between the two on 11 November 1865, Bhutan had to cede territories in the Assam Duars and Bengal Duars, apart from 83 square kilometres of Dewangiri in south-eastern Bhutan, to British India, in exchange for an annual subsidy of Rs 50,000.

Following the death of the Shabdrung in 1903, the British successfully brought an end to slavery and serfdom in Bhutan and appointed Ugyen Wangchuk as the hereditary king of the country in 1907.

The later political development led to the signing of the treaty of Punakha between British India and Bhutan on 8 January 1910. It was signed by the political officer of Sikkim, Charles Alfred Bell, and the first Druk king, Ugyen Wangchuk. The treaty was viewed as an amendment covering all terms of reference of the earlier treaty of Sinchula in 1865. It guaranteed Bhutan's independence in return for British India regulating Bhutanese external relations.

After 1947, Bhutan opted to retain its independence; this was acknowledged by independent India on 8 August 1949 and culminated in the signing of the Indo-Bhutan treaty on 8 August 1949.

End of Bhutanese theocracy

It is not clear why the British, at the beginning of the twentieth century, put an end to the 250-year-old Bhutanese theocracy—perhaps they did so in collusion with the Bhutanese political elite. It could well have been driven by a power struggle or perhaps underpinned by the strategic factor of countering Tibetan hegemonic influence over the Himalayan region.

It is said that when Jigme Dorji, the seventh incarnation of the Shabdrung, was born in 1905, the two powerful regents (Deb Raja and Dharma Raja) decided not to enthrone him as the Shabdrung. Instead, the duo, in connivance with British rulers, formed a monarchy in 1907 and installed Ugyen Wangchuk as the hereditary king of Bhutan.[2] The institution of the Shabdrung was banned by Royal Bhutan in 1931.

Some people allude to a brother of the Seventh Shabdrung who was rumoured to have met Mahatma Gandhi in the 1920s to garner British India's support for the restoration of the Shabdrung's authority.[3] However, the Seventh Shabdrung was rumoured to have been killed in 1931. Similar controversy surrounded the fate of his incarnate, the Eighth Shabdrung Jigme Tenzin, who probably died in 1953.

The Ninth and last Shabdrung, Jigme Ngawang Namgyal, was born in 1955. During the 1962 war, he was rescued from Tawang by the then chief secretary of Assam, Nari Rustomji. He was kept in Rewalsar (Himachal Pradesh) under police surveillance, for he feared getting killed by the Bhutanese authorities.

Despite the ban in Bhutan, the Shabdrung enjoyed wide popularity among the people. Public records suggest that some political forces including the Druk National Congress stood in favour of resurrecting the institution of the Shabdrung within the Bhutanese constitutional framework. However, when he visited Bhutan clandestinely in 1985, he was nearly caught by the authorities.

It was a view that the Shabdrung was India's reserve card.[4] However, there are hardly any documents available that point conclusively to whether India ever wanted to play the Shabdrung against the Druk king.

Since Jigme Singye Wangchuck, the king at the time, was close to the Indian establishment, such an occasion perhaps may never have arisen. In fact, those who were associated with Jigme Ngawang Namgyal faced persecution by Indian authorities. It seems that Prime Minister Rajiv Gandhi had arranged a face-to-face meeting between King Jigme Singye Wangchuck and the Shabdrung in New Delhi in 1988.

The Shabdrung probably lived among the Tibetan refugee community but there is not much information available about his political activities in India. He may have remained under surveillance. The only exception was the Indo-Bhutan Friendship Society (IBFS), formed in 1999 by Satya Prakash Malaviya and Professor Anand Kumar of Jawaharlal Nehru University (JNU), which made a vain attempt to rally support around him.

However, when the Shabdrung was about to take interest in the issue of Bhutanese refugees (*sharchop*) living in camps in Nepal, he died in a Vellore-based hospital in April 2003.[5] Sonam Dorjee, the secretary of Shabdrung Jigme Ngawang Namgyal, dismissed media reports of a conspiracy theory surrounding his death and denied the rumour that the Rinpoche had any involvement with Bhutanese refugees in Nepal.[6] Sonam Dorjee had also confirmed that 'Rinpoche had been vomiting in the hospital but this was due to side effects of chemotherapy'.[7]

Nevertheless, Bhutanese media, including *Kuensel*, later wrote extensively about how he died after a prolonged illness—probably due to a bout of cancer.[8] Surely, another claimant of the Ninth Shabdrung also existed in Tibet.

For a Tibetan-origin Vajrayana state, the recurring politics of reincarnation has always remained hazardous for the government for its impact on internal political dynamics. Months after the Ninth Shabdrung passed away, a young boy, Pema Namgyal, was born in November 2003 in Trashiyangtse (Bhutan). He was found to be the tenth incarnation of the Shabdrung. However, according to Dhurba Rizal, the Ninth Shabdrung emanated one year and four months before he had passed away on 5 April 2003.[9]

But another claimant had been born in Paro four years prior to the demise of Jigme Ngawang Namgyal. However, a powerful Bhutanese oracle, Choechong Tseurama, and a senior spiritual master, Khenpo Tshoki Dorji, authenticated Pema Namgyal as the true incarnate. Pema was reportedly smuggled out of Bhutan to Bodh Gaya in India.[10]

Interestingly, Khenpo Tshoki Dorji, a supporter of the Tenth Shabdrung, Pema Namgyal, managed to get Pema ordained clandestinely by the Seventeenth Karmapa, Ogyen Thinley Dorji, in December 2004.[11] It was not clear whether the move had a political angle or was meant to forestall a rival claimant, but the news of the Karmapa being instrumental in the ordination of the Tenth Shabdrung sent alarm bells ringing in Bhutan and India.

The Bhutanese authorities did not take the issue lightly, especially when the matter also involved interference by a Tibetan lama exiled in India. The Bhutanese government, through the embassy of Bhutan in New Delhi, did raise strong objection to the Tibetan government-in-exile in Dharamshala regarding the Karmapa's role in the Shabdrung issue.

It is not clear how the issue was resolved but it appeared that the Bhutanese government did manage, through diplomatic pressure, to subsequently get the recognition letter of Shabdrung Pema Namgyal revoked in writing from the Karmapa.

It seems the Bhutanese authorities panicked as they quickly arranged to pass a resolution in this regard in the 83rd Session of the National Assembly held in June 2005.[12] The National Assembly constituted a five-member Reincarnation or Verification Committee under a senior member of the state clergy. It was tasked with setting the traditional procedures and rules for the formal *ngedzin* (recognition) of reincarnations of lamas and tulkus.[13] The intention was possibly to deal with the issue of the Tenth Shabdrung, already recognized by the Karmapa. The committee finally laid down a fourteen-point procedure for recognition by traditional norms, which included verifying the candidate through a biographical sketch and his previous life.

The committee then invited the Ninth Shabdrung's reincarnation claimants to face the verification process. Of the two claimants, the first was eight years old and belonged to Paro, and the second was the two-year-old Pema Namgyal, who was born to Tashi Dawa and Yeshi Lham from Trashi Yangtse.

Pema Namgyal, living in India since 2004, returned to Bhutan with the hope of receiving the official seal of recognition from his country. Along with his parents, the main patron, Khenpo Tshoki Dorji, and oracle Choechong Tseurama, he appeared before the verification committee on 17 October 2005. The verification process was done under the supervision of Bhutan's chief clergy, the Je Khenpo, along with eight other members.

Many argued that it was a pre-decided exercise to denounce any claimants to the Shabdrung's incarnation that emerged against the will of the State. The Je Khenpo spelt out at first that there had been no precedence of obtaining recognition of the Shabdrung from outside the country.

The committee found the first candidate to be invalid on the grounds that the boy was already eight years old, which meant that he was born a few years prior to the demise of the Ninth Shabdrung in 2003. In the case of Pema Namgyal, the Je Khenpo conveyed that in his Soeldeb prayer, he showed no extraordinary signs and circumstantial situation indicating him to be the true reincarnation. He therefore ordered that there was no need to go on to the next stage that required exhibiting the personal belongings of the previous Shabdrung for identification by the boy.

The committee then announced the following findings:

First, the oracle, Choechong Tseurama, who was the medium who had initially authenticated the boy, went against the law by directly approaching the Karmapa in India for Pema's recognition. The authorities had convicted Choechong of the crime of misguiding several people in the past.

Second, the Ministry of Home and Cultural Affairs produced two letters from the Karmapa, one in favour of recognizing the boy and the second revoking the recognition.[14]

Third, the committee found that the boy had not completed even two years and was not old enough to identify himself.

Based on these findings, the committee rejected Pema as the reincarnation of the Shabdrung. Khenpo Tshoki Dorji and his associates were reported to have acknowledged or accepted their mistakes and gave assurances that they would abide by the laws and traditions and not repeat such mistakes in future.

Soon after the recognition process was over on 20 November 2005, the National Assembly of Bhutan, after a lengthy debate, resolved that hereafter the formal recognition of tulkus and lamas born in Bhutan would be conducted according to Bhutanese traditions and the rules of procedure framed by the committee.[15] The assembly also invoked the resolution of the 30th Assembly (1969) which stipulated rules regarding those incarnates who were not Bhutanese citizens but were born in Bhutan, and those Bhutanese lamas who lived outside Bhutan. For them, the option was given to renounce Bhutanese citizenship.

Since then, the government has strictly sought adherence to rules and procedures and discouraged false claimants within or outside the country. The Ministry of Home and Cultural Affairs has also warned people not to interfere in Bhutan's internal matters with ulterior motives.

The ministry instructed the *dzongdags* to carry out a census of incarnated lamas in the country along with their personal details. This number exceeded sixty, with many of them residing outside Bhutan as they were reincarnations of Tibetan lamas. A circular issued by the authority said that the two claimants of the Shabdrung were false and people should refrain from recognizing them as such.

It seems that on completion of the recognition process by the committee, Pema Namgyal expressed his desire to return to Bodh Gaya. The authorities, however, put him under house arrest.[16] He is presently being educated in a monastery in Chirang. This information is not verified. Hardly any details are available about young Pema Namgyal, except a photograph that appeared on social media in September 2012 after a gap of seven years, but without any details.[17]

Pema Tenzin, the regional head of Kuensel Corporation at Kanglung, told this author in 2013 that the young Shabdrung was able to learn good English in a week's time.[18] Pema's whereabouts continue to remain a matter of concern to his followers, mostly concentrated in the Bodh Gaya–based Druk Ngawang Thubten Choling (Buddhist Institute for Higher Studies and Research).

Not to be ignored, the Shabdrung institution remains a subject of power politics in Bhutan, even though it is a thing of the past and scarcely has any relevance in the present. Clearly, the Shabdrung factor is still critical for Bhutan's internal and external politics. By de-authenticating Pema Namgyal, the authorities managed to bury the Shabdrung question. They also made sure there was no Tibetan influence in their internal spiritual affairs. Pema was most likely prevented from leaving the country so that he did not fall into the hands of the powerful body of Buddhist hierarchy outside Bhutan.

As it stands, Pema Namgyal is viewed as the true transmission of the Shabdrung at least by Kagyu followers outside Bhutan. They say that Pema was born amidst auspicious indications like the 'blooming of unseasonal flowers, and the appearance of spring water in a village that went dry after the death of ninth Shabdrung'.[19] The Karmapa too is said to have predicted in 2004 through his 'wisdom eyes' at Dharamshala that the incarnate had been born to a couple in eastern Bhutan.

Apparently, Pema's consecration as the Shabdrung was done by the Karmapa in the presence of the Dalai Lama at Bodh Gaya in December

2004. Besides, his local patron, Khenpo Tshoki Dorji, and oracle, Choechong Tseurama, enjoy spiritual legitimacy in their own right.

It is unclear how the new democratic Bhutan would be able to curb the Shabdrung's emotional appeal amongst its people. This is akin to China's policy of the State controlling the reincarnation of living Buddhas in Tibet. Interestingly, China too adopted a similar policy concerning the Panchen Lama and other reincarnated lamas in Tibet.

The Druk king gave up absolute power in favour of a democratically elected government in 2007. But as Bhutan's polity becomes more pluralistic, the Shabdrung factor emerging centre stage in the country's politics remains a possibility.

Fixing boundaries

By the end of the nineteenth century, almost all the States in the Himalayas sought accommodation with the British. In return, British India promised to preserve their independence and protect their interests from the regime in Tibet under the administration of the Qing Dynasty. The only areas outside British India's control were a fringe in the western Himalayas, mainly Ladakh, and the hill tracts of upper Assam.

In the western Himalayas, the kingdom of Ladakh (the ancient Ngari) comprising Ladakh, Guge, Purang, Zanskar and Spiti had faced many invasions from Tibet. As mentioned in the previous chapter, in the seventeenth century, Ladakh had to seek help from the Mughal emperor against the advancing Tibetan–Mongol army. The Mughal Empire helped Ladakh to repel the Tibetan–Mongol troops in 1683, but under the 1684 treaty of Temisgang, Ladakh had to cede its eastern part (Guge and Purang) to the government of the Dalai Lama.

Even while Ladakh's rulers paid tribute to Kashmir, they retained political autonomy until the area fell under the control of the Hindu Dogra ruler in 1834. When the Dogra general Zorawar Singh Kahluria moved further east, the Tibetan–Qing army butchered him at Mayum-la (the mouth of the Sutlej) in 1842. General Cunningham finally drew the Tibet–India border under the treaty of Temisgang in 1842. Ladakh became a part of India in 1947.

Undoubtedly, the biggest challenge before British India was to fix its boundary with Tibet in the eastern Himalayas along the hill tract of Assam. This is the region of Monyul (land of Monpa) or Lho-Mon, inhabited by ethnic Monpas. From British India's perspective, Monyul was a colony under Tibetan rule for over two centuries until the Qing Dynasty collapsed in 1911–12.

The British knew little about the Mon people but established contact with the local ruler, the Deb Raja, from 1844 onwards. Captain F.M. Bailey became the first British officer to explore the Tawang area. His report, 'Explorations on the North-East Frontier 1913', noted that the 'Monpas are very distinct from the Tibetans and resembled more the inhabitants of Bhutan and Sikkim'.[20]

Bailey's expedition was followed by a visit to the area by Captain G.A. Nevill (political officer of the North-East Frontier Tract, 1914–1928). In his 1928 report, Nevill wrote to the Indian government, 'should China gain control of Tibet, the Tawang country is particularly adapted for a secret and easy entrance into India'.[21]

From then onwards, British India wasted no time in ending the Tibetan feudal colonization of Monyul and bringing the area under its direct administrative control. The Tibetans not only resisted British India's influence in Tawang but also either sought to form an anti-British common front with the Qing or hide behind the facade of Chinese imperial authority.[22]

British India finally managed to get the Tibetan Ganden Phodrang authorities to agree to define the border with Tibet and China. The Simla Convention was signed on 3 July 1914 to settle the boundary as per the line drawn using watershed principles by Sir Henry McMahon, thereafter called the McMahon Line.

From the Tibetan side, the convention was signed by their plenipotentiary, Lonchen Shatra. And as per the drawn line, the Monyul area or Tawang Tract fell south of the McMahon Line; except for some private estate, the Tibetans agreed to cede the area to British India.[23] Controversy, however, erupted immediately when China's plenipotentiary withdrew from the meeting and refused to sign the 1914 Simla Convention.

The Tibetans signed the Simla Convention but never actually ratified, it on the pretext of Beijing's non-acceptance of the boundary line. Experts now contend that the 1914 Convention was contingent upon China's acceptance of the boundary line.[24] The Chinese government never recognized the boundary, but there is also an argument that the Tibetans retracted while suggesting that Ganden Phodrang authorities were in fact dissatisfied with Lonchen Shatra's unilateral decision to agree to the drawn line.

Other than this, the larger Tibetan perspective has been that the Tawang monastery is an integral part of the Tibetan Gelug theocratic institution; hence, it can never be parted from Tibet. All in all, the Tibetans too remained ambiguous and considered the McMahon Line 'invalid'.[25] More details on the Tibetan perspective will be addressed elsewhere.

In effect, Lhasa continued to exert full spiritual and temporal authority over Monyul, and British India could do little to enforce the Simla Convention until 1938.[26] It was only on 10 December 1951 after the Government of India tasked the Assam Rifles to evict Tibetan troops from the area south of the Sela Pass that the end of Tibetan theocratic control over Tawang was marked.

Meanwhile, British India had administratively brought Tawang under the jurisdiction of West Kameng District, which was then a unit of the North-East Frontier Tract under the charge of a political officer with headquarters at Charduar. The unit was renamed the Balipara Frontier Tract in 1919, which was further divided in 1946 into the Se-La Sub-Agency and the Subansiri Area.

Many reasons have been cited for the delay in British India taking full control of the area. Apart from the Tibetan refusal to cooperate and their about-face, the immediate transfer of Sir Henry McMahon from India is a factor.[27] Financial severity was another reason, and obviously, the subsequent outbreak of the two World Wars (1914–18 and 1939–45) meant little attention was paid to the Frontier Tract.[28] British India's attention was diverted elsewhere, but the Government of India seemingly abstained from doing anything except for regulating inter-tribal relations and redressing in some ways the grievances of local Monpas.

However, when the authorities did make it to Tawang in the 1930s, they found it to still be a colony under Lhasa's authority. Yet, it was not until the arrest of a British botanist, Frank Kingdon Ward, in 1935 by the Tibetans, on the charge of trespassing in the area, that the government refocused its attention on Tawang. This episode is often cited by the Chinese to underscore the point that Tibetans held full jurisdiction over Tawang and never surrendered to the British.[29]

Clearly, the 1928 report of Captain G.A. Nevill as well as Kingdon Ward's arrest in 1935 prompted the British Foreign Office to depict the Tawang Tract and the McMahon Line in its map publications.

The Constitution Act of 1935 for Excluded and Partially Excluded Areas Order, 1936, resulted in creating the Frontier Tract on the line of the Balipara Frontier Tract. Tawang was brought under the direct administration of the governor of Assam from 1 April 1937.

More affirmative action followed. In September 1937, the Assam government instructed its political officer of the Balipara Frontier Tract to delimit the Indo-Tibetan frontier as per the 1914 Simla Convention from the 'eastern frontier of Bhutan to the Isu Raji Pass on the Irrawaddy-Salween water parting'.[30]

Subsequently, the Indian government decided to implement the 1914 policy to send a political officer to Tawang, held in abeyance thus far. In doing so, caution was maintained to avoid any friction with the vested interests of the Tawang monastery. And as per the instructions left by Sir Henry McMahon in 1914, an experienced British officer was dispatched to run the administration there.[31]

According to some sources, Britain and Tibet secretly ratified the McMahon Line in 1938, and for the first time, a reference to the Simla Convention was highlighted through an open publication.[32]

It wasn't clear whether it really happened because the Tibetans continued their defiance even thereafter. When the British dispatched a military contingent to Tawang on 30 April 1938 under Captain G.S. Lightfoot (political officer of the Balipara Frontier Tract), he was met with strong resistance by the Tibetans. The Tibetan cabinet, the Kashag, accused him of entering the area without Lhasa's permission. This episode of Tibetan resistance too finds prominent reference in Chinese arguments.[33]

But the Assam government never gave up. In fact, an officer from Sikkim, Norbu, in 1941 worked for pushing British India's case vis-à-vis the Tibetans.

In 1944, James Philip Mills, district commissioner of the Naga Hills and 'adviser' to the Assam governor, reorganized the North East Frontier Tract. The Sela Sub-agency was created out of the Balipura

Frontier Tract in 1946. A post for the Assam Rifles was set up at Dirang Dzong and the region was placed under the North-East Frontier Agency (NEFA) in 1946.

Following China's declaration to 'liberate' Tibet in 1949, a more forward position was adopted to strengthen its control over Tawang. On 10 December 1950, the Government of India informed Nari Rustomji, 'adviser' to the government of Assam, to 'effectively occupy it'. Rustomji then tasked Major R. Khating of the 2nd Assam Rifles and assistant political officer of the Tirap Frontier Tract to lead an expedition to evict Tibetan troops from the area lying south of the Sela Pass.[34] Major Khating's mission was successful. The event decisively marked the liberation of Monyul, which finally became a part of the Indian Union in 1951.[35]

Monpa liberation

It might be helpful to mention here that British India was strongly motivated to free the Monpas and Sherdukpens from the excessive subjugation they were facing under the Lobas of Akas and Mijis, as well as exploitation by the Tibetan lamas. Invariably, the British officers in their notes never missed mentioning how harshly the Monpas were exploited, suppressed and murdered by the Tibetan government.[36]

The *East Kameng, West Kameng and Tawang Districts Gazetteer*, published in 1996, is a valuable document that authentically documents the area's socio-economic profile.[37] It is a repository of information on the people inhabiting the Tawang Tract, their history, culture, and customs, and their social, economic and political activities.

For example, Captain G.A. Nevill found the living conditions of the Monpas and Sherdukpens rife with extreme poverty. In the villages of But and Konia, the Monpas were in a 'miserable' state. They were forced to cultivate land for others. The *Gazetteer* quotes from Nevill's report, 'Lobas harassed people and indulged in blackmailing raids . . . they look on the Monpas as their lawful prey and talk of their visits as collecting taxes. These things must be stopped at once, and the Lobas be clearly told that this state of things cannot continue.'[38] To protect the Monpas, Nevill had even suggested setting up police posts at Dirang and Rupa.

They were not only greatly harassed by the Lobas and Mijis but also oppressed by Tawang's monastic establishment, which levied its own tax on the farmers who had taken monastic land on lease. The taxes were excessive and unjust and taken from the farmers in kind. The *Gazetteer* notes that prior to British control, the locals paid annual tribute to Tawang Dzong, but the Tibetan officials provided no security against the constant raids carried out on them by the Akas and the Mijis.

Among others, Nevill wanted the value of taxes collected by Tibetan lamas to be assessed carefully, and also suggested that the government of India pay subsidies directly to the Tawang monastery instead of sending them to the Drepung monastery in Lhasa.

A more damning report came from Captain G.S. Lightfoot, who reached Tawang on 30 April 1938. It said, 'The Tibetan Government should be asked to withdraw their officials because only with the departure of these officials would automatically end their exactions of tribute and forced labour, the oppression which the Monpas bitterly resented.' Lightfoot noted further, 'Tawang monastery belonged to the Monpas, but so inextricably are State and religion intermingled that till the Tibetan monastic officials are withdrawn, Tibetan influence and intrigue must persist in the surrounding country.'

Similarly, British authorities had to send an expedition to Nakhu and adjoining areas to stop the oppression of the Monpas. Later, the Assam Rifles' outposts were established in Rupa in 1941 and at Dirang in 1944 in order to prevent extortion of taxes from the Monpa and Sherdukpen areas.

The Monpas continue to carry memories of the persecution at the hands of their Tibetan rulers. For example, as late as 2006, journalist Randeep Ramesh of the *Guardian* wrote about eighty-one-year-old Pema Gombu of Lhou village who had lived under three flags: Tibetan, Chinese and Indian.[39] 'Although Gombu's living room is decked with pictures of the current Dalai Lama, he said the Tibetan administration in the early 20th century was the worst. Gombu narrated: "The [Tibetan] officials in that time were corrupt and cruel. I am sure His Holiness did not know this. In those days if a Tibetan stopped you they could ask you to work for them like a slave. They forced us to pay taxes. Poor farmers like me had to give over a quarter of our crops to them. We had to carry the loads 40 kilometres [25 miles] to a Tibetan town as tribute every year."'

The journalist quoted Pema Gombu as saying 'such treatment turned Tawang away from Tibet'.

When the Tibetans were expanding towards Dirang in 1830s, the local Monpas had to build a dzong to repel them.[40] Dozens of Monpas were killed in the conflict. A memorial *chorten* (stupa) came up later for the martyrs; now a symbol of local resistance against the Tibetan forays.

Apart from being the symbol of Monpa resistance, Dirang also symbolized British India's final victory, evicting Tibetan troops from the Tawang Tract. Seemingly for these reasons, Tibetans never visit the memorial stupa in Dirang—this includes the Dalai Lama.[41] A local politician, Maling Gombu, said that despite an earlier promise the Tibetan spiritual leader skipped a planned visit to the memorial site in Dirang in 2017. It is indicative of how the undercurrents of political, ethnic and sectarian dynamics still have a bearing on the politics in Tawang.

3

The British Game in the Himalayas

Indians had no strategic knowledge of the Himalayas until British explorers in the latter part of the nineteenth century carried out clandestine surveys into High Asia, which had hitherto remained terra incognita to the outside world.

By the end of the nineteenth century, they had completed mapping and had gained an understanding of the Himalayan terrain—the dynamics, numerous classifications, spatial differentiations, distinctness, their interactions and relationships.[1] This was a crucial part of British India's geopolitical power game against Tsarist Russia. The key objective was to counterpoise its interest against an advancing Russian threat from the north. Finally, the 'Great Game' or 'Tournament of Shadows' was played against the Russian Empire, mostly in Afghanistan and in the Himalayas.[2]

At the same time, geographical knowledge and that of cultural variations was essential to define the limits of India's northern frontiers, for they could be used for military advantage and defence, as was done by Colonel Francis Younghusband when he led a military mission to Tibet in 1904.

As for most British officers, the mountains beyond the Himalayas or Tibet proper wasn't so much of an attraction. In fact, they tended to dismiss Tibet as a 'worthless piece of territory'.[3] Possibly, the lack of economic stakes in Tibet may have been one reason for British indifference to it. Lord Curzon, viceroy of India from 1899 to 1905, remarked in 1901: 'It would be madness for us to cross the Himalayas to occupy Tibet.'[4] He later did pursue a 'forward policy' only within the context of counterpoising the Russian rather than Chinese expansion in Tibet. For the British Empire, defining Tibet's political status was important to safeguard its own interests.

For that reason, Curzon had sent an expeditionary force to Lhasa in 1903–04 under the command of Colonel Francis Younghusband. The aim was: a) to establish diplomatic ties with Lhasa; b) to solve the border dispute between Sikkim and Tibet; and c) to seek Tibetan permission to set up three British trade agencies in Tibet.

Of course, it was ostensibly a part of Curzon's strategy to prevent Tibetans from establishing ties with the Russian Empire. Curzon had learnt in 1900 about the Tsarist Russians making inroads into Tibet and striking a secret alliance with the Dalai Lama. The British suspicion grew further with the news that a Russian Buriyat lama, Agvan Dorjiev, who was studying in Lhasa and was a close aide of the Dalai Lama, had visited St Petersburg in 1901.

Typically, the Tibetans refused to play ball with the British. Instead of negotiating with Younghusband, Tibetan troops stiffly fought against his Indian escorts, though in vain. Thousands of Tibetans were killed.[5] The Thirteenth Dalai Lama fled to Mongolia's capital Urga or Niislel Khüree (capital monastery).

Though the Russians had never advanced beyond the Pamirs, the British suspicion probably proved somewhat correct. The Dalai Lama was escorted to Urga by the Buriyat Lama, Dorjiev. Following their meeting with Shishmaryov, the Russian consul in Urga, Dorjiev was quickly rushed to St Petersburg with a letter from the Thirteenth Dalai Lama and one from the Kashag to seek Russian support against the British.[6]

Though in hindsight, Younghusband's mission would have brought about ineradicable consequences for the Tibetan status, the 1904 mission was instead termed a 'British invasion of Tibet'.[7] Younghusband returned after signing the treaty of Lhasa with the three Gelug centres (Sera, Drepung, Ganden) headed by Ganden Tripa Lobzang Gyeltsen who was the regent in the Dalai Lama's absence.

While in Urga, the Dalai Lama didn't get along at all with Jebtsundamba Khutuktu, the chief lama and celestial head of Mongolia. Mongol historians allude to several reasons, but the differences seem to have been mainly over hierarchy and protocol of seating arrangements.

My Mongol Buddhist teacher Kh. Nyambo had confided privately that the local clergy didn't want the Dalai Lama to stay put in Urga for too long and conspired to send him back.

Eventually, his stay in Urga became untenable. Meanwhile, during his absence from Tibet, the British signed the Anglo-Chinese Convention of 1906, which accepted China's suzerainty over Tibet. Similarly, the Anglo-Russian Convention of 1907 agreed that neither side would act in Tibet—both recognized China's suzerainty over Tibet. When he learnt about Britain no longer being keen to act in Tibet, the Dalai Lama left for Lhasa in 1908 via Peking.

En route from Mongolia to Peking, he stopped at Wutai Shan Mountain in Shanxi, which is sacred to the Bodhisattva Manjushri—the symbolic centre of Tibetan, Mongolian and Manchu unity. This is where he encountered William Rockhill, the American ambassador to China.

While in Peking, the Dalai Lama also established contact with the Japanese ambassador and military adviser. After he returned to Lhasa in 1909, Japanese military advisers arrived in Lhasa to train the Tibetan army against British India. When he returned from exile, the Dalai Lama was received by Ngawang Lobzang Tenpai Gyeltsen, who was then serving as the galden tripa, and other members of the Kashag. A few days after his arrival a grand ceremony at Potala Palace was held where the Kashag presented the Dalai Lama with a 'gold seal', portraying his authority of being 'indestructible as a diamond'.[8]

An independent Tibet

As the Qing Dynasty collapsed in 1911, the Tibetans too declared their independence. The two Inner Asian theocracies (Tibet and Mongolia) mutually recognized each other's independence in 1913.[9] This event and the period from 1912 till China regained its hold in 1951 is considered proof of Tibet being a de facto independent state. Tragically, neither did the world community recognize Tibet's independence nor did it ever question China's sovereignty over Tibet.

While India, America and the rest of the world broadly went by accepting the British idea of China's political 'suzerainty' over Tibet, they failed to underpin the insight of the most dynamic spiritual nuances that had Tibet's political ties intertwined with China.

This book does not intend to analyse the nature of the Tibet–China relationship—already the subject of a major propaganda war.[10] But the two enjoyed a symbolic relationship that according to the Tibetans was more in the nature of priest–patron (cho-yon,[11] or *tanyue guanxi* in Chinese) rather than a relationship of sovereign and subject. Tibetans also argue that their past submissions to the Yuan and Qing courts were more metaphysical than political, more symbolic than substantive.

The fact remains that the last Qing Empire (1644–1911) held complete spiritual, political and military control over Tibet. Even in the post-Qing period, for example, in the case of selecting the present Dalai Lama, the Tibetans directly or indirectly sought political and spiritual legitimacy from the central government in Beijing.

The Tibetans, though, omit or overlook the role played by the Kuomintang government in the selection of the present Dalai Lama, born in 1935. The Chinese have been arguing how Beijing authorized its envoy, General Wu Zhongxin, to supervise the process of search, confirmation and ratification of the present Dalai Lama that had been completed between December 1938 and February 1940.[12]

This aspect of Tibet's peculiar relationship with China had been known to British historians and experts, but the Americans who took over the mantle of Tibetan politics in the early 1950s fell short of understanding this rather intrinsic and inimitable proximity between the two.

Juxtaposition of American-style political logic on the metaphysically multifaceted value orientation of the region may have entailed a policy failure of great magnitude, in the case of Tibet at least. In fact, the cho-yon bond would have survived if China had not taken the course that it did since 1949.

The British seemingly learnt about Tibet the hard way from the nineteenth century onwards. A British army officer, Laurence Austine Waddell, studied Tibetan religious practices and published a book in 1895 titled *The Buddhism of Tibet: Or Lamaism, with Its Mystic Cults, Symbolism and Mythology, and in its Relation to Indian Buddhism.*

Waddell was a physician with the Indian Medical Service and served in India, China, Tibet and Burma. While in Tibet, he was shocked to find that the Buddhism he encountered there wasn't a purely intellectual 'philosophy' but utterly a 'degraded, superstitious' form of ancient Indian Buddhism.

Early Western scholars like Waddell, therefore, studied Tibetan psychology more in the context of Lamaism—an institutionalized system of relationships between the people with their deities and demons through sacred rituals and use of violence. Politically, Lamaism was a political hierarchy run by landowning princely lamas through the system of tulkus or 'dharma princes'. Generally, the tulkus were incarnated lamas but they can wield political authority to manage society and economy with complete religious sanctity, with people paying obeisance to the lama.

Since the time the Chinese communists took charge in Tibet, the exiled Tibetan has astutely modified the discourse by abandoning Lamaism to replace it with the more suitable scholarly phrase 'Tibetan Buddhism' as a new form of Tibetan identity more acceptable to the modern world. The Dalai Lama, for instance, describes Tibetan Buddhism as a 'science of the mind'.[13] There has been dialogue between the Dalai Lama and a group of Western physicists and philosophers taking place since the mid-1990s.[14] But that's easier said than done. A majority of Tibetans still need a lama and they continue to practise Lamaism in some form or the other centred on the lama and not the Buddha.

Antipathy towards the British

The British learnt about the Tibetans and their Lamaist conception of loathing the Europeans rather early. Noted Tibetan scholar Dawa Norbu quotes from Sarat Chandra Das that Tibetan monks and officials had a terrifying image of the English and dreaded them as incarnations of *lha-mayin* (giants or anti-gods) who fought against *lha* gods.[15]

Although they had some idea about the Phyiling (Englishmen) who had taken over the Himalayan estates of Bhutan, Sikkim, Ladakh, Kashmir and Nepal, they understood little about the nineteenth-century phenomenon of British imperialism and the wave of colonialism that had taken over much of Asia.

In fact, Tibetan antipathy for the British dated back to the eighteenth century, to when English soldiers had taken part in the 1791–92 Nepal–

Tibet conflict. Even at that time, the Eighth Dalai Lama, Jamphel Gyatso, and the Panchen Lama were whisked away to safety from Lhasa. The conflict with Nepal was about a trade dispute, but Lhasa sought Chinese help.[16] The emperor, Qianlong, then dispatched Commander Fuk'anggan and his troops to chase the Nepal forces until they reached Nuwakot and signed the treaty of Betrawati.[17]

The 1791 Sino-Tibetan war against Nepal had in fact critically changed the status of Tibet under Chinese control. The Twenty-Nine Article Imperial Ordinance of 1793 by the Qing Empire envisaged the Dalai Lama's authority to control border inspections and maintain communication with Peking. The ordinance issued by the Qing Empire also instituted the lot-drawing process using a golden urn to select the high Tibetan lamas.[18] The Chinese then explained that the reincarnation system was to facilitate a man-made procedure in order to eliminate controversies and disputes over the selection of high lamas. The ritual involved the names of candidates written in the Manchu, Han and Tibetan languages to be placed in the golden urn.

The Tibetans argued that the real purpose was to allow the Qing emperors to control the selection process of top Tibetan and Mongolian lamas.

Tibet's peculiar relationship with China could be underrated, and it was here that the British found it hard to deal with the Tibetans. As Dawa Norbu succinctly says, 'When the British approach Tibet directly, the Tibetan authorities tend to hide behind the facade of Chinese imperial authority. On the other hand, when they were indirectly approached through the Chinese, the Tibetan authorities objected and refused to honour any Chinese orders.'[19]

One such example of Tibetan deception relates to the 1914 Simla Convention. The Tibetan Ganden Phodrang authority first wilfully signed the Simla Convention on 3 July 1914 regarding the McMahon Line. But it refused to ratify the treaty on the pretext of Beijing's non-acceptance of it.

When British trade agents and officers tried to set up a police force and a modern school in Tibet in the 1920s, gullible Tibetans defied it as a proselytizing move. The school had to be closed but one British officer while returning back to India remarked that the Tibetans would 'regret this decision one day when they are Chinese slaves once more, as they assuredly will be'.[20]

Here, I recall my two-year stay in Outer Mongolia in the mid-1980s, where I realized how much the Mongols also hated the Kyahtad (Chinese) but never the Oros (Russians).

My teacher Kh. Nyambo once narrated how the Mongolian ecclesiastical leader, Jebtsundamba Khutuktu or Bogd Khan, could declare independence for Mongolia from the collapsing Qing Empire on 29 December 1911. Nyambo explained how the Mongols felt gratitude to Tsar Nicholas II whose support was critical to the signing of a tripartite agreement between Russia, China and Bogd Khan's government that ensured autonomy for Mongolia under the Kyakhta treaty of June 1915.

When the Chinese army reoccupied Outer Mongolia in 1919, the Bolshevik Red Army supported the Mongols in driving out the Chinese and proclaimed the country as the Mongolian People's Republic. The rest is history.

Things probably didn't work out for the Tibetans the same way as the Mongols, though their political cases resembled each other.

Clearly, the Tibetan conception of alien Phyiling-pa was a greater threat as compared to the Chinese with whom they lived for centuries and shared a similar culture. It was one of the reasons that the doors of Tibet remained closed to Westerners. Possibly, such excessive 'anti-Western phobia' eventually proved detrimental to the Tibetans' political future.

The tragedy was that while the British did not really find substantial evidence of Russian presence in Lhasa, their actions in Tibet in 1904 worked to invigorate extra anxiety in the Chinese mind about intimidating external threats.

Until then, China faced threats only from the nomadic Mongols and Manchus from the north. It suddenly realized that Tibet could become an 'open backdoor to China'.[21] The British infringement therefore 'sensitized' China of Tibet's strategic importance to it. In fact, Chinese writings tend to cite this as 'iron-clad proof' of how the British coveted Tibet to use as a base to attack China.

Dawa Norbu argues that if Tibet was strategically important to British India, it was no less so to the Chinese Empire.[22] It was rather a classic security dilemma for China: 'If we did not take over Tibet, India would, so let us take it over,' writes Norbu. As one Manchu official put it, 'Tibet is the buttress on our national frontiers—the hand, as it were, which protects the face.'[23]

Younghusband's expedition therefore quickly prompted the Chinese to dispatch troops to Tibet in 1906 under General Zhao Erfeng, who ruthlessly captured the Kham region. The battle in Kham seemingly earned Zhao the nickname 'Butcher of Kham'. Thereafter, Dartsedo town was renamed Kangding, short for 'Kangfang pinding' or 'Pacification of Kham'.[24] Since then, Khanding has been known as 'the gateway to Tibet'. The Luding Iron Bridge built then is considered a historical landmark to cross into Tibet from Sichuan. In 2018, when I visited Khanding, it was a modern city and could be compared with any city in modern China.

Shifting power equations

In 1910, General Zhao's forces quickly crushed the Tibetan resistance in Lhasa. The Thirteenth Dalai Lama once again fled Lhasa after handing over charge to his regent. And this time he escaped to India.

While the Dalai Lama was in India in 1911, he was declared deposed by the Qing emperor. But the same year, the Qing Empire itself fell, to be replaced by the Republic of China. The outbreak of civil war in China meant that the Chinese warlord Liu Enhui was able to control eastern Kham. Amdo was controlled by the warlord Ma Bufang.

While he was in India, roughly three months, the Dalai Lama was under the liaison of a political officer of Sikkim, Charles Bell. However, to his utter disappointment, the British rejected his plea for military help against General Zhao. The British were bound by the Anglo-Russian Convention of 1907 that forbade Britain from intervening in Tibet.

Charles Bell writes, 'The order came through from London that our attitude towards him [the Dalai Lama] was to be one of neutrality.'[25] He goes on to say that when he delivered this message to the Dalai Lama, the latter 'was so surprised and distressed that for a minute or two he lost the power of speech'.

Interestingly, the Thirteenth Dalai Lama was hosted in Kalimpong by a Bhutanese Lonpo, Ugyen Dorje, at the newly built Bhutan House, *mi 'gyur ngon dpar dga ba'i pho brang* (Palace of Unchanging Supreme

Joy). The Tibetans claim that the Dalai Lama, as a gesture, gifted a part of Doklam in Chumbi Valley to Ugyen Dorji, who also served as the intermediary between British India and Tibet at the time.[26] Doklam was the site of the 2017 India–China stand-off over which the Dalai Lama refrained from making any comments.

The Dalai Lama returned to Tibet in 1912, but by then many Tibetans had sided with the Chinese. Fortunately for him, the Chinese hold over Tibet had weakened due to the regime change in Peking. The Dalai Lama was able to reassert his authority in 1913. He once again proclaimed independence and ordered the severance of all traditional 'priest–patron' ties with China to let it 'fade like a rainbow in the sky'.[27] The Chinese settled in Tibet were asked to leave within the next three years.

By this time, the Dalai Lama had gained some exposure to the world and embarked on a modernization drive that included political and social reform. Among others, he sent Tibetan boys to study in England and invited Westerners to build schools in Tibet. A Japanese military expert even trained the Tibetan army, and some weapons were bought from the British.

As the Chinese presence weakened in Tibet, the Dalai Lama sent his prime minister (*srid blon*), Lochen Dhastra Peljor Dorje, to Simla in India in 1913 to attend a tripartite conference of China, Britain and Tibet to decide on the boundaries.

In the negotiation, while the Tibetans sought the return of all Tibetan territories occupied by the Chinese in Kham and Amdo, the British suggested an 'Inner and Outer Tibet' formula, wherein Tibet surrendered territories east of the Drichu River (Upper Yangdze) in return for China accepting Tibet's independence.

In 1914, the representatives of Tibet, China and Britain initialled the draft of the Simla Convention, but none actually ratified the agreement. In 1917, when the Tibetan army tried to regain control over Kham, the British tried not to encourage them to do so. The Tibetans went ahead but not without paying an internal cost. The war soon led to an eruption of differences over the government's decision to levy a war tax on monasteries and wealthy estates. Lhasa's decision to impose one quarter of the cost of the army on Tashilhunpo (the Panchen Lama's estate) caused a serious rift between the Dalai Lama and the Panchen Lama.

During the Tibetan war with Nepal in 1791, the Panchen Lama had paid one-quarter of the military costs that Lhasa incurred to fend off the Gurka attack on Tashilhunpo. Apparently, the Dalai Lama used this as a precedent to retrieve one-fourth of the costs of the 1912–13 Chinese war. Similarly, the Panchen Lama was asked to pay one-fourth of the expenditure during the Tibeto-British wars of 1888 and 1904. American Tibet scholar Melvyn C. Goldstein quotes the value amounting to 27,000 ke (*khal*) of grain, which Tashilhunpo strongly disputed.[28]

In the ensuing dispute, and fearing detention by the Tibetan government, the Panchen Lama fled Shigatse in November 1923 to take refuge in China. In fact, the internal rifts resulting in the Panchen Lama's flight inevitably sealed Tibet's future political history. The Ninth Panchen Lama never returned to Tibet, and his next reincarnation, the Tenth Panchen Lama, Lobzang Trinle Lhundrub Chokyi (1938–89), played a key role in accommodating Chinese rule in Tibet.

But the Chinese were not the only enemy. Major hindrances to change came from within. Not only did the Tibetan monks resist the influence of Western education, metaphysically obsessed lamas prevented Western-trained engineers from developing gold mining, arguing that such actions would hurt the *Sadag* and *Lu* (the earth spirits).

Then there were the sectarian rifts. For example, the Thirteenth Dalai Lama's effort to take along other Tibetan sects was stiffly opposed by senior Gelug lamas. For example, the Dalai Lama's taking religious ordination from Nyingma lamas invoked the displeasure of the influential Gelug lama Pabongkha Dechen Nyingpo (1878–1941), who even sought atonement from the Gelug proctor deity, Dorje Shugden. The sectarian factor and myth of Gelug supremacy continue to divide the Tibetan community, serving as a natural handy tool for the Chinese.

These apart, a host of internal dynamics and contradictions that are difficult to comprehend helped provide greater manoeuvring space for the Chinese in Tibet. The British found it difficult to figure out Tibet's political conceptions. When Younghusband wanted to engage with the Dalai Lama in 1904, he fled to Mongolia, and when General Zhao came to negotiate in 1910, the Dalai Lama and his cabinet fled to India. It was equally hard for the Chinese to deal with the Tibetans, but between the British and the Chinese, the latter had a far greater advantage in its ability to comprehend Tibetan complexities.

No psychological evaluations are available as to why the Dalai Lama was repeatedly sent into exile. In the past, the Dalai Lama escaped from Tibet to China in 1792, to Mongolia in 1904, to China in 1908, to India in 1910, and to India again in 1959. The same pattern was seen in the case of the Panchen Lama as well. Such a trend exhibited more opacity and less clarity regarding the Tibetan political behavioural pattern. Constantly seeking asylum abroad meant that the Dalai Lama left the field open to the British and the Chinese to do whatever they wished in his absence.

Outside powers found it challenging to deal with Tibetan political behaviour. For many scholars of oriental history, the Dalai Lama was only an instrument of Mongol or Manchu (Qing) power. The famous American orientalist Owen Lattimore wrote, 'Politically, Tibet's supreme pontiffs acted throughout as the agents of one or another alien overlord.'[29] This was what the tributary or feudatory status of Tibet exactly meant.

The elusive nature of Tibetan polity probably compelled the British to finally set the limits of its overreach not beyond the Himalayan frontiers. For them, it also meant diminishing returns in terms of economic costs that finally led to their abandoning their 'forwards policy'.

In all, from 1876 to 1914, the British brought forth eight major conventions affecting the status of Tibet. Notable among them was the Anglo-Chinese Convention of 1906 which accepted China's suzerainty over Tibet.[30] This meant that Tibet had internal autonomy but not over the conduct of its foreign affairs and external trade relations. In short, Tibet was turned into a buffer state between British India and China. Similarly, the Anglo-Russian Convention of 1907 agreed that neither side would act in Tibet—both recognized China's suzerainty over Tibet.[31]

British India finally settled for an ambiguous working relationship with Lhasa. The formulation of suzerainty not sovereignty, autonomy not independence was meant to entail a weak Chinese presence in Tibet. A suzerainty status was meant to: a) protect India's commercial interests, b) deter Russian expansion, and c) impede Tibetan irredentist claims over the Buddhist Himalayas. Whereas autonomy for Tibet ensured no direct military threat from China.

By late 1940, the nationalist Kuomintang government lost the civil war against the Communist Party of China (CPC). In India, Jawaharlal Nehru tried to lay the ground even prior to India's independence by inviting a Tibetan delegation to participate in the Asian Relations Conference held in New Delhi in March 1947. Thereafter, when New Delhi asked the Tibetans to visit India for ratifying the 1914 Simla Convention, not only did the government in Lhasa rebuff India's request, it also refused to send a delegation to participate in India's independence celebration. The Tibetans had already changed their mind to come to terms with the Chinese, which they did in March 1951.

The Seventeen-Point Agreement signed on 23 May 1951 between the Central People's Government and the government of Tibet affirmed Chinese sovereignty over Tibet.

The Dalai Lama and his government-in-exile later repudiated the agreement on the ground that it was signed under duress and that the Chinese allegedly used forged Tibetan government seals.[32] This was, however, denied by the head of the Tibetan delegation, Ngapoi Ngawang Jigme, who signed the agreement. But the most authoritative account is provided by Melvyn Goldstein, who writes that public disavowal of the agreement under 'duress' was done on American behest as a precondition of its support for the Dalai Lama's departure from Tibet.[33]

One of Ngapoi Ngawang's sons, whom I met in Beijing in 1992, told me that his father had signed the 1951 agreement with China in all fairness and in the interest of the Tibetan people. Jigme Ngapoi was then keen on setting up a firm to produce yak milk powder in Tibet.

In sum, Tibet's failure may have stemmed from the following reasons:

First, it lacked the essential elements and instruments required for building a modern nation;

Second, the lack of geopolitical understanding and inability to deal with neighbours meant Tibet's isolation from global realities; it did not even apply to join the UN until 1950; foreigners were viewed as disreputable lha-mayin (anti-gods);

Third, the excessive belief in epistemology and metaphysics meant rejection of worldly attachment and hence less attention was paid to the development of social and economic interests;

Fourth, excessive expenditure incurred on religious activities (ceremonies, rituals and festivals) was out of mode and wasteful;

Fifth, the authority of Ganden Phodrang was ineptly feudal; its elite monastic community blocked economic, demographic and military growth.

Surely, the Thirteenth Dalai Lama meant well for Tibet, wishing to protect his country from foreign powers, but a year before he died, in 1933, he warned during a teaching at the Reting monastery of the 'danger awaiting Tibet in the time to come'.[34]

It was also a curious case of two contrasting situations. For example, when the Qing Dynasty collapsed in 1911, the Jebtsundamba of Mongolia could easily deal with Tsarist Russia, which in turn helped Mongolia gain a semblance of political autonomy from China. The Dalai Lama of Tibet too proclaimed independence from China, but British India was reluctant to do so. And this was largely to do with Tibet's lack of clarity in their political conduct.

Being a theocracy also meant that Tibet under the Dalai Lama and his monk officials were unable to fully fathom power politics, especially the imperatives of modernization and the subsequent pressure from foreign powers. They didn't know the process of British colonialism taking place elsewhere but were resentful of British India getting a foothold in the Himalayas (Sikkim, Bhutan, Nepal, Ladakh and Monyul).

Regime changes

A series of wars against China, the last being the Boxer Rebellion (1900), resulted in defeats. Eventually, the Wuchang uprising in 1911 led to the declining power of the Manchu Qing Dynasty, which also meant the end of Tibetan feudal theocracy.

The Bolshevik Revolution in Russia in the early twentieth century had threatened Gelug institutions in Mongolia, Tannu Tuva and Buryatia. In Outer Mongolia, the new Communist government officially banned the search for the reincarnation of Jebtsundamba after his death in 1924. The Stalinist-style brutal repression and complete obliteration of the Lamaist feudal order in Mongolia in the 1930s represented a setback for Tibet.

Bhutan did not follow the Gelug order, but the theocratic rule of the Shabdrung there ended after the British successfully installed a secular figure, Ugyen Wangchuk, as the hereditary king of the country in 1907.

In Sikkim, the theocracy under the Chogyal Dynasty since 1642 had come under British influence from the middle of the nineteenth century. By 1890, Sikkim became a British protectorate and its theocratic Chogyal ruler became a titular ruler under the directive of the British governor. With the Government of India creating a political agency in Gangtok in 1888, the Tibetan hegemony over Sikkim had come to an end.

In the kingdom of Ladakh, the ancient territory of Ngari comprising Ladakh, Guge, Purang, Zanskar and Spiti, had long spurned domination by Tibet. The combined Mughal and Ladakh army decisively pushed the invasion of the Tibetan–Mongol army in 1683. Since then, Ladakh paid tribute to the durbar in Kashmir. General Cunningham finally drew the Tibet–India border under the treaty of 1842.

Monyul or Tawang had been freed from Tibetan–Qing control by the British under the Simla Convention of 1914. However, the Tibetan government continued to administer the area until 1951, when the Assam Rifles evicted Tibetan troops from Tawang and marked the end of Tibetan theocratic control over Tawang.

In the upper Himalayas, Lo Manthang or the Mustang kingdom had fallen into the kingdom of Nepal in 1795. It was on the Salt Route between India and Tibet. Legend has it that the Mustang Gyalpo (king) traced his lineage directly back to Ame Pal, a descendant of the Gungthan Empire. Lo Manthang and Dolpo maintained direct ties with the Ladakh, Purang and Lumia kingdoms for centuries. But, following the Gorkha kings conquering the valley of Kathmandu in the eighteenth century, the kingdom of Lo Manthang was annexed to become a part of Nepal.

Clearly, against these sweeping political changes taking place in the nineteenth to the twentieth century, the Lamaism or Lamarchy (rule of Lama) presided over by the Dalai Lama since 1641 was on the decline.

The Thirteenth Dalai Lama had warned before his death in 1933: 'If not protected, the joint spiritual and temporal system cherished for long by the holy lamas including the triumphant father and son, the Dalai Lama and the Panchen Lama, will be eliminated without a trace. The properties of the reincarnate lamas will be seized; our political system will be reduced to an empty name; my officials, deprived of their patrimony and property, will be subjugated as slaves for the enemies; and my people, subjected to fear and miseries, will be unable to endure day or night. Such an era will certainly come.'[35]

Whatever the case may have been, the events that followed since 1951 in Tibet decisively changed the terms and the geopolitical context of India and China in the Buddhist Himalayas, although in a way, that was not exactly of their choosing.

Not much seems to have changed since. In fact, the Tibetans being feted by the West with the help of India continues to weigh on Chinese calculations. They remain apprehensive about the prospects of anti-China forces (the Western world) exploiting Tibetan irredentism built around the idea of Tibetans as distinct peoples with no common bond with the Han Chinese.

Since the 1950s, the direction of Tibetan politics has been impacted by the Americans. It is widely known that the United States aided the Dalai Lama in 1951 on the condition that he publicly disavow the Seventeen-Point Agreement, depart from Tibet, and preferably take asylum in Ceylon.

Instead of relying on knowledge rooted in the Indian experiences, especially on the statecraft carefully evolved during the British period, India's policy objective for the Himalayas and Tibet is subservience to US policy goals.

4

Peace in the Himalayas

In the past, the spirituality of India and China overlapped in the Himalayan space. This probably resulted in forming a long period of Sino-Indian cultural congruence, at least in a non-territorial sense. The sacred Mount Kailash in the Himalayas signified the earthly manifestation of the cosmic site of eternal peace, a pilgrimage site. It was also considered the site of Mount Meru, the epicentre of the Indian mythical world order, which finds mention in the beliefs of every Indian religion.[1]

It might seem a strange contradiction then that two ancient nations, India and China, bordering each other and sharing a spiritual destiny for thousands of years, have become bitter geopolitical rivals, especially in the Himalayas.[2] The trend showed little sign of abating in spite of the colossal amount of diplomatic capital that had been invested since 1988 to attain a certain level of normalcy in India–China relations.

Most tend to believe that the mutual mistrust has its genesis in colonial history when Indian troops fought for the British against the Chinese anti-colonial uprising (the Boxer Rebellion) between 1899 and 1901.[3] The event, though unintended, was to underpin the course of the relationship between the two countries in modern times.

Nehru's India

China and India, from the early days of their independence, shared a common outlook on a range of global issues, especially in the 1950s. The bonhomie resulted in many goodwill gestures; China provided emergency food aid to India in 1951. India, on its part, not only advocated for China's admission to the UN but also pushed for its permanent membership of the Security Council. The seat was then held by the Republic of China (Taiwan).

, Scores of books are available on the 'peaceful coexistence' era, as well as those that question the merits of Nehru's naivety towards China.

There was hardly any ideological congruence between the two countries, though. China opted for Soviet-formulated Marxist socialism.[4] India followed a benign 'socialistic pattern' of development. Unlike China, India chose not to abandon its 'cultural traditions', while both attempted to espouse the desirable traits of Western-style modernity, social and economic transformation.

But it was because of Jawaharlal Nehru's grand intellectual outlook and his passion for anti-colonial struggles, anti-imperialistic and anti-fascist views that drove him to extend open solidarity with the people of China. In the mid-1930s, Nehru described China as a 'sister nation'.[5]

On the home front, he was able to contain reactionary and imperialistic tendencies, especially the right-wing religious groups asserting to define India as a 'Hindu' State. Yet, Nehru neither opted for a Soviet-style socialist model nor did he choose a capitalist model. Instead, he wanted India to be a welfare state based on the four pillars of parliamentary democracy, secularism, non-alignment and economic planning. Nehru left no space for the communists to flourish, nor did he give a free hand to the right-wing forces which were bent on equating nationalism with religion.

At the global level, Nehru's 'non-alignment' foreign policy appealed to other world leaders, but the 'Nehruvian model' was found to be too idealistic and impractical by his opponents at home. Almost every piece of essential writing invariably critiqued his foreign policy follies—the Himalayan blunders, the China War, among others.

From the details that surfaced in recent decades, Nehru seems to not have faced any strong opposition, but there always existed reactionary groups (underpinned by ideological differences) which opposed Nehru's inflexible principles and ideals, both in terms of domestic politics and foreign policy.

The United States especially despised Nehru's rhetoric of Asian solidarity. On his part, Nehru abhorred the pro-imperialist causes espoused by the West. He did not trust the United Kingdom even a bit, for the Kashmir issue at the United Nations was a good example of why he thought it would be prudent to do otherwise. Yet, he found the British to be more reasonable than the Americans.

Unlike Korea, India never joined the US-led global struggle against communist expansion, nor did it have any intention of an ideological clash with China. In fact, India was among the first powers to recognize the People's Republic of China (PRC) on 30 December 1949.

India's contrarian position towards most international issues in the early 1950s—that is, on the Korean War and on Indo-China countries (Cambodia, Laos and Vietnam)—led the Americans to view Nehru and Krishna Menon as enemies of the West.[6] For Nehru, as one side of an argument goes, was deeply aware of India's weaknesses, and hence he wanted to avoid a direct row with China. Meanwhile, the other view is that he was too moralistic to be a part of the zero-sum rivalry among the great powers.

The other side argued that Nehru's soft corner for China stemmed from his fervour for Asian solidarity—an idea that he first advocated in 1927 at the International Congress against Colonial Oppression and Imperialism held at Brussels.[7] Interestingly, a joint India–China declaration at the Brussels conference, purportedly drafted by Nehru, held the British responsible for fostering enmity against India in China. It said, by employing Indian troops 'in support of British capitalist brigandage', Britain destroyed the over 3000-year-old close cultural ties between the people of India and China.[8]

Sarvepalli Gopal quotes Nehru as saying, 'We must now resume the ancient personal, cultural and political relations between the two people. British imperialism which in the past has kept us apart and done us so much injury is now the very force that is uniting us in a common endeavour to overthrow it.' Nehru also wanted Indians to be educated about China urgently, and British imperialism to be 'simultaneously engaged on two of its most vital fronts'.

But Nehru's critics blamed him for his misplaced idealism and failing to grasp realpolitik on the international front. Surely, many Congress leaders including J.B. Kripalani questioned India's wisdom in pressing for China's admission to the United Nations at so early a stage.

Peace-building efforts

It was against this curiously appalling trend of ideological struggle that Nehru probably felt less concerned about China's military forays in Tibet in the early 1950s. Also, until the time it became a republic, China was too weak to assert effective control over the region, even if it claimed de jure sovereignty over it.

Nehru appeared quite clear that India had no political or territorial claims in Tibet.

India would have certainly continued with the earlier British policy of accepting a suzerain rather than sovereign status of China over Tibet, therefore retaining Tibet's buffer status against Russia and China. However, India was neither in a position to assert for a buffer state in Tibet, nor could it ignore the fact that the Chinese intermittently held control over Tibet, depending on the strength of the regime in power. In fact, no country had acknowledged Tibet as an independent country. As such, Nehru may have found it unnecessary to continue to control Tibet or encourage it to assert its independence.

Possibly, India was also aware of Tibet's irredentist claims over territories in the Himalayas earlier administered by British India. For this reason alone, Nehru had advised the British and the Americans not to bring up the Tibet issue at the UNSC.

Nehru made a clarification on 6 December 1950 that India was not keen to challenge China's suzerainty over Tibet. On 12 February 1951, he expressed grief in Parliament over the military crackdown in Tibet and also said, 'We didn't allow that to affect our policy or our desire to maintain friendly relations with China.'[9]

On 23 May 1951, the Dalai Lama's representatives signed the Seventeen-Point Agreement with the Chinese leadership, thereby affirming Chinese sovereignty over Tibet.[10] India, on its part, sent troops to evict Tibetan troops from Tawang in February 1951. India's action to gain control over Tawang didn't face much opposition from China.[11] It was only later that China began to blame India of having occupied Tawang by pursuing a policy of 'expansionism'.[12]

The Seventeen-Point Agreement meant that India lost its diplomatic profile in Tibet. India had a full-fledged mission in Lhasa. The India

House in Lhasa was called Dekyi Linka until it was downgraded to the Indian consulate general in 1952.

Interestingly, neither the Seventeen-Point Agreement nor India taking military control over Tawang (1951) impacted ties. In fact, it was only after the Tibetans surrendered to China and accepted Chinese sovereignty over Tibet that India began negotiating for a peace treaty with China in December 1953. Instead, the two countries promised to follow the 'Five Principles of Peaceful Coexistence' or Panchsheel that was signed on 29 April 1954 in Beijing and which explicitly recognized Tibet as part of China.[13]

The peaceful coexistence between the two Asian nations was expressed in the slogan 'Hindi Chini Bhai Bhai'. When Premier Zhou Enlai paid a brief visit to India in June 1954, the friendship between the two countries was noticeably warmer and followed the 'Bhai Bhai' spirit.

In October that year, Nehru paid a return visit to Beijing, where he met Mao Zedong. The visit was held up as a triumphant symbol of Asian solidarity reflecting the 'ancient' and 'cultural' continuum of the Buddhist era, from the second and third century BC to the present.

Nehru has been criticized on his China policy since. The opponents saw the Panchsheel as the last nail in the coffin. According to J.B. Kripalani, Panchsheel was an 'agreement born-in-sin'.[14] When the Bharatiya Janata Party (BJP)–led government came to power in 2014, Nehru's critics spared no time in reminding people of his worst blunder.[15] For many, Panchsheel had put a legal end to Tibet's existence as a distinct nation even though there is no explanation as to how Tibetan culture could have been saved if India had not signed the agreement.

'The "friendship" reached such a height that on 20 October 1954 India had decided to supply rice to the PLA stationed in Tibet,' writes Claude Arpi. 'Can you believe it! New Delhi offered food to the Chinese troops engaged in building a road [crossing the Aksai Chin] on Indian Territory!'

Nehru's astute move

Nehru could not push the Tibetan case, possibly for India's own self-interest; he was nevertheless able to secure India's spiritual and commercial ties with Tibet through the 1954 agreement with China.

Nehru's proponents considered the idea of the 'Five Principles of Peaceful Coexistence' as his greatest gift to India's foreign policy.

In fact, if one goes by Article I of the 1954 agreement, India and China mutually agreed to establish Chinese trade agencies at New Delhi, Calcutta and Kalimpong, and at India counterpoints at Yatung, Gyantse and Gartok in the Tibet region of China; both parties agreed to accord similar protocol and treatment (privileges and immunities for couriers, mailbags and communications in code).[16]

Both sides agreed to allow traders to customarily engage in trade between the Tibet region of China and India at (1) Yatung, (2) Gyantse and (3) Phari in Tibet, and (1) Kalimpong, (2) Siliguri and (3) Calcutta on the Indian side.

The Chinese government also agreed to specify on its side (1) Gartok, (2) Pulanchung (Taklakot), (3) Gyanima-Khargo, (4) Gyanima-Chakra, (5) Ramura, (6) Dongbra, (7) Pulang-Sumdo, (8) Nabra, (9) Shangtse and (10) Tashigong as markets for trade, while the Indian government agreed that when in accordance with the development and need of trade in future, specific markets in the corresponding district in India (Ladakh) adjacent to the Ari district of the Tibet region of China would be considered on the basis of equality and reciprocity.

Article III of the agreement said that pilgrims from India of Lamaist, Hindu and Buddhist faiths may visit Kang Rimpoche (Kailash) and Mavern Tso (Manasarovar) in the Tibet region of China in accordance with custom. In reverse, pilgrims of Buddhist faith from Tibet may visit Banaras, Sarnath, Gaya and Sanchi in India in accordance with custom.

Similarly, pilgrims customarily visiting Lhasa were allowed to do so. And according to Article IV, traders and pilgrims of both countries could travel through six passes: Shipki La, Mana, Niti, Kungri Bingri, Darma Pass and Lipu Lekh. The agreement also stipulated the use by traders and pilgrims of the customary route of Demchok-Tashigong along the Singge-sangpu (Indus) River as was customary.

The clause demanded diplomatic personnel, officials and nationals of the two countries to hold passports with valid visas, but the traders (and their wives and children) who were customarily engaged in trans-border trade should be allowed entry on the production of certificates issued by the local government.

Importantly, inhabitants of the border districts crossing each other's borders to carry on petty trade or to visit friends and relatives were not to be restricted to the passes and route specified in Article IV and were not required to hold passports, visas or permits. As for pilgrims, they were not required to carry documents but only register at the border checkpoints and receive a pilgrimage permit.

While the 1954 treaty covered the general provisions of trade and cultural ties, a separate exchange of notes signed later specified the actual regulation of certain matters which inter alia agreed that (1) the Government of India will withdraw within six months the military escorts stationed at Yatung and Gyantse, (2) Indian postal and telegraph services together with equipment in Tibet will be handed over to China at a reasonable price, and (3) twelve Indian-owned rest-houses would be handed over at a reasonable price to China.

China allowed all buildings within the compound walls of the Indian trade agencies (ITAs) at Yatung and Gyantse to be retained by India and the land within its agency compound walls to be leased from the Chinese side. Similarly, the Chinese trade agencies (CTAs) at Kalimpong and Calcutta could lease lands from India for the construction of buildings thereon. China agreed to render assistance for housing the ITAs at Gartok and India agreed to reciprocate for the CTAs in New Delhi.

In fact, an exchange of notes signed on 29 April 1954 specified details of laws and regulations related to trade and pilgrimage facilities, including the protection of persons and properties of each other's nationals, laws and regulations for hiring employees, transportation and other privileges to carry out normal trade on both sides.

From all angles, the 1954 treaty was an astute move. Had the agreement been followed in true spirit, the consulate and agencies opened on the ground would have ensured a lasting friendship between the two nations.

But things have not turned out quite as the two might have wished. The hard reality was that by the late 1950s, some intrinsic contradictions eventually surfaced between India and China.

First, India could not possibly escape Mao Zedong's politico-militaristic approach to shape the course of China's relations with its Asian neighbours, including India.[17] Mao's known admiration for using military strength—'political power through the barrel of a gun'—and his belief in the 'inevitability of war', largely in the context of East–West ideological confrontation, had given rise to the idea of China as an expansionist power.

The second issue was the differences that stemmed from the pressing concern of defining the national territorial boundaries of the two countries. (This book does not intend to deal with the boundary question but simply to underscore the complexities that confronted the two great ancient nations for accepting a common cartographic line in the 4000-kilometre-long Himalayas.)

There exist enormous storylines of claims and counterclaims between the two countries. But China's opting for a narrower 'Sino-centric' perspective for its territorial boundaries meant it would reclaim imperial-era land which it asserted having lost to foreign powers when China was weak.

Strangely, even the CPC which took power in 1949 had taken a cue from the 'Middle Kingdom' that functioned under the tributary system of the centre, dominating the peripheries through economic, trade and spiritual relationships.[18] The PRC then called for re-establishing its control over Manchuria, Mongolia, Xinjiang and Tibet after a lapse of nearly forty years (1911–49).[19]

In 2018, Chinese Tibetologists explained to me the Chinese concept of Li—a 'ritual' or 'rites'-based order in which were embedded all norms of behaviour, codes of conduct, ceremonies, gifts, surnames and so on. China's links with Tibet for them were historically rooted in the ritualistic Li order that functioned along an open-ended 'concentric circle' of relationships.[20]

Though the Indians never jettisoned the epistemological outlook of their geographic continuum in a spiritual sense, the modern Indian state sought a national boundary in conformity with the British-era administrative boundaries in the trans-Himalayas.

A mystical outlook

To digress a bit, India's traditional world order is best conceptualized in Kautilya's 'Rajamandala' (circle of sacred and friendly space) which revolved around the core (centre) rather than the periphery (boundary). Here, the sacred Mount Kailash in the Himalayas signified the earthly manifestation of the cosmic Mount Meru, which was the epicentre of the Indian mythical world order.[21]

Fundamentally and mythically, there wasn't any difference. The name 'China' itself comes from the Sanskrit 'Cina'. The word 'Cina-de'se' or 'China country' actually formed an intrinsic component of Indian political and spiritual dispositions—best found during Emperor Harsha's reign in the sixth century. In fact, one of the best depictions of the Indian political and spiritual disposition of China is found in Emperor Harsha's *Ashta-Maha-Sri-Chaitanya-Stotra*.[22] The Chinese conception of Sukhavati (Western Paradise) referred to the Buddha Amitabha (boundless light), a popular deity in China.[23] Of course, a host of books has been written in China and India on the early cultural confluence between the two civilizations.[24]

In all possibility, the Tibetans would have introduced the mythical aspect of the Himalayas to the Chinese emperors from the time they came in spiritual contact with each other.

Sakya Pandita Kunga Gyeltsen was the first Tibetan spiritual master to have reported to the Imperial Court during the Yuan period (1206–1368). He initiated the process of a spiritual bond between the Chinese, Tibetans and Mongols that was further strengthened during the Ming period (1368–1644) as well.

Later, during Manchu rule (1644–1912), the Qing emperors formally adopted the Tibetan Gelugpa sect as China's official religion, and the bond between the trio was formalized through a celestial and devotional order.

The Dalai Lamas and Panchen Lamas of Tibet were quick to confer the Qing rulers the emanation titles of the Great Celestial Manjushri King (Bodhisattva of Wisdom). In return, the Dalai Lama of Tibet was christened 'Avalokiteshvara incarnate' (Bodhisattva of compassion) and the Mongol kings were the 'Rulers of Vajra Beings' or 'Vajradhara' (bearer of the thunderbolt).

As a consequence, the Buddhist Himalayas probably fell in the peripheral circle of Chinese imperial tributary influence, albeit circuitously through a tribute or homage paid by Tibetan lamas to the court in Peking.

The Buddhist Himalayas when placed in a narrower, 'Sino-centric' geopolitical perspective became complicated for India, especially when it tried to define national boundaries on the basis of cartographic lines drawn by the British. This apart, the divergent approaches and interpretation of their deemed 'traditional customary boundary'—through history, norms, beliefs and practices—further accentuated the quarrel that inevitably led to a serious and long-term rivalry in the Himalayas. Of course, none of the imaginary claims including the archival and official documents helped alter the material reality of the boundary question between India and China.[25]

Trade, not Tibet, was the dispute

Tibet was never an issue of public importance in India even months after the March 1959 uprising in Lhasa. In fact, until 1958, there were hardly any serious differences between India and China, even though the need to sort out the discrepancies in boundary maps along with minor readjustments was felt by the two sides.

Indian concerns related more to the difficulties faced by Indian traders in Tibet. The notes exchanged between the two countries in the early 1960s suggested that managing trading activities for India had become untenable because of the constant harassment faced by Indian traders.[26]

The Indian side complained that the privileges it enjoyed in Tibet had to be surrendered; Indian escorts had to be repatriated; the postal and telegraph services had to be abandoned. Similarly, the wireless sets of the ITA were confiscated by the Chinese. Among others, the ITA was prevented from reconstructing its building in Gyantse destroyed by flash floods in 1954.[27]

As the Chinese were consolidating their hold in Tibet, there were reports of the PLA moving towards the Aksai Chin plateau and Barahoti area.[28] In July 1958, the Indian authorities complained that the PLA had crossed the Kharnak fort in Ladakh. Earlier, in September 1957, China announced the completion of the Sinkiang–Tibet highway that India claimed as its territory through a new map published in 1954.

Chinese military activities at this point only impacted the Indian trading community in terms of the obstacles and hardship it faced in Tibet. The problems were caused especially to the Bhutia community that engaged in trans-border trade. Likewise, India found it increasingly difficult to sustain its diplomatic presence in Tibet, but that had seemingly arisen directly in response to the deteriorating political situation and increased Chinese anxieties in Tibet.

For example, on 6 August 1959, a member of Parliament (MP), Braj Raj Singh, demanded an adjournment motion in the Lok Sabha about China's discriminatory practices against Indian traders in Tibet, such as freezing merchandise stocks of Indian traders, charging arbitrary prices for Indian stocks, and difficulties in border supplies into India. The question was based on the statement of the chief minister of Uttar Pradesh that trade from Almora to Tibet had been shrinking and had adversely affected the economic condition of the Bhutias. The MP demanded a full statement from the prime minister on this.[29]

Prime Minister Nehru in his reply said that the matter did not call for an adjournment motion. However, he acknowledged that 'Indian trade within Tibet has suffered very considerably in the last few months, more especially since these disturbances in Tibet'. Nehru also gave some figures about the fall in trade volume, that is, 'in February last, our trade with Central Tibet was Rs 15 lakh imports and Rs 10 lakh exports. By June the corresponding values declined to Rs 2 lakh imports and Rs 3 lakh exports'.

Nehru admitted reports having been received about the difficulties in the way of Indian traders. He said it was true that 'they cannot travel about. They cannot get transport. They cannot send their goods. All these difficulties have arisen'.[30] Nehru, however, said the Government of India has been communicating with the Chinese government on this subject quite fully and repeatedly.

Clearly, the debate in the Indian political circle then wasn't so much about the situation in Tibet but about the concern for Bhutia traders suffering economic losses in border trade. But here too, as Dr Sampurnanand replied, 'There was nothing new or urgent about the problems of Bhutia traders. Since the Chinese occupied Tibet, the Indian traders encountered many difficulties.' Perhaps the Chinese wanted to put restrictions on Indian traders. But they did not altogether stop trade with India. However, the Indian government's position was that India's consul general in Lhasa was in touch with the Chinese authorities in Peking about it.[31]

Interestingly, the Speaker of the Lok Sabha while rejecting the motion made a telling remark, 'I only wanted to make up my mind as to whether this matter was of such importance, whether it arose only recently, whether it has not been going on for some time and whether it is a proper method for ventilating this grievance or having discussion. I am not satisfied that adjournment motion is the proper method of having a discussion on this subject. Restrictions have been placed from time to time. The government is also taking steps and is doing all that is possible to do. Under these circumstances I do not feel I am competent or it will be proper that I should give consent to this motion.'

But even the nature of concerns raised by Braj Raj Singh pertained more to the shrinking border trade that affected the livelihood of Bhutia traders.

Even while Indian leaders were concerned about the possibility of friendly ties with China becoming embittered on this account, fifty Indian shops at Yatung and twenty-two at Phari had been reduced to eighteen at Yatung in the post-1959 Lhasa events. When the Panchsheel agreement lapsed in April 1962, there was no point in renewing it.

The border question

Up until 1959, the border was not a serious issue even though there had been a few skirmishes arising out of discrepancies in maps, especially in the Aksai Chin and Barahoti areas.[32] It was a time when the Chinese were consolidating their hold on Tibet.

Chinese leaders admitted that there was no territorial controversy on the border with India. Zhou Enlai wrote to Nehru on 23 January 1959 that the boundary between China and India had never been delimited and no treaty or agreement had ever been concluded between the two governments.[33] Enlai further said at the 1955 Afro-Asian Conference in Bandung that China was yet to fix a border line with some neighbours, and 'until they defined it China is willing to maintain the status quo and also ready to restrain from crossing even one step across our border. If such things do happen, we shall like to admit our mistake.'[34]

The controversy only erupted between September–November 1955 over Chinese troops preventing an Indian detachment from entering Damzan (south of the Niti Pass). The Indian government contested that

Damzan was clearly within Indian jurisdiction and also a recognized trading point under the 1954 agreement and hence amounted to trespass.[35]

In July 1958, Indian authorities handed over a protest note on the violation of the border near the Kharnak Fort in Ladakh. In September 1957, China completed the Sinkiang–Tibet highway traversing Aksai Chin, which an Indian reconnaissance party discovered later. India considered Aksai Chin to be indisputably a part of Ladakh.

In 1954, during Nehru's visit to Peking, Indians were surprised to find an official Chinese map showing 50,000 square miles of Indian territory as part of China. The Chinese leaders explained to the Indian officials that 'they were old maps and need not be taken seriously'.[36]

Even as the Chinese started negotiating with the Burmese to settle the boundary on the basis of McMahon Line principles, they refused to recognize the same principles for defining the Sino-Indian border.

In December 1958, when Nehru wrote to Zhou Enlai to recognize the boundary with India, China instead brought out a new map published in *China Pictorial* magazine that showed a large part of India's NEFA as part of Chinese territory.[37]

Worried that such distortions in maps by China would affect the bilateral relationship, Nehru further wrote,[38] 'I gave answers to the effect in our Parliament that these maps were merely reproductions of old ones and did not represent the actual facts of the situation. But you will appreciate that even nine years after PRC came to power, the continued issue of these incorrect maps is embarrassing to us as to others. There can be no question of large parts of India being anything but India and there is no dispute about them. I do not know what kind of surveys can affect these well-known and fixed boundaries.'

Zhou Enlai in his response on 23 January 1959 made it clear that the 'Sino-Indian boundary has never been formally delimited and that historically no treaty or agreement has ever been concluded. So far as the actual situation is concerned, there are certain differences between the two sides over the border question. In the past few years, the border question has been taken up on more than one occasion by two sides through diplomatic channels.'

On the western sector, China clarified that 'the Indian government recently claimed that a southern part of China's Sinkiang Uyghur

Autonomous Region (Aksai Chin) was Indian Territory. All this shows that border disputes do exist between China and India'. It was true that India did publish a new map in 1954 that included Aksai Chin within the boundaries of India.

On the issue of the McMahon Line in the eastern sector, Zhou Enlai said:[39] 'The so-called McMahon line was a product on the British policy of aggression against the Tibet region of China and aroused the great indignation of the Chinese people. It has never been recognized by the Chinese Central Government. Although, related documents were signed by a representative of the local authorities of the Tibet Region of China, the Tibet local authorities were in fact dissatisfied with this unilaterally drawn line.'

Nehru replied on 22 March 1959 by saying, 'It is true that the frontier has not been demarcated on the ground in all the sectors but I am somewhat surprised to know that this frontier was not accepted at any time by the Government of China. The traditional frontier, as you may be aware, follows the geographical principle of watershed on the crest of the High Himalayan Range, but apart from this, in most parts it has the sanction of most specific international agreements between the then Government of India and the Central Government of China.'[40] Nehru drew his attention to some of these agreements:

- The boundary of Sikkim was defined in the Anglo-Chinese Convention 1890;
- The boundary of Ladakh was defined under the 1842 treaty between Kashmir and the emperor of China and the Lama Guru of Lhasa;
- The McMahon Line that runs eastwards from the eastern borders of Bhutan to the India–Burma border was drawn after full discussion and was confirmed subsequently by a formal exchange of letters.

Nehru, in his letter, hoped to reach an understanding on this issue with the Chinese premier.

Obviously, before the boundary discrepancies could be addressed effectively between the two countries, the Americans quickly stoked the fire by fixing the revolt in Lhasa. They had anyway been waiting in the wings to create a rift between India and China. They had never approved of Nehru's soft attitude towards China and were irritated with India's non-alignment policy.[41] In fact, Nehru's refusal to toe the US-led discourse had sowed the seeds of the Cold War syndrome reaching the Indian doorstep.

Revolt in Tibet

Trouble started immediately after the outbreak of the Tibetan rebellion on 10 March 1959 and the subsequent escape of the Dalai Lama to India. The Chinese not only blamed India but also accused its forces of colluding with Tibetan rebels. In fact, such accusations had been made by the Chinese for months leading up to the Lhasa revolt.

When Mao Zedong embarked on a campaign to consolidate China's administrative control over Tibet in the early 1950s, he had found Tibet's links with India, customary or trade-related, to be obstacles. China also openly rebuked India for deliberately trying to obstruct its sovereign rights to exercise control over Tibet.

India, of course, rubbished Chinese allegations that its forces could in any way be in collusion with Tibetan rebels. The reply note said, 'The Government of India has no information about any rebel activities in this area, and if there are any, they are in no way responsible for them.'[42]

It had appeared that the Indian prime minister didn't know about the revolt immediately. News of the widespread rebellion was released in New Delhi on 20 March 1959, even though it had broken out on 10 March. Nehru informed the Lok Sabha of it only on 23 March when he said the Indian consul in Lhasa had rightly decided not to interfere in the ensuing events, even though a group of 5000 women had approached the Indian consulate for help.[43]

It is rather well known that the Dalai Lama's escape in March 1959 was plotted by the US and Nehru was asked to provide asylum to the Tibetan leader. The entire story of the Central Intelligence Agency's (CIA) clandestine operations in the lead-up to the March 1959 Lhasa revolt is well documented.[44]

Yet, there appeared a strong case of dichotomy in the Indian narrative. On the one hand, the prime minister of India had no idea what was happening inside Tibet, and on the other, everything had been prearranged to rescue the Dalai Lama from Tibet.

The Dalai Lama's entire journey from Lhasa to the Indian border was coordinated by the CIA's Special Activities Division. The US 'requested' Nehru to provide asylum to the Dalai Lama and CIA operatives conveyed India's acceptance by radio to the rebels in Tibet. As a result, the Dalai Lama crossed into India on 30 March 1959 with Rs 2,00,000 provided by the CIA.[45] The Dalai Lama was indeed offered ready asylum and officially received by a senior Ministry of External Affairs (MEA) official, P.N. Menon, upon his arrival in Tezpur.

China's accusation was that the CIA had built a guerrilla base inside the Indian border for raids into Tibet. Nehru immediately refuted Chinese charges that Kalimpong was the commanding centre of intrigue. He questioned how a small group of people sitting in Kalimpong would have organized major unrest in Tibet, whereas the Khampa revolt had started three years ago. Nehru categorically repudiated the allegation by saying, 'I cannot conceive this could happen without the Indian Government not knowing about it.'[46]

The situation in Tibet worsened after India gave asylum to the Dalai Lama. China, since then, has constantly accused India of interfering in its internal affairs.

The CIA operation in Tibet will be dealt with separately, but the conflict arising from the Dalai Lama's arrival in India soured the friendship between India and China and led to a brief armed conflict in 1962.

The thirty-three-day war left far-reaching collateral consequences that decisively changed what had hitherto been a friendship between India and China into a moral and psychological conflict, not to mention a military one. For nearly six decades, the Indian political and bureaucratic class and even academia and media got trapped into the psychological effect of a catastrophic 'betrayal' by China.

The effects of the China war and the humiliation thereafter have been serious and long-lasting. It decisively altered the Indian public's psyche and perception of China. It cast a shadow on Nehru's approach to foreign policy, and his 'idealism' was blamed for letting the country down. A lingering feeling has since developed that India yielded its interests in Tibet without getting in return from China a fair deal on the boundary issue.

5

Wrecking the Himalayas

The situation as it unfolded after 1959 certainly put India in a tight spot in terms of maintaining its sovereignty on the one hand, and seeking foreign aid to accelerate its modernization process on the other. In the process, India was inevitably drawn into the broader conflict among bigger powers pursuing their own ideological and economic goals.

For Mao Zedong, the 'inevitability of war' was in the context of a struggle against US-led imperialism. The Americans, on the other hand, perceived their destiny in a global struggle against communist expansion to save Western civilization. This meant India had few options.

Chinese troops marching into the Tibetan plateau in the late 1950s meant Nehru couldn't possibly not worry about the security of India's border areas in the Himalayas. PLA troops had already moved down from Chamdo to Aksai Chin (Ngari) in western Tibet. Many Indian leaders including Sardar Vallabhbhai Patel saw the events in Tibet as Chinese communist expansion.

Nehru then modified his stance a bit to follow the British principle of recognizing China's suzerainty over Tibet subject to the condition that Peking agrees not to challenge Indian frontier areas that were under Indian political jurisdiction.

Nehru also talked about protecting India's traditional trading rights in Tibet.[1] When Nehru conveyed India's concerns over Tibetan affairs through Indian envoy K.M. Panikkar, the Chinese premier Zhou Enlai is said to have not taken them kindly. Instead, Zhou Enlai in his reply reiterated the commitment to restore China's control in Tibet by all means, either through negotiation or by military force.

Inevitably, there was a sea change in Nehru's China policy post-1959. India decided to draw the limits of its boundary with Tibet in conformity with the McMahon Line. For Nehru, that was final, 'map or no map'.[2] For he even asked China to decide whether it wanted amity or confrontation with India.[3]

For the Chinese, the boundary was not a settled matter as they wanted negotiations to be carried out between India and China. Nehru's firm position on the boundary was explicable, though many blamed him for taking a unilateral view without taking the Chinese perspective into consideration.

China was also irked by Nehru's attempt at negotiating new treaties with Nepal, Bhutan and Sikkim. All this may have given birth to suspicions in the minds of both Indian and Chinese strategic communities.[4]

However, Nehru's soft spot for Tibet (advocating for its autonomous status) on the one hand while demanding strict conformity with the McMahon Line on the other put his statesmanship to its sternest test.

While the Chinese criticized Nehru for his doublespeak, his opponents at home started to question his wisdom in befriending China in the first place. Sardar Patel, the home minister, publicly condemned China's 'unjustified' actions in Tibet. Patel had even cautioned Nehru on 7 November 1950 against adopting a complacent approach towards Tibet. There were others who were pushing for direct intervention.

Nehru's naivety on China has been well analysed by many commentators. Defenders of his policies suggest that he was doing fine so long as he was the sole maker of the China policy, even though he faced opposition from the media and also colleagues within his own party, especially from Patel, whose view on China stood in stark contrast to Nehru's.

Americans and the CIA

One of the lesser-known facts is the manner in which the US from the early 1950s had begun the groundwork to derail Nehru's priorities. By the late 1950s, the US fully outmanoeuvred his non-aligned policy by secretly machinating a divergent ideological view in India. Quite clearly, a pro-American lobby had succeeded in getting Nehru to acquiesce to the 'Chinese danger' plans.

Benjamin Zachariah's seminal new book[5] on the life and work of Jawaharlal Nehru alludes to how the secret, behind-the-scenes, outside interventions affected Nehru's policies on India's everyday domestic affairs. Zachariah tellingly notes how the US had started encouraging what it perceived to be anti-communist forces in India.

Among others things, the CIA had funded a 'cultural front'—the Congress for Cultural Freedom (CCF)—in India to propagate the Western narrative of the Cold War, especially to fund academic and cultural activities for Western liberal ideas. The CCF was headed by a well-known veteran politician, Minochar Rustom Masani, who earlier worked within the old socialist group, and along with Jayaprakash Narayan and others formed the Congress Socialist Party (CSP). Later, he became a propagandist for capitalism and supported free economy as opposed to the Soviet-style socialist economy.

Masani operated the CCF for a long time without revealing its source of funding. It was only in 1967 that it became known that the CCF was a front for the CIA. The CCF also operated under the cover of the Bhoodan movement.[6] The CCF was able to penetrate a wide section of prominent Indian academics and intellectuals. It seemingly seduced some who served as members of the cabinet, and who may have attempted to constrain Nehru's socialist leanings in favour of aligning more closely with the US. Zachariah's biography reveals how more details have begun to emerge about 'some extremely prominent members of Nehru's inner circle' who were working for the CIA.

According to Zachariah, even Nehru was not above suspicion in the eyes of the Americans when it came to pro-communism lobbies in India. In 1959, the case of M.O. Mathai, who served as Nehru's personal secretary, came to the fore. Mathai was accused of having disproportionate wealth ostensibly as payment for supplying information from the CIA and Indian businessmen. Sarvepalli Gopal, in his book on Nehru, notes, 'It can safely be assumed that from 1946 to 1959, the CIA had access to every paper passing through Nehru's secretariat.'[7]

The role of the CIA, initially dismissed as paranoia by many, turned out to be severely understated. Zachariah quotes 'prominent members of Nehru's inner circle who were working for the CIA from at least 1955' including, according to him, Bhola Nath Mullick,[8] who served as director, Intelligence Bureau from 1950 until the year Nehru died in 1964.

Mullik, according to Zachariah, worked for the US during the Cold War and 'trained under him large numbers of anti-communists as Indian intelligence agents, and worked closely with the CIA to sponsor Tibetan guerrillas in India'.

He further notes that 'intelligence sources' warnings to Nehru of the 'Chinese danger' seem to have been in keeping with their anti-communism, and may have eventually turned out to be a self-fulfilling prophecy.

Among the dispassionate analysts in India, at least in the academic circle, veteran China expert Giri Deshingkar wrote in his article 'The Nehru's Years Revisited', published by the Indira Gandhi National Centre for the Arts, New Delhi, in 1998,[9] 'Following Patel's demise in 1950, Nehru's China policy ran into difficulties only due to B.N. Mullik, Chief of the Intelligence Bureau (IB), who in the late 1950s owing to his direct access to Nehru (perhaps as a result of his success in Kashmir) was able to convince Nehru to consider China as an adversary.' He goes on to say, 'Not once did Nehru disagree with Mullik's intelligence assessment, nor did he ever object to the IB's overt and covert actions.'

Deshingkar quotes from B.N. Mullik's *My Years with Nehru: The Chinese Betrayal*[10] that he fought his own private war with China through rebellious Khampas inside Tibet. He asserts further that the Kongka Pass incident of October 1959 in the Chang-Chemno Range on the Line of Actual Control (LAC) in Ladakh, which led to a 'brutal massacre of an Indian police party', was engineered by Mullik. The incident led to the Sino-Indian war of 1962—a turning point in India–China relations for which Mullik's colleagues in the army and the MEA accused him and the IB of 'aggression' and 'expansionism'.

Deshingkar further says that Mullik's private war with China continued until the two armies clashed in 1962. 'Although a mere civil servant, he must be counted as a major contributor to the making of Nehru's China policy. In fact, it is difficult to say whether the tail was wagging the dog or whether Nehru had a split-level approach towards China.'

Consequently, Nehru was in favour of abandoning the British colonial policy of playing the 'Great Game' on the Himalayan frontiers, and his view post-1958 was solely influenced by 'Mullik's mindset' that finally culminated in the humiliating defeat by China in 1962.

Heat over Tibet

Nehru had turned seventy in 1959 and his declining physical and mental energy meant 'people with lesser integrity' began to dominate the government. By implication, foreign policy issues were handled by lesser mortals.

Even so, Prime Minister Nehru never wanted to spoil India's friendship with China for the sake of Tibet, and avoided Tibet becoming a domestic public debate. However, following the outbreak of a rebellion on 10 March 1959, he was perhaps compelled to make a statement in the Lok Sabha on 17 March, when he said, 'I have seldom referred to Tibet except in answer to some criticism. Again, it is embarrassing to discuss events happening in a neighbouring country about which we know something of course but naturally, what we know is limited. It is not easy get a full picture.'[11]

He further said, 'No country had ever recognised the independence of Tibet, we certainly did not and it was inevitable, therefore for us to recognize the suzerainty . . . call it sovereignty—these things are fine distinctions and they depend upon the power of the state, how far it goes.'

In a statement in the Lok Sabha on 30 March 1959, Nehru mentioned the long tradition of cultural and religious ties between India and Tibet but cautioned the House against doing anything that might worsen an already difficult situation.[12]

Clearly, Nehru, being a cautious politician with a deep understanding of global affairs and aware of India's own social milieu, upheld the Indian Parliament's right to discuss any matter of its choice. However, he cautioned that the method of government, legislatures and organizations in China were different from that in India and underlined that the right of discussion and action by Indian authorities has to be exercised always with wisdom and thinking of the consequences.[13]

For Nehru, solutions could not ensue from war-like speeches and talking a fiery language, and the anger over the events in Tibet had to be conveyed in a fairly effective language.

Clearly, reports of border skirmishes with China and the escape of the Dalai Lama had created a fair amount of hysteria in India. Passions were inflamed within and outside Parliament in favour of retaliation despite the government's efforts to hold the peace and not worsen the situation. But by then, mounting foreign and domestic pressure was brought to bear on Nehru to grant asylum to the Dalai Lama. People flocked to see the legendary Tibetan phoenix when he arrived in India.

There was an upsurge in sympathy for Tibet and a rise in anti-China sentiments in India.[14] In April 1959, the opposition Socialist Party–led protesters raised 'Free Tibet' slogans. Fiery slogans led to vandalism and mutilation of Mao Zedong's portrait on the wall of the Chinese consulate in Mumbai. When Zhou Enlai complained about the protection afforded by the Indian government to the Dalai Lama, Morarji Desai compared his status to that of Karl Marx, whom the British had given sanctuary to after he was exiled from his native Germany.[15] The support for the Dalai Lama and insult to Mao invoked Chinese ire.

Beijing conveyed that such a huge insult to the beloved leader of the Chinese people would not be tolerated. New Delhi in its reply deplored such incidents but pointed out to the Chinese that such protests and processions could not be banned under law. However, the Chinese warned that if the matter is not resolved reasonably, '[The] Chinese side will never come to a stop even for one hundred years.'[16]

Obviously, the matter was further accentuated by Opposition parties raising the tide of nationalist outrage both inside and outside Parliament on the issue of China's cartographic aggressions, construction of roads in Aksai Chin and reports of Indian soldiers killed by Chinese troops.

On 3 April 1959, Nehru informed Parliament that the Dalai Lama would be treated respectfully if he were to seek asylum in India, but made a clear-cut policy statement four days later in which he said:

- The Dalai Lama had come to India on his own volition and not on the suggestion of the Indian government;

- He was entirely responsible for his statements that he had made in India;
- There was no Indian hand in the drafting or preparation of those statements.

Nehru thus made it clear on 20 April 1959 that 'while the Dalai Lama would be free to pursue his religious activities in India, he could not participate in the political programmes in India'.[17] This position has not changed till date, as can be read from the MEA statements issued from time to time.

Even so, Nehru could not escape criticism from China. The Chinese view until then was that Nehru was a 'captive of reactionary forces'[18] that he couldn't control, but that he might eventually break free.

But after the Dalai Lama took shelter in India, the Peking newspaper *Ta Kung Pao* on 25 April 1959 accused Indian 'expansionists' of plotting to make Tibet a vassal state of India.[19] For the first time, Nehru was upset with China, which according to him had used the 'language of cold war' in its statement. Nehru refuted the Chinese allegation that India was following the British policy of expansionism.

The New China News Agency immediately alleged that the Dalai Lama had entered India 'under duress' and that he had been kidnapped by 'Indian expansionists'.[20] When, on 18 April, the Dalai Lama denied being kidnapped, the Panchen Lama issued a statement from Peking saying that the statement made by the Dalai Lama 'was imposed upon him by the foreigners'[21] but he didn't specifically mention 'Indians'. The Chinese, of course, protested India rendering asylum to the Dalai Lama.

Nehru refuted the Chinese allegation that the Dalai Lama was being detained in India. He further said that it was up to the Dalai Lama to return to Tibet or go wherever he wished to. He also rejected that the revolt was confined to a number of 'upper-strata reactionaries' and said that it was a crisis of 'considerable magnitude'.

Yet, there was no doubt that Tibet falling in Chinese hands caused genuine concern for India if not put it in an acute dilemma.

India's stand

Nehru then perhaps decided to take the cue from advice he received from British prime minister Clement Attlee. In an eight-point memorandum sent on 27 October 1950, Attlee had advised among others that 'India should do what it can for Tibet short of military assistance' and that 'recognising Tibetan independence must be ruled out'.[22]

A former senior Indian diplomat, Ranjit Kalha, quotes that similar British advice to the US on Tibet worked on the following points: a) Britain was 'always' prepared to recognize Chinese sovereignty over Tibet, but on the understanding that Tibet is autonomous, and, b) Tibet's inaccessibility makes it impracticable to do anything to stiffen military resistance to China.

Finally, Nehru went by the government's assessment that inter alia conveyed two points: a) Tibetans themselves are incapable of doing anything than putting up nominal resistance, and b) 'Neither India nor any external power could prevent the Chinese takeover of Tibet.'

These hard realities and a consciousness of India's military weakness forced Nehru to define India's Tibet policy thus:

- To ensure the security and integrity of India
- To accept Chinese suzerainty/sovereignty over Tibet
- To maintain friendly relations with China.

Nehru followed a middle way; he welcomed the Dalai Lama and expressed sympathy for the Tibetan people, but he refused to censure China's occupation of Tibet.

Nehru, at the end, felt 'this is a correct policy not only for the present but even more so for the future . . . it would be a tragedy if the two great countries lived peacefully as neighbours for ages past, should develop feelings of hostility against each other'.[23]

At the same time, Nehru did not support the Jan Sangh's Resolution on Tibet introduced in the Lok Sabha on 21 August 1959, which called for the Tibet issue to be referred to the UN.[24] That Nehru felt sympathy for the Tibetans was evident in his offering refuge to the Dalai Lama and 13,000 Tibetans, but to go beyond this would be mere futility.

For the international prospects of the Tibet issue, Nehru said the UN could respond only on two grounds: violation of human rights, which would not apply to China as it was not a member of the UN; and aggression, which was difficult to justify because Tibet had never been acknowledged as an independent state.

Further, Nehru believed that sponsoring the Tibet question at the UN would only produce a Cold War–like atmosphere that was not desirable for India's long-term interests.[25] Nehru's unambiguous position not to challenge China on Tibet may have compelled the Tibetans to appeal to the UN, which they did on 9 September 1959.[26]

It seems that India had even advised the British and the Americans not to bring up the Tibet issue at the UNSC. When a joint Malay–Irish resolution on the restoration of fundamental human rights in Tibet was adopted by the UN on 21 October 1959, the Indian delegation abstained from voting on it. As a result, the Tibetan question was never allowed to proceed beyond the preliminaries at the UN. It died a natural death for by then even the US had decided to play it safe.

To be sure, there may have been more than one reason that prompted India to hold back from pushing the Tibet agenda, both at home and at global forums. But while clarifying India's policy stand, Defence Minister Krishna Menon stated, 'The Government of India wants to make it clear that they did not recognize any separate Government of Tibet and there is therefore no question of a Tibetan government under the Dalai Lama functioning in India.' For further clarification, he stated, 'Our abstention [sic], however, will be in no sense . . . a lack of concern or a lack of feeling in regard to the Tibetan people or any reflection upon our relation with China.'[27]

Nehru also may have found no reason to opt for war with China on the Tibetans' behalf, for India had enough problems of its own, especially on the economic front.

Nehru had the option of handing the Dalai Lama back to the Chinese as he had two years earlier in 1956, when the Dalai Lama along with the Panchen Lama came to attend the 2500th anniversary celebrations of the Buddha's birth. That was a wise decision taken after consultation with Ram Rahul, who was an expert on Himalayan studies.[28]

In 1959, Nehru did provide political asylum to the Dalai Lama, but wasn't really happy about hosting him in India. In spite of the fact that many in India viewed the Tibetan issue as a leveraging point vis-à-vis China, Nehru wished to steer clear of it and privately told the Dalai Lama to leave according to recently declassified CIA documents.[29]

It said, 'For Nehru, who on the one hand was compelled by the presence of Dalai Lama on Indian soil to defend him and on the other hand was reluctant to further strain Sino-Indian relations, he told the Tibetan leader to limit his activities in India to religious affairs, and Indian officials were probably reflecting Nehru's real anxiety when they stated privately that the government would not be sorry to see the Dalai leave the country.'

The Soviet Union and its leader Nikita Khrushchev were opposed to Chinese actions in Tibet and were unhappy that Mao Zedong had allowed the Dalai Lama to flee towards India. Possibly, Khrushchev wasn't happy about China embroiling India in what he might have viewed as a Sino-US confrontation.

As for China, Mao Zedong was apparently quite happy with the Dalai Lama in India, which perfectly suited Beijing. According to a former foreign secretary of India, as told to this author, Chairman Mao had conveyed to Prime Minister Nehru through an Indian communist leader visiting China in the late 1950s that 'he should keep the Dalai Lama in India'.[30]

Nehru could neither keep the Dalai Lama in confinement nor could he stop the public from flocking to seek audience with the Tibetan spiritual leader. An added problem was the growing domestic hysteria over the border issue. Nehru could hardly do anything. Moreover, he was beginning to get annoyed with the Chinese arrogance. He perhaps felt that China was undermining his foreign policy besides sullying his reputation.

But the fact remains that both before and after the arrival of the Dalai Lama in India, Tibet was not a factor that could by itself derail India–China relations. Nehru clarified in Parliament on 4 May 1959 that India's basic policy towards China remained unchanged and it would continue to support China's entry into the United Nations.[31]

Nehru's failure in handling the Dalai Lama adequately probably furthered India's dispute with China. Obviously, there has been no win for India, but China also lost by being tainted as an aggressor and a betrayer. The epic tale of the 1962 war still hangs heavy in India.

But the critical factor, as the CIA report suggests, was the US approach and the role it played by casting its lot with the Dalai Lama.

This changed the context of the game in the Himalayas. Obviously, the Dalai Lama expressed his deep gratitude to Prime Minister Nehru and his colleagues in the Government of India for the kind reception received upon his safe arrival in India.

CIA's covert operation

The US from day one had tried to induce the Dalai Lama to disavow the Tibetan agreement with China and planned for his flight into exile. In *A History of Modern Tibet*, Melvyn C. Goldstein provides the most authoritative account of how the entire operation started with US Secretary of State Dean Acheson approving a verbal message transmitted to the Tibetans in August 1951. It said, 'The US government repeats its belief you can best serve your people and country by evading Communist control at earliest opportunity and by denouncing agreement with Communist China after you will have reached safe asylum.'[32]

The final official letter to the Dalai Lama was sent by the US ambassador in New Delhi, Loy W. Henderson, on 17 September 1951 which said, among other things, 'Your Holiness will understand, of course, that the readiness of the United States to render you the assistance and support outlined above is conditional upon your departure from Tibet, upon your public disavowal of agreements concluded under duress between the representatives of Tibet and those of the Chinese Communist aggression.'[33]

Goldstein's book provides a fascinating depiction of how the Tibetan issue factored in the US calculus vis-à-vis China against the backdrop of the Korean War, the Sino-Soviet alliance, and the American Cold War doctrine.

India was not with the US on the Korean War, but what angered China the most was the way the Dalai Lama was received by Indian officials in March 1959; the fact that he was allowed to indulge in political activities; and how the border town of Kalimpong was allowed to be used as a hub for exiled Tibetans and CIA agents, supported by prominent members of Nehru's administration.

Two months later, the Chinese foreign ministry in its note of 23 June 1959 claimed that over 200 Indian troops equipped with radio stations and weapons of various types were intruding and building military works around Migyitun, Samgar Sanpo and other places in Tibet. More seriously, China accused Indian troops of 'entering into collusion with the Tibetan rebel bandits'.[34] India, in its reply on 26 June 1959 denied any violation of territory in Tibet near Migyitun and asserted that the 'traditional international frontier with China coincides with the McMahon Line, and accordingly Migyitun is within Chinese territory in Tibet and so are Samgu Sampo, Molo and Gyala'.

New Delhi also regretted that 'China should have believed the allegations that their forces could in any way be in collusion with Tibetan rebels. The Government of India has no information about any rebel activities in this area, and if there are any, they are in no way responsible for them.'

The frictions later escalated into border skirmishes resulting in the 'Longju incident' of 25 August 1959 that marked the first armed encounter between the border forces.

As the reports of border incidents flashed across the country, passions were inflamed against the government's China policy. Nehru was terribly distressed after receiving Zhou Enlai's letter of 8 September 1959 that among other things alleged Indian troops having trespassed, 'invaded and occupied' a number of places; accused India of shielding armed Tibetan rebels in the frontier areas and accused Indian aircraft of repeatedly violating Chinese air space.

Nehru in a twenty-nine-paragraph rebuttal to Zhou Enlai on 26 September 1959 wrote: 'I must frankly say that your letter of the 8th September has come as a great shock to us. When our two countries signed the 1954 Agreement I hoped that the main problems which history had bequeathed to us in the relations between India and China had been peacefully and finally settled. Five years later, you have now brought forward, with all insistence, a problem which dwarfs in importance all that we have discussed in recent years and, I thought, settled.'

Nehru deeply resented the allegation that India was seeking to reap benefit from the British aggression against China as he wrote: 'The Government of India voluntarily renounced all the extra-territorial rights enjoyed by Britain in Tibet before 1947 and recognised by treaty that Tibet is a region of China.'

Clearly, the 1959 episode that occurred five years after the 1954 Panchsheel agreement finally resulted in China calling the McMahon

Line an 'imperialist fabrication' while in India it was called the 'Chinese betrayal'. It only suggested that Nehru was already losing control over his China policy.

As explained before, Nehru was doing fine so long as he was the sole maker of the China policy. He admitted that existing border lines were vague and needed further discussion, but he didn't find it worth going to war to protect barren land. Even after the first clashes on the border towards the end of 1959, Nehru told the American journalist Edgar Snow 'the basic reason for the Sino-Indian dispute was that they were both "new nations" and therefore it was natural that a certain degree of conflict should be generated before they could stabilize their frontiers'.[35]

Nehru in May 1962 told the Lok Sabha, 'If you start thinking as the Chinese do . . . on the assumption that the territory in Ladakh, especially in the Aksai Chin area, is theirs and has been theirs, well, everything we do is an offence to them. But if we start on the basis of thinking that the territory is ours, as it is, then everything the Chinese do is an offence. It depends on with what assumption you have started.'[36]

But by then people like Bhola Nath Mullik had influenced Nehru to acquiesce to act on the premise of the 'China threat'. Kalimpong was turned into a hub of CIA agents. A plethora of books and papers published since allude to the CIA's overt operation under the code-named ST CIRCUS project[37] with Indian collaborators, perhaps without the knowledge of Nehru.

The Opposition too was adamant against talking to the Chinese despite intervention by the USSR in July 1962 to start negotiation between the two sides. Fiery public speeches then drew India's 'mystical affinity' with the Himalayas. In the run-up to the January 1962 elections, even Lal Bahadur Shastri rhetorically threatened China with a fate similar to that of Goa, which had recently been liberated from the Portuguese in December 1961.

The war rhetoric brought the Congress back to power, winning 358 of 491 seats in the Lok Sabha with 44.78 per cent of the vote share. But the Opposition parties, after gaining more vote share, blocked boundary talks with China and thought it tantamount to surrender.

A CIA Staff Study entitled 'The Sino-Indian Border Dispute',[38] covering the 1959–62 period published in 2007 revealed how China promptly agreed to Krushchev's intervention against India's hardened stand. In July 1962, despite Soviet advice and Chinese willingness to negotiate, the Opposition remained steadfast—'boundaries were not negotiable' and the situation became dangerous.[39]

Nehru became 'captive' to a domestic hysteria he couldn't control. He was forced to abandon his friendship with China; instead a provocative 'forward policy' was pushed—sending ill-equipped border patrol into disputed territory. Many other adventurous acts were in play, perhaps without Nehru's knowledge. The Chinese denounced Nehru becoming the 'running dog of imperialism'.[40]

War and its aftermath

In September 1962, Krishna Menon ordered the eviction of Chinese troops south of the McMahon Line—possibly against military assessment. On 20 October 1962, the Chinese assault began and Indian troops faced a humiliating defeat.

Krishna Menon quickly became the scapegoat—a familiar tactic—and the rest is history.

But the war weakened Nehru. He was attacked for compromising national security. A hysterical nationalism once again gripped the country with an unprecedented outburst of passion among ultra-nationalists who turned to voicing fabled 'analogies of Indian invincibility' and power.

Chinese-owned shops were vandalized and Communist Party of India (CPI) offices were attacked. It was that simple to manipulate nationalist pride in a new state around the idea of defending national borders.

Nehru's anti-socialist groups manoeuvred the defeat into a conflict between communism and democracy.

The US quickly offered military aid to repel Chinese troops, and the war ended after China declared a ceasefire on 20 November 1962, and unilaterally withdrew its troops from NEFA. According to the US assessment, the Chinese may have been frightened by the idea of a major US intervention.[41] But several authors including Neville Maxwell, the author of *India's China War*, conclude that from the Chinese perspective the 1962 war was a 'punitive expedition, not an invasion'.[42]

China quickly made a unilateral announcement on 21 November seeking both sides withdrawing 20 kilometres to the position held as on

7 November 1959, which would be the LAC before any negotiation for a settlement begin.

Nehru ignored the Chinese call but he conveyed to Zhou Enlai through the Sri Lankan prime minister that 'India would not move back to the McMahon Line'.[43]

The end is interestingly summed up by Zachariah, who writes, 'At talks in Colombo, India avoided an explicit settlement; it was impossible even now to acknowledge the simple reality that on the ground the Chinese victory had settled the issue. On the Chinese side, a generous willingness to allow Nehru to save face prevented their forcing an explicit agreement; but the border issue remains, theoretically, unresolved, as it was before 1962.'

The net result of the war was devastating. Nehru came under attack for compromising national security. The defeat was further fed into the national discourse to target Nehru's socialist policies even by many within the Congress. As it is, when Asia was experiencing a sudden outbreak of competing ideologies, anti-socialist groups, especially the Swatantra Party, possibly manoeuvred the defeat by China into a conflict between communism and democracy.

Washington achieved the aim of roping in New Delhi in its CIA-run Tibet project. Radar stations were placed in the Himalayas for surveillance, and by early 1963 the CIA freely operated a covert war, parachuting Tibetan warriors trained since 1957 at Camp Hale in Colorado into Tibet from an Indian military base.

As Zachariah writes, 'By 1964, Nehru had given free rein to the CIA to use Indian territory in its war against China in Tibet, and US spy planes were given refuelling rights in India on their way into Tibetan airspace.'

The entire sequence of events covering 1959–62 has been documented by various authors who had accessed CIA documents. In Jack Anderson's disclosures, *The Anderson Papers*,[44] Thomas Powers' book on the quintessential CIA director Richard Helms, *The Man Who Kept the Secrets*,[45] Kenneth Conboy and James Morrison's *The CIA's Secret War in Tibet*,[46] among others, reveal how the CIA during the thick of the Cold War carried out its secret war in the Himalayas; rescued the Dalai Lama from Tibet; and set up a guerrilla commando force in Mustang (Nepal) and a Tibetan Special Force in India to be deployed along the China border.

America and India were secret partners, and details of Indian and Tibetan intelligence are revealed in these papers. In fact, more publications have come out detailing the most compelling account of the US agency enterprise.

The ST CIRCUS file,[47] a documentation created by Bruce Walker, is quite revealing. Walker played a direct role in CIA's ST CIRCUS project for training and arming the Tibetan Chu-shi Gang-druk guerrilla fighters. Walker initially studied at the Namgyal Institute of Tibetology in Gangtok and later became part of the training staff at Camp Hale in Colorado where the Tibetan guerillas were trained.

Mikel Dunham's book, *Buddha's Warriors: The Story of the CIA-Backed Tibetan Freedom Fighters, the Chinese Invasion, and the Ultimate Fall of Tibet*,[48] is another fascinating account of the events unfolding in the 1950s and 1960s. Dunham spent seven years interviewing Tibetan fighters, as well as Indians and Americans involved in CIA operations.

Missions to Tibet[49] author Dr Joe F. Leeker alludes to how the Tibetan resistance leaders first approached the Americans for help as early as in 1950. It was President Dwight Eisenhower who approved the provision of training and equipping Tibetans with modern weapons and finally to be dropped into Tibet by parachute.

Initially, the CIA picked up six Tibetans in India for training at a secret CIA base at Saipan. They were later taken to Okinawa for parachute training in the summer of 1957. The CIA's Operation ST Barnum carried the ammunition drops in the fall of 1957.

In early October that year, the trained guerillas were flown by the B-17 from Kadena, Okinawa, to an emergency air base in Kurmitola located near Dhaka (East Pakistan). Later, they were dropped near the Brahmaputra, south of Lhasa.

President John F. Kennedy succeeded in roping India into the CIA's Tibet programme. Kennedy offered economic aid to India, and when the Chinese troops attacked NEFA in October 1962, the US offered military aid to India. The weapons came through Europe in the first week of November.

In the following years, after the 1962 war and China's conduct of its first nuclear tests in the next-door Xinjiang province in 1964, the CIA, along with the Indian agencies, clandestinely installed a nuclear-powered sensing device on the Nanda Devi peak in the Garhwal Himalayas for the purposes of surveillance.[50] The episode has remained shrouded in mystery but more facts have come out in the public domain in recent years.[51]

Nevertheless, between 1963 and 1967, the tensions between India and China continued to be alive, as China constantly threatened India's Himalayan border, forcing the country to spend more and more money on weapons.

As for the Tibetans, a Southern Air Transport DC-6 in November 1962 made three shuttles between Takhli in Thailand and the Charbatia airfield in eastern India, bringing in an assortment of weapons and communication sets for building up a Tibetan resistance force.[52]

By the fall of 1963, the CIA set up Air Ventures Inc. inside Nepal to do the airlift, and by late 1963, India agreed to airlift the Tibetans directly close to the Tibetan border in Mustang.

As mentioned earlier, the CIA/RSS DD/I Staff Study of May 2007 declassified some more facts with redactions.[53]

By now, we are sufficiently hard-wired to conform to our own world view, 'we could have done no wrong', conveniently attributing the defeat to either Chinese 'treachery and betrayal' or Nehru's 'idealism'. The truth is that the differences originally limited to trans-border trade and pilgrimage issues until 1959 suddenly got conflated into a military conflict in 1962.

The frenzied war hysteria that followed thereafter eternally turned India and China against each other, with all the perceived threats and trappings of a geopolitical rivalry. Against these intersecting interests, the two states have sought to constrain each other through proxies and alliances. Pakistan is one of the tools in this 'Great Game' at play between India and China.

The 'Great Game' in the Himalayas has only intensified since and continues unabated, though in different formats, despite the best efforts of both India and China to resolve the boundary issue. It only seems that the burden of Cold War politics and pressures continues to impinge on the India–China rivalry in the Himalayas without really comprehending what the two sides actually want, least what the third factor (the US) would do to decide the end game.

The assumption whether India would go to war or not has always had its limitations. In 1959, India sought a guarantee from the US to ensure that Pakistan would not attack India in case of an India–China conflict. A potential two-pronged military threat still exists.

A lasting India–China conflict serves Pakistan to prolong its conflict vis-à-vis India while putting into action its strategy of 'Bleed India with a Thousand Cuts'.

India as a nation ought not to fall prey to provocation, for national hysteria could once again get hijacked for sabotaging India's economic rise or even be used as an instrument for creating more enemies. India will have to craft a more perfect strategic alignment with Russia, America and China. In fact, for a long period of time in history, China had been India's spiritual neighbour and brother, which needs reigniting. China has acquired a composite national strength that enables it to defend itself against foreign aggression. There is also much for India to learn from the way China deploys its economic leverage to retaliate against those harming its interests.

6

Indian Perspective: Strategic and Economic

For India, its jurisdiction over Tawang was completed in 1951. It remained a part of NEFA—a British-created administrative unit under the Assam state government—until it was made into a Union Territory of Arunachal Pradesh in 1972.

A separate Tawang district was created in October 1984 out of West Kameng district as a result of the promulgation of Arunachal Pradesh (Reorganisation of Districts) Act, 1980, and the Second Amendment Act, 1984.

In 1987, India declared Arunachal Pradesh a full-fledged state of the Indian Union. But the state has remained the subject of a sovereignty dispute between India and China, with the latter refusing to recognize the McMahon Line as the boundary between the two countries and denying the legitimacy of India's legal control of the region.

Of course, India inherited the British legal claim to the region defined as per the 1914 Simla Convention, in which Tawang fell south of the McMahon Line. However, Indian nationalists have built a narrative of the region being a historic part of the Indian sphere of influence.[1]

According to this narrative, the area of Arunachal Pradesh is referred to as Prabhu Mountains in the ancient Hindu scripture *Kalika Purana* and the epics Mahabharata and Ramayana.[2] It was under the control of the Sutiya kings until the Ahoms took over in the sixteenth century. The archaeological site of Malinithan, which consists of the ruins of a fourteenth-century Hindu temple on the banks of the Brahmaputra River in west Siang, was built during the Sutiya period.

The nearby Akashiganga temple is believed to be associated with the legend of Goddess Parvati, narrated in the eighth-century *Kalika Purana*.[3] Similarly, present-day Bhismaknagar, located near Roing in the Lower Dibang Valley, was a stronghold of the Sutiya kingdom until the sixteenth century. Bhismaknagar was associated with Sadhayapuri.[4] This is why the area was rechristened with a Sanskritized name, 'Arunachal Pradesh' (Land of the Rising Sun), given by Bibhabasu Das Shastri, the then director of research, NEFA, and K.A.A. Raja, the then chief commissioner of Arunachal Pradesh, on 20 February 1987. Arunachal Pradesh became a state on 20 January 1971.

India, like the British, perceives Tawang as a strategic point that if left undefended could become an easy corridor for the Chinese into India. The British forced the Tibetans to give it up under the Simla Accord so as not to give the Tibetans and the Qing army the advantage of height.

When independent India's government was formed in Delhi, it inherited the British borders. In February 1951, a small force accompanied by political and administrative officers reached Tawang and instructed the lamas that they need not pay tribute to Lhasa. This region became part of NEFA and gradually the administrative gap was filled by Indian officials. A brief war occurred in October 1962 at the Thagla Ridge in Zimithang after Chinese troops intruded in the area.

Without going into the details of the contestation between India and China, be it the boundary issue or strategic rivalry, the underlying key variables in the conflict are not limited to India vis-à-vis China but the Tibetans themselves, who have been relentlessly playing their own game with the support of Western powers, namely, the United States.

The 'Great Game' has taken various forms, military, strategic and economic, but it has certainly engulfed the entire Buddhist Himalayas in a way where the end is not in sight. Rather, it is becoming more complex and asymmetrical.

Tibet's economy

If Chinese claims are eclectic and contextual (the Tawang–Dalai Lama factor), then Beijing also does not hide its intention to covet the region strategically and economically.

It is rather commonplace to read about the Himalayas and Tibet in their geostrategic settings. In fact, the current India–China contestation is being viewed as a replication of the nineteenth-century 'Great Game' between the British and Russian Empires.

But the Chinese, as also the Tibetans, argue how the Himalayas' vulnerabilities have been exploited in the past by forces inimical to them. They cite the British invasion of Tibet in the beginning of the twentieth century as a case in point.

Since the 1960s, China has gone in for massive economic transformation accompanied by the massive militarization of Tibet. Widespread infrastructural developments along with a network of airstrips, roads and railways built throughout the Tibetan plateau have inevitably posed a greater challenge to India.

Tawang's economic utility often gets embedded in China's calculations. One argument often made by Chinese experts is that the entire tract of Tawang is endowed with rich natural resources, minerals and agricultural and water resources that could support a third of Tibet's economy.[5]

In the past, Tawang, like the Chumbi Valley, historically served as a gateway between India and Tibet. A regular and flourishing trade was carried out in the past through the Kuriapara Duar. The *Gazetteer of India*, Arunachal Pradesh, notes that valuable goods traded regularly along this route included rice, coarse silk, iron, lac, skins, buffalo horns, pearls and corals from Assam and Bengal. In return, woollens, gold dust, salt, musk, horse's cowries and Chinese silks came from Tibet.[6]

Traders traditionally met at Udalguri in Darrang district, where they bartered goods and religious items. The Monpas and Sherdukpens played an important role as middlemen. They sold chillies, oilseeds and radishes in Assam and bought rice and cloth in return. Of course, the region was not without problems even in the past. Constant turmoil in Assam and adjoining areas, including Burmese forays, impacted trade, especially in the early nineteenth century.

Economic and trans-border trade, therefore, very much forms a good deal of Chinese calculations. In addition to Tibet's geostrategic setting, the latest source of concerns for India is China's aggressive attempts to make Tibet a logistical hub and gateway to South Asia under its Belt and Road Initiative (BRI).

Essentially, Tibet is now being embedded as a vital entryway for China's BRI cooperation with Nepal, Bhutan and Sri Lanka. And this does not exclude the use of Tibet and its Buddhism to forge the soft power needed to engage these countries.

Make no mistake, this is a well-thought-out strategy, especially when India is unable or unwilling to play its Buddhist legacy card. The most recent debates and discussions involve Tibetan monks and scholars to explore how best Tibetan Buddhism could better serve China's BRI.[7] The soft power of Buddhism will become yet another vital tool in the already growing asymmetry of power between India and China. So far, India held back from joining China's BRI for geopolitical reasons.

Securing trade and cultural (pilgrimage) rights in Tibet formed India's primary goal until the late 1950s, but not any more. Post-1962, India took the defensive mode amidst apprehensions that Tawang and the Chumbi Valley (Doklam) could provide easy military access to the PLA to enter the Assam plains and the rest of north-east India.[8]

Also, a strong fear psychosis prevails in India about China's plan to divert the Brahmaputra—which begins in Tibet but passes through Arunachal Pradesh—to feed its arid northern and western regions. This is an issue that gets featured heavily in Indian security calculations. A specific elaboration is made on this in a separate chapter.

Ecological concerns

According to the exiled Tibetan government's publications, China has been exploiting more than 126 identified minerals in Tibet. The plateau is endowed with high reserves of the world's deposits of uranium, chromites, boron, lithium, borax and iron.[9] Reserves of corundum, vanadium, titanium, magnetite, sulphur, mica, caesium, rubidium, arsenic, graphite, lepidolite and potash are found in abundance.

In 2007, Chinese geologists discovered more than 600 new sites of copper, iron, lead and zinc ore deposits on the Qinghai-Tibet plateau since 1999, according to the results of the latest geological survey.[10] The discovery included large-scale high-grade iron ore deposits of 300 million to 500 million tonnes in Nyixung. Large quantities of oil shale resources besides hydrocarbon resources are said to have been found in Tibet.[11]

In 2010, Chinese media reported that geologists have discovered 102 types of mineral deposits in over 3000 mine beds worth $100 billion. Among the variety of mineral reserves, they reportedly found large chromium and cuprum (copper) deposits of a higher grade than what is found other regions of China.[12]

With improved infrastructure and connectivity, Chinese minerals and metals companies are already flocking to the Tibetan plateau to extract these rich deposits and natural resources.

Much has been written about the environmental destruction in Tibet as part of the Tibetan struggle for freedom. Most of them argue that the Chinese have unearthed limitless raw materials principally for the benefit of China and against the interest of upsetting Tibet's delicate ecosystems and the survival of the Tibetan people.

The exploitation of Tibet's natural resources has been made one of the major planks by the exiled Tibetan government to attract global attention. It prepared a comprehensive report titled 'Tibet: Environment and Development 1992', first for circulation at the United Nations Earth Summit in June 1992, followed by another report in 2000. The second report detailed the litany of China's environmental exploitation and abuse in Tibet. But the Chinese foreign ministry official expectedly dismissed it by saying that the report was 'not worth commenting on', calling it 'full of distortions of the real situation in Tibet'.[13]

In 2007, a third report, 'Tibet: A Human Development and Environment Report', detailed another insight into the socio-economic situation in Tibet, from environmental and development perspectives, with a particular focus on human development issues.[14] The report acknowledged some positive developments, but called on China to reconsider its development policies. The Central Tibetan Administration (CTA) continued with their campaign and urged world leaders even at the UN COP21 Climate Change Summit in 2015 to put Tibet on their agenda.

In a message to world leaders, the Dalai Lama himself gave a clarion call to protect the environment of the Tibetan plateau when the campaign 'Tibet Climate Action for the Roof of the World' was launched by Sikyong (Tibetan prime minister) Lobsang Sangay in 2015 that sought to make Tibet central to global climate change discussions. 'This blue planet is our only home and Tibet is its roof.

As vital as the Arctic and Antarctic, it is the third pole,' said Lobsang Sangay. The Tibetan plateau, according to Sangay, is environmentally a strategic area constituting 46,000 glaciers; the third-largest store of ice and the largest source of accessible fresh water on the planet.[15] Sangay links the global significance of the Tibetan plateau in the context of climate change and global warming.

Tibetan concerns and anguish are certainly genuine and deserve the world's attention. Their cause has been receiving support from international environmental and Tibet solidarity groups. However, it still remains a normative position that lacks political realism—their position is getting reduced to engaging in Western-style climate activism.

The population transfer of the Chinese and their exploitation of resources in Tibet are facts. The Tibetans in exile believe that the infrastructural and resource development programmes initiated in Tibet since the 1980s only benefited China's economy. But the Chinese think Tibetans are ungrateful to the government that poured in billions for Tibet's development.

By ignoring the economic dimension and singularly focusing on Dalai Lama–led politics, India may have inadvertently allowed the Chinese to exploit Tibet's gigantic mineral and hydro wealth.

7

The Game of Imperfect Information

We have only been told about Nehru's blunders, his 'innocence and gullibility'[1] in surrendering India's rights and interests as a 'gesture of goodwill to Communist China'.[2] That in his quest for becoming nice towards China, Nehru hastily signed the Panchsheel agreement at India's own peril.

It is rather difficult to substantiate Nehru's 'goodwill gesture' theory, but barely two months after India's independence, he was apparently shocked to receive two telegrams from the Tibetan government in Lhasa asking newly independent India to return its lost territories.

In 1947, the Fourteenth Dalai Lama was only eighteen years old and too young to understand geopolitics, but his government demanded pockets of territory in the Buddhist Himalayas administered by the British until 1947, including Tawang, be returned to Tibetan authority.

The telegram, dated 16 October 1947, forwarded through the Indian mission in Lhasa, sought the return of territories 'such as Sayul and Walong and in the direction of Pemakoe, Lonag, Lapa, Mon, Bhutan, Sikkim, Darjeeling and others on this side of the Ganges River and Lowo, Ladakh, etc. up to boundary of Yarkhim'.[3]

Nehru was apparently stunned by these demands but concealed them from Parliament. He seemingly rejected the Tibetan claim and instead advised Lhasa to maintain status quo until new agreements could be reached. This most preposterous claim by the Tibetans, which was fraught with incalculable consequences for India, is mentioned in the then IB chief B.N. Mullik's book, *My Years with Nehru: The Chinese*

Betrayal. Mullik characterized it as an 'ill-advised claim' by the Tibetan authority.

New Delhi's expectation, on the contrary, was that Tibet would accept independent India's call for ratifying the 1914 Simla Convention or the McMahon Line treaty, which would have defined Tibet's own political status. Not only did Lhasa apparently rebuff India's call, it also refused to send a delegation to India's Independence celebrations.

The negative response from Lhasa came as a shock to New Delhi, especially since Nehru had already prepared the diplomatic groundwork for the Tibetan case by inviting a delegation from Tibet to participate in the Asian Relations Conference in March 1947. Clearly, the Tibetans had already changed their mind and instead agreed to terms from the Chinese, which they did in March 1951.

The events marked a decisive turn in India's view on Tibet and prompted Nehru to make a clarification on 6 December 1950 that 'he was interested in Tibet's autonomy but without challenging China's suzerainty over it'.[4] On 12 February 1951, Nehru only expressed grief in Parliament over the military crackdown in Tibet, but said, 'We didn't allow that to affect our policy or our desire to maintain friendly relations with China.'[5]

India was perhaps greatly relieved when the Dalai Lama's representatives signed the Seventeen-Point Agreement with Chinese authorities on 23 May 1951 affirming Chinese sovereignty over Tibet.[6] It was only after the Tibetans accepted Chinese sovereignty that India signed the peace treaty with China on 29 April 1954 which explicitly recognized Tibet as part of China.[7]

Interestingly, after his escape to India in 1959, the Dalai Lama absolved himself of any missteps by saying that he was only eighteen years old and had no active control over his regent. Regrettably, the Tibetan faux pas turned into a great benefit for China.

To their credit, the Tibetans finally accepted their blunder after almost sixty years when the former kalon tripa, or prime minister, Professor Samdhong Rinpoche, while addressing the participants of the Five-Fifty Forum in October 2017, said:[8]

'When India got its independence, it was open to dealing with Tibet as an independent nation. However, the Tibetan leadership at that time was completely ignorant of the world and we lost the opportunity to assert our sovereignty. In fact, the Indian leadership reached out to Tibet at that time to discuss the continuation of the trade treaties that Tibet shared with British India. However, Tibet didn't respond, thereby compelling India to talk to China instead.'

Dalai Lama's Tawang card

India's failure to get China's endorsement on the McMahon Line is a contentious subject. When it comes to Tawang, however, the key stakeholder is Tibet. The Tibetans continued to play their own subtle game in Tawang even after Chinese troops took control of Tibet in 1951. The Dalai Lama himself is a major actor and has been playing Tawang as a card, which he uses both vis-à-vis China and India.

When the Dalai Lama crossed into India on 30 March 1959, he went straight to the Tawang monastery before being escorted to Tezpur in Assam on 18 April. There are, in fact, some private narratives that suggest that Tibet's state oracle, Nechung, advised the Dalai Lama in a prophetic trance to establish a government in South Tibet. He even drew the directions to reach Tawang on a piece of paper.

It appeared that the Dalai Lama had other options. A revelation emerged in 1984 when the Dalai Lama told veteran journalist Bertil Lintner in an interview that he actually intended to go into exile in Burma (Myanmar) rather than India.[9] More precisely, he had wanted to settle in one of the ethnic Tibetan villages north of Putao, in northern Kachin state. As per the interview, 'He wanted to be among his own people and he thought Myanmar, a Buddhist country with a neutral stance in regional great power games, would respond positively to his presence.' Feelers were, in fact, sent out to Burmese leaders, but Prime Minister U. Nu declined, fearing it would derail their sensitive talks with Beijing to finalize the boundary settlement with China.

Another option had been offered by the United States when it was persuading the Dalai Lama to flee Tibet in 1951. The American ambassador in New Delhi, Loy W. Henderson, in his letter of 17 September 1951, advised the Dalai Lama to seek asylum in Ceylon or some other country from where he could continue his struggle for Tibet's autonomy. An offer was also made to take asylum in the US in case it should seem impractical to do so elsewhere.[10]

One can wonder, then, why he opted to come to India despite its reluctance to give him asylum. More importantly, upon reaching India, he refused to recognize India's sovereignty over Tawang and Arunachal Pradesh. After four decades of his stay in India, the Dalai Lama, while touring Tawang in 2003, said, 'Arunachal Pradesh was actually part of Tibet.'[11]

It was in 2006 that the former Tibetan prime-minister-in-exile, Samdhong Rinpoche, started articulating that Arunachal Pradesh was an 'inseparable part' of India.[12] However, Samdhong's statement came on the eve of Chinese President Hu Jintao's visit to India in November 2006. It also came against the backdrop of a provocative claim made by the Chinese ambassador in India, Xun Yuxi, who had said that the whole of Arunachal Pradesh was 'Chinese territory'.[13]

Samdhong refuted the Chinese claim over Arunachal on the grounds that the Tawang monastery had once been a part of Tibet, and that Tawang was part of Tibet before the McMahon Line was drawn.

Dharamshala's changed position on Arunachal Pradesh was also viewed in the context of the diminishing scope of continuing a Tibetan dialogue with China. Clearly, the intention was also to build pressure for resuming talks between the Dalai Lama's representative and China. Beijing had even sought reversal of the Dalai Lama's position as a precondition for the resumption of talks with his envoys, which were interrupted in 2008.

In June 2008, the Dalai Lama finally changed his position and said that both the Tibetan government and Britain recognized the McMahon Line in 1914. In fact, the statement was seen in the context of the March 2008 bloody riots in Lhasa that took place five months before Beijing hosted the Olympic Games.

It was the year when US President Barack Obama decided not to meet the Tibetan leader, emboldening Beijing to further step up its anti–Dalai Lama rhetoric. In the same year, China's rising financial clout compelled the United Kingdom to change its long-held position of describing Tibet as 'suzerain' to the 'sovereign' part of China. The change of position by the British government recognizing China's direct rule over Tibet for the first time fully undermined the Dalai Lama's position vis-à-vis China.

The Dalai Lama had almost lost hope of reaching an agreement with China. In October 2008, he said his exiled government could hereafter harden its position towards Beijing. This new position has been reiterated several times since 2008, but that is done while keeping in mind political compulsions, especially when it is left with little choice but to toe India's position over Arunachal Pradesh.

Moreover, the Dalai Lama, in recent years, has been rather shrewdly played the Tawang card. He has tried to stoke the fire while suggesting that 'Arunachal Pradesh is a part of India and not China'. Such statements have evoked immense sentiment for him among the Indian people.

This apart, the Dalai Lama has often used the 'guru–chela' idiom in order to gain sympathy among the Indian people. He has often said, 'I am the longest staying guest in India' and 'I am a son of India', which can be viewed as a dual but deceptive tactic he applies to both threaten China and enthral India. In recent years, he has used the phrase 'son of India' to describe himself more than two dozen times. Such insidious statements serve to create an atmosphere of mistrust and a 'negative public persona' in India against China, recurrently preventing the two countries from settling their boundary dispute. There lies the real game!

The Chinese termed the Dalai Lama calling himself a 'son of India' 'disgraceful' and a move meant to humiliate and split China,[14] saying that declaring himself a 'foreigner' wouldn't affect China's position on Tibet and boundary issues. Chinese Tibetologists deemed the Dalai Lama's actions as a betrayal and an attempt to sell out the people and the country. In comparison, the Thirteenth Dalai Lama, Thubten Gyatso, had never sold the motherland to a foreign country, they asserted.[15]

Political expediency

Rhetoric apart, Tibetans still maintain in private an ambiguous approach on Arunachal Pradesh at best, and this would be subjected to repudiation in future.

As elaborated elsewhere, Tibetan officials are known for repudiation as per political expediency. The Dalai Lama's government initially signed the Simla Convention on 3 July 1914 to define the border between Chinese Tibet and British India drawn by Sir Henry McMahon, but in practice it never ratified the McMahon Line on the pretext of Beijing's non-acceptance of it. In fact, at various points in history, the Tibetans opted in favour of taking protection under Beijing against British India's efforts to deal with them directly.

In the current context of Tibetans having lost autonomy, they do admit to having legally ceded Tawang to the British in 1914, but they also assert that Tibetan authorities exercised de facto power over Tawang until 1951.

Not to forget, the government in Lhasa initially signed the Seventeen-Point Agreement with Beijing affirming Chinese sovereignty over Tibet in 1951 only for it to be repudiated later on the grounds that the agreement was signed under duress.

The Tibetan position on Tawang was subject to political expediency too. In other words, had Tibet been independent or had it not been caught in a conflicting situation as it is today, Tawang would have continued to be claimed by Lhasa on the very same principle that the 1914 Simla Convention was ratified neither by Peking nor Lhasa.

From the Tibetan perspective, to justify Arunachal as part of India they will have to equally justify the rest of Tibet as being part of China. Yet, they are unable to express this openly as long as the exiled government is in India.

Even if the Tibetan government-in-exile comes up with a fresh position, it doesn't enjoy any legal authority or status to sign treaties. And, despite what the Dalai Lama and his officials say, Tibetans would continue to hold on to their inherent perception about their history, and for them Tibet would remain central to the future of Tawang's status.

Tibetan scholar Tsewang Dorji concludes in his article, 'Tibetan Narrative on Tawang', 'Despite numerous flimsy interpretations and narratives made by Chinese, Indian and Western scholars, academicians, politicians and adventurists, the foundational facts and the history of Monyul remain unflinching. The historical facts and accounts of Monyul can be explored in the history of Tibet. Hence, the Tibetan narrative on Tawang in the context of historical approach is a key to understand the most reliable historical account of Monyul.'[16]

Dorji may be right because both India and China rely on the same history of Tibet for staking their respective claims over Tawang.

The argument Tibetans often make privately is that 'India cannot have it both ways'—if it wants China's acceptance of the McMahon

Line, it has to recognize Tibet as an occupied country. Without giving sovereign political status to Tibet, India cannot seek validation to its claim over Arunachal Pradesh. In other words, the Simla Convention was a bilateral treaty between British India and Tibet, so how could India expect to have the McMahon Line without recognizing Tibet as an occupied territory?[17]

A very sound Tibetan perspective came up in 2014, the centenary year of the McMahon Line.[18] In a well-researched article titled 'The Centenary of the McMahon Line (1914–2014) and the Status of Monyul until 1951–52', Lobsang Tenpa says, 'Even while the geographical area of Monyul had been included within the sphere of the McMahon Line, the Lhasa-appointed twin authorities *bla gnyer* (abode manager) of the Tawang monastery and *rdzong dpon* (governor) of Tsona Dzong continued to sway power until 1951 when the area was incorporated into the "North-East Frontier Agency".'

Tenpa interestingly refers to the 'status quo rights' document signed between the Tawang monastery (estate and subjects) and the newly established assistant political officer, the Sela Sub-agency, on behalf of the Government of India on 8 July 1952. The document, according to Tenpa, put an end to the quandary and established the final implementation of the 1914 Simla Convention.

The main contention of Tenpa's argument is: a) Tibet was an independent state and it enjoyed sovereign control over Tawang till the 'status quo rights' document was signed by Tibetan officials with the assistant political officer of the Government of India on 8 July 1952, and b) the document is significant to the ongoing Indo-Tibetan or Sino (Tibetan)-Indian boundary negotiation in the eastern Himalayas. It implies that Tibet is still a party to the final border settlement.

Tenpa contends that Monyul's incorporation into the Indian Union was a gradual process as it was completed only after the last Tibetan official left Tawang following the 'acceptance cum requisition' paper being endorsed by the Indian political officer on 8 July 1952.

Very importantly, Tenpa argues that the status of Tibetan officials in Tawang and the 'requisition' were based on the continuity of the 1844 and 1853 treaties and the 1680 edict issued by the Fifth Dalai Lama. Here again, the argument is that Tibet exercised its autonomy until it signed the document on 8 July 1952.

The emphasis on the 1952 document signed with the Indian Union is meant to underscore the point that it was signed after the Tibetan government signed the Seventeen-Point Agreement with the Chinese communist regime in 1951.

The distinction Tenpa makes between the two documents is that the latter (1951) was forced to be 'signed and accepted' and the former (1952) was '[acceptance cum] requisition' to maintain the Tibetan status.

The fact that Monyul was 'legally' incorporated into the Indian Union in 1952 and Tibet was illegally (under duress) incorporated into China in 1951 is a brilliant academic argument. However, two years later, India (under the Sino-Indian Agreement on Regulating Trade and Pilgrim Traffic signed on 29 April 1954) recognized Tibet as a part of China—a fait accompli which is unlikely to alter any time soon.

Tawang's abbot and monastery

The subtle nature of contestation today relates to who controls Tawang. For the Chinese, control over Tibet is incomplete without Tawang. From the Tibetan point of view, Tawang is an extension of the Drepung gonpa in Lhasa and as such cannot be separated from Tibet.

From India's perspective, Tawang and its estate tenants had been legally incorporated into India after the signing of the 1914 Simla Convention or even if we accept the Tibetan claim of the signing of the 'acceptance cum requisition' paper in July 1952.

Accordingly, the authority of the Tawang abbot has extremely important symbolic significance, for he not only presides over the temporal charge of the monastery but also influences the place and its people.

There appears to be little official clarity now as to who should be appointing the abbot of Tawang. As per legal jurisdiction, only an Indian national (a Monpa in this case) should have been appointed as its khenpo (abbot) to run its affairs.

An elderly monk at the Tawang monastery, where he made the statement, recalled that until 1951, the head lama of the monastery had been appointed by the Tibetan theocracy based in Lhasa, and the Indian government had only a token presence here.

It seems that till date, the practice of appointing the abbot or head lama of the Tawang monastery by Tibetan theocracy is still in practice. In the present case, the appointment of the abbot is being decided by the Dalai Lama and, in effect, it is Dharamshala that exercises firm control over the Tawang monastery and its subjects. Which means the Government of India, which provides funding, and the local Monpas, who make offerings, are not the major stakeholders and do not have a say in the affairs of the monastery.

Here, the Dalai Lama's visits symbolize reaffirmation of his authority over Tawang or the region of South Tibet. In a conversation with a high lama of the Mon region, the Fourteenth Thegtse Rinpoche told me in private that Dharamshala has restored the old Tibeto-Qing era tradition of appointing a monk from Drepung as head lama of the Tawang monastery. He suspected that was done with a political motivation and on the advice of the former prime minister, Samdhong Rinpoche, who is still an adviser in the Dalai Lama's private office.

Obviously, the arrangement of non-locals serving as temporal heads of the Tawang monastery has not been without contestations made by local Monpas.

In 2016, the Dharamshala-appointed abbot, Guru Tulku Rinpoche, a non-Monpa, had to step down because of his interference in local affairs. In fact, the large presence of Gelugpa monks in the May 2016 protests had been viewed as a total rebellion against the Dalai Lama who appoints the abbot. The abbot's resignation last year is said to have hurt the Dalai Lama as he also threatened later that he would no longer appoint the abbot.[19] However, months later, he named a new abbot for the Tawang monastery.

In fact, an underlying mix of religion, political, ethnic and sectarian dynamics seems to still have a bearing on India's tenuous control over Tawang. The general impression is that the Dalai Lama–appointed Tawang abbots, who wield influence over the local populace, maintained close ties with powerful political families. Controlling the Tawang monastery is also significant for the Dalai Lama for he claims his sixth incarnation, Tsewang Gyatso, was born there in 1683—an assertion China also makes in order to reassert its claim on the area.

The politics mainly revolves around the influence of the powerful Khandu family, headed earlier by former chief minister Dorje Khandu, and now by his son, Pema Khandu.

One of the main issues pertains to the construction in the area of the National Hydroelectric Power Corporation (NHPC)-run 780 MW mega hydropower station, Nyamjang Chhu (Phase I and Phase II). As per media reports, the Khandu family has been lobbying for the projects for which an upfront payment of Rs 37.5 crores each is said to have been made to the Arunachal government in 2008.[20]

Against this, a popular local movement, Save Mon Region Federation (SMRF), has been spearheading protests since 2011, opposing large hydro projects in the ecologically sensitive region.

The twist in the story came when the Dalai Lama's appointed abbot, Guru Tulku Rinpoche, was seen undermining the popular anti-dam movement spearheaded by locals. Two persons including a monk were killed in police firing during the SMRF protest in May 2016.[21]

Instead of mammoth hydel projects, the local Monpas including monks of the Tawang monastery have been demanding the building of mini dams like the 6 MW Mukto Shakangchu in the interest of protecting the environment. According to the media, the National Green Tribunal (NGT) had concurred with the SMRF in April 2016 for the suspension of environmental clearance of the project.

Earlier, the call for the construction of mini dams was led by famous local religious figures such as Tsona Gontse Rinpoche, who had died under mysterious circumstances in Delhi in 2014. Similarly, former chief minister Kalikho Pul also committed suicide in a mysterious circumstance in 2016—it is not clear, though, whether the incident was linked to the controversy.

Given this context, even though the Dalai Lama's visits are dubbed 'purely religious' and organized on 'people's demand', they have underpinnings in local politics, power, governance and government-sponsored developmental projects involving huge financial stakes.

Another interesting point is the Dalai Lama's ability to connect with the sentiments of the local population, especially his ability to spiritually oblige (bless) local politicians. Pema Khandu's father Dorje Khandu was a 'very good friend' of the Dalai Lama.[22] In 2017, Pema Khandu invited the Dalai Lama to inaugurate his late father's memorial park where a stupa and a museum are being built in his memory.[23]

The Dalai Lama's visits are also meant for creating the rhetoric of India's assertive stance vis-à-vis China by local politicians such as Kiren

Rijiju and Pema Khandu. Such ultra-nationalist political posturing certainly gives them political dividend, but for others, such moves become far less reassuring.

Any attempt to curb his visits to Tawang by New Delhi, therefore, risks politically alienating the Buddhist constituency in the region. A local politician, Maling Gombu, felt that the Dalai Lama's visits get counted as an important factor for mobilizing popular support during the local elections by the ruling party—either the Congress or the BJP. This raises the point that the Dalai Lama's visits are often manipulated by vested interests.

In 2017, Pema Khandu announced his plan to organize a Kalachakra initiation in Tawang during 2018 that would have paid huge political dividends for his party, disregarding the fact that such events would cause another round of tension with China.

The agenda of getting the Bodhi (Tibetan) language included in Schedule VIII of the Indian Constitution is also very much on the politician's mind. Pema Khandu also talked about popularizing and teaching Bodhi to people, especially in schools.

There is also the important sectarian dimension of reinforcing the primacy of the Gelugpa sect that controls the Tawang monastery. The area was originally dominated by the Nyingmapa and Kagyu sects until the Tawang monastery was established in the seventeenth century on the wishes of the Fifth Dalai Lama.

Tawang is also historically important for the Karma Kagyu sect. In fact, the Government of India had facilitated a visit by the Seventeenth Karmapa, Lama Ogyen Trinley Dorje, to Tawang which did not anger the Chinese much. The motive of Dorje's visit wasn't clear, though.[24] It couldn't have been meant for reviving the Kagyu tradition at the cost of Gelug. In all probability, it was linked to boosting India's claim over Tawang. He was accompanied by Amitabh Mathur, a former R&AW officer and adviser on Tibetan affairs until 2018.

The Karmapa was taken to Sera Je Jamyang Choekorling monastery, Sangyeling monastery and Tawang monastery where he was received by the chief minister, Pema Khandu. He was also taken to Dirang, West Kameng district and Bomdilla.

In Tawang, Karmapa talked about maintaining sectarian harmony. It appeared as if the Indian authorities had fallen short of grasping the undercurrents of sectarian rivalries that are embedded in Tibetan politics and are detrimental to Indian interest in Tawang. The Karmapa is recognized by both China and the Dalai Lama, but his visit to Tawang did not anger Beijing as much compared to the Dalai Lama's visits.

Despite the Dalai Lama's acknowledgement of the Karmapa, the latter's ties with the Gelug-dominated Dharamshala have never been smooth and it has a lot to do with the politics of who controls the Himalayas. The Karmapa has been allowed to claim some space in India as long as he remains under the control of Dharamshala. In June 2017, he fled India mysteriously and hasn't returned since from the United States.

Geostrategic ramifications

All the points mentioned above would appear metaphorical today considering the fact that the Dalai Lama and his exiled government now acknowledge all of Arunachal Pradesh, including Tawang, as an integral part of India.

But, hypothetically, should the Tibetans, at some stage in future, regain autonomy or independence from China, would they then not reassert their reclaim to Tawang? For political watchers like Ashis Chakrabarti, 'This question may seem rhetorical today, but a future twist in the Himalayan power game might make it relevant someday.'[25]

But to rely on such rhetoric would remain risky considering the memories of Tibetans having made several twists and turns with regard to Tawang's historical status.

The fact remains that India gained control over Tawang because of its military strength, when Major Khating of the 2nd Assam Rifles evicted Tibetan troops from the area lying south of the Sela Pass, marking the end of Tibetan theocratic control over Tawang. It was also because of the Chinese PLA's intrusion in 1962 that India woke up to guard its strategic hold over the Tawang region.

However, unnecessary emphasis on Tawang's connection with the Dalai Lama seems rather an ill-thought political strategy of India's, for it might come back to haunt it in future. In fact, many points relating to Tibetan irredentist assertion over the Himalayas are deliberately hidden from the public domain or overshadowed by the fear of threats posed by China.

Instead, reckless policies mixing the Dalai Lama with Tawang may have only served to confuse the status of Arunachal Pradesh, which will eventually conflict with India's own interests.

It is rather paradoxical how the Dalai Lama, whose predecessors conquered and ruled Mon-Tawang (an integral part of India) from 1681 to 1951, is being hailed by the Indian State as a bulwark against China. The Dalai Lama's belated endorsement of the Indian position on Tawang would not make any difference to the Chinese position. The possibility that China will ever use the military route is rather dim. Instead, the Chinese would rely more on the Tibetan card and the Dalai Lama's own record to ease the Indian hold over the region.

China views the Dalai Lama issue as having a bearing on the political foundation of China–India relations. The Chinese argue that when the two countries have already reached a level of consensus to address the boundary question, why then does the Tibet issue always get propped up?

India under the Modi government since 2014 has made a few flip-flops on China and the Dalai Lama. The symbolic gesture of inviting the Tibetan prime-minister-in-exile to Prime Minister Narendra Modi's swearing-in ceremony did irk the Chinese.

But Modi's historic visit to Mongolia in 2015 and the purported game of sending the Dalai Lama to Mongolia in 2016 besides hosting other outreach programmes for him during 2017 proved somewhat counterproductive.

It was symbolically satisfying to use such diplomatic posturing to score a point, but the ultimate success of a strategy depends on other leverages, including economic clout, to deal with a country like China.

In the 1950s, instead of asserting the status of Tibet, India fought for Mongolia's membership to the UN. It was a smart move. But this time around, India's diplomatic posturing evidently did not pay off. It needs a strategic sense to realize that Mongolia is not the same thing for India as Nepal is for China.

The Chinese clamped down heavily on Mongolia over the Dalai Lama's visit, and Ulaanbaatar had to almost apologize for its misplaced audacity—it vowed never to invite the Dalai Lama again. Mongolian foreign minister Tsend Munkh-Orgil told the media, 'The government feels sorry for this,' adding that the Dalai Lama 'probably won't be visiting Mongolia again during this administration'.[26]

India's announcement of a $1 billion credit line to Mongolia in May 2015 was a costly strategic move. Earlier in April 2016, a similar repudiation was seen when India had to withdraw a visa for an Uyghur to visit India.

The Dalai Lama issue, however emotional it may be, has often made Indian policy go astray. Such policies were never pragmatic or based on geopolitical realism, as they should have been from an aspiring great power like India.

8

Tibet–China–India: A Shadowy Game over Tawang

China's claim on Tawang was initially linked to a territorial dispute. In the late 1950s, it expressed its willingness to recognize the McMahon Line as the boundary in the east (Tawang) in exchange for India accepting China's claim in the west (Aksai Chin). The boundary issue is not the focus of this book. However, to underline here briefly, China has made a shift in its position from the western sector since 1957 to the eastern sector in the mid-1980s. This has been known for a long time but more facts have recently come to the fore even to insiders who have been dealing with the India–China boundary dispute.

Shivshankar Menon, former foreign secretary and India's special representative for border talks, in his book *Choices: Inside the Making of India's Foreign Policy,*[1] alludes to how Chinese officials since the 1980s had begun saying 'if India made major adjustments first in the East, China would make concessions in the West'.[2] By 1985, Beijing specifically suggested the return of Tawang ostensibly in exchange for Aksai Chin as part of the swap deal.

A firmer position came in 1993, when China proclaimed almost all parts of Arunachal Pradesh to be integral to the Tibet Autonomous Region, termed as South Tibet. It is further split among six border counties such as Cona, Lhunze, Nang, Mainling, Medog and Zayu. Tawang is included in Tibet's Cona county.

The boundary negotiations are not revealed to the public, but it was none other than Dai Bingguo (Chinese boundary negotiator from

2003 to 2013) who confirmed China's stand when he said in 2017, 'If the Indian side takes care of China's concerns in the eastern sector of their border, the Chinese side will respond accordingly and address India's concerns elsewhere.'[3] What Dai Bingguo was talking about was that the border dispute could be resolved if New Delhi accepted Beijing's claim over Tawang.

'The disputed territory in the eastern sector, including Tawang, is inalienable from China's Tibet in terms of cultural background and administrative jurisdiction,' said Bingguo. 'Even British colonialists who drew the illegal McMahon Line respected China's jurisdiction over Tawang and admitted that Tawang was part of China's Tibet.'[4]

Surely, Indians never accepted China's new line of thinking, often dismissing it as neither practical nor possible. But a conformity to Dai Bingguo's assertion from the Indian side came from his former India counterpart, M.K. Narayanan, who wrote, 'During several rounds of my discussions, Dai Bingguo made it amply clear to me that Tawang was non-negotiable [even though] the Agreement signed in 2005 on the Political Parameters and Guiding Principles for the Settlement of the India–China Boundary Question stipulated that areas with settled populations would not be affected in any exchange.'[5]

Tit for tat?

With this, it became fairly clear that Tawang, a non-negotiable point for China, remains the stickiest point in the boundary dispute. Narayanan commented, 'Even before the ink was dry, China began to dissimulate as far as Tawang was concerned, even though Tawang is the most "Indianised" place in the entire Northeast. All this leaves little scope for compromise with regard to areas like Tawang.'

The Chinese believe in sifting through history to find facts. According to Narayanan, Chinese thinking is eclectic, contextual, relational and convoluted, and its methodology obtuse. Narayanan notes, 'China constantly flaunts its exceptionalism and its uniqueness. Chinese exceptionalism tends today to be largely historical and revivalist. A combination of Mao's utopianism and Deng Xiaoping's realism has left China in a kind of philosophical vacuum. It has led to an excess of nationalism and nationalistic fervour, making China's objectives clear-cut.'[6]

It is hard to say whether it is true or not. Even the Indian way of thinking is abstract and open-ended without reaching a conclusion.

There exists a new-found enthusiasm among Chinese officials and academics for Tawang while touching on the Dalai Lama's history on the following points: (a) Tawang is historically woven into the fabric of Tibetan religion and culture, (b) 'Monyul', populated by Monpas, Sherdukpens, Membas and Khampas, traditionally had deep links with Lhasa, (c) the Tawang monastery (Galden Namgey Lhatse) was built by Lama Lodre Gyatso in 1680–81 in accordance with the wishes of the Fifth Dalai Lama, Ngawang Lobsang Gyatso, (d) the Sixth Dalai Lama, Tsangyang (Tsewang) Gyatso, was born in 1683 in the family of Lama Tashi Tenzin, a descendant of Pema Lingpa, who was a treasure revealer, and Tsewang Lhamo, a Monpa girl of a royal family of Bekhar village.

Since the early 1990s, the Chinese authorities have publicly referred to Tawang's importance as the birthplace of the Sixth Dalai Lama. According to a study by the International Campaign for Tibet (ICT) in 2014,[7] Chinese state media and the authorities intended to recover at least the birthplace of the Sixth Dalai Lama if not the entire territory. The study quotes an article entitled 'China Will Not Abandon Birth Place of Sixth Dalai Lama in Dawang [sic] Area', written by Liu Silu in the Chinese-owned Hong Kong newspaper *Wen Wei Po* in 2008, stating, 'Due to special significance of Dawang area, China can never give up the place. However, recovery of the entire 90,000 square kilometres of land will be very difficult. At least, the birthplace of the Sixth Dalai should be recovered. This writer is convinced that China will not give up Dalai's birthplace now and will never give up the place in the future.'[8]

In 2003, a Chinese academic, Zhao Gancheng of the Shanghai Institute of International Studies, said in New Delhi that Tawang is deeply associated with Tibet and its surrender to India would 'hurt the sentiments' of the Tibetan people.

'Tawang is part of the Deprung monastery in Lhasa' is a new line in China's cultural argument—a point made by Lian Xiangming of the government-run China Tibetology Research Center (CTRC) in Beijing.[9] This fact is not only true but also one that the Dalai Lama subscribes to till now.

During my last visit in September 2018, Tibetologists of the CTRC brought out fresh documents to attribute Tawang's origin to the

Fifth Dalai Lama, who in turn paid his ritual obeisance to the Chinese emperor under the tributary system.[10]

China's increasing confidence and reliance on the Tibetan narrative is rather telling. However, most Indians doubt whether Tawang's linkage with the Dalai Lama is China's central point of argument.

This is where Indians have gone wrong always. Narayanan got deluded by the 2005 agreement on the 'Political Parameters and Guiding Principles' for the boundary settlement that excluded settled areas from any exchange.

Similarly, the Indian side went by the June 2003 agreement signed during Prime Minister Vajpayee's visit to Beijing that explicitly recognized the Tibet Autonomous Region as a 'part of China'—without perhaps realizing that officially China covers Arunachal Pradesh as part of the Tibet Autonomous Region. Or was it done in exchange for Beijing agreeing to restart border trade with India through the Nathula Pass in Sikkim, amounting to China's acknowledgement of India's de facto sovereignty over Sikkim?

The truth came back to haunt New Delhi. A month after Vajpayee's visit, a Chinese foreign ministry spokesman said that 90,000 square kilometres of land in Arunachal Pradesh was not part of Indian territory.[11]

China did recognize India's sovereignty over Sikkim in 2005, but held on to its old stand when China's envoy to New Delhi, Sun Yuxi, said, 'The north-eastern state of Arunachal Pradesh was still a disputed area between India and China.'[12] Sun said this ahead of Premier Wen Jiabao's visit to New Delhi in April 2005.

Clearly, China's recognition of Sikkim wasn't quid pro quo. And all of these factors have left a sense of confusion in India.

Instead, most Indian analysts view China's key contestation vis-à-vis India as stemming from its deep-seated concerns about political vulnerabilities within Tibet. It was none other than the former Indian foreign secretary Kanwal Sibal who in a commentary wrote that China's oft-raised objections are merely 'diplomatic bluster'[13] and shouldn't be taken seriously.

It becomes emotionally satisfying for Indians to use the 'Tibet card' to score a point or to provoke China, but in reality, they may only be inadvertently contributing to reinforcing China's position, if not falling right into China's trap vis-à-vis its position in the Himalayas.

India's claims

Curiously, if India's sovereign claim over Arunachal Pradesh is based on the legality of British inheritance (defined as per the 1914 Simla Convention) but never ratified by either China or Tibet, why does India need to play the Dalai Lama card to prove its rights?

Clearly, the India–China conflict in the Himalayas has become almost like a reckless battle of wits. The trend so far suggests that by inserting the Dalai Lama factor, India has participated in making the Himalayan region a theatre of conflict with China.

Hardly anyone had heard of the Tawang monastery before it became a battle zone in 1962 due to the unsettled long border with China. Since then, it has been a flashpoint largely due to oft-repeated visits by the Dalai Lama ostensibly in the guise of religious activities.

Since 1983, the Dalai Lama has visited Arunachal Pradesh several times. In 1983, he spent one-and-a-half months in the state and visited Miao, Tenzingang, Bomdila, Tawang, Dirang and Itanagar. In 1996, he travelled to Miao, Tezu, Mirig, Tenzin Gang, Bomdila, Dirang and Tawang. In 2003, he visited the area twice. But it was his last two visits (8–15 November 2009 and 4–13 April 2017) that became the most controversial.

A bolder diplomacy?

India's MEA denies having any 'Tibet card', but it maintains that India has a long-time commitment and consistent position to treat the Tibetan spiritual leader as a guest as he is well-respected and revered by people in India.

In 2016, the Government of India, though, denied having departed from the past practice of letting the Dalai Lama go wherever he wanted to. But never before were other organs of government seen going out of their way to involve the Dalai Lama in official events, as was done during the year 2016–17, including his presence at Rashtrapati Bhavan in December 2016. This was in stark contrast to the government carefully maintaining the strict protocol of avoiding the Dalai Lama's interface with high officials beyond the exchange of private courtesies and greetings.

For instance, in 2009, Lodi Gyari, formerly a close associate and special envoy of the Dalai Lama in Washington, had advised India's national security adviser, Shivshankar Menon, to float a Buddhist platform in order to counter China's aggressive promotion of Buddhism since 2006. The idea led to the formation of the International Buddhist Confederation (IBC).[14]

Lama Lobzang, who headed the IBC since 2010, virtually turned the body into a propaganda machine for the Dalai Lama and the Tibetan cause, instead of countering China through the spread of Indian Buddhism in the world.

In 2011, China objected to the presence of the Dalai Lama at the IBC-organized event, the Global Buddhist Congregation, in New Delhi. Beijing even threatened to call off the fifteenth round of border talks between the special representatives if India refused to yield and cancel the conference. Eventually, the prime minister and president had to skip the event.

Clearly, this time round, India, under Prime Minister Narendra Modi, was signalling a bolder diplomacy with China. In fact, from day one, the Modi government has shown scant caution for China's sensitivities and broken past convention of avoiding any official meeting for the Dalai Lama with high constitutional authorities. Allowing his presence in such large public events and seating him with the Indian president was still rare.

As such, the Dalai Lama inevitably became a part of India's diplomacy toolkit—more a tactical motive to settle scores with China and less a sign of change in India's Tibet policy. In fact, the Dalai Lama 'card' is being used in a calibrated manner as a way readily available for tit-for-tat action.

Attempts to alter the approach started with the dramatic move to invite CTA head Lobsang Sangay to Narendra Modi's first swearing-in ceremony as prime minister along with the heads of South Asian Association for Regional Cooperation (SAARC) States on 26 May 2014. The tendency to play the 'Tibet card' has only increased since then, despite Modi not appearing to be very inclined in its favour.

In fact, a trend of New Delhi proactively using the Dalai Lama through 2016–17 was apparent. The Tibetan spiritual leader was seen getting greater public outreach; politicians and officials openly received and shared platforms with him—something the Indian government had avoided earlier.

A sequence of major events that involved the Dalai Lama included the following:

- In April 2016, Dharamshala was allowed to hold an 'inter-ethnic conference' with Uyghur and Chinese dissenters participating in it.
- In October 2016, India permitted the US ambassador in New Delhi, Richard Verma, to visit Tawang to attend a festival. Months later, in January 2017, Verma hosted a dinner for Kiren Rijiju and the prime minister of the Tibetan government-in-exile, Lobsang Sangay, at the US embassy in Delhi.
- In November 2016, the Dalai Lama paid a four-day visit to Mongolia despite China's strident warning to Ulaanbaatar.
- On 30 November 2016, the Indian government facilitated a visit by the Karmapa, Ogyen Trinley Dorje, to Tawang.[15]
- In December 2016, President Pranab Mukherjee for the first time hosted the Dalai Lama at Rashtrapati Bhavan at the Laureates and Leaders for Children Summit.
- In March 2017, the Dalai Lama inaugurated the three-day international Buddhist conference on 'The Relevance of Buddhism in the 21st Century' at Nalanda, Bihar where he shared the stage with the minister of state for culture and tourism, Mahesh Sharma, among other officials.
- On 24 March 2017, New Delhi, in a snub to China, allowed the visiting Australian cricket team to meet the Dalai Lama in Dharamshala. The Indian media described it as a fitting reply to China, which had earlier objected to the permission given to the Dalai Lama to visit Arunachal Pradesh.[16]
- In April 2017 came the most controversial visit by the Dalai Lama to Arunachal Pradesh after a gap of eight years since 2009. His visit was announced well in advance in October 2016.

Obviously, among the wide range of views prevailing in New Delhi in 2017 was that India would gain leverage vis-à-vis China by the Dalai

Lama's visit to Arunachal Pradesh.[17] Many had long suspected that his visits to Tawang were prearranged by the Indian government.

In fact, during a conversation with a prominent political activist from Tawang, it came to light that New Delhi had sought an invitation from the chief minister of Arunachal Pradesh to the Dalai Lama to visit the state.

But while doing so, New Delhi is also careful about China's sensitivities related to Tibet and Taiwan which are non-negotiable for China. If there is indeed a Tibet card, then New Delhi plays it in a calibrated way so that the fallout does not become politically difficult to reverse.

It also means that India has a full grip and the Dalai Lama is at New Delhi's beck and call. Surely, the Dalai Lama himself has little option left after Beijing managed to pin the Tibetan leader down by deploying every political and economic threat in its arsenal to constrict his global outreach.

The Modi government's approach to the Tibetan cause was welcomed by the Western world, for they thought a new 'Great Game', albeit as a 'soft diplomacy' was being launched against China.[18] The world certainly viewed the President inviting the Dalai Lama to Rashtrapati Bhavan as an indication of a change in the Indian policy vis-à-vis the Tibetan issue.

Beijing strongly reacted to the Dalai Lama's outreach activities, especially his presence at Rashtrapati Bhavan and his meeting with President Pranab Mukherjee. Chinese foreign ministry spokesperson Geng Shuang said, 'India must respect China's "core interests" and take effective means to remove the negative impact caused by the incident so as to avoid any disturbance to bilateral ties.' Beijing claimed that Delhi 'insisted' on his presence at Rashtrapati Bhavan and that he share the stage with the president.[19]

India ignored China's reservations, with an MEA spokesperson saying, 'India has a consistent position. The Dalai Lama is a respected and revered spiritual leader and it was a non-political event organized by Nobel laureates dedicated to the welfare of children.'[20]

China also strongly objected to Richard Verma's Tawang visit by saying that any interference by Washington in the Sino-India boundary dispute would only complicate it.

On the Karmapa's November 2016 visit to Arunachal Pradesh, Beijing told India to abide by consensus and refrain from taking any action that might complicate the boundary dispute.[21] It was unclear, though, why Ogyen Trinley Dorje visited Tawang.[22] It couldn't have been to revive the Kagyu tradition at the cost of Gelug. In all probability, the Karmapa's visit was also linked to boosting India's claim over Tawang. He was accompanied by Amitabh Mathur, former R&AW officer and adviser on Tibetan affairs until 2018.

Of course, Mongolia took the more courageous step of inviting the Dalai Lama despite facing Beijing's ire. China's foreign ministry strongly objected, saying, 'China resolutely opposes the Dalai Lama visiting any country to carry out anti-China separatist activities in any name or in any capacity. We also stand firmly against all forms of contact between officials from any country and the Dalai Lama. We strongly demand that Mongolia, for the purpose of maintaining the general picture of a sound and steady development of bilateral ties, earnestly stick to its commitment on Tibet-related issues, do not allow the visit by the Dalai Lama and do not provide any form of support and convenience to the group of the Dalai Lama.'[23]

Similarly, China lashed out at India for insisting on inviting the Dalai Lama to attend the international conference on Buddhism held by the Indian government despite China's opposition.[24]

China's tough warning came a day after Dai Bingguo said Beijing would be willing to leave Aksai Chin if New Delhi gave up Tawang. It also came soon after Foreign Secretary S. Jaishankar visited Beijing for the first bilateral 'strategic dialogue' with the aim of resetting relations between the countries. It was held against the backdrop of both nations having faced an unclear situation relating to US President Donald Trump's approach to Asia.[25]

Contentious visit

The sternest rebuke from Beijing came about the Dalai Lama's visit to Arunachal Pradesh in April 2017. It warned India of 'serious damage' to the relationship if the Dalai Lama's visit was allowed to go ahead. India responded by saying that there was nothing 'unusual' about his visit and underlined that the border state was an integral part of the country.

But this time, the idea was to taunt China, for the visit was almost for two weeks, starting in Assam on 1 April and ending in Tawang on 13 April 2017. Surely, the Chinese displayed both irritation and anger over the Dalai Lama's visit, which they thought was 'obstinately arranged' by New Delhi. Beijing expressed its anger in October 2016 after it became known that the Dalai Lama may visit Arunachal Pradesh in early 2017 at the invitation of the state's chief minister, Pema Khandu.

Again, in a departure from past practice, the Dalai Lama was escorted to Arunachal Pradesh by the Union minister of state for home, Kiren Rijiju. In fact, this was the highest point of provocation. To add fuel to the fire, Chief Minister Pema Khandu made a zealous comment that his state (Arunachal Pradesh) shared a border with Tibet (not China), which was interpreted as questioning the 'One China' principle.

The visit was built up gradually. It started with the Dalai Lama's visit to Guwahati from 1 April 2017, where he attended a couple of functions, including the government-sponsored Namami Brahmaputra Festival along with the chief minister of Assam, Sarbananda Sonowal.[26] He delivered a talk in Dibrugarh before embarking on a nine-day tour of Arunachal Pradesh.

Beijing was initially throwing barbs mostly through the media, but as the Dalai Lama's arrival in Tawang drew closer, it upped the ante, issuing a stern warning that the visit could cause 'serious damage' to bilateral ties.

Indian officials asked China not to create 'artificial controversy' over the visit and argued that the Dalai Lama was not doing anything that was a departure from his usual activities, and his visit to Arunachal Pradesh was a result of the long-standing demand of his followers there. New Delhi also rubbished China's concerns as the official spokesperson Gopal Baglay said, 'We have no say on his travels in India. No political meaning should be assigned to the visit.'[27]

Close to the time when the Dalai Lama was to travel to Tawang from Bomdila, Beijing summoned India's envoy, Vijay Gokhale, on 5 April 2017 to 'immediately stop the erroneous move'.[28] Beijing furiously said it will take 'necessary measures'[29] to preserve its territorial sovereignty and legal interests if India goes back from its commitment on Tibet. Beijing also warned India it would have a negative impact on the boundary settlement, besides damaging bilateral ties, and even threatened to downgrade the bilateral relationship.

China probably wanted to make sure that its protests did not go unheeded. A day before the Dalai Lama reached Tawang, Chinese official media warned that 'if New Delhi chooses to play dirty . . . Beijing should not hesitate to answer blows with blows' and even issued a veiled threat to retaliate by interfering in Kashmir.

China accused India through an article titled 'New Delhi Using Dalai As Diplomatic Tool Harms Sino-Indian Ties' in *Global Times*, a CPC-run daily. The report said, 'Amid Beijing–New Delhi conflicts, the Dalai Lama is now openly used by India as a diplomatic tool to win more leverage. New Delhi is dissatisfied with Beijing's stance over its membership bid to the Nuclear Suppliers Group and its request to name Masood Azhar, head of Pakistani militant group, to a UN Security Council blacklist. Therefore, Delhi attempts to play the Tibet card against Beijing.'[30]

When the Dalai Lama finally reached Tawang on 7 April, everything suddenly went quiet. Union minister Kiren Rijiju was missing from the scene, though he had earlier announced he would receive the Tibetan leader at Tawang. Earlier, on 6 April, he, along with Pema Khandu and other senior functionaries, was seen accompanying the Dalai Lama in the Bomdila and Dirang monasteries.

No significant report emerged thereafter from Tawang. China, too, stopped protesting. Clearly, the two sides had decided to pull back from the brink. At worst, India had caved in to threats from China.

On his part, the Dalai Lama avoided making any comments on the status of Tawang and stuck to making indistinct comments such as 'I am a messenger of Indian thoughts', 'Happy to visit Arunachal Pradesh', 'Thank the Indian government for taking care of me' and so on.

He also steered clear of political comments, stating, 'There is nothing new in China's objections,' as he also rejected the view that 'India has never used him against China'. But he used the occasion to clarify his own position: 'We don't want independence from China . . . Chinese government must give us meaningful self-rule or autonomy.'[31]

So, what came out finally was a statement by the MEA on 14 April 2017 that said, 'There is no change whatsoever in India's policy towards the TAR [Tibet Autonomous Region] of China, and its approach to seeking a fair, reasonable and mutually acceptable solution to the boundary question remains unchanged.' This meant the Dalai Lama wasn't a factor in the boundary issue.

The question however remained why the Indian government made such unprecedented moves around the Dalai Lama's visit and why it defended his Arunachal visit so vociferously in 2017.

No clarity was available on whether the issue became a litmus test for Indian democracy or whether the Dalai card was so essential for India's legitimate claim over Arunachal Pradesh, or was there any other hidden agenda in this? Officially, India maintains an unambivalent stand on the status of Arunachal Pradesh.

The Chinese official reaction came four days later, surely after making a full assessment of the Dalai Lama's visit. Spokesperson Lu Kang said on 17 April, 'I have noted relevant statements. For some time, due to reasons known to all, the political foundation for China–India relations has been damaged, casting a shadow over bilateral relations and the boundary negotiations. What is imperative now is for the Indian side to take concrete actions to honor its solemn promises, in particular never again using the 14th Dalai Lama to undermine China's core interests.'[32]

The popular perception both within and outside policy circles was that India was using the Dalai Lama simply as a pressure point to settle scores with China, especially to retaliate for the way Beijing had at the time blocked the listing of Masood Azhar on the UN terror list, prevented India's entry to the Nuclear Suppliers Group, pressed ahead with the China–Pakistan Economic Corridor (CPEC) project in Pakistan-occupied Kashmir, adopted an unyielding stance on the boundary issue, and so forth.

Another act that could be seen as a blunder was letting Lobsang Sangay unfurl the Tibetan national flag at the strategic location of Pangong Lake in Ladakh on 5 July 2017. It is not clear whether it was an amateur decision taken by the government without adequate understanding of its implications. It could be seen as the first such act by a Tibetan in Ladakh since 1683 when the Tibetan army was pushed back by the Mughal–Ladakhi army.

Journalist Jyoti Malhotra has hinted how Indian policymakers were desperate to make full use of the Dalai 'asset' before he was no more—a point 'vulgarly described' in security circles.[33] Although the Dalai Lama denied he was being used, he did make a visit to Tawang where the minister of state for home affairs escorted him like a virtual minister-in-waiting.

The Dalai Lama's Tawang visit was hailed by many in India as a big feat. The media especially created a strong emotional current for having responded to China both effectively and appropriately by hitting them where it hurts. It was like the 'straw breaking the camel's back' for some.[34] Others thanked the Dalai Lama for giving India a big 'victory' in the battle of wits—a symbol of India's emergence as a confident nation.[35] Some viewed the move by India as some sort of a 'surgical strike'—thus the ghost of 1962 has been buried at last![36]

With this, India not only hoped to reset its ties with China on more equal terms but also to leverage its ties with the US. To an extent, New Delhi sent the right signal, and even seemingly worked to pinprick China, which also faces vulnerabilities in Tibet, Xinjiang and Taiwan.

So, did China succeed in getting India to concede never to use the 'Dalai Lama card' in future, similar to what it had successfully done in Mongolia recently? We don't know yet.

India might not have any interest in Tibet per se, but it does have useful deterrence value vis-à-vis China. Coming back to Arunachal Pradesh, when the Dalai Lama wrapped up his week-long trip to Tawang in April 2017, he had promised to return for initiating a Kalachakra ceremony that was to be held in January 2018 on the invitation of Chief Minister Pema Khandu.[37] The Kalachakra ritual was never held in Tawang.

Upset with this turn of events, Beijing issued a stern warning of 'negative consequences' on the boundary settlement, and on bilateral ties in general. Two months later, the Indian army intercepted road-laying efforts by the PLA in the Doklam plateau, leading to a military stand-off that lasted for seventy-three days. Everything that has happened since is well known.

Whether playing the Dalai card yielded any results is hard to tell, but in 2018 the government may have averted Doklam 2.0 by stopping the Dalai Lama's ten-day visit to sensitive Sikkim in March 2018.

India, Mongolia and Dalai Lama

It wasn't clear whether playing up Tibet was an Indian foreign policy priority. In a speech in 2016, then foreign secretary S. Jaishankar said, 'India and China have put a premium on developing a bilateral relationship and not allowing other considerations to unduly influence their progress' and that 'three lost decades compel us to still play catch-up in the relationship'.[38]

That said, it was also true that India was trying to play the Tibet card to counter China's strategic moves. Among others, there was a sense that Indian agencies fed by Dharamshala or at the behest of the US seemed to be preparing to start thinking of the future of the Dalai Lama.

So, even as Beijing appeared poised to find its own Fifteenth Dalai Lama, New Delhi seemed determined to forestall any such plan. According to one version, as the Karmapa would be viewed as the Dalai Lama's interim political successor, New Delhi was tempted to boost his profile. Another view was that preparations should be made to start mobilizing the support of the clergy in other Vajrayana countries like Mongolia to decide the future Dalai Lama. Thinking in this direction assumed importance in the light of the new administration in the United States. As president-elect, Donald Trump had hinted at the US ending its 'One China' policy. Of course, that never happened when Trump assumed the office of president.

In fact, for a while it seemed India was seeking to play the Inner Asia geopolitical chess game over Lamaism that Chinese imperial courts had historically played. There might have been a strategic consideration behind Prime Minister Modi's trip to Ulaanbaatar in May 2015. Surely, there was bilateral content in his visit as he also announced a $1 billion credit line to Mongolia that surprised many at home.

This is a separate issue, but his visit was followed by a five-day visit to Mongolia by the Dalai Lama in November 2016. Clearly, the visit was aimed at letting the Dalai Lama stir up the game his institution used to play in the past. And the game was linked to reviving the sixteenth-century Mongolian ecclesiastical institution built around the 400-year-old spiritual figure of the Jebtsundamba Khutukut or Bogd Khan, whose lineage was terminated when the communist government came to power in 1921.

The ninth and last Jebtsundamba was born in Tibet but spent most of his life in Karnataka until November 2011, when he went to Mongolia where he passed away in March 2012.

At the heart of the Dalai Lama's visit to Mongolia lay the exercise of identifying the new Jebtsundamba. On the fourth day of his visit, he announced that he was convinced (through his wisdom eyes) of the recent rebirth of the Jebtsundamba in Mongolia. He, however, desisted from revealing the boy's identity. It is possible that the Mongolian state may have aborted the plan fearing a Chinese rebuke. Another rumour, quite credible, though, spread that the Mongolian president privately told the Dalai Lama to select his son to be a reincarnation of Jebtsundamba.[39] The Dalai Lama probably didn't entertain the idea.

It is also possible that the Dalai Lama himself withheld the identity for a possible future negotiation with China to jointly agree to identify the Tenth Jebtsundamba just as he and Beijing did for the Seventeenth Karmapa in the 1990s. The visit of a high-level Tibetan delegation from China to Mongolia prior to the Dalai Lama's visit may have been linked to the recognition of the Jebtsundamba.

Unsurprisingly, Beijing censured Mongolia for taking the 'erroneous' step of inviting the Dalai Lama and took strong retaliatory action, calling off loan negotiations, imposing border tariffs and cancelling key bilateral talks. China appeared angrier this time, especially after it had in recent years succeeded in curtailing the Dalai Lama's outreach to world capitals.

Weeks later, the Mongolian foreign minister, Tsend Munkh-Orgil, seemed to have extended an apology to the Chinese government and promised never to invite the Dalai Lama to Mongolia again. 'Under this current government, the Dalai Lama will not be invited to Mongolia, even for religious reasons,' the foreign minister told the Mongolian media on 22 December 2016.

The Chinese foreign ministry hoped that 'the Mongolian side can really learn the lessons from this incident, earnestly respect China's core interests, and abide by its promises and work hard to promote the improvement of China–Mongolia ties'.[40]

Why did Mongolia play the Dalai Lama and India cards against China? Mongolia had previously said that the Dalai Lama's trip had nothing to do with the government and that he had been invited by Mongolian Buddhists. But the real answer lay in the terrible financial soup it found itself in 2014–16. The country was worst hit by the downturn, especially by China's slowdown, resulting in its growth rate crashing from 17.3 per cent in 2011 to negative in 2015.

Mongolia had gone into a massive sovereign default with an external debt of $22.5 billion—twice the country's GDP. It needed to clear a commercial debt of \$2 billion as well as another \$2.3 billion currency swap agreement with the Bank of China due in 2017. Critically, Mongolia's negotiation with China for a \$4.2 billion bailout hadn't worked.[41]

Also, since the end of the Cold War, Mongolia had been unable to play its two giant neighbours—Russia and China—against each other. Then, it included the US and Japan as its 'third neighbours' to play its strategic game. But clearly, Mongolia's 'third neighbours', whom China despises, seem unable to bail it out of its repayment obligations. And it is here that the Dalai Lama and India come in.

One interesting outcome of the Dalai Lama's visit was Mongolia turning to its 'spiritual neighbour' India for financial support. When the Dalai Lama card failed to yield results, Mongolia quickly sought an Indian financial bailout on 'spiritual' grounds, as well as 'clear support' against China's transport obstruction, imposed following the Dalai Lama's visit.

The Mongolian envoy in New Delhi told the media that India not raising its voice could be construed as giving China a 'pass' for its 'behaviour'.[42] The underlying suggestion was that India had a hand in the Dalai Lama's Mongolia visit and its fallout. China had already warned Mongolia against seeking Indian help. Its official media termed the step 'politically harebrained' and said that 'Mongolia cannot afford the risks of such geopolitical games'.[43]

The issue was about India's credit line of \$1 billion offered during Prime Minister Narendra Modi's visit in 2015 that Mongolia now wanted released to meet its fiscal needs. However, it was difficult to imagine how India could help solve the country's debt burden. There seemed to be no precedent of India converting its line of credit to service the debt of another country. Nevertheless, the MEA spokesperson said India was 'ready to work with Mongolian people in this time of their difficulty'.[44]

While Mongolia's plea on 'spiritual' grounds was appealing, others cautioned against playing such a game, knowing what had happened when India went out of its way to help Nepal. Also, it was not that India would get anything in return, Mongolia being a distant country with which India could not trade without transiting through China.

Mongolia quickly withdrew from standing up for India despite its strong commitment to work together on issues like terrorism.

Barely a year after Prime Minister Modi's visit to Ulaanbaatar, it was disappointing in its response to the attack in Uri. The Mongolian foreign ministry issued only a meek statement expressing 'regret'. The country's opportunism became clearer when its foreign ministry refused to meet the Indian envoy in Ulaanbaatar for months. Mongolia has no substantive ties with Pakistan, but it was surely acting on China's advice to stay away from lending wholehearted support to India on terrorism.

India certainly should have been sympathetic to Mongolia in terms of providing financial relief besides implementing its own promised $1 billion credit line to support Mongolia's economic capacity and infrastructure. But an attempt to play traditional Gelug politics put India and Mongolia in a tight geopolitical spot. It was certainly an ill-thought-out move that caused hardship for the Mongols. India should have been mindful that until very recently, the Mongols, Tibetans and Manchus were bound in an intricate symbiotic relationship and together they affected the geopolitics of Inner Asia.

China, however, made a canny remark to India's move. The *Global Times* in an article described India's $1 billion aid to Mongolia as a 'bribe' and said that there may be 'endless trouble' in Sino-India ties if New Delhi viewed China's cargo service with Nepal as a threat to the sale of Indian goods.[45]

The article further said, 'China won't be overly sensitive about India's cooperation with Mongolia, and won't mistake India's assistance as a counter to China. China's influence on Mongolia's economy cannot be replaced by India in the short run, and efforts will be in vain if India attempts to bribe Mongolia's loyalty with only one billion dollars.'[46]

Meanwhile, state-run news agency Xinhua quickly compared India's 'bribes' to Mongolia with China's 'help' to Nepal, saying that dozens of trucks carrying $2.8 million worth of products such as clothes, appliances, electronics and building materials had left mainland China for the Nepalese border with an aim to boost trade under BRI with the South Asian neighbour.[47]

The *Global Times* commented further that 'when it comes to cooperation with other countries, both China and India should refrain from excessive sensitivity', while adding that 'China's efforts to connect itself with Nepal will be conducive not only to the export of Chinese-made products, but also to the import of goods from Nepal or even from India'. It appeared that China had perceived India's Dalai Lama card and offer of $1 billion aid to Mongolia as a ploy to counter China's BRI programme.

The US factor

The Dalai Lama and Tibet are an American project—a residual product of the Cold War. But in reality, apart from attraction for Tibetan Buddhism, the issue of Tibet has drawn little official attention in the Western world. For the US, Tibet is viewed in the bigger geopolitical context of the India–China rivalry in Asia, and this is where the entire problem lies.

The Dalai Lama himself has certainly acquired phenomenal influence as a global icon, but despite all the publicity and support he received from the US Congress, Western parliaments and the Human Rights Caucus, support for the Tibet issue at best remains equivocal. Their governments are still obligated by global political exigencies to consider Tibet as a part of China, and as such, no country would risk jeopardizing ties with China over Tibet.

Even Tom Lantos, the Democratic congressman known for his profound moral convictions and deep commitment to human rights, wrote in 1988, 'Tibet in the eyes of the State Department remains somewhat of a bothersome orphan whose demands for attention are more trouble that they are worth.'[48]

However, the human rights concerns—a domestic political exigency for politicians in the West—keep issues like Tibet in a reasonable limelight despite all the pulls and pressures. At the same time, this contextual issue follows a specific pattern.

First, Tibet's case is episodically brought to the forefront of global attention by Western lobbyists under the human rights rubric to prevent the United States from pushing for warmer ties with China.

Second, the issue gets a global spotlight whenever tensions between India and China cross a certain threshold. To cite a few examples, Tibet caught the global spotlight in 2008 when China started curtailing countries around the world from receiving the Dalai Lama. In September 2008, Barack Obama decided not to meet the Tibetan leader, emboldening Beijing to step up its anti–Dalai Lama rhetoric.

Following the March 2008 bloody riots in Lhasa, Beijing increased the frequency of personal attacks against the Dalai Lama, calling him a 'splittist'. No one has been able to damage China's rising global reputation as much as the Dalai Lama has done singlehandedly through his network of sympathizers worldwide.

Despite Beijing's intense efforts, the Dalai Lama visited Taiwan to pray for the survivors of Typhoon Morakot in 2009. Beijing also failed to stop him from visiting Japan for nine days to attend a conference from 13 October 2009.

Against this backdrop, the easiest way to offset the trend is to counterpoise India against the domineering Chinese moves while working on the faultlines of the India—China boundary disputes in the Himalayas.

An influential section among the Indian elite has felt obliged to follow a Western agenda. Of course, there are also a number of lobbyists to press Indian politicians to lend stronger support to Tibet. They work in the corridors of power in New Delhi and Washington.[49]

Seemingly against the backdrop of unrest in Tibet during the 2008 Olympics, Dharamshala gave a press briefing about a proposed week-long visit by the Dalai Lama to Arunachal Pradesh to begin on 8 November 2009. The briefing led to mounting pressure on New Delhi by Beijing, and for about two months, between September and November, a fresh round of a scathing war of words erupted, reminiscent of the atmosphere of tension that prevailed in 1962.

It would be useful to dwell here on the 2009 episode of the Dalai Lama's Tawang visit for a better understanding of the nuances of how the Tibet issue became an additional bone of contention between India and China.

China then strongly reacted to the Dalai Lama's planned trip to Arunachal Pradesh. Chinese foreign ministry spokesman Ma Zhaoxu said on 20 October 2009, 'China is greatly concerned over the news and we believe this exposes the Dalai Lama's nature of anti-China separatism.'[50] The *People's Daily* accused India of 'recklessness and arrogance' and of harbouring 'the dream of a superpower . . . mingled with the thought of hegemony'.[51]

India remained adamant and made its position clear when the minister for external affairs, S.M. Krishna, said that Arunachal Pradesh is part of India and the Tibetan leader was 'free to go anywhere in

India'.[52] India's foreign secretary, Nirupama Rao, reiterated the point that the Dalai Lama was free to visit any part of the country as long as he did not indulge in any political activity.[53]

On the issue of the Arunachal Pradesh dispute, Rao was firm. 'I can say with all honesty both governments are convinced that there is no other way to resolve this without dialogue. One has to resolve it through dialogue. I remember our first late Prime Minister, Jawaharlal Nehru, speaking to Parliament in 1962, saying, "We cannot march to Peking," and I am quoting his words.'

Reaffirming India's position on Chinese objections to Prime Minister Manmohan Singh's visit to Arunachal, the foreign secretary said, 'Of course, we take this [Beijing's objections] seriously, and we have been very, very particular and very clear and unambivalent in expressing our position to the Chinese. In that way, we have said that Arunachal Pradesh is an integral part of India, it is an inalienable part of India.'[54]

The Dalai Lama's visit to Tawang did become serious this time and even compelled Prime Minister Manmohan Singh to make a statement after he had met Wen Jiabao in Bangkok. He said that the exiled Tibetan leader was an 'honoured guest' of India and was free to travel anywhere he wished to.[55] It was a reiteration of India's implicit stance maintained since 1954 that the 'Tibetan leader will be allowed stay in India till the time when he himself feels that it is time for him to return to Lhasa'.

Underlying this position was Nehru's view that 'neither the UK nor USA, nor indeed any other power, is particularly interested in Tibet or in its future. What they are interested in is embarrassing China.'[56]

Yet, for years, India's moral stand of providing spiritual sanctuary to the Dalai Lama was viewed by many as a geopolitical move and masterstroke of diplomacy vis-à-vis China. Obviously, many Indian politicians in private at times have taken a position on Tibet contrary to the one adopted by the government. On his part, the Dalai Lama, through an expression of diplomatic proviso, described his relationship with India as that between a guru and a chela.[57] He has gained, over fifty years, enormous sympathy from a wide range of Indian society and a section of Indian politicians to keep up the tempo of their support to him.

It wasn't clear, though, why China was hung up on opposing the Dalai Lama's visit to Arunachal Pradesh this time, for it wasn't the first time that he was visiting Tawang. Many analysts thought it may have been linked to Chinese paranoia following the stir in Tibet and Xinjiang.

But what may have actually concerned Beijing was the change in the Dalai Lama's position on Arunachal Pradesh in 2006, when he started to describe Tawang as an inseparable part of India.[58] Beijing had even sought the reversal of his position as a precondition for the resumption of talks with his envoys, which was interrupted in 2008.

The view was also expressed in various circles then that the trip to Tawang was to do with deciding the Dalai Lama's future. For example, former foreign minister of Singapore, George Yeo, wrote in *YaleGlobal* on 8 September 2009, quoting the Dalai Lama, saying, 'He was born to accomplish certain tasks, and as those tasks were not completed, it was "logical" that he would be reincarnated outside China.'[59] Many believed then that 'outside China' meant Tawang in India where the Sixth Dalai Lama was born.

War of words

Whatever the concerns the Chinese may have had, India's strong stand on the Dalai Lama this time received avid appreciation from the Western press. The *Wall Street Journal* of 28 October 2009 had an editorial titled, 'India Shows the World How to Stand Firm with China', that said, 'As Barack Obama prepares for his trip to Beijing next month, he'd be wise to cast an eye toward New Delhi, where Prime Minister Manmohan Singh is showing the rest of the world how to deal with Beijing when it gets into a bullying mood.'[60]

The editorial further said, 'Singh's stance stands in sharp contrast to Obama's decision not to meet with the Dalai Lama earlier this month. His cave-in broke Presidential precedent and emboldened Beijing to step up anti-Dalai Lama rhetoric . . . Singh to stand firm on the principles for which India stands—the very same principles of democracy and freedom that America holds. Therein lies a lesson for Obama, too.'[61]

After India stuck to its ground, the Dalai Lama drew up schedules for his visit to the US, Canada and Japan to mobilize support.

Meanwhile, in Arunachal Pradesh, Chief Minister Dorjee Khandu had declared that the Dalai Lama would be accorded the honour of 'state guest' during his stay in the state from 8–15 November 2009. But days before the Dalai Lama began his travels, China's *People's Daily* called the Dalai Lama a 'liar' and said he was pursuing a 'hidden agenda' to split China.[62]

It was not that the government hadn't faced flak for its Dalai Lama policy. Several critics suggested the government discouraged the Dalai Lama from visiting Tawang in the interest of saving the close relations that had been built with China over the years.

Prem Shankar Jha, for example, cautioned the government to understand the depth of Chinese concern over the Tibetan issue. He wrote, 'The resulting confrontation has now acquired a life of its own and is leading the two countries towards a war that neither wants. The calibrated escalation of China's demands and actions suggests that the point of no return will be the Dalai Lama's visit to Tawang in November. Wen Jiabao's request for a meeting with Manmohan Singh in Bangkok should, therefore, be seen as a last ditch effort to avert war. Fortunately for India, reversing the escalation does not require making humiliating concessions. All that New Delhi needs to do is clear up the misapprehensions that have taken root in the Chinese leaders' minds . . . India never has, and never will, support the demand for an autonomous "Greater Tibet". This is a carefully considered position, for any departure would open a Pandora's Box within India that New Delhi would never be able to close. Time, however, is running short. The immediate need is to persuade the Dalai Lama to postpone his visit to Tawang. This should not prove difficult for he could hardly be relishing the prospect of setting the house he has been living in on fire. A postponement will buy time for the two countries to clear misunderstandings and evolve a policy that brings peace to Tibet.'[63]

Jha's comments heavily influenced the minds of many Indians; they may even have put the government in a dilemma.

When the Dalai Lama set foot in Tawang, he did make a politically loaded statement: 'My stand that Tawang is an integral part of India has not changed.'[64] He said, 'The Tibetan spirit in Tibet is very strong. On the other hand, China has taken a hard line.'[65]

The Dalai Lama dismissed China's complaints that he was promoting anti-China unrest in Tibet and that he was encouraging a separatist movement as totally baseless. On China's claims over Tawang, he said when 'the People's Liberation Army of China had occupied Tawang and nearly reached Bomdila in 1962, why then China declared a unilateral ceasefire and withdrew [its forces]. Now the Chinese have got different views. This is something which I really don't know. I am little bit surprised.'[66]

The Dalai Lama's statement not only upset the Chinese but also rattled the Indian government. New Delhi, worried about the matter going out of control, suggested amending his programme on 11 November 2009, and ordered reporters to leave Tawang as their Inner Line Permits (ILPs) could not be extended beyond Tawang.[67] The government had initially restricted journalists from asking him questions on political matters while foreign journalists had been banned from covering the event. This measure by New Delhi had come immediately after Beijing censured the Dalai Lama's statement and issued a veiled threat to India for deliberately provoking China while using the Dalai Lama card to further its own agenda.

On 11 November 2009, the *People's Daily* in a provocative article titled 'India Covets Dalai Lama's Visit' quoted an anonymous scholar as saying that the Dalai Lama's presence in the 'disputed region' was a 'double insult' to China. 'India may have forgotten the lesson of 1962, when its repeated provocation resulted in military clashes warning. India is on this wrong track again.'[68]

A Chinese security analyst, Hu Shisheng of the China Institutes of Contemporary International Relations (CICIR) was quoted as saying that the Dalai Lama was sent to South Tibet by Indian agencies to foment an anti-China sentiment among the people living in the region. 'When the conflict gets sharper and sharper, the Chinese government will have to face it and solve it in a way India has designed . . . India may make use of the Dalai Lama to solve the decade-long territorial conflict by encouraging his visit to southern Tibet,' he said.[69]

Another expert, Zhao Gancheng, had said, 'India's encouragement of the Dalai Lama's visit betrays its promise to China to oppose any anti-Chinese activities.'[70]

The Chinese reactions put India in a spot. Minister of State for External Affairs Shashi Tharoor rejected the contention that the government had any role in his visit. He said that 'the initiative would have come from him and the government would have coordinated his visit'.[71] Even former national security adviser Brijesh Mishra commented that India had done what it had been doing on the issue in the past.

But crucial support came from US Undersecretary of State Maria Otero, who said, 'The Dalai Lama is a religious leader and he, of course, can travel to carry out that role . . . he is visiting a monastery, a holy place.'[72]

The government's unambivalent stand on Arunachal Pradesh was explicable but the intriguing aspect was the way New Delhi defended his Tawang visit so vociferously.

No clear explanation was available as to why New Delhi had to ratchet up the Tawang visit so seriously that it required the prime minister to make a statement; whereas the matter could have been handled in a subtler manner without creating further rift in India–China relations.

Many in India applauded the Manmohan Singh government for standing up to China, signalling to Beijing the reaffirmation of India's claim over Arunachal Pradesh.

Beijing chose to tone down the issue while shifting the blame on to the Dalai Lama for damaging India–China ties. Chinese foreign ministry spokesman Ma Zhaoxu said, 'The Dalai Lama often tells lies . . . he's a national separatist. This attempt to damage relations between China and the relevant countries will not succeed.'[73]

Interestingly, a Chinese scholar at the CICIR told this author in 2017 that China would actually have no problem if the Dalai Lama visited Tawang with the consent of Beijing, otherwise his visit would be 'illegal' for China.

The tactical change in China's stance was significant as it came after leaders of both countries, Prime Minister Manmohan Singh and President Hu Jintao, met in Brazil in April 2010. It appeared that China's anger was less to do with the dispute with India over Arunachal Pradesh and more about the Dalai Lama's political activities allegedly sponsored by the US.

Beijing's sensitivity to the Dalai Lama's activities was heightened since bloody riots erupted in Lhasa during the build-up to the 2008 Beijing Olympics. But a section of the Indian government might have taken a tougher stand considering China's unambiguous criticism over the visit by the prime minister and president of India to Arunachal Pradesh. Perhaps the need to take a strong position to rebuff Chinese assertions was felt.

Another consideration involved the sentiments of the local population of Tawang. Any curb would have risked political alienation of the Buddhist constituency in the Himalayan region. Besides, the visit would have factored in the local elections in the state, which the ruling party would not have risked.

On his part, the Dalai Lama had shrewdly stoked the fire not only while making several anti-China statements in Tawang but also by playing to the gallery in India by saying he considered Arunachal Pradesh to be a part of India and not China. The statement served to evoke immense sentiment among the people for him, and by implication the Dalai Lama had taken his cause to the Indian public. This did give an impression not only to the Chinese but also to the people of India that India was deliberately playing the Dalai Lama card vis-à-vis China.

However, a lacuna did prevail. After staying firm on his visit citing the principles of freedom and democracy, why did the government curb his programme in the middle of his visit? How did Tawang become a 'sensitive area', with reporters covering his trip asked to leave Tawang?

There were reports that the government had seemingly turned down the Dalai Lama's request to visit Tawang in 2008 but felt it necessary to push for it in 2009.[74] This and other questions remain largely unanswered pertaining to who decided the Dalai Lama's Tawang visit: Dharamshala/Washington or New Delhi.

It could have been that Dharamshala made a pre-emptive move while announcing the Dalai Lama's plans in advance through the media instead of waiting for the government's approval. This meant the government had no prior information even though the MEA had upgraded its office in Dharamshala since 2008 to a director-level official.

Yet another pertinent question often raised is whether India's claim over Arunachal Pradesh is really contingent on the Dalai Lama. If so, how will India handle Arunachal Pradesh once the Dalai Lama is no more, unless the next Dalai Lama decides to be reborn in India? Even if it did happen that way, it would not be without strategic implications, and this is what the Americans must be envisaging. Not surprisingly, the Dalai Lama said in March 2019[75] that his reincarnation could be from India. This has immediate implications for where the future course of India–China relations would move. To be sure, it means prolonging the stand-off to another lifespan.

Beijing, of course, insists on following the old rule and would do anything to prevent the Dalai Lama deciding the future of his status—this will be the most important game in the Himalayas that could last for another century.

Clearly, the Dalai Lama's 2009 visit to Tawang was arranged to coincide with President Obama's visit to China in November 2009. The idea was to get Obama to pressurize Beijing to resume talks between China and the Dalai Lama which had been interrupted following the March 2008 events in Tibet. Obama was to offer third-party assistance to the dialogue. In fact, several important American leaders wanted Obama to push for an invitation for the Tibetan leader to visit China. Of course, the context was also to exploit China's vulnerability after the bloody riots in Lhasa in March 2008 and the fear of Tibetans disrupting the Beijing Olympics.

The Dalai Lama's 2017 Tawang episode appeared well-scripted to concur with President Donald Trump's two-day summit with President Xi Jinping planned for 6 and 7 April at the Mar a Lago golf club in Florida. The Tibetan spiritual leader had originally planned to be in Tawang on 5 April 2017, but bad weather conditions forced him to reschedule the trip; he travelled by road to reach Bomdila next day.

There were many expectations of a looming showdown between Xi and Trump over trade at the summit. The anticipation was that Trump would push Xi to the edge, while the Dalai Lama would shoot a salvo from Tawang. In fact, the cue came from how badly Richard Verma's Tawang visit had irked the Chinese.

But the salvo went seemingly off target, with Trump having made a complete U-turn on his anti-China policy. Trump showed little interest in pushing a human rights agenda, leave aside the Tibet issue with Xi.

Strategic renaming

Beijing made a counter move that was equally cultural in nature. In fact, weeks after the Dalai Lama's visit to Tawang in 2017, China's Ministry of Civil Affairs unilaterally renamed several places in South Tibet (Arunachal Pradesh)—a move China's *Global Times* said was meant to reaffirm China's territorial sovereignty.[76]

At least six places in the Tawang area were declared standardized in Chinese characters, Tibetan and Roman alphabet, including Wo'gyainling, Mila Ri, Qoidengarbo Ri, Mainquka, Bumo La and Namkapub Ri. These names are spelled in India as Urgelling, Daporijo, Upper Siang District, Menchuka, Bum-La and Namka Valley respectively.

China justified the move and said the renaming was done on the basis of its historical, cultural and administrative jurisdiction over the area.

The *Global Times* quoted Xiong Kunxin, a professor of ethnic studies at Beijing's Minzu University, as saying, 'The standardization came amid China's growing understanding and recognition of the geography in South Tibet.'

The legalization of names, according to the Chinese, was a part of the rule of law and done in accordance with the regulations of the State Council. The *Global Times* also quoted Guo Kefan of the Tibet Academy of Social Sciences saying that the names had existed since ancient times but had never been standardized before. Importantly, Kefan believed that new standardized names would serve as a reference point for China for its border negotiation with India in future.

China rejected India's charge that it was inventing names to make its territorial claims over the area legal. The Chinese foreign ministry responded by saying, 'Relevant names have been used by ethnic Monpa and Tibetan Chinese who have lived here for generations. So it is a fact that cannot be changed. To standardise these names and publicise them is a legitimate measure based on our lawful right.'[77]

'South Tibet [Arunachal Pradesh] is historically part of China and names of the places there is part of the local ethnic culture. It is legitimate for the Chinese government to standardise the names of the places,' the foreign ministry said.

The move was defended by saying that the Chinese government was conducting a second nationwide survey to standardize geographical names in the languages of ethnic minority groups, and more names would be announced later.

Clearly, there was a larger purpose. The *Global Times* said, 'China has been making efforts to solve the territorial disputes with India, but over the past decades, India has not only increased migration to the disputed area and boosted its military construction there, but it also named Arunachal Pradesh, China's South Tibet, as a formal state of India in 1987.'

China was reaffirming its cultural affinity with the region, not only to retaliate against the Dalai Lama's visit to Tawang but also to harden its stance on Arunachal Pradesh.

It is a fact that the Chinese have scant historical records to support their claims, except for the fact that the Sixth Dalai Lama was born in Tawang and the monastery there was controlled by the Drepung monastery in Lhasa.

The renaming of the Ugyenling monastery as Wo'gyainling is significant from this angle. It is possible that China may have obtained older maps and archival records from Taiwanese sources to prove its historical, cultural and administrative control over South Tibet.

While doing so, China was also perhaps trying to get India to concede that it would never ever use the Dalai Lama in future, a move they had made successfully with Mongolia in 2017.

India rolled out some symbolic kneejerk responses, one of which came from Union minister M. Venkaiah Naidu, 'China has no right to rename our cities, every inch of Arunachal Pradesh belongs to India; let them rename. How does it matter? It's like you renaming your neighbour. It does not change his name,'[78] Naidu said in a tit-for-tat response to Beijing's symbolic snub.

At the same time, renaming places cannot be dismissed as a play of nomenclature. Both India and China have changed names of places to reflect a certain political narrative. In fact, China has been applying Sino-centrism as a tool for cultural dominance for centuries.

India, too, has played the name game before. Tawang was part of the NEFA until it got the Sanskritized name 'Arunachal Pradesh' (land of the rising sun), given by Sri Bibhabasu Das Shastri when it became a Union Territory on 20 January 1971, and later a state on 20 February 1987.

Renaming is certainly not a new thing. Bombay was renamed Mumbai, Peking as Beijing. The Chinese have Romanized the spelling Mao Tse Tung to Mao Zedong.

What is likely to happen is that India and China may get into a cartographic battle if China is able to enforce global search engines and websites to use standardized Chinese words.

As this book is being written, Chinese customs officials ordered the destruction of three lakh maps that did not mention Arunachal Pradesh and Taiwan as part of its territory. In February 2019, the Chinese destroyed 30,000 world maps printed in the country for incorrectly showing the borders with India and depicting Taiwan as a separate country.

Clearly, any attempt at Tibetanizing or Sinifying names in the Himalayas serves China's interest, for the epicentre of Tibetan culture is China—it makes more sense for it to get the names of places in Arunachal Pradesh codified.

The fundamental basis of India's claim rests not on the Dalai Lama but on its record of the 1914 Simla Convention under which Tibet ceded Tawang to British India. While China continues to exploit its occupation of Tibet by opening its remote regions to increased development activities, India views its situation vis-à-vis China from the Dalai Lama's perspective, which is essentially a Chinese-created politico-religious institution devised for controlling the Tibetan world.

At the popular level, especially amongst the informed circle, the move to play the Dalai Lama card wasn't seen to be normal behaviour on the part of the government. In fact, many were baffled by the China–India stand-off over the Dalai Lama amid improving ties. Possibly, it may have been done to let out our long-festering anger against China for pinpricking India on a number of occasions.

Quite possibly, it may have been done under some special circumstance, especially to bring the Tibet issue back on the table when Donald Trump took over as the new US President. But the decision to use the Dalai Lama's Tawang card may have crippled New Delhi's strategic vision. The matter was, however, defused and the anger did not extend beyond a verbal outburst, though months later, tension in the Himalayas erupted in the form of Doklam.

In fact, the Dalai Lama episode is getting linked to India's internal security—the problems in Kashmir, the north-east and in Naxal-infected areas, Pakistan-sponsored terrorism, etc. are not unrelated to it. Indian security agencies have been indicating close links between ULFA (I) and other armed outfits in the north-east and China. In fact, in an unprecedented move, ULFA (I) chief Paresh Barua in a statement on 28 March 2017 cautioned the Dalai Lama against speaking out against China 'in private or public' from 'the soil of Assam'.[79] This couldn't have been issued without Chinese direction to signal to India that they too could challenge India's sovereignty in the north-east. In fact, China messaging against India's 'Tibet card' through the rebels in the north-east is something quite new.

Recently, in the wake of the Pulwama attack on 14 February 2019, Pakistani media had likened the Dalai Lama to the terrorist Masood Azhar.[80] A senior Pakistani journalist retweeted a decade-old news article whose headline described the Tibetan leader as a 'terrorist'.[81]

This was meant to suggest that China's blocking India and other nations from listing Azhar as a global terrorist in the UNSC was linked to India sheltering China's 'enemy' since 1959.

The notion that China respects power is correct but the show of power cannot be displayed through senseless acts. The Chinese media called India's use of the Dalai Lama card as 'tactless'.

9

The Karmapa and the Sectarian Power Struggle

Traditionally, the Indian Himalayas are the main bastion and stronghold of the Kagyu lineage. The Karmapa is the legitimate stakeholder by virtue of being one of the major Kagyu leaders. There is a murky subterranean power struggle for sectarian dominance being fought between the Gelug (yellow)-dominated Tibetan and Kagyu (red)-dominated Himalayan regions.

That the Tibetans, from clergy to laity, are riven by sectarian fissures is well known, but the issue is too obscure in nature for common observers to understand. It is beyond the gaze of even well-informed Indians, but the game is played very shrewdly by none other than the Dalai Lama himself.

Over the years, Tibetan sectarianism has had huge geopolitical underpinnings that are not easy to decipher. It is not easy to make a dispassionate analysis of the subtexts involved. Yet, it is important to sift through critical trends emerging among major Tibetan sects that would have an impact on India's national security.

Understanding Tibetan sectarian complexity is a separate topic altogether, and it is not necessary here to discuss in detail the Karmapa controversy that erupted ever since the Seventeenth Karmapa, Ogyen Trinley Dorje, landed in India on 5 January 2000.

To briefly recount, Dorje had made a daring escape from Tibet, which caused huge embarrassment to the Chinese government. Many theories centring on the Karmapa are shrouded in mystery—especially about the rituals and intrigues of succession politics. The Chinese, unfazed by his flight, claimed in 2000 that Dorje had gone to India just to collect the 'sacred black hat' from Rumtek (Sikkim), which belonged to his predecessor.

The plot thickened after his arrival in India, when the Dalai Lama's administration and the Indian establishment began to wrestle for control over the Seventeenth Karmapa for geopolitical reasons.

In an interview in April 2001, the Karmapa said he feared the Chinese were using him for political purposes such as separating the Tibetans from the Dalai Lama. He said he would not return to Tibet until the Dalai Lama did.

Considering the Karmapa's importance in the Tibetan Lamaist order, the Dalai Lama in 1992 endorsed Dorje—the candidate chosen by the Chinese—as the Seventeenth Karmapa, possibly as a trade-off plan to get his chosen Panchen Lama released from Chinese captivity. That, of course, was not realized. Beijing, instead, installed a Panchen Lama of its own.

But the Karmapa's sudden arrival in India in 2000 had raised many eyebrows in India. Many believed his escape was facilitated by the Chinese for the purpose of him getting hold of the 'sacred black hat' lying in Rumtek. But sections of the Indian media were then quick to label Dorje a Chinese spy.[1]

A reference was made about the Karmapa having left behind a secret note in the Tsurphu monastery in which he promised to return to Tibet soon. Interestingly, in a video message on 26 June 2017,[2] he said he desired to return to the 'Land of Snow' (Tibet) within the next two or three years.

In India, he was confined to the Gyuto Tantric monastery near Dharamshala under the tight surveillance of the CTA and Indian intelligence agencies. The government imposed travel restrictions on him, notably banning him from visiting the Rumtek monastery.

Ups and downs

In 2011, the Karmapa was caught in an unsavoury controversy over the illegal recovery of a large stash of cash ($1.4 million), including Chinese currency, at his monastery as well as a benami land deal in

Himachal Pradesh.[3] Such incidents fuelled suspicion about his being a Chinese plant.

According to some, Dharamshala may have created suspicion in the minds of Indian officials to ensure the Dalai Lama's popularity doesn't dip, but this is unsubstantiated since it is also known that among many iconic religious masters, the CTA has played up the Karmapa's stature to ensure that he has a pivotal role in the post–Dalai Lama scenario.

The general impression created was that the Karmapa is the second-most important Tibetan figure and will be a kind of successor to the Dalai Lama. For most Indian analysts, the issue was as naive as that.

In May 2017, the Karmapa suddenly disappeared from the radar of Indian intelligence.

Amidst rumours, he was finally traced to Europe and later to the United States, where he was staying under the pretext of poor health. The Karmapa has since been reportedly located in New Jersey's Wharton State Forest area.[4]

Some media reports suggested the Karmapa may not return to India, where he had spent eighteen years, but in an interview to Radio Free Asia,[5] he said he was talking to the Indian government about coming back; reportedly, he was to do so by November 2018. Earlier, he had promised to return by June 2018. Sources said that the mood among intelligence circles has been tense after the Karmapa's disappearance months before the Doklam stand-off began.

Clearly, Dorje's escape has caused huge embarrassment to the CTA, especially the Dalai Lama, who had been vehemently defending his authenticity (as the true Karmapa) and had also dismissed accusations of him being a Chinese spy. Dorje's disappearance right under his nose raises several key questions, especially about the activities of Tibetan refugees in India.

His slip is an embarrassment for the government as well, because the decision to revoke the travel restrictions imposed on him by the Cabinet Committee on Security (CCS) in 2000 was taken only in 2017, in spite of intelligence agencies cautioning against it.

Not surprisingly, both New Delhi and Dharamshala seemingly tried their best, though in vain, to persuade him to return. A number of special emissaries were also sent to convince him to return, to no avail.

Shocking revelations

In March 2018, the Karmapa made some stunning revelations in a thirty-seven-minute 'special message'[6] telecast from the US that sent shock waves among his supporters and opponents alike. It was part of a 'special message' to his devotees, with English and Chinese translations, broadcast on the last day of the thirty-fifth Annual Kagyu Monlam (prayer) ceremony in Bodh Gaya (26 February–5 March 2018).

The Karmapa revealed how his journey from the age of seven was manipulated by others. At an early age, he didn't understand what it meant to be put on the Karmapa's throne. As he grew up in the Tsurphu monastery in Tibet without any freedom, his *changtsos* (adult attendants) controlled his childhood. They even opened his gift packets on the pretext of checking for 'bomb or poison', and once taken away, they were never brought back. People at times offered money 'surreptitiously', quickly slipping it under his cushion when no one was looking.

Similarly, he felt he was misguided by advisers to be the best. Also, Dorje had no motivation for 'competing with everyone else'; perhaps he meant with his other claimants.

The Karmapa said his tutors in Tibet were 'not the greatest'— the reason why he fled to India in 1999 at the age of fourteen. But he admitted that he hadn't received adequate religious training even in India. The reasons cited included the non-availability of Kagyu lamas/khenpos who were scattered around India and abroad and were preoccupied with their own dharma centres. Besides, he was frustrated to see the internal disarray and rift within the Karma Kamtsang lineage.

Due to restrictions placed on his movements by Dharamshala and the Indian government, he virtually lived a prisoner's life in the Gyuto monastery under tight surveillance and was kept away from the main Kagyu masters. As a result, he did not have enough opportunity to learn in an orderly manner from qualified teachers as compared to past Karmapas. To become a good scholar, he had even thought about undergoing training in a Gelugpa school, but decided against it after realizing that it would become problematic in future, especially since he carried the title of Kagyu head.

'I have been downcast and depressed,' he said, and added that he couldn't meet his obligations. He honestly admitted his shortfalls as the Karmapa and head of the 900-year-old institution with sixteen reincarnation lineages. He humbly admitted to having no high 'qualities and abundance realizations' of the type that his previous incarnations had. 'I don't even have the confidence that I can even hope for such. And I don't really believe it would ever happen,' he confessed. He said that despite his best efforts, the situation was 'beyond me', although he has received blessings to some degree.

'Many people think to themselves that being the Karmapa is some incredible thing, but for me, that hasn't happened, even if I am the Karmapa. I have no reasons for me to say that I am the reincarnation of any great Lama to meet the limitless hopes of people.' Dorje asserted he was 'an ordinary person' and not qualified to teach what was required of him and he couldn't continue 'deceiving the public'.

Interestingly, Dorje said he came to India hoping it was a free and democratic country. But upon his arrival (due to the lack of a reliable guide), he confessed to having run into 'disharmony and disagreement' with the Indian government that caused some suspicions to the point of labelling him a 'Chinese spy'.

For him, the eighteen years of 'hassled life' in India were disappointing. He said he continued to stay for the sake of his education and for the benefit of Tibet. He, nevertheless, expressed satisfaction over having met His Holiness the Dalai Lama and other profound Kagyu masters in India. But he regretted that while the teachers (the 'heart sons') lived elsewhere, he remained confined to the Gyuto monastery, therefore, 'there has never been a place for us to spend an extended period of time at the same place. It's like we've all been scattered.'

Dorje was blunt about the bitter rift in the lineage. Without going into details (caused due to the dual recognition of a Karmapa candidate), he referred to how he had to helplessly witness his sect being torn into rival factions. He confessed to having tried in vain, despite people vociferously discouraging him, to heal the wound and seek 'reconciliation' by talking to the opponent group led by Kunzig Shamar Rinpoche, who passed away in 2014.

The Karmapa confessed that though no specific result came out of his meeting with Shamar Rinpoche, it was a comforting feeling to meet him and tell him what he thought. Now that Rinpoche had passed away, Dorje advised everyone to have respect for the historical line of Shamarpas. He appealed to devotees to refrain from removing the Shamarpa lineage from their supplication prayers. 'No matter how much the Rinpoche was wrong, we must think positively about him in the interest of both Buddhism and the lineage,' he said.

He particularly sought 'reconciliation' so that having a situation of two different reincarnations of Shamar Rinpoche could be avoided. 'Looking at each other as enemies and continuing to cling to [our] own factions would cause further harm to the Kamtsang,' he said.

The Karmapa cited his concurrent medical problem as also the ill health of his attendant as reasons for his prolonged stay in America. Another reason was that he wanted to avail the opportunity to give rest to both his body and mind. 'Once I get back to India, there'll be a lot of busyness and franticness', and 'I stay here to think about the long term'. He denied any intention of personal benefit or 'insidious plans' for staying in America.

The Karmapa conceded that he feared people putting pressure on him to play a political role both in Tibet and India. But from his perspective, the Karmapas have historically acted as spiritual rather than political leaders.

While he certainly believed that Tibet at present required a political direction and a leader, for him to give political directions would be inappropriate, especially when he was holding the Karmapa title. 'I wouldn't know how to play politics and I never wished to do it,' he said.

Dorje said that many people had doubts and anxiety about his intentions, but in reality 'he has been feeling quite depressed', for he also repeatedly talked about his desire for 'giving up'. 'There's no reason for me to pretend and if I keep deceiving people, I will be accumulating negative karma,' he said. 'I have no feeling of delight, no desire to get rich, power and confidence that many people want me to have' and that 'I also felt strongly in recent times that it would be better to live just as an 'ordinary Dharma practitioner'.

The Karmapa called for community support and said that the Gyalwa Karmapa is like the father of the big Karma Kamtsang family, but the father can't take all responsibility alone. 'A single pillar can't hold up a single building, can it,' he asked. Interestingly, he said, 'you need somebody to take care of you', as an underline in the Buddhist view of interdependence in relationships.

Dorje cited the example of how the Kagyu lineage suffered terrible losses in the past, especially during the times of the Mongol army raids and during the Cultural Revolution. He called all the heads of factions to seize the opportunity for forging unity and revival while taking into consideration the longer-term perspective. Finally, he didn't ask people to support him, but advised them to keep in mind that they should respect the leader no matter who the future leader might be. The Karmapa offered an apology if he had said anything inappropriate.

Analysing the revelations

When the Karmapa said he couldn't take the responsibility of the lineage all alone, did he mean he wanted to jointly share it with his opponent Karmapa, Trinley Thaye Dorje, who was recognized by Shamar Rinpoche?

Ogyen Trinley Dorje underlined that the issue of whether one is a pure Karmapa or not comes down only to the 'practice in the mind-streams'. On his statement that he wanted to live as an 'ordinary person', many people probably thought he wanted to step down and lead a married life, just like the other Karmapa, Trinley Thaye Dorje, who got married to Rinchen Yangzom in 2017.[7]

In fact, Trinley Thaye Dorje hoped that his karmic connection with his wife would further strengthen the Karma Kagyu lineage. On 9 March 2018 his official website shared the joyous news of the couple expecting their first child. Trinley Thaye Dorje had already hinted that the child would bring great benefit to the Karma Kagyu lineage. It could have been an indication that the child would be a reincarnation of Thaye Dorji's mentor, the late Shamar Rinpoche. A boy was born to Trinley Thaye Dorje and Rinchen Yangzom on 11 August 2018 in France.

Importantly, Ogyen Trinley Dorje in his message foresaw the potential problems confronting the lineage on account of Shamar Rinpoche's reincarnation. He warned that should there be two candidates, it would cause further damage to the unity of the lineage. To be sure, there was a link between the two events taking place in the factions.

Dorje referred to attempts being made to push him to play a political role against his wishes and the interest of Karma Kagyu unity. One might ask the question why and who was pressing him to take up a political role. Curiously, the Karmapa had to webcast a special message about his personal struggles from the US. This smacked of something serious.

His confession came on the heels of new developments relating to Tibet and the Tibetan issue, both inside and outside Tibet—when Xi Jinping was elected lifetime president and when the Western world including the US had significantly reduced their interest in raising the Tibet issue with China.

Similarly, New Delhi too was changing its 'Tibet policy' in the interest of having better relations with Beijing. Besides, there had been considerable discord among Tibetans living in exile, including schisms and differences within major Tibetan sects.

At such a time, the Karmapa's confession could have serious implications for the Tibetan cause, especially with the Dalai Lama's advanced age. Many hitherto unknown issues related to Tibetan affairs in exile were uncovered. The Karmapa's revelations could encourage others to air their issues and frustrations, especially in the post–Dalai Lama period.

The Karmapa was certainly candid while sharing his personal struggles with genuine humility and honesty. At the same time, he wasn't sufficiently clear about what he wanted to do in the future except for some subtle hints, which might become clearer in the time to come.

He said he regretted how he was pressured to play a political role against the historical legacy of the Karmapa institution. For he also saw politics as being about seeking short-term benefits, profiting from 'dividing people into factions', whereas dharma offered limitless prospects to serve people.

His main frustration pertained to his inability to meet the obligation of the title 'Karmapa'. The important point was that he felt squeezed after running into 'disharmony and disagreements' with the Indian government.

Several pertinent questions arise from the Karmapa's revelation as to who was conspiring against him; why was he confined to a monastery for eighteen years; why was he denied Kagyu teachings; why was he pressurized to undergo training in the Gelug tradition; who pressed him to take up a political role; who created a rift in the Karmapa lineage; was he not the real Karmapa or was there an error in identifying the Karmapa; why was he thinking of stepping down and living as an ordinary person; and why was the ban on his travel suddenly lifted prior to his flight to the US?

There have been many developments since March 2018. The Karmapa has refused to come back on some pretext or the other despite several attempts made by Dharamshala and Indian officials to get him back.

Possibly, there is a fear in his mind that he will not get a fair deal if he returns to India. Already, many senior Kagyu monks and individuals associated with the Karmapa have faced restrictions on their travels within and outside India.

Second, he has wanted to avoid confrontation on all other odds including stiff competition in India from a rival group seeking legal control over the Rumtek monastery in Sikkim, built by his previous reincarnate, the Sixteenth Karmapa.

Third, one of the reasons cited for his escape was his disappointment over multiple hindrances to get a suitable plot of land for building a replica of Tsurphu in India. After he left India, media reported that he was finally offered a plot in Dwarka (New Delhi) at the cost of Rs 22 crore an acre. But by then it was too late.

Another reason was the restriction on him to travel to Sikkim and visit the Rumtek monastery. Again, in a belated attempt to woo him back, the CCS in March 2018 allowed the Karmapa to visit Sikkim, excepting the Rumtek monastery. There is also a lawsuit filed by a rival claimant over Rumtek and the matter is currently subjudice. The decision to lift the ban also came after monks in Sikkim went on a hunger strike.

Against all this, the Karmapa might have weighed the option of seeking asylum in the US, thereby getting a green card and freely travelling to China and elsewhere and also meeting anybody he wished to. Sources said that hordes of visitors, including top artists from Tibet, have attended his birthday celebrations.

As per reports, the Karmapa had obtained the passport of the Commonwealth of Dominica, a Caribbean island nation, in 2018. The decision to do so was born of the 'too many restrictions' that the Indian government had imposed on his movements.

In a video message, Dorje explains, 'I need to travel often, I have many responsibilities towards communities around the world. I thought it necessary to have a passport, but I asked the Indian government for a visa to get back to India as soon as possible.'[8]

Union of the two Karmapas

Meanwhile, the astonishing news of a meeting between the two Karmapas, Ogyen Trinley Dorje and Trinley Thaye Dorje, in France in October 2018 took the Buddhist world by storm.[9]

This is, by far, the most significant development in the recent history of Tibetan Buddhism. After obtaining a foreign passport, this was the Karmapa's second major move since he left India in 2017. It came at a critical juncture, with far-reaching consequences for Tibetan politics, Himalayan security and China–India relations. The union of the Karmapas also came as a big blow to those who probably never wished for this to happen, and may have been thrown off balance by this meeting.

A joint statement[10] following the meeting said the purpose was to 'get to know each other personally and work together to strengthen the Karma Kagyu lineage and heal the division'. It said, 'We both had this wish for many years, and we are gratified that this wish has now been fulfilled.'

The Gyalwang Drukpa, head of the Drukpa Kagyu, was the first spiritual leader to react on social media,[11] saying, 'The meeting has set an example of how spiritual masters can resolve internal problems.' He also wished the younger generation of spiritual masters to follow suit. Earlier, Ogyen Trinley acquiring the citizenship of the Commonwealth of Dominica may have led to tension within intelligence circles and in Dharamshala—both tried their best, although in vain, to get him back.

A thaw between the Karmapas shouldn't have come as a surprise. Ogyen Trinley Dorje had earlier signalled it through a special message sent in March 2018, wherein he said he was helplessly witnessing his own sect being torn into rival factions.

Among other things, he revealed how his position as Karmapa was manipulated by others and how he virtually lived a prisoner's life in Dharamshala (under tight surveillance) and stayed away from his teachers. But most importantly, he revealed how he even tried in vain to heal the wound and seek 'conciliation' by talking to the opponent group, led by Kunzig Shamar Rinpoche, despite people vociferously discouraging him against it. Nothing came out of the meeting, but it comforted him.

The birth of Thaye Dorje's son in August 2018 may have pushed him to seek reconciliation with the former, and prompted him to travel to France—ideally suited for a meeting, away from the gaze of Dharamshala. It is unclear whether the Karmapas discussed the issue of selecting the next Shamar Rinpoche.

As for settling the Karmapa title, both would possibly recognize the other as an 'emanation' or 'manifestation' of the self—probably acceptable in an esoteric tradition, along the lines that 'the union of two rays always becomes a line'.

Of course, it is too early to speculate about a final settlement, given the disputes over property, especially the fate of the Rumtek monastery in Sikkim where the 'sacred black hat' is preserved. A lawsuit was filed by the rival groups Tsurphu Labrang (supporting Ogyen Trinley Dorje) and the Karmapa Charitable Trust (supporting Trinley Thaye Dorje).

Also, whether the lower ranks of the factions would accept such a deal is debatable. In fact, a much-speculated possible holding of a joint Kagyu Monlam (the sect's annual prayer festival) did not take place in Bodh Gaya in February 2019.

One thing is certain: the Kagyu lineages are no longer going to accept interference in their intra and inter-sectarian affairs.

Unlike Ogyen Trinley Dorje, Trinley Thaye Dorje is not recognized by the Dalai Lama and Beijing. Even so, he has a large following in both India and Bhutan. It is also unclear what the coming together of the Karmapas would entail, especially when people have been split by the claim to the title of Karmapa.

It is unlikely that Ogyen Trinley Dorje has any insidious plans, but he may still fear not getting a fair deal if he returns to India, especially in terms of free movement. In 2018, the government had cleared the deck to offer him a plot in New Delhi to build a Buddhist centre. Trinley Thaye Dorje already has a centre at Qutub Institutional Area in New Delhi.

Travel document controversy

The Karmapa's failure to show up for the much-publicized event, the Thirteenth Religious Conference of the Schools of Tibetan Buddhism and Bon Tradition, scheduled from 29 November 2018 in Dharamshala, seriously hit the CTA's plans.

Just a few days before the conference was scheduled to begin, on 24 November, the CTA suddenly deferred it indefinitely on the grounds that the supreme head of the Nyingma sect, Kathok Getse Rinpoche, had passed away recently in Nepal. Kathok Getse's presence would have been important, but the absence of the Karmapa at the meeting would have adversely affected the CTA's plans. His failing to show up exposed the rifts among the Tibetans.

It wasn't just the issue of the Karmapa acquiring citizenship of the Dominican Republic; the two rival Karmapas coming together was probably a big blow to CTA. The two Karmapas pledged to 'work together to strengthen the Karma Kagyu lineage and heal the division'. The CTA doesn't recognize Trinley Thaye Dorje.

The other factions such as the head of the Drukpa Kagyu sect showed scant interest and stayed away from the CTA's planned event. However, the story has been told in such a way as to project that the issue was the Karmapa's unwillingness to return to India on the travel identity certificate (IC).

During his stay in the United States, the Karmapa obtained a passport of the Commonwealth of Dominica in March 2018. This created a controversy related to his travel document as he obtained it without surrendering the 'certificate of identity' that the Indian government had issued him for travel purposes. The media report from Dharamshala misreported that India had refused to issue a visa to the Karmapa to attend a Tibetan religious leaders' conference at the end of November 2018.[12] Technically, he didn't require a visa as Tibetans travelling abroad on an IC needn't obtain a return visa.

However, it seemed that the Karmapa wanted to return to India on the Commonwealth of Dominica passport and that he wanted a multiple-entry Indian visa on it. The Karmapa argued that he had acquired the passport of a Caribbean island country for the convenience of travel to various countries where he has centres and followers.

In his video message[13] recorded in Germany in January 2019, the Karmapa said that he had requested the New York consulate to accept the surrendered IC and grant an Indian visa.

'As that was the case, as soon as I got the new document, I went to the Indian embassy in New York to turn it to them. I went there and told them that I wanted to turn in my old document and further requested them to grant me a visa in the new passport. But the people in that office said that they were not authorised to do so and needed to ask the offices in Delhi about it. There was a lot of back and forth which took a bit of time and in the end, I could not get things done.'[14]

The Karmapa may probably have contravened Indian rules that require a Tibetan to surrender his IC prior to obtaining the passport of another country. Apparently, India has also not allowed him to surrender his IC in the consulate general's office in New York as he was asked to do so only in India. The rule suggested that the IC, which was given to Tibetan refugees to travel abroad, could only be surrendered in India.

The Karmapa also flouted rules that required him to return to India within the stipulated period. By overstaying abroad (since May 2017), he may have annoyed the Indian authorities. Yet, this was not the key issue. He could have been allowed to return if the government really wanted it. Even so, it was noted that the document became automatically invalid once the bearer acquired a foreign passport.

Amidst these contradictory reports, the Government of India in December 2018 had conveyed to the Karmapa that he was free to come to India any time he wanted to. The only condition was that he could not return on the IC which had become invalid, but on a visa on his Dominican passport for which he had to apply at the Indian consulate or mission. According to media reports, despite instructions given to Indian missions in the United States to grant the visa, the Karmapa has not even applied for it till date.[15]

The matter probably got stuck because the Karmapa wanted multiple Indian travel visas to be stamped so that he could return to the US. But the Indian government said that the type of visa will be a 'sovereign decision' and 'not a matter of negotiation'.[16] The stand-off between the Karmapa and the Indian authorities continues and this has also led to a higher level of mistrust. This is perhaps unavoidable since the issue of the Karmapa is highly sensitive, with consequences for national security.

The situation has reached an impasse. It was none other than India's former adviser on Tibetan affairs, Amitabh Mathur, who said that the matter had now been put on hold. 'There are no restrictions on his travel, however,' he was quoted as saying.[17] But the fact is that the Karmapa has been on a retreat since then and has altogether avoided the issue of his possible return to India.

The Karmapa's unwillingness to return to India is already impacting the travel movements of other high Karmapa lamas. In April 2019, Tai Situpa Rinpoche told me that his planned visit to Switzerland for medical treatment had been stalled by the home ministry. Tai Situpa Rinpoche also complained that he was unable to get in touch with the Karmapa and didn't know his whereabouts.

In a huge turnaround, perhaps in a threatening tone, a report on India Today TV had quoted government sources saying that New Delhi does not recognize Ogyen Trinley Dorje as the 'sole' Seventeenth Karmapa.[18] Of course, this is the subject of another controversy, but the process of delegitimizing Ogyen Trinley Dorji as the true Karmapa perhaps began when he decided not to sing to the tune that Dharamshala wants him to sing.

The bigger context

During a recent trip to Tibet, Chinese officials mentioned that Ogyen Trinley Dorje is listed among China's officially recognized tulkus (living Buddhas). 'He is most welcome to return if he wishes to,' said a Tibetan official in Kanding.

The Karmapa's importance lies in his utility in deciding the successor of the Dalai Lama. The Chinese seem adamant on finding his successor as per the 'prescribed rituals, conventions and China's laws' relating to the Tibetan Buddhism Living Buddha Reincarnation Management Measures under the National Bureau of Religious Affairs' Order # 5 enacted in 2007.[19]

So far, only the United States has made a position through a resolution by the US Senate which said that the responsibility of identifying a successor would rest with the Fourteenth Dalai Lama's private office.[20] Clearly, and knowing China's browbeating approach, Beijing will repeat the procedures followed for installing the Eleventh Panchen Lama in November 1995.

Now that Ogyen Trinley Dorje has not returned to India, one can conjecture whether he might go to the Tsurphu monastery in Tibet: his seat. This would fit into Beijing's succession plan. For example, in a situation of conflict over two different reincarnations of the next Dalai Lama, Beijing will have two Tibetan stalwarts, the Seventeenth Karmapa and the Eleventh Panchen Lama, Gyaincain Norbu, to bestow legitimacy on the candidate found to be the Fifteenth Dalai Lama. The Karmapa's institution is nearly three centuries older than the Dalai Lama's—China knows this would matter in the esoteric-driven politics.

Seemingly, China's State Council is already talking to Mongolian officials and clergy on religious and cultural exchanges, possibly to come to an understanding on the Fifteenth Dalai Lama. The rest of the Buddhist world or any other country doesn't matter in any case, said Tibetologist Xiaobin Wang of the CTRC in Beijing. Such being the current trend, it became clear that any country unwilling to endorse Beijing's candidate would risk affecting ties with China.

In fact, New Delhi not being so forthcoming on the matter of issuing a travel visa to Ogyen Trinley Dorje on one pretext or the other smacks of subtle diplomacy at work by Beijing.

The Karmapa's disappearance from India is certainly not without a plan. It especially comes at a critical juncture, with far-reaching consequences for Tibetan politics and China–India relations. It is certainly a loss for India and the Himalayan region.

If the rumours are to be believed, the government itself may have scuttled the planned Religious Conference of the Schools of Tibetan Buddhism and Bon Tradition scheduled for 29–30 November 2018 in Dharamshala. The conference was to decide on the issue of finding a successor to the Dalai Lama. Such an impudent move by Dharamshala would have once again provoked the Chinese which meant the derailment of the normalization process that had begun in Wuhan. The simple thing for the government was to deny a travel visa to Karmapa. And without the Karmapa's presence, the meeting would have had no tangible meaning.

Future scenario

No one knows how things will unfold for the future of the Karmapa, but the issue has certainly created confusion at several levels, which will have implications for the Himalayan region. It is quite possible that he will play the waiting game and rather do it from where he has a larger audience with a vast network of followers—in the West, China, South East Asia and Tibet itself, rather than in India. He may possibly be trying to buy land in the US or in Europe to set up his seat in exile.

It would be another matter if the Karmapa were to end up becoming a strong asset for the US. He is already being courted by the House of Representatives, which invited him to a function in July 2018 at the Capitol Visitor Center, attended by Democratic leader Nancy Pelosi and other Congresswomen.

Also, the Karmapa's escape provides an opportunity for China to convince the Tibetans, both within and outside Tibet, about the futility of the 'India card'. Beijing can say: look what India does to Tibetan Lamas. The Karmapa episode may have allowed the Chinese to further confuse the exiled Tibetan community. On its part, Beijing will continue to support Ogyen Trinley Dorje in the hope that he will return to Tibet.

In fact, if the rumours are true, the Karmapa may also opt to return to the Tsurphu monastery, located 70 kilometres from Lhasa, renovated by the Chinese government. In 2017, he talked about wanting to visit Tibet to meet his parents.[21]

Overall, there is a limited possibility of the Karmapa returning to India—the only exception that may work is moral pressure or the trust factor of the Dalai Lama. But the efforts of emissaries who went to plead with the Karmapa have so far failed to yield the desired results.

New Delhi, therefore, needs to assess the implications and options that lie before it. To prop up the rival Karmapa, Trinley Thaye Dorje, in place of Ogyen Trinley can be one option. His recognition is not endorsed by the Dalai Lama, even though he has an equally large following that includes a vocal faction of the Himalayan Buddhist community in India. The prospect for cultivating other high-ranking Tibetan lamas to ensure a succession in India is rather bleak. They remain deeply divided on sectarian and sub-sectarian lines. The Chinese may have worked to operate on their faultlines already.

The assumption that the Tibetan lamas of the Gelug sect (including the Dalai Lama) offer a degree of strategic depth for India in the Tibetan plateau vis-à-vis China is a misplaced one. It is neither proven nor will it happen in future. On the contrary, the Chinese may already be acquiring a reverse strategic depth in India—there will be every possibility of New Delhi getting caught off guard by such storms in future.

What actually matters for India are the sects that traditionally have a strong presence in the Indian Himalayan borderlands, which include the Karma Kagyu, Drukpa Kagyu, Drikung Kagyu, Sakya and Nyingma.

The ambivalent situation created for the Karmapa's stay in India could be a deeper conspiracy with roots in who will control Himalayan Buddhism—the Gelugpa led by the Dalai Lama or the Kagyupa led by the Karmapa. The Bhutanese, Sikkimese and other Himalayan people are conscious of this fact, with the exception of the Indian state.

The Karmapa's stay in India has never been easy. Right from the beginning, he has been kept under the watchful gaze of Dharamshala. He had been labelled a Chinese agent, fuelling suspicion about him among the Indian intelligence community. The Karmapa's staying away from politics was further seen as proof that he was sent by the Chinese. In fact, it has been a success story how Dharamshala built up a feeling of mistrust in the Indian government about his political leanings.

The key issue is not about India and China or about Tibet and China but about the intrinsic sectarian power struggle over who will control the Indian Himalayas—the main bastion and stronghold of the Kagyu lineage. And here the Karmapa is the legitimate traditional stakeholder by virtue of being one of the major Kagyu leaders.

The Karmapa has a troubled history in India, which is linked to the territorial issue in Sikkim; the dispute over Rumtek; the controversy over rival claimants of the Karmapa, among others.

The Karmapa was recognized by the Dalai Lama, perhaps in good faith or perhaps dictated by political exigency then. But after he arrived in India, he was never allowed to get a free hand as compared to other lamas who flocked to support the Dalai Lama's cause.

India's Tibet folly

The history of India's adoption of myopic thinking on the Tibet issue had its genesis in the Western perspective that actually began much before the arrival of the Dalai Lama in India in 1959. Swati Chawla, a historian of modern South Asia and an expert on Himalayan Buddhism, sums it up in her paper thus, 'Archival records of Tibetans applying for Indian citizenship in the 1950s show an emerging bureaucratic shorthand in which markers of allegiance, viz. "Buddhist" and "Communist" became synonymous with the territorial markers "Tibetan" and "Chinese".' According to her, 'incoming Tibetan monks were required to prove that they had "Buddhist leanings" and were "opposed to Communism"'.[22]

Probably, this was the narrowest approach India could have adopted that defined the course of events, eventually to the detriment of India's own policy failure. Accordingly, anyone who followed the Dalai Lama was pro-India, and any Tibetan who was a bit educated was termed pro-China. It was the most ridiculous policy distinction even the Chinese probably had never opted for.

Swati Chawla makes the argument in the context of India's mistrust towards the Karmapa who would not be accepted because he was born in Tibet under the Communist regime, recognized and trained by communist Tibetans. If it is true, the biggest flaw in this policy is that six million Tibetans living in Tibet under Chinese control now cannot be trusted. The only Tibetans who can be trusted are the Dalai Lama and the 80,000 Tibetans who accompanied him into exile in March 1959.

One thing is clear, the Tibet factor is overly played and remains overly securitized. The sectarian affiliations across India's borderlands are quite clearly defined between the Gelug-dominated Tibet and Kagyu-dominated Himalayas.

Even if there is a wider Lamaist affiliation with Tibet, it doesn't come in the way of Himalayan historical and political loyalties towards India. As such, any undue keenness for India seeking high-stakes bidding for the Tibetan Gelug lamas will remain an exercise in futility. Unless India wishes to confuse the situation further, like it has done in the case of Tawang and Ladakh already.

The Dalai Lama, who has turned eighty-four, recently expressed his wish to return home but China has not responded to him. To build further pressure on China, he has threatened to be reborn in India.

10

China's Game Plan

The Tibetans were a distinctly identifiable people living on the high plateau, but they were never delinked from Chinese history, especially since the seventeenth century and the reigns of the second Qing emperor, Kangxi (1661–1722), and the Qianlong emperor (1736–95); this situation lasted until 1911 when the Qing Empire collapsed.

It must be underlined that it was the Mongol ruler Gushi Khan who invented the idea of creating the entity of the Dalai Lama and the institution of Ganden Phodrang authority in 1642—post-facto starting from the Fifth Dalai Lama. The Qing rulers later inherited the Mongol-style sponsorship of Tibetan Lamaism.

During the Qing period (1644–1912), the Mongol–Tibetan–Manchu trio formally created a new celestial and devotional order under the unified command of the Tibetan Gelugpa sect, headed by the Dalai Lama and aided by the Panchen Lama.

Within a span of nearly 300 years, the Qing emperors, through their celestial ties with the Mongols and Tibetans, were able to transform the vast area they controlled beyond the Great Wall including Mongolia, Tibet, Xinjiang, Manchuria and parts of Siberia. China tripled in size under the Qing Empire. It is believed that the Qianlong emperor was able to Sinicize 450 million non-Chinese and integrate them to become a part of one tributary state.

One can say it was the biggest experiment of acculturation that ever took place in world history. In fact, the process of Sinicization was far more intense and effective than the Sovietization experiment of the twentieth century.

The massive acculturation process the Tibetans have gone through under prolonged Chinese influence, therefore, cannot be ignored. The relationship was that of cultural intermingling and interface between the Hans and all other ethnic groups of tributary states in terms of art, culture, religion, philosophy and exchange of goods and commerce.

The maximum trans-acculturation took place during the Qianlong emperor's time when cultural traits, behaviours, food habits and life norms were adopted. Of course, the process was also not without affinity, and bonds developed through intermarriages among the ruling classes. There did exist a Qing emperor rhetoric of having created 'one family' (*neiwai yijia*) out of the majority Hans and the minority Mongol, Tibetan and Uyghur populations. In fact, the ruling classes among the Mongols, Tibetans or Uyghurs were ingratiated to the Qing emperors in return for receiving legitimacy for their own rule.

The multilayered interface canvas among the Manchus, Mongols and Tibetans developed into a symbiotic relationship which was embedded in the Tibetan political and cultural institution of the Dalai Lama.

The first Tibetan cultural interface with the Chinese started during the Mongol period (1206–1368) when the Yuan Dynasty patronized the Tibetan lama, Sakya Pandita Kunga Gyeltsen, as an instrument for its political ambition. Later, it developed into a spiritual bond between the Chinese, Tibetans and Mongols that was strengthened during the Ming period (1368–1644) as well.

The Tibetan power hierarchy is based on the tulku (reincarnation) system that has both political and spiritual underpinnings.[1] Its origins were also in the evolution of the Dalai Lama institution that was originally backed by the Mongol and Qing courts. By implication, the Peking court controlled the tulku institutions that governed ties between Tibet and China. This unique Tibetan system of rule by reincarnation and acceptance of the lama as an object of devotion has survived for centuries.

Their political integration was based on celestial kinship wherein the Dalai Lama enjoys an ascribed status of a soul being born into a particular person. It operates on a widespread belief in celestial and non-physical allegiances that are meant to keep the bond alive irrespective of political developments.

In fact, Tibetan Lamaism has been part of China's imperial grandeur, reflecting every symbolism of the Qing Empire's legacy and rhetoric. The intimate political and spiritual alliance helped the Qings establish an Inner Asia order.

Tibetan lamas performed rituals for the emperors and prayed for their success. The Qing emperors in return patronized them and built several temples for them in China. For example, the Putuo Zongcheng temple was built in 1771 in Chengde for the Eighth Dalai Lama. The Xumi Fushou temple was built in Chengde in 1780 for the Sixth Panchen Lama. There are several Tibetan temples in Beijing built for Tibetan lamas in the seventeenth century. Among them are the Yonghe temple, popularly known as the lama temple, and the Xihuang monastery, where the Sixth Panchen Lama, Lobsang Palden Yeshe, died of smallpox on 2 November 1780.[2]

While it is correct to say that the Mongols, Tibetans and Uyghurs are separate people with separate histories, one cannot ignore the historical reality of their assimilation and acculturation into the Chinese way or their gradual Sinification that started long before the communists took over China in 1949.

The Qing-era system obviously could not survive after 1911, but whether nationalists or communists, they all relied on imperial history to define modern China's boundaries. History is a key instrument of statecraft to define China's diplomatic, military and cartographic ties vis-à-vis its neighbouring countries.

China–Tibet and the Himalayas

As described elsewhere, China's claim over Tibet is based on the 'Middle Kingdom' or ritualistic Li order theory that functioned on the imperial tributary system of the core dominating the peripheries through economics, trade and spiritual relationships.

The Himalayas fell in the peripheral circle or zone of influence, albeit circuitously, through the tribute paid by Tibetan lamas to the court of Peking. Essentially, the Chinese view the Himalayas, along with Mongolia and Tibet, to be within the pale of Manchu influence, hence fair game for inclusion into the modern Chinese state.

Tibetan lamas persistently played a key role in expanding the influence of Chinese empires to outlying regions of the Himalayas.

Hence, even for Chinese communists, Tibetan Lamaism became a useful vehicle of influence in the Himalayas. The Chinese were also aware that Lamaism is not only a cementing factor but also a powerful social force that underpins nationalistic sentiments both among the Han Chinese and Tibetans and Mongols alike. The Buddhist Himalayas could not but fall into this orbit.

Clearly, Mao Zedong was playing the Himalayan Buddhist game as early as the 1950s when he said, 'Xizang [Tibet] is China's right hand's palm, which is detached from its five fingers—of Ladakh, Nepal, Sikkim, Bhutan and Arunachal Pradesh (formerly NEFA). As all of these five are either occupied by, or under the influence of India, it is China's responsibility to "liberate" the five to be rejoined with Xizang [Tibet].'[3]

Mao must have been prompted by the Tibetan perception of the extent of their territories in the Himalayas. As mentioned earlier, the Tibetan authorities much before Mao had written to the Indian prime minister in October 1947 to return all the territories in the Himalayas that belonged to Tibet.

It is an irony that the 1959 Tibetan revolt and the subsequent escape of the Dalai Lama from Tibet may not have been without advantages for China. It is likely that China's military showdown in Tibet was pre-planned and calibrated. For example, Mao was said to be least concerned about the possibility of the Dalai Lama leaving Tibet, for he thought the Tibetan leader to be an impediment to Chinese plans for Tibet.

There are references about Mao's conversation with Soviet premier Nikita Khrushchev on 3 October 1959, where Mao admitted that China was waiting for an opportunity to crush resistance in Tibet. 'We could not launch an offensive without a pretext. And this time we had a good excuse and we struck.'[4] It is said that when Khrushchev confronted Mao for letting the Dalai Lama escape, Mao said: 'We could not keep the Dalai Lama, for the border with India is very extended and he could cross it at any point.'[5]

While the world was quick to decry Mao's actions in Tibet, the Chinese may have felt relieved and even considered it an opportunity to promote internal dissension and at the same time consolidate their hold on Tibet.

Externally, instead of containing the Tibet crisis within its borders, Mao may have calculatingly approved its spilling over into the Indian side of the Buddhist Himalayas. This probably fit into China's policy of leveraging the Qing-era network of Lamaist institutions to achieve its frontier assimilation objectives. In a way, China, through the Dalai Lama, is trying to prove its palm-and-five-fingers analogy to make its inroads into the Himalayas. In fact, the pattern of China's boundary claims follow the pattern set by the Tibetans.

There is no case here to term it 'war by proxy' carried out covertly by China. This proxy war, if any, is being fought on two fundamental political accounts. First, it was the sheltering of the Dalai Lama and the manner in which the Indian prime minister received the Tibetan leader, which offended the Chinese. India also allowed the Dalai Lama to run a parallel government from Dharamshala.

Second, despite the border between China and India yet to be settled, India sending troops (though ill-equipped) to the border provoked China's hostility, putting an end to Panchsheel solidarity and 'Bhai-Bhai' feelings towards each other.

Obviously, these actions by India had consequences and India has been paying heavily for supporting the Dalai Lama since 1959. It would be rather asinine to assume that one can maintain normal ties with a neighbour while harbouring its enemy. The question is therefore invariably asked by many even in India: how is the Dalai Lama India's baby?

India faced a humiliating defeat in the 1962 war but got away with its missteps because China was completely isolated both from the Western world and by the Soviets. The world sympathized with the weaker of the two: India. The story told to the Indian masses was that China betrayed Indian trust by attacking its borders in Ladakh and NEFA.

Be that as it may, unlike Pakistan, which is directly involved in proxy wars against India on several fronts, China has been engaged in asymmetrical soft-power warfare since the 1960s.

The Chinese knew that the Himalayas belonged to the Tibetan cultural ecosystem and the Qing-era religious allegiances between China, Mongolia and Tibet (inclusive of the Himalayas) couldn't be severed formally. They knew that millions of people in Inner Asia continued to revere the Dalai Lama and other Tibetan high lamas.

However, they continue to be painfully conscious of the limitation of playing the Lamaist card as long as the current Dalai Lama is alive.

To be fair, the Chinese are not seen opposing the Dalai Lama's cultural activities, except for his anti-China stand in the Himalayan region.

Surely, India and China inherited a boundary issue that had its genesis in their past colonial and imperial histories. The Chinese have so far not accepted the McMahon Line, for they know that after having claimed Arunachal Pradesh, they cannot just give it up. It would mean loss of face (dignity) for China. However, they also know they cannot get it back and hence will accept the status quo when the time comes.

Seemingly, neither country wants differences over the border to escalate into disputes. But the developments in the Himalayas since the 1990s have become more complex and hot, the objective of which seems to offer no solution to the boundary question.

It is the Dalai Lama factor that has caused the Buddhist Himalayas to be in a state of flux, especially in the current context of India–China relations. In fact, his restricted goal is to play the religious card to thwart any India–China rapprochement until the Tibet issue is resolved. But the role he plays outside Tibet could very well be paying some dividend to China as well.

Quite visibly, the enormity of Tibetan religious activities in the Buddhist Himalayas seems to have only increased since the 1990s, with the exception of Nepal and Bhutan, where the governments seem very cautious of the fallout due to their historical sense of threat vis-à-vis Tibet rather than China. India, on the other hand, systematically allowed its own Himalayan consciousness and identity that had historically evolved vis-à-vis Tibet to fade away.

Scores of students from the Himalayan region are taken to Tibetan establishments such as Sera, Drepung and Ganden created in Mungod (Karnataka) since 1966. They are educated in the Gelug tradition that propagates Tibet-oriented nationalistic feelings.

The Dalai Lama Foundation,[6] founded in 2009 as a US-based non-profit charitable organization (registered in New York), has been running several activities in the Himalayas. The aim of the foundation is to support the activities of individuals or institutions working for the welfare of the Tibetan people, the advancement of the culture and heritage of the ancient civilization of Tibet, and to help promote educational opportunities for deserving students, etc. It also aims to evolve strategies that will encourage a sense of universal responsibility in youth through the educational system, foster meaningful dialogue between science and religion, promote the preservation of the environment, encourage and cultivate ahimsa and non-violence as a method of both individual growth and broader social change, and provide relief and assistance to underserved communities of all faiths and origins.

However, according to several local monks, the activities of the foundation boil down to supporting institutions of the Gelug sect that propagate the Tibetan cause.

For example, in Ladakh alone, the Dalai Lama Foundation is said to be supporting three newly created schools which include the Siddhartha High School[7] in Stok run by the school's founder, Khenpo Lobsang Tsetan of the Tashi Lhunpo monastery; the Ngari Institute of Buddhist Dialectics in Saboo village run by Geshe Tsewang Dorje;[8] and the Jamyang School[9] established in Leh for the students of the Drokpa tribe (Arayan tribe) of Ladakh who are not traditionally Buddhists by faith.

These schools are supposed to have been created to teach Tibetan Buddhism to the Himalayan populace, but not everyone seems to be happy about such activities being sponsored by the Dalai Lama outfits. There seems to be an undercurrent of resentment and resistance at various levels against such trends of Gelug assertion which could have a destabilizing effect in the years to come. Surely, the pattern would be the same in other parts of the Himalayas.

Importantly, the agenda of getting the Bodhi (Tibetan) language included in Schedule VIII of the Indian Constitution was initially set by Dharamshala through its proxies from the Himalayan region. The move is gaining momentum and being embedded in the agenda of local political parties. In fact, the Dalai Lama and other Tibetan institutions have become rallying platforms for the Himalayan people to assert their cultural causes.

The other critical points include the subtle insertion of Tibetan sectarian history, culture and religion in the curriculum of local government schools. This has been achieved successfully at least in Ladakh. According to a lama from Temisgang, Gelug forces have even managed to insert texts relating to the propagation of Je Tsongkhapa, the fourteenth-century Tibetan founder of the Gelug tradition, in the school curriculum in Ladakh. Similarly, in 2017, Arunachal Pradesh chief minister Pema Khandu also talked about popularizing and teaching Bodhi to people, especially in schools. And, here, it is difficult not to imagine why the further intensification of Tibetan culture and language in the area will not be leveraged by China.

Trends and the tide

In the current context, and given the Chinese propensity to reflect on the past in their strategic overview, there is no doubt about the probability of China playing lama politics once again, especially in a scenario where their political differences with the Dalai Lama get resolved, perhaps sooner or later.

George Orwell said, 'He who controls the past controls the future.'[10] This is relevant in this case, since much of the contemporary political differences between the Chinese and the Tibetans are strongly historical by nature. Also, given the fact that the Tibetans and the Chinese have shown an inclination for revisionist tendencies, they are poised to eventually seek reconciliation.

Most Indians are oblivious to the fact that China is already in the midst of harvesting the devotional potential of Tibetan Buddhism—a religion it had attempted to destroy several decades ago. A gradual process of reconciliation and the spiritual merger of Tibetan and Chinese Buddhism are already underway. The Dalai Lama's teachings are now translated in Chinese.[11] His teachings are attended by hundreds of Han Buddhists.[12]

The future is being built on the very same premise that Chinese rulers followed in the past. They not only readily embraced Lamaist hierarchy but also patronized lamas. In a way, a very subtle process of a doctrinal merger of the Han and Tibetan schools seems already at play. This might mean a gradual reinstatement of the imperial-era harmonious and spiritual coexistence between Tibetan and Han Buddhism, if not a complete hierarchical acceptance of Tibetan Buddhism into Han Buddhism.[13]

India is yet to figure out the Chinese ability to play on political anthropology in a low-intensity conflict. Instead, India may have for decades played into Chinese hands. Paradoxically, China may have already thrown India off balance in ways that the latter is made to feel proud in supporting Chinese dissidents. Most Indians rejoiced in harbouring the Dalai Lama since 1959, and that suited Beijing perfectly. This is because India does not realize that it was being ensnared into a game plan where the ultimate victory would be China's.

Of course, the narrative built up in India in the 1960s was based on US thinking. The Americans in all fairness had their ideological interest in using Tibetan Lamaism as a potent weapon against communist China, just as the Afghan Mujahedeen were used against the Soviets during the Cold War. But the Indians should have at least advised the Americans that the lamas would not pick up Kalashnikov guns. Tibet's history suggests that from the seventeenth century onwards, after the Dalai Lama took the reins, the Tibetans never fought any major wars, and if they did, they got the Mongols and the Chinese to fight for them. Tibetan raids into the Himalayas were always led by Mongol generals.

There is no case here to term the Tibetan engagement in the Himalayas a proxy war carried out covertly by China because the lamas are not connected to the Chinese state, but that does not absolve them of the fact that ties between the Chinese and the Tibetans are intrinsic in nature. This provides the Chinese state the deniability advantage of sponsoring covert Tibetan soft power in the Himalayas.

India should have been mindful that Tibetan Gelugpa politics has an intricate symbiotic relationship with the Chinese and the Mongols. Together, they ruled Inner Asian regions for centuries. It was certainly an ill-thought-out move that has put India in a tight geopolitical spot, causing sufficient strain on Indian resources.

The prolonged presence of the Dalai Lama has already blurred the distinction created by the British between the Indian Himalayan frontiers and Outer Tibet, which was under Qing control.

The owning of China's imperial history and its imagined geographical frontiers by India will have highly destabilizing strategic consequences. Clearly, India's deliberate policy to sponsor Tibetan cultural strength will ultimately help the Chinese restore their old hegemonic tributary influence over the Himalayas.

It is also clear that the Himalayas are not the most suitable cultural terrain for India to do well in; it can do little except rely on military strength. Instead, it is ideal terrain for the Tibetan lamas who thrive in the Himalayas like fish in the sea. Clearly, the notion that those who have mastered the past control their present and will chart their own future may come true. This naivety on the part of India could cause it immense difficulties in the future.

The trend that has been seen so far is that excessive Tibetan influence (Tibetanization) in the Indian Buddhist Himalayas has become a considerable concern for the Indian defence. This has come about via a gradual process of taking over every Indian monastery in the Indian Himalayas by Tibetan lamas.

The picture on the ground is already hair-raising. A case in point is the struggle over the Rumtek monastery in Sikkim. The Tibetan takeover of almost all the big monasteries in Ladakh has been rather hassle-free despite Article 370 which impedes even an Indian citizen from owning monastic property in Jammu and Kashmir.

Sectarian discord

The growing inter-Tibetan sectarian strife has become another instability factor in the Buddhist Himalayas. Of course, there is a strategic calculation involved in this. It is an old Chinese method of playing on various faultlines to keep the Tibetans divided, while at the same time furthering their own key objectives. This author has witnessed in Kazakhstan the Chinese managing to break up over 2,50,000 people of the Uyghur diaspora into at least eighteen different factions.

Sectarian suitors of all sorts—most likely armed with foreign funding—seem to have found a way to build their network while skilfully manipulating Indian law and influential individuals, politicians and local institutions. They have built mega-religious infrastructure all along, from Ladakh to Arunachal Pradesh.

To top it all, they have brought in sectarian discord among people hitherto devoid of any such differences. This is a major cause for worry that could push local communities deeper into the throes of anxiety and tear apart Himalayan stability. For example, in the western Himalayas, a small incident took a critical turn in 2015 when the Dalai Lama issued a virtual gag order against facilitating the visit of the rival Karmapa, Trinley Thaye Dorje.

While the majority for a variety of reasons did not ignore the Dalai Lama's directive, the other sects, barring the Gelug sect—Drukpa Kagyu, Drikung Kagyu, Nyingma and even the Sakya—defied the gag and accorded a reception to Trinley Thaye Dorje. The incident almost risked the society getting divided and led to a split in the All-Ladakh Gompa Association (LGA), which is the equivalent of a local sangha. The LGA office remained locked to avoid any direct conflict for several years.

The main motive for the Dalai Lama's actions couldn't be ascertained. It could either be meant to undermine the Kagyu hold in Ladakh or relate to the dual appearance of the Karmapa. The Dalai Lama and China had recognized Ogyen Trinley Dorje as the true Karmapa and not Trinley Thaye Dorje.

Similarly, Sikkim has been on the boil for decades over contesting sectarian parties claiming rights to Rumtek's ownership. In Nepal, the Chinese have been supporting Buddhist projects through Tibetan monks. In May 2016, Drukhang Thubten Khedrup Rinpoche, vice chairman of the Buddhist Association of China (BAC), supervised the Buddha Jayanti celebration in Lumbini. In Bhutan too, though less successfully, the Chinese have been using the Tibetans to influence the trend of Buddhism.

A rift within the Dalai Lama's own Gelug ranks has widened after he banned the worship of the sect's protector deity, Dorje Shugden, in 1996. He has good political reason to do so, but his opponents in this regard, mostly Western converts, have been trumpeting the iniquity of the Dalai Lama, calling him a 'Muslim' and 'the worst dictator' in modern times.

The Tibetan presence makes the situation in the Indian Buddhist Himalayas rather perilous and one whose end is not in sight. Worse, no finger can be raised in such issues for it would be dubbed as 'China's hand'. For example, the unrest in Tawang in May 2016 in which a monk was killed was described as the handiwork of China.

In the coming years, such recurring issues would inevitably spark pent-up sectarian and inter-ethnic strife, and convert the Himalayas into a bigger tinderbox, while India's own Buddhist institutions are speedily undermined to the detriment of its interests. This is where China would try to win both the Tibetan and the Himalayan Buddhist games.

To be sure, a power struggle among various Tibetan sects will get heightened in the post–Dalai Lama scenario, for the issue is linked to the Gelugpa sect retaining its supremacy over the Tibetan order.

Future of the Dalai Lama

Himalayan stability would also depend on the future of the Dalai Lama. So far, the Dalai Lama's ambivalent stance on his next birth has confused everyone. It is clear that the Tibetans would certainly need and want a Dalai Lama to lead them, and Beijing too is determined to find a successor of its own choice.

Given the Tibetan track record of ensnaring India in its murky agenda, there would be every attempt to build a case for the rebirth to occur in India. The simple logic for the Americans to play Tibet politics in future would depend on controlling the Tibetan leader's next reincarnation. Not surprisingly, the Dalai Lama has already hinted that he expects his reincarnation to be born in India. Clearly, this would mean he will be born in the Indian Himalayas, either in Arunachal Pradesh or in Ladakh, and possibly also among the Tibetan refugee population in India. No one knows what it would mean but it will cause the Himalayas to become further prone to conflict. And it would animate the sectarian cause of retaining the Himalayas as a Kagyu bastion, as against the Gelug taking control of the region.

In the past, the news of the Dalai Lama possibly installing his chosen Karmapa, Ogyen Trinley Dorje, to be the next interim leader was stiffly resisted by the Gelug faction. They would not like the Dalai Lama's selection process to be handled by non-Gelug Lamas. A situation where he could be chosen from outside their area of influence would be strongly resisted by the Gelugpas. In fact, a media report highlighted communication between the Dalai Lama's aide and the chairman of the Gelug Monastic Disciplinary Council, Jangchup Choeden, and Chinese authorities about a joint project, for 'offerings in monasteries in Tibet', to decide the successor of the Fifteenth Dalai Lama.[14] Choeden later denied having such a communication about warming up to the Chinese.

All in all, the Buddhist Himalayas will continue to remain a contested geo-cultural landscape between the various competing narratives of India and China. However, in the current scenario, India's interests in the Buddhist Himalayas remain even more compromised than during the colonial period, when British strategists were able to play the Himalayan game more perceptively.

For example, in the early twentieth century, the viceroy of India, Lord Curzon, was able to visualize the Himalayan regions of Ladakh, Sikkim, Bhutan and the north-east frontier as an 'inner defence line for India protected by a Tibetan buffer region'.[15]

However, in the contemporary situation, India's lack of sufficient wherewithal to understand the critical interplay between Buddhism and the Himalayas may have led it to weigh heavily on the minds of the Dalai Lama and his government-in-exile. Of late, the 'Tibet card' is being redefined, albeit on the grounds of Buddhist diplomacy.

The 2017 Doklam crisis brought into focus what will be one of the most difficult issues that will unfold in the Himalayas in future. It indicated the tensions rising from conflicting territorial claims by both India and China which will almost certainly keep recurring and continue raising the risk of war.

11

Water and Himalayan Geopolitics

Any prospect of a stand-off between India and China would less likely hinge on Tibet than over the control of trans-Himalayan water resources. This is the stark reality. And as the economies of both India and China grow, the need to control water resources has assumed greater significance and will potentially risk heightening the geopolitical conflict in the Himalayas.

Previously deemed too remote to exploit, the Chinese have lately been looking at Tibet's primordial water resource to solve the country's numerous dilemmas. According to Chinese sources, the Tibet Autonomous Region alone is said to be having 354.8 billion cubic metres (BCM) of surface water resources (13.5 per cent of the nation's total) and 330 BCM of glacial water resources.[1] The figure is 448.2 BCM according to the Tibetan government-in-exile in Dharamshala.[2]

What concerns India is the annual flow of an estimated 354 BCM of water from Tibet into India, of which 131 BCM is accounted for by the Brahmaputra.[3] The fear has been that China is seeking a water diversion plan by damming the Tsangpo (Brahmaputra) at the Great Bend at Shuomatan Point as a bumper solution to tap the water and divert it to the north.

In August 2006, the news of China's river plan sent shock waves through India, especially in Assam and Arunachal Pradesh.[4] Some Western writers were convinced that work had already begun.[5]

The news of China building a 510 MW hydroelectrical project at Zangmu was confirmed in March 2009. The Indian government was then trying to ascertain the fact. But India's own National Remote

Sensing Agency (NRSA) confirmed that construction was indeed underway. The Indian intelligence agency National Technical Research Organisation (NTRO) had even claimed that it had alerted the government in May 2008 about the project 'moving from discussion to planning stage'.[6] It had pinpointed activities in nine suspected locations near the Great Bend on the China side.

Beijing said it was a run-of-river project and assured New Delhi the dam would not impact downstream flow. However, China's actions since then have caused confusion and even sparked off an emotive public response in India. What added to India's edginess was China's opaque position on the matter. The official Chinese organs, though, denied the diversion project, but its hydropower lobby was seen pressing for a mega project to meet China's water woes.

Diversion plans

Surely, the diversion plan had been on the drawing board of Chinese planners for several decades. Chinese hydrologist Guo Kai was the first to moot the idea of a *shuo-tian* (reverse flow) plan to divert Brahmaputra[7] water to end chronic water shortages in China's north and north-west regions. The idea inspired others, such as the former PLA officer Li Ling who wrote the book *How Tibet's Water Will Save China* in 2005.[8] This resulted in Jiang Zemin issuing a vision document titled 'Xibu Da Kaifa' (Great Western Extraction) in 1998 that gained support from 118 PLA generals, politburo members, National People's Congress (NPC) deputies and the engineering community.[9] Since then, hundreds of media reports, op-eds and anecdotes have been making the rounds in support of the diversion project.

The diversion idea gained new currency in the mid-2000s, possibly because of China's growing domestic water crisis arising from the industrial upsurge. It appeared as if water would become a potential catalyst for domestic turmoil in China at some stage. The stakes were huge as the Chinese also desired to turn millions of arid hectares into arable land.[10]

The diversion project was part of China's $62 billion South–North Water Transfer Project (SNWTP), a dream of Chairman Mao Zedong that was given the go-ahead in 2002.[11] The aim was to send 45 BCM of water annually from the Yangtze and Yellow Rivers to the arid north.[12]

The first phase of the SNWTP was completed in March 2013. The middle route was to feed water to the north by 2014. A section of the route was completed to meet water requirements during the Beijing Olympics.[13] The third stage involves the Tsangpo's diversion. The aim is to build a dam for generating 40,000 MW of hydropower and divert 200 BCM of water annually to the north.

The news reports of the Brahmaputra's diversion suddenly came into the limelight following the completion of the Qinghai–Tibet railway in 2006. Even while the Indian government adopted a cautious approach, the media and a section of think-tank experts set alarm bells ringing.

It was difficult to ascertain the status of the diversion plans because of conflicting information from different sources.[14] But media reports suggested the project would involve an enormous engineering complexity on the scale of the Tibet railway and the Three Gorges dam.[15]

An imaginary threat perception was built about China's manipulation of the river as a subtle coercive measure if not a politico-military tool vis-à-vis India.[16] Such perceptions might have emanated from the Western world, though Indian pundits like Brahma Chellaney argued that the building of dams on the headwaters of the Brahmaputra, Sutlej and the Indus 'implies environmental devastation of India's northern and eastern plains and thus be akin to a declaration of water war'.[17]

Similarly, Tibetan activists such as Claude Arpi have been pushing the argument that if China goes ahead with the diversion project, it would risk India's national security and practically be considered a 'declaration of war' against India.[18]

Abruptly, an old report of China's plans to use nuclear explosives to divert the river, that had originally appeared in the *Scientific American* in June 1996, was pulled out by Tibet supporters in an attempt to antagonize the issue.[19] Scores of articles have been giving credence to the publication along with other such study reports that originated from the West.[20]

In fact, Indian media reported that the Chinese conducted several nuclear blasts near the Great Bend in 2005. No details were found but the Indian government had shared the information with the then American defence secretary, Robert Gates, in 2008; Gates had admitted the complete failure of US satellites in detecting the blasts.[21] According to the report, China's plan for building a 200-kilometre-long canal passing through Mount Namcha was first presented by experts in December 1995 at the Chinese Academy of Engineering Physics.

The Great Bend and other projects

One cannot ignore the point of the Tibetan mythological angle.[22] The area around the Great Bend is called *tsari* (pure crystal mountain) and *pemako* (array of the lotus).[23] This is considered a sacred mountain and major pilgrimage site for the Tibetans—among the three holiest places along with Mount Kailash and Lapchi. The area has significance for the Tibetans as the abode of the protector deity Dorjee Phagmo or Vajravarahi—a wrathful form of Vajrayogini.

Intensification of other large-scale infrastructural projects, including roads, railways, airports and dams on the Tibetan plateau, also meant increased thrust on India along the borders. In fact, media reports[24] have continued to come as recently as in 2017 that tunnels were being tested to transfer water from Yarlung Tsangpo to the Tarim Basin in Xinjiang, although China denied such a plan on account of engineering difficulties and high-cost implications.[25]

But what really heightened Indian edginess included China's ravenous exploitation of the Himalayan rivers, which had a perilous downstream impact. Fears were raised that the Great Bend was at a geologically fragile knick-zone with very rapid bedrock exhumation rates.[26] The seismic rate beneath the massif is believed to be exceptionally active.[27] In case of an earthquake, there could be ominous consequences for millions living in downstream areas.

Other fears include upland diversion offsetting the silt and nutrient-rich sediment flux that could affect livelihoods of riparian areas, apart from destroying the biodiversity of the downstream Assam plains and Bangladesh's delta. It would also cause the sea water to encroach.[28]

The fear that it would enhance Chinese engineering capability to turn the taps on or off, leaving India at the mercy of China to release water during the off season, and for prevention of floods during the monsoons, cannot be ignored.

From India's perspective, China is entitled to take up any upstream projects, as long as the existing flow of 79 BCM of water into India remains unimpeded. Most of the Brahmaputra's catchment area, providing an annual average runoff of 585.60 BCM, almost 80 per cent, falls within Arunachal Pradesh.[29] The volume becomes ten times higher during the monsoon. Allowing China to divert a constant volume of water during that period could help mitigate floods in India and Bangladesh. Non-consumptive exploiting of water by China for power generation may also be beneficial for India, as the flow is expected to increase by 10 to 20 per cent during the dry season.

But India's key concerns stem from environmental threats. Suspicions and fears have also been caused by the sudden rise and fall in water levels of the Brahmaputra. There have also been reports of increasing incidents of landslides and deluges in the Himalayan rivers.

Until 2005, India was unaware about the Zada dam on the Sutlej basin and even appeared clueless when the Chinese announced they were building dams at Dagu, Jiacha and Jiexu. In 2000, the Pare-Chu deluge created havoc in the Sutlej, leaving a trail of destruction.[30] The cause of the June 2000 floods in Arunachal Pradesh is still not known. More such hydropower projects may have probably come up in the Sutlej tributaries.[31] Also, little is known about the Shiquanhe and Zhikong projects on the Indus. Locals have observed that the Singe-Tsangpo too has been tapering over the years. Therefore, the fear remains that the Chinese would be able to repeat the manipulation of water flow into India at a much bigger scale.

India managed to sign a Memorandum of Understanding (MoU) with China on data-sharing over trans-boundary rivers in 2002, and an expert-level committee was set up in 2006 for monitoring hydrological activities along them.[32] In 2014, a new provision for sharing data twice a day from 15 May to 15 October was added.[33]

However, it is not clear whether these mechanisms have fully mitigated the problems, including that of floods. In fact, Beijing has at times shown reluctance to exchange data with India.

During the prime minister's visit to China in 2008, Beijing only assured the 'protection and rational use' of water resources in the trans-Himalayan rivers.[34] It also refused India's requests to set up two additional hydrological monitoring stations for the Brahmaputra.

The diversion threat since then has become a recurring theme of debate in India and also in Bangladesh,[35] but certainly not serious enough to become a central agenda in India–China ties. The Indian government appeared hesitant to raise the issue forcefully with Beijing. At the same time, it never tried to push the issue aside either.

For the first time, the issue featured in Indian official strategic thinking in 2008, when the then external affairs minister Pranab Mukherjee was outlining India's security challenges at the National Defence College in New Delhi. He said that China was a security 'challenge and a priority' and not an opportunity. He admitted that India was not fully equipped to deal with the challenges that China poses. Importantly, he cited an instance that 'during Prime Minister Manmohan Singh's visit to China in October 2008, he told journalists that his conversation with Chinese President Hu Jintao focused a lot on the future of trans-border rivers . . . While India does not articulate this concern often, it's clearly very high priority.'[36]

Yet, there was certainly no evidence of the Chinese diverting the waters of the Brahmaputra. Successive Indian governments continued to allay fears of Chinese projects affecting India's water usage. In November 2009, Indian external affairs minister S.M. Krishna clarified in Parliament that 'China is a responsible country and would never do anything to undermine any other country's interests'.[37]

In April 2010, China finally admitted to building a hydropower project on the Brahmaputra. The reports suggested that the 510 MW Zangmu run-of-river project was being built by China's Gezhouba Group, a construction and engineering company. The Chinese admission, however, came against the need for cooperation from India at the 2010 climate summit at Cancun.

However, when Prime Minister Manmohan Singh proposed in March 2013 in Durban a joint mechanism for verification, President Xi Jinping gave no clear answer except reiterating that China would bear in mind its responsibilities and the interests of riparian states.

A threat multiplier

Indian apprehensions further grew when in 2013 China completed the vital Medog motorway in the Nyingchi prefecture—30 kilometres from the Indian border in Arunachal Pradesh.[38] Obviously, China's assurances had been taken with a pinch of salt. In 2013, an inter-ministerial panel report had asked the government to closely monitor China's plan for a series of cascading run-of-river projects in the middle reaches of the river. Again in February 2014, the external affairs minister, Salman Khurshid, admitted that the ministry of water resources had been asked to verify whether the dams built on Yarlung are run-of-river or storage dams.[39]

In December 2015, External Affairs Minister Sushma Swaraj responded to a question in Parliament by stating, 'Government, in close cooperation with various state governments, continues to carefully monitor the water flow in the Brahmaputra River for early detection of abnormality so that corrective and preventive measures are taken to safeguard livelihood of peoples of these states of Union of India.'[40]

The same reply was repeated on 26 December 2018 by the minister of state for external affairs, V.K Singh, when he also said that the government had consistently conveyed its views and concerns to the Chinese authorities, including at the highest levels, and had urged them to ensure that the interests of downstream states are not harmed by any activities in upstream areas.[41] He informed the House that 'the Chinese side has conveyed that they are only undertaking run-of-river hydropower projects which do not involve diversion of the waters of the Brahmaputra'.

The government gave a reassurance that various issues relating to trans-border rivers are discussed with China under the ambit of expert-level mechanism and under the MoU on sharing hydrological data that was renewed in June 2018.[42]

The Zangmu dam was completed in 2015, but three more dams are currently under construction at Dagu (640 MW), Jiacha (320 MW) and Jeixu.

However, the threat of an imminent water war is a premature assessment because there is no evidence of China having given approval for river diversion projects. However, India does have a genuine strategic concern for the reason that China could possibly link the water issue to a border settlement.

In fact, soon after India and China signed the Strategic Partnership Agreement in 2006, a prominent Chinese writer, Wang Weiluo, asked a provocative question in an article, 'The Chinese government's desire to solve its northern water shortages depends on projects that in the long term will require the use of water resources currently under the de facto control of India. I can only ask our policymakers, what should China do?'[43]

The contention of Wang Weiluo's statement meant that the actual catchment area of the Tsangpo basin (92,000 square kilometres) falls under de facto Indian control, hence going ahead with the SNWTP is meaningless. During the same year, the Chinese ambassador to India, Sun Yuxi, made the assertion that 'in our position, the whole of what you call the state of Arunachal Pradesh is Chinese territory. And Tawang is only one of the places in it. We are claiming all of that.'[44] Since then, China's position on Arunachal Pradesh has only hardened. The fear of water becoming a threat multiplier thus draws merit.

In fact, the occasional flaring up of disputes along the border tends to overshadow the sharing of hydrological data. For example, China went ahead and signed the extension of the 2002 MoU on data-sharing even after the border incursion incident in the Depsang Plain in 2013. However, it stopped sharing hydrological data in 2017 after the seventy-three-day Doklam stand-off.[45]

While the Chinese side cited technical reasons such as the upgradation of hydrological stations, Bangladesh continued to receive discharge-level data on the Brahmaputra from China. China resumed providing hydrological data only after Prime Minister Modi and President Xi Jinping held detailed discussions on bilateral and global issues at their informal summit in Wuhan in May 2018. While refusing to share data during the Doklam border stand-off, China demonstrated its intentions to use water for political leverage.

The runoff of 629 BCM of water on the Indian side provides huge potential for hydropower and irrigation schemes. Logically, and to pre-empt any future move by China, India will have to start building storage capacities if it wishes to strengthen its rights on the Brahmaputra downstream. Otherwise, China would have a right to divert the water.

India has commenced construction of fourteen hydropower projects in Arunachal Pradesh as an effort to establish its 'lower riparian right' to counter China's first-use priority rights. However, barring one, all projects continue to remain stuck due to non-issuance of environmental clearances.[46]

An interesting observation made by a journalist was that 'while the concerns regarding Chinese diversion plans may be genuine, India also maintains the "China threat" to a certain extent to veil its own administrative lapses and justify dam-building activities to its domestic audience'.[47]

Nothing much can be done on the matter as China is not a signatory to any important treaty governing trans-border management. There are some international laws, but China would not abide by them.[48] Beijing has refused to join the Mekong River Commission. China has also not ratified the UN Convention on Non-Navigable Use of International Watercourses (1997), which requires states to share information relating to the use of international water courses. But China believes the convention adequately takes care of the interests of upstream states. But the underlying intentions of both China and India in not signing the UN Convention are driven by geopolitical considerations.[49]

As a result, other riparian states too are worried about China's plans. The Xiaowan dam on the Mekong has been stirring up passions across South East Asia. Last to join the chorus is Myanmar, vehemently opposing China building the Myitsone mega dam on the upper Irrawaddy. The project could potentially rupture China's longstanding bonhomie with Myanmar. In Central Asia, diversion of several trans-border rivers, including Illy and Black Irtysh by China, have caused concern. Tragically, countries like Kyrgyzstan, Kazakhstan and Tajikistan neither have the courage nor a public protest culture to raise their voice against China.

Currently, India has very little leverage with China. The only option is diplomacy, but in most cases, diplomacy has failed due to suspicions emanating from a host of contentious bilateral and international issues. Past experiences have shown that a denial by China cannot be taken seriously. Even if an agreement is signed, there is no guarantee that China will honour it.

Many experts suspect that the reason for China's gesture of cooperating to share hydrological data with India is only part of its political strategy of portraying an image of a 'responsible neighbour'. From China's perspective, it has no obligation at all but is doing it out of a sense of 'trust'.[50] So essentially, cooperation with India remains a goodwill gesture from the Chinese side.

Clearly, both China and India will be water-stressed in coming years because of the rising demand for food security and clean drinking water. Even if China does not go ahead with the project, cross-border tensions over water seem likely as China builds more reservoirs for drinking supplies.

The way out should be to prevent water becoming a catalyst for future conflict. In the absence of a treaty or some other protective mechanism, water issues could become a destabilizing factor, especially when unilateral actions are undertaken by one side.

It becomes more challenging when countries sharing common rivers carry unresolved political issues. While border disputes are generally of great significance, water becomes a matter of life and death. But in the case of India–China relations, both problems seem intertwined. It is here that China's persistent claim over Arunachal Pradesh seems linked to its water agenda, especially in terms of seeking to leverage its position over boundary negotiation. In fact, Chinese planners had conducted the Tsangpo feasibility studies project when India–China relations had already entered into a higher gear.

Hydro-related infrastructure in Tibet would enhance China's military capability, which would finally enhance China's manoeuvrability of negotiating on the boundary issue. Therefore, some security analysts have suggested that disputes over water potentially tend to become a 'threat multiplier' in fragile regions.[51]

The Indus

The Himalayan river conflict is also potentially exacerbated by the strategic nexus between China and Pakistan. In fact, little is known about Chinese hydro projects on the Singe-Khabab Tsangpo or the Indus.

What is being widely reported is that China has built a dam on the Indus opposite the Indian border point of Demchok. It was first reported by Alice Albinia, a British journalist and author of the book *Empires of the Indus*, as a hydroelectric installation. It seems the Sengye Tsangpo Hydropower Station located in Ali produces 6400 kilowatts of power.

Ali (Gar) is a major military settlement. It is surrounded by arid land. The storage of water is, therefore, essential for irrigation and agriculture. Gar is the capital of the Ngari prefecture that borders the Aksai Chin and Demchok areas of Ladakh. The area is strategically located on the Tibet–Xinjiang Highway and is critical for the Chinese military to manage deployments on the border with Ladakh, Aksai Chin, Himachal Pradesh, Uttarakhand and Nepal. It is suspected that more dams will be built in the area with the aim of promoting tourism because of its location near Mount Kailash, a favourite destination for both religious and adventure tourists. In coming years, Gar is likely to become a major hub for air connectivity for flights to Kashgar, Lhasa, Chengdu and other major cities in western China.

The people of Ladakh have observed that the flow of Singe-Tsangpo too has been falling over the years. Therefore, the fear remains that the Chinese would be able to repeat the manipulation of water flow into India on a much bigger scale.

In fact, a more serious matter was earlier reported by Western commentators. This relates to the possible diversion of water from the Indus River in western Tibet to the Tarim Basin in Xinjiang to become a part of China's grand Western Diversion Route.

Claude Arpi wrote a piece about a smaller 'pilot' project to divert the Indus River towards Xinjiang.[52] The main conclusion is that the diversion will help in maintaining long-term stability in Xinjiang.

In 2015, Arpi reported yet another proposal for diverting the Yarlung Tsangpo or Brahmaputra to Xinjiang that was mooted by about twenty scholars of the Urumqi Xinjiang University of Finance and Economics. Arpi quoted a professor from the university, Ren Qunluo, as saying, 'Water from rivers such as the Yarlung Zangbo River can help turn vast deserts and arid lands into oasis and farmlands, alleviate population pressure in the east, as well as reduce flood risks in the countries through which the river travels downstream.' Ren Qunluo was quoted in the *Global Times* saying, 'Xinjiang has 1.1 million square kilometres of plains but less than 70,000 square kilometres are arable due to a shortage of water. If all these plains are greened, another China will have been created.'[53]

A concern for India is that the Indus Waters Treaty it has signed with Pakistan involves the China factor even though China is not a party to the treaty. In fact, this makes it geopolitically more threatening than the Brahmaputra.

Much has been said about India possibly making a case for the abrogation of the Indus Waters Treaty or blocking the flow of water to Pakistan from its eastern rivers in order to punish it for abating terrorism in India. There have been no responses officially from China in this regard. But Beijing has been quietly sending subtle messages to India through think tanks and conversations on the cocktail circuit that any alteration to the treaty to punish its friend Pakistan will entail consequences for India as well.[54]

What it means is that China will be under no obligation to allow water from the Indus or Sutlej Rivers to flow should India abrogate the treaty with Pakistan. Inevitably, any such action by China would mean that a large area of north India will be deprived of water, and this would also impact the flow into the Bhakra dam, the Karcham Wangtoo hydroelectric project, and the Nathpa Jhakri dam, all of which generate colossal amounts of electricity.

Alarming reports have emerged indicating rapid depletion of the Himalayan cryosphere or its glacier space due to climate change. According to recent reports, rising temperatures would lead to the Himalayas losing two-thirds of its glaciers by 2100.[55] As a result, countries will be 'stressed' for water, and it will be water, not oil, which could become the world's next biggest catalyst for conflict.

It is here that India and China would feel the greatest impact. Some interesting observations in this regard have been made by Geoff Dabelko, director of the Environmental Change and Security Program at the Woodrow Wilson International Center for Scholars in Washington, D.C. 'Water is seen as a strategic asset for China . . . nearly two billion people are dependent on the Tibetan water . . . by definition, that makes it high politics and critically important in a politically strategic sense.'[56] Similarly, for Aviva Imhof, the campaign director of the International Rivers Network, 'Pressure on the Asian rivers is going to get worse before it gets better.'

There is simmering doubt about the political issues swirling around Tibet and China getting more complex, and for Rajendra K. Pachauri, 'A staggering number of people will be affected in the near future by the declining glacial flows on the Tibetan Plateau.' Sandra Postel of the Global Water Policy Project once predicted that conflicts over water could ricochet across Asia.[57]

It has been proven that water scarcity has historically worked in favour of cooperation rather than conflict between states.[58] The Indus Waters Treaty is a case in point, and there are other examples.

Any forward movement on ensuring hydro security in the Brahmaputra basin would require a long-term understanding between the two countries. India's hydro-diplomacy thus faces the daunting challenge of engaging China in a sustained dialogue and securing a water-sharing treaty that serves the interests of both countries.

While the demand for Tsangpo's diversion may get louder in China, growing environmental disasters are also fuelling mass protests[59] in the country against mega projects. In fact, the greater resentment to manipulating the Shuomatan Point could emanate from China. India should evolve a comprehensive strategic plan, which cannot be handled by the water resources ministry alone.

While India–China relations have shown a significant upswing, fuelled by burgeoning trade and investment, the dispute over water could add to the existing mistrust emanating from a variety of issues. It is prudent that both India and China strive to set up a water governance regime with a binding legal agreement.[60] Both countries should also jointly explore the prospects of ecological cooperation to save the Himalayas and mitigate the threat posed by climate change.

12

Western Himalayas: Resituating Menser and Darchen-Labrang

The Instrument of Accession signed by Maharaja Hari Singh on 26 October 1947 warranted India's control over the entire territory of the erstwhile princely state of Jammu and Kashmir. And Section 4 of the Jammu and Kashmir Constitution defined the state's territory as comprising all the territories which, on the fifteenth day of August 1947, were under the sovereignty or suzerainty of the ruler of the state.

Consequently, the geographical extent of Jammu and Kashmir included areas now under Pakistani occupation, that is, Pakistan-occupied Kashmir (PoK), as well as the Trans-Karakoram Tract or Shaksgam valley, and the Aksai Chin plateau.

One important fact that is generally ignored is that when Maharaja Hari Singh signed the Instrument of Accession with the Dominion of India, he referred to himself as 'Shriman Inder Mahinder Rajrajeswar Maharajadhiraj Shri Hari Singhji, Jammu & Kashmir Naresh Tatha Tibbet adi Deshadhipati', which meant that he was not just the ruler of Jammu and Kashmir but also of the areas of eastern Ladakh including Aksai Chin as well as the territory he controlled inside Tibet.

Accordingly, Jammu and Kashmir's territory included jurisdiction over the Minser (Menser) estate, which consisted of a cluster of villages located 296 kilometres deep inside Chinese territory at the foot of Mount Kailash on the bank of Mansarovar lake.

Menser: An Indian estate in Tibet

Menser continued to remain a part of Ladakh even after Tibet snatched the eastern half of Ladakh during the 1679–84 war. It is a cluster of villages in Ngari-khor-sum or the Guge kingdom in western Tibet, located near Mount Kailash.

The villages were retained by the then ruler of Ladakh, Deldan Namgyal (1642–92), when the area was annexed by troops of the Fifth Dalai Lama, Ngawang Lobsang Gyatso (1617–82), who frequently launched brutal attacks on Ladakh during 1679–84. The area was part of Ladakh during the reign of King Singge Namgyal (1570–1642) when he ruled over all of western Tibet—covering Rudok, Guge, Kailash and Burang up to the Nepal border junction.

In 1684, the Tibetans defeated Ladakh and wrested away half its territory. As mentioned before, a peace treaty was later signed in 1684, which was brokered by the Sixth Drukchen Rinpoche Mipham Wangpo (1641–1717) of Bhutan.

The sectarian affiliation, as mentioned earlier, was strong between Ladakh and Bhutan as both kingdoms followed the same Drukpa Kagyu tradition of the Ralung lineage. According to legend, Singge Namgyal, as a mark of respect, offered legal rights over a series of monasteries near Mount Kailash to the Bhutanese theocratic ruler Shabdrung Ngawang Namgyal in the seventeenth century. The monasteries included Darchen, Kangri, Diraphu, Zuphu, Rizong, Chaskip, Yarigon-phu, Yazer, Somgu and Shara—located either at the foot of Mount Kailash or near Gartok.

India's jurisdiction over Menser

Under the Temisgang treaty (1684), Ladakh reserved its right to govern the villages in Menser: a) to have a transit place for Indian traders and pilgrims to Mount Kailash, and b) to meet the expenses of religious offerings to the sacred Mount Kailash. The treaty also confirmed delimitation of the Tibet–Ladakh boundary at Demchok, as well as trade regulations between Ladakh and Tibet.

Since 1846, the maharajas of Jammu and Kashmir followed the obligations of the 1684 treaty and collected tax from Menser villagers. For over 300 years, the enclaves of Menser and Darchen-Labrang served as key outposts for India and Bhutan for defence and trade and for pilgrims visiting Mount Kailash. Both countries exercised full administrative jurisdiction and collected annual tributes from their respective enclaves until the 1960s.

According to British Ladakhologist John Bray's article, 'Ladakhi and Bhutanese enclaves in Tibet',[1] the wazir of Ladakh, Mehta Basti Ram, collected Rs 56 as revenue from Menser in 1853. The collection had gone up to Rs 297 in 1905. According to Indian censuses in 1911 and 1921, Menser had forty-four houses, eighty-seven males and seventy-three females. The final settlement report of Jammu and Kashmir in 1958 showed Menser among 110 villages in Ladakh tehsil.

Among the official Jammu and Kashmir revenue collectors from Leh were Dr Kanshi Ram, British trade agent (1939), Tsetan Phuntsog (1941), Abdul Wahid Radhu (1942), Lumberdar of Rupshu, Sonam Khansar of Leh and many others who continued to visit Menser until 1962.

Sonam Khansar told this author that the annual tribute to the maharaja consisted of sixty sheep, twenty goats, six yaks and sixty lambskins, besides Rs 60 towards the travelling expenses of the officials. More details can be found in the 'Notes, Memoranda and Letters Exchanged and Agreements Signed between the Governments of India and China' White Paper IV for the period September 1959–March 1960, published by the MEA, Government of India.

It looked like Jammu and Kashmir officials had stopped going to Menser after the Indo-Pak War of 1965, but it is now becoming apparent that India actually stopped exercising sovereign rights over Menser in the early 1950s, that too discreetly.

Interestingly, Tibetologist Claude Arpi in his articles, 'Little Bhutan in Tibet'[2] and 'One Country Which Has Not Been Nice',[3] said, 'Nehru, wanting to be nice and have his Panchsheel Agreement signed, had unilaterally renounced all Indian "colonial" rights over smaller principalities including the Indian estate of Menser in 1953.' Arpi says Nehru, though, knew about the maharaja of Kashmir's suzerainty over Menser, but felt uneasy about this Indian possession near Mount Kailash—hence, he surrendered it as a 'gesture of goodwill towards Communist China'.

Arpi says Nehru's instructions to Indian negotiators on the Panchsheel agreement signed in Beijing were as follows: 'Regarding the village of Minsar in western Tibet, which has belonged to the Kashmir State, it is clear that we shall have to give it up, if this question is raised. We need not raise it. If it is raised, we should say that we recognise the strength of the Chinese contention and we are prepared to consider it and recommend it.'[4]

At the same time, however, Nehru added, 'We should not come to a final agreement without gaining the formal assent of the Kashmir government.'[5] Clearly, the Bhutanese enclaves of Darchen-Labrang in Tibet also met with the same fate.

Nehru's 'goodwill gesture' theory cannot be substantiated, though most critics have blamed him for the situation India found itself in with China. No clear answer is found as to why India had to keep mum on the territory located near Mount Kailash that was jointly owned by Jammu and Kashmir and Bhutan. Menser was critical for India's forward defence, especially to offset the Sino-Tibetan threat to India's Himalayan frontiers.

Possibly, and as outlined earlier in the book, Nehru was shocked to receive two telegrams in 1947 from the Tibetan government in Lhasa asking India to return the (lost) territories of Tibet that included Ladakh as well. Lhasa did not accept India's call to ratify the 1914 Simla Convention and the McMahon Line treaty, nor was it willing to send an official delegation to attend India's Independence celebrations.

The Tibetan assertion may have caused a dilemma in Nehru's mind whether to follow the traditional customary treaties with Tibet or stick to British conventions for resetting boundaries with China.

For Nehru, the British colonial legacy involved a risk of being called an 'imperialist'. But continuing with the old treaties with Tibet risked opening a can of worms in the Himalayas, especially when the Tibetans themselves were asserting claims over territories from Ladakh to Arunachal Pradesh.

Hence, the decision to forego the Indian and Bhutanese principalities inside Tibet and also not making any reference to the discrepancies along the Sikkim–Tibet border and the Bhutan–Tibet border or Doklam (tri-junction) in the early 1950s probably stemmed from Nehru's dilemma vis-à-vis Tibet.

India, therefore, may have preferred to opt for continuing with the British policy of accepting suzerain and not sovereign status for Tibet, with one of the underlying objectives to check Tibetan irredentist claims over the Indian Himalayas. That is why India probably decided not to push the Tibetan question in the United Nations beyond the preliminaries, thus leading to a natural death of the issue. Moreover, the British government's advice then was that neither India nor any external power could prevent the Chinese takeover of Tibet.

Nehru started to challenge Beijing's motives, when barely five years after the 1954 Panchsheel agreement was signed, China appeared set to 'betray' him. Nehru was terribly distressed after receiving Zhou Enlai's letter of 8 September 1959 that described the McMahon Line as a product of the British policy of aggression on a weak Tibet.

Among others, Zhou Enlai claimed an additional 40,000 square miles of Indian territory; accused India of using all sorts of pressure tactics including using force on China; raised the issue of China's non-ratification in 1842 of the Tibet–Ladakh border; reminded Nehru of Lhasa's 1947 correspondence; claimed the frontier east of Bhutan as the traditional frontier; repudiated the Sikkim and Bhutan boundary issues falling within the scope of the India–China discussion; asserted China had a 2000 kilometre boundary instead of 3530 kilometres as claimed by India; alleged Indian troops had trespassed, 'invaded and occupied' a number of places; accused India of shielding armed Tibetan rebels in frontier areas; alleged Indian aircraft repeatedly violated Chinese air space, et al.

The correspondence and Nehru's aggrieved response has been discussed earlier in the book. Nehru deeply resented the allegation that India was seeking to benefit from British aggression against China. In his reply, he wrote, 'The Government of India voluntarily renounced all the extra-territorial rights enjoyed by Britain in Tibet before 1947 and recognised by treaty that Tibet is a region of China.' Clearly, Nehru's misjudgement finally resulted in China calling the McMahon Line an imperialist fabrication—hence 'illegal'.

Change of tack

The turnaround in Nehru's position against China's provocations has reflected in India's reassertion over issues relating to the Sikkim and Bhutan boundaries.

In para 17 of his September 1959 letter, Nehru, though, never questioned the validity of the 1890 Sikkim–Tibet Convention, but insisted that it only referred to northern Sikkim and not to the tri-junction. Nehru explicitly objected to the discrepancy in Chinese maps showing a sizeable part of the tri-junction (Doklam) area of Bhutan as part of China, which needed to be discussed with Bhutan and Sikkim.

The matter, in fact, had earlier been affirmed by Nehru with Zhou Enlai, besides references made by India on matters pertaining to Bhutanese rights in Tibet. China, however, has been refusing all along to discuss or exchange maps related to the Tibet–Sikkim and Tibet–Bhutan borders with India.

Critically for India, their non-inclusion would not only impact Indian security but also impinge on its own negotiating position vis-à-vis China on the boundary issue. India, therefore, had to file a separate statement showing the eastern part of Bhutan adjacent to the Kameng Frontier Division (today's Tawang district). India's position on the valid boundary between India and China is reflected in the 'Notes, Memoranda and Letters Exchanged and Agreements Signed between the Governments of India and China' White Paper IV for the period between September 1959–March 1960, published by the Government of India.[6]

Consequently, India remained more confirmatory about Sikkim exercising full administrative and jurisdiction control all along the traditional/customary 'boundary alignment' that had been recognized by both sides.

With regard to Bhutan, the 1961 Report of the Government of India and the Republic of India on the Boundary Question (Part 3),[7] published by the MEA, mentions:

- The State of Bhutan has been maintaining check posts and exercising effective administrative jurisdiction all along her boundary with Tibet.
- The Government of India has already taken up with the Government of China various matters on behalf of Bhutan, including the delineation of Bhutan's external boundaries.
- The official map was more or less correctly drawn except Bhutan's eastern border with India.

- Since the traditional India–Tibet boundary run along the Himalayan watershed, Bhutan's eastern boundary was a matter concerning India and Bhutan only.
- The whole of Bhutan's eastern boundary with India had been studied jointly during 1936–38 and formally accepted by the Governments of India and Bhutan.

The report interestingly highlights, 'Chinese officials have illegally dispossessed the designated authorities of the Government of Bhutan in the following eight villages situated in western Tibet over which Bhutan has been exercising administrative jurisdiction for more than 300 years: Khangri, Tarchen, Tsekhor, Diraphu, Dzung Tuphu, Jangehe, Chakip and Kocha.

'Bhutanese officers governed these villages, collected taxes from them and administered justice. Tibetan authorities consistently recognised that these villages belonged to the Bhutan Government.

'At the request of the State of Bhutan the Government of India in their notes of 19 August 1959 and 20 August 1959 have represented to the Chinese Government to restore the rightful authority of the Bhutan Government over their enclaves.'

As mentioned earlier in the book, following Sardar Patel's demise in 1950, Nehru's China policy ran into difficulties because of the misguided advice he received from his key adviser, B.N. Mullik, chief of the IB, who in the late 1950s owing to his direct access to Nehru was able to convince him to consider China an adversary.

Though Nehru was in favour of abandoning the British colonial policy of playing the 'Great Game' in the Himalayas, his view post-1958 was solely influenced by 'Mullik's mindset' that culminated in the humiliating defeat by China in 1962.

The Sikkim–Tibet boundary now emerged as most contentious—the scene of the military stand-off in 2017. China has been repeatedly issuing statements that as per 'Article 1 of 1890 convention, the alignment of the boundary line between Tibet and Sikkim is clearly established'. Also read the fifteen-page document issued by the Chinese embassy in New Delhi on 3 August 2017. In all its statements, China has been deliberately and selectively obfuscating the facts of India's seeking clarification since 1959 over the discrepancy in Chinese maps showing a sizeable part of the tri-junction (Doklam) area of Bhutan as part of China.

The Menser mystery

Coming back to the subject of India's rights over Menser, the 1961 official report[8] provides a full account, including India's historical, administrative and revenue records since the time the five villages near Mansarovar came under the Kashmir maharaja's jurisdiction.

Menser was one of 108 villages that fell under the Ladakh tehsil, and the official report is backed with documents that include the Jammu and Kashmir Revenue Assessment Report of 1902 and the Settlement Report of 1908, Census Reports from 1901 to 1937, and revenue records from 1901 to 1948, among others.

But the report surprisingly mentioned nothing about India's sovereign claim over Menser in the same manner as India did through its 'Notes' on 19 and 20 August 1959 asking the Chinese government 'to restore the rightful authority of the Bhutan Government over their enclaves'.

We do not as yet know the full story regarding Nehru's discreet surrender of Menser to China, but some pertinent questions surrounding the case should still be raised even if they are of only academic relevance.

First, if the Tibetans and Chinese authorities acknowledged Ladakh/Kashmir and Bhutan holding certain rights in the Mount Kailash area, why did India pre-decide to hand over those rights to China?

Second, on record, Beijing apparently did not challenge Indian sovereign rights over Menser, and neither did India raise the issue in talks with China in 1953–54. So does Menser legally still belong to India?

Third, Menser's surrender was neither referred to in Srinagar nor was it ratified by the Indian Parliament. Members of Parliament from the Ladakh constituency have been seeking in vain a clarification relating to Menser since 1982 in the Lok Sabha. Till date, no convincing answer has come from the government. Was it a case of self-betrayal for which the government still owes an answer to the people of Jammu and Kashmir?

Fourth, if the Government of India was the competent authority to take up matters concerning Bhutan's territory, what prevented India from raising its own issue regarding Menser with Beijing?

Fifth, having decided to forego the enclaves, why didn't the Government of India ever seek any compensation for either Ladakh/Kashmir or Bhutan?

Clearly, the fate of these enclaves has not been negotiated or settled legally so far. As John Bray wrote,[9] 'The status of Minsar (Menser) is no more than a minor footnote to these concerns, but one that has still to be cleared up.' Therefore, the Menser question shouldn't be considered by India to be entirely closed.

Strangely, not only the Chinese but even the Dalai Lama remains silent on the status of Menser and the Darchen-Labrang enclaves.

We must note that China in 2015 insisted on opening Nathu La instead of Demchok as an alternative pilgrimage route to Mansarovar. Beijing had done this ostensibly to put to rest any future discussion on the Menser and Darchen-Labrang enclaves located near Mount Kailash, knowing very well that they held great spiritual, emotional and political significance for Indian and Bhutanese pilgrims.

Importantly, we know that the Chinese assert their claim to Tawang based on the argument that the Sixth Dalai Lama was born there and the Tibetans paid obeisance to the monastery for centuries—hence, they cannot be parted.

By the same analogy, Menser and Darchen-Labrang along with eight other monasteries owned respectively by Ladakh and Bhutan were visited by their people for pilgrimages to Mount Kailash (Gang Rinpoche) or the holy abode of Lord Shiva (Chang-chub-chen-mo) for centuries—hence they cannot be parted and swept away.

Importantly again, India needs to remain cautious about China possibly claiming in future people and places in Ladakh based on the argument that Lama Staksang Repa (Stagsang Respa), the sole legal owner/caretaker of the Hemis monastery, is a Chinese national. Hemis continues to hold legal ownership to large amounts of Ladakh's agricultural land. Critically, key Indian monasteries in Ladakh have already fallen into the hands of high-ranking Tibetan (refugee) lamas and this will entail long-term implications for India.

In addition to the Menser enclave, China is today sitting on a 38,000 square kilometre area of Aksai Chin and a 5000 square kilometre area of

Shaksgam in Jammu and Kashmir. According to a 2013 report (which was not made public) by Shyam Saran, former foreign secretary of India, India has over the decades allowed the Chinese PLA to nibble away 645 kilometres in Raki Nallah in north-east Ladakh, Pangong Tso and Skakjung in eastern Ladakh. Consequently, the original LAC defined in 1959 had been pushed westward and the territory controlled by India has considerably shrunk. Even now, Chinese on-ground assertion in Depsang, Trig-Height, Hot-Spring, Chuchul, Spanguur, Demchok and Chumur continues unabated.

To be sure, pushing for a formal settlement in the western sector, where it has nothing to lose, could be one of China's objectives. In fact, swapping the claim over Aksai Chin for Arunachal Pradesh is also entertained as a pragmatic idea even in India.

A smart Chinese move would be to let India, in the first step, forego its claim over the 38,000 square kilometre area of Aksai Chin, thereby delinking Ladakh or the Jammu and Kashmir sector from the overall boundary dispute. By doing so, China intends to remove the Aksai Chin, Shaksgam and Menser areas from the dispute. A similar trick was applied while settling China's borders with three Central Asian states in recent times. Ceding Aksai Chin would then alter the status of Jammu and Kashmir and would mean by implication ceding Gilgit-Baltistan to Pakistan.

Once India falls for the magnanimous Chinese position over Aksai Chin, Beijing will shift focus to Arunachal, considered by it as South Tibet. They would then emphatically convey that India was occupying 90,000 square kilometres of Chinese territory, but state that Tawang was 'non-negotiable' in a final settlement of the border issue. China's 'minimal demand' has been aired through unofficial and academic channels. This 'minimal demand' tactic worked profitably in China's favour in Central Asia as well.

Clearly, China would want to resolve issues with India along three essential points: a) settle the boundary dispute on its terms, b) solve the Tibet problem without Indian interference in the post–Dalai Lama scenario, and c) prevent India–US congruence in Himalayan frontiers. Finally, the reopening of the hitherto forgotten question of Menser and enforcing a residual sovereign claim by India over it is rather difficult. But Menser is historically, emotionally and commercially more important for Ladakh when compared to Aksai Chin.

But now that the Chinese have reopened the Doklam issue, it is an opportune time for India and Bhutan to talk more loudly on Menser and Darchen-Labrang in addition to Aksai Chin and Shaksgam under the illegal occupation of China.

Menser cannot be seen in isolation from the issue of PoK and the launch of the CPEC by China. If India's sovereign claim over PoK, including Gilgit-Baltistan, hitherto in diplomatic abeyance, has been given a renewed impetus, why not Menser?

India's strategy should also enable it to push to restore the web of historical, spiritual and commercial links with the Kailash–Mansarovar region. If nothing else, it would help deter China's and the Dalai Lama's claiming of Tawang and other places in India on the basis of religious affiliations.

Those who insist on playing the 'Tibet card' should know that the only residual issue, if at all, is the retrieval of India's own lost territories, including Aksai Chin and Menser near Kailash–Mansarovar, from Sino-Tibetan occupation. Clearly, these are not easily achievable, but the least India can do now is normalize its traditional trade and cultural ties with Tibet. Instead of investing so much in the CTA's agenda, they should ask the Dalai Lama to make an explicit statement, while he is still alive, that Tawang as well as the areas around Kailash–Mansarovar have historically been a part of India.

13

India's Shifting Tibet Policy

It is not clear whether the aggressive use of the Dalai Lama and Karmapa cards by the government throughout 2016–17 yielded anything. India's tokenism on Tibet for almost seven decades failed to counter Chinese activities in PoK and did not deter it from extending BRI connectivity lines to Nepal. Yet, many have found the Tibet issue to be of useful deterrence value vis-à-vis China, a valuable means of forcing China's reciprocity, especially in dealing with the boundary issue.

In 2018, there was a sudden policy U-turn that saw a downscaling of the Dalai Lama's activities. The prime minister got a new foreign policy team after Foreign Secretary Vijay Gokhale assumed office.

In a remarkable move, Gokhale wrote to the cabinet secretary in March 2018 asking state functionaries to avoid events planned by the Tibetan government in March and April to mark the sixtieth year of the Dalai Lama's exile. The events included one in Delhi on 1 April called 'Thank You India', where the government-in-exile intended to invite a number of Indian dignitaries.

However, the government said that India's stance on the Dalai Lama had not changed and its position is 'clear and consistent'. 'He is a revered religious leader and is deeply respected by the people of India,' the ministry said. 'There is no change in that position. His holiness is accorded all freedom to carry out his religious activities in India.'[1]

The Indian government's advisory note had, however, caused disappointment to the CTA and embarrassment to the Tibetan spiritual leader personally, and evoked predictable criticism from the usual quarters. They argued that it was imprudent for India to give up the 'Tibet card' and cave in to China's bullying tactics when the pay-off from Beijing was uncertain.[2] At the same time, there were also countering voices on social media calling for the Modi administration to abandon this 'card' and put the interests of 1.2 billion Indians first.[3]

This debate begged a more fundamental question on whether the so-called 'Tibet card' had helped India harvest adequate diplomatic pay-off vis-à-vis China. The fact is that there was never such a card from day one. India was left with no choice in the matter after the Tibetans themselves relinquished their wish for independence by signing the Seventeen-Point Agreement with China on 23 May 1951. It was only after their explicit decision to join China that India accepted Tibet as a part of China on 29 April 1954.

The Dalai Lama wants to return home

This turn of events also came against the confirmation of Xi Jinping as 'lifetime president'[4] in China. Both Xi Jinping and the Dalai Lama seem to want a resolution of their differences. To start with, the Dalai Lama may possibly make a short trip to China in the near future. He is now more vocal about his willingness to follow the 'One China' policy and 'stay with China'. In that case, the negotiation process with Beijing could start soon.

It was against this backdrop that the MEA probably wants to pursue a policy of 'quiet diplomacy' with China. It wanted to carefully weigh the 'Tibet card'—its utility, sustainability, costs and benefits—vis-à-vis the need for opening a new page with China. But to be sure, other operatives may derail the government's plans.

All in all, the Dalai Lama and the 'Tibet card' are Cold War–era relics. The issue has been kept alive for almost six decades, mainly due to the games being played, some at the behest of Western powers. The Dalai Lama and Tibet 'cards' have not served any deterrent purposes for India; rather, they have prolonged mutual suspicion and hostility with China.

In fact, there may have been more to the Dalai Lama's desire to return home than meets the eye.[5] The Tibetan leader's statement on 23 November 2017—'The past is past, Tibetans want to stay with China'—carried a serious political overtone, coming as it did immediately after the Nineteenth Party Congress and the Doklam stand-off between India and China.

Earlier, in April 2017, he said in Tawang, 'I think more than 90 per cent of Tibet is keen to bring me back . . . many are waiting for me. Even millions of Chinese Buddhists want me back. Just when the right signal comes from the Chinese government . . . I will go back. The Chinese government is against us and has a hard-line [stance] there. I am not seeking independence for Tibet.'[6] Media also quoted him saying, 'Tibet is materialistically backward but spiritually highly advanced. We want to develop materialistically by remaining with China and it should also feel the same way for mutual benefit.'[7]

The Dalai Lama's statement that he is not seeking independence for Tibet and wished to stay with China is not new; however, his declaration that he would 'return to Tibet at once, if China agrees' sparked fresh speculation of a possible rapprochement with Beijing.

The sign of the thaw strangely came on the heels of President Donald Trump's November 2017 visit to Beijing. Most likely, Trump wouldn't have made Tibet a pressure point in his dealings with Beijing; rather, he would have dumped the Dalai Lama (whom the US had fostered for over half a century) on the altar of a better trade deal and for securing China's commitment to exert pressure on North Korea. During the trip US officials made to Dharamshala prior to Trump's visit, this prospect might have been discussed.

The inevitability of this change was clear when the US had started faltering on Tibet even earlier, when Barack Obama had to welcome the Dalai Lama through the back door of the White House, signalling Washington's inability to withstand Beijing's pressure.

Trump was not even inclined to embrace the issue as he refused to meet the Tibetan leader and instead proposed zero aid in 2018 to the Tibetans, reversing a decades-old American policy.[8] The State Department has also not appointed a special coordinator for Tibet.

Surely, it couldn't have been a coincidence that a week after Trump's China visit, the Dalai Lama abruptly selected two personal emissaries to represent him in all 'global engagements' for an indefinite period.[9] He cited increasing physical fatigue, but the decision to appoint two 'trusted friends'—former prime minister-in-exile Samdhong Rinpoche and current president of the government-in-exile, Lobsang Sangay—was meant to send a calibrated signal to China.

This appointing of personal emissaries has satisfied China. Beijing has been emphatically asking the Dalai Lama to stop travelling to Western capitals if talks are to resume. At the Nineteenth Party Congress, the Tibet Work Forum (TWF) chief told reporters that international figures have no excuse for meeting with the Dalai Lama.

Global freeze

Tibet was once a strong pretext for foreign powers to block China from international forums, but not any more. Beijing has practically won the diplomatic war against the Dalai Lama. By 2016, it appeared that Beijing had finally managed to pin the Tibetan leader down by deploying every political and economic tool in its arsenal to constrict his global outreach.

Until recently, international pressure had worked to get a dialogue going between the Dalai Lama and Beijing. This is no longer the case. The leaders in the West, who propped him up once as an 'ascetic Buddhist superstar'[10] and used him for domestic electoral gains, as also to win market access in China, are abandoning him one by one.

No wonder then that the Dalai Lama had to be admitted to the Mayo Clinic in Rochester on 24 September 2016[11] when world leaders including Pope Francis met for the annual UN General Assembly meeting in New York. No details came forth about his mystery health probe except that he had been advised to rest. Media reported later he was admitted for prostrate gland treatment.[12]

The West's economic downturn turned the game for China. Beijing no longer felt compelled to entertain anyone on Tibet. Instead, it started to call the shots, frowned on those who met the Tibetan leader and punished them through an assortment of coercive diplomatic measures. Call it bully-diplomacy or realpolitik, no country, big or small, wants to face Beijing's wrath. Instead, they prefer the 'quiet diplomacy' route to win over China.

The world has seen how the United Kingdom grovelled to Beijing. Former prime minister David Cameron mended his ways after being rebuked by China for meeting the Dalai Lama in 2012. Unable to jeopardize billions of dollars of investment and trade, he afforded red-carpet treatment to Xi Jinping in 2015. Even Prince Charles, who has called Chinese leaders 'appalling old waxworks' in the past, bowed before him.[13]

In 2001, dozens of leaders received the Dalai Lama. The count is twenty-one between 2005 and 2008; since 2009, it has dropped to two. In 2013, he met only the heads of Lithuania and Poland.[14] Germany and France no longer provoke China. Australia, the Netherlands and New Zealand stopped entertaining him in 2007. Pope Francis was among those who snubbed him recently, along with Denmark, South Africa and even Norway, which had conferred the Nobel Peace Prize upon him in 1989.

Except Japan, no other Buddhist country invites the Dalai Lama. Even Mongolia, from where the title 'Dalai' (ocean) was conferred by Mongol Khan in the sixteenth century, stalled his visit in 2014, but allowed it in 2017 only to face insuperable wrath from Beijing.

Strangely, the United States under the Barack Obama administration gave him a frosty welcome; getting him to the White House through a side entrance and making him exit through back doors—at times into a 'mound of trash'.[15]

In a first, President Obama met with the Dalai Lama publicly in 2014, but at the National Prayer Breakfast where the US President referred to him as a practitioner of 'compassion'. It seems even the photo-op practice was dropped.

The issue bears so much on China's sensitivity that Beijing doesn't even spare artists and singers who have links with the Tibet campaign. The list of those whose shows have been nixed in China included the Los Angeles band Maroon 5, Icelandic singer Bjork, Britpop group Oasis, Elton John and others.

Policy shift

In his host nation, India, the BJP initially stunned Beijing and the world by inviting a Tibetan delegation comprising the head of the government-in-exile, Lobsang Sangay, and his home minister, Dolma Gyari, as guests to Modi's swearing-in ceremony in 2014.

The Tibetans were certainly delighted to see their leader seated with the Indian prime minister and president and the heads of SAARC countries. They hoped Modi would turn the page on India's Tibet policy. But their hope soon turned to despair when it was revealed that the invitation to the event was obtained in connivance with some BJP and Sangh Parivar members.[16]

Apparently aware of this implication, the official group photo of the heads of states that featured Sangay in the line-up was withdrawn. But his presence raised hackles in China. Beijing issued a demarche to India protesting the invitation.[17] This was followed by Foreign Minister Wang Yi rushing to New Delhi to seek a clarification. New Delhi probably struggled hard to make up for the diplomatic goof-up.

China apparently chose not to escalate the matter, considering the prospects of building closer relations with the new government. But the damage was done.

Quite clearly, the incident may have made the government more cautious regardless of what some Sangh Parivar members thought about the Tibet issue. Things have only seemed to worsen on the Tibet front since then.

Prime Minister Modi and the Dalai Lama had an extremely guarded meeting in August 2014. According to a story published in *India Today* in July 2015, the Dalai Lama was 'virtually kidnapped' in an unmarked car and spirited into 7 Race Course Road through a side entrance. The media reported that the meeting had gone off very badly and the Dalai Lama looked 'visibly shaken' by the encounter.[18] It was 'horrible', the Dalai Lama's younger brother Ngari Rinpoche told me privately in 2015.

In a marked departure from protocol, Modi apparently didn't come out to receive the Tibetan leader, who was frisked at the entrance. It did not stop there. Modi spoke to the Dalai Lama in Hindi, which had to be translated into English. A close aide of the Dalai Lama recalled how the two had comfortably conversed with each other in English when they met in Baroda in 2010.

Modi's snub could not have been inadvertent, and China could not have been the only reason. The *India Today* story referred to the BJP government being unhappy over a probable meeting between the Dalai

Lama and Xi Jinping during the latter's 2014 Delhi visit fixed by the Dalai Lama's advisers and a Hong Kong–based Chinese businessman friend.

In May 2015, Modi asked for the cancellation of a scheduled meeting between BJP president Amit Shah and the Dalai Lama, fearing it would affect his trip to China.

Quite clearly, an uneasy tension, according to foreign policy analyst Jyoti Malhotra, had 'reached such a stage that the Dalai Lama travelled to California to celebrate his eightieth birthday' in July 2015.

Was Modi, like other world leaders, opting for 'quiet diplomacy'? It seems the government was carefully weighing the 'Tibet card'—the utility, sustainability, strategic costs and benefits of the Dalai Lama's presence vis-à-vis the need for opening a new chapter with China.

Even so, the Modi government knows it cannot ignore public sentiment. In a marked departure from protocol, the government dispatched cabinet ministers to attend several Tibetan events, including the Dalai Lama's eightieth birthday celebrations in 2015. It seems the Modi government was attempting a balancing act, signalling unwillingness to abandon the Tibet option, considering a view held by many in India that China could eventually implode due to a possible uprising of the Tibetans and Uyghurs. But that scenario may have changed after the Wuhan summit in 2017. Most people were not amused when the Tibetan leaders were not invited to Prime Minister Narendra Modi's swearing-in ceremony at Rashtrapati Bhawan this time on 30 May 2019.[19]

There is another important context, probably linked to Modi's passion for rebooting India's own Buddhist heritage for geopolitical and economic interest. As he learns to grapple with the challenges of 'Buddhist diplomacy', he might understand the critical space that Buddhism occupies in the Asian balance of culture, economics and politics.

Modi has China already expanding its influence through Buddhism, and it may soon take over the discourse of Buddhism. Beijing is taking serious steps to reclaim the Buddhist space for itself. It has been holding international conferences on Buddhism for several years now. In 2014, China, for the first time, organized a conference of the Bangkok-headquartered World Fellowship of Buddhists (WFB). It is even funding other countries like Nepal to restore its Buddhist sites.

Worried about India losing the leadership role in Buddhism, Modi has been trying to reconnect India directly with major Asian Buddhist institutions in Japan, Korea, Mongolia, Russia and China. While many in India might respect the Tibetan Buddhist legacy, Indians are also beginning to understand that the Dalai Lama's prolonged stay in India has created an enduring source of tension with China.[20] What Modi appears to be doing is to ensure that India's own Buddhist traditions are strengthened, which would open up the prospect for India playing a larger role in Asia.

Modi seems aware of these undercurrents, since he is keeping the Dalai Lama out of major events, even as the latter continues to enjoy huge sympathy and admiration among the ranks of the BJP and RSS. It is no wonder, then, that the Dalai Lama would be angry, for he also gave a thinly disguised signal about the lingering boundary issue and cautioned not to go around Tibet if India and China want peace. Annoyed by the developments, the Dalai Lama told *India Today* in July 2015 that he would rather 'go home to Tibet, as well as meet his friend Xi Zhongxun's son, President Xi Jinping'.[21]

India's longest-staying guest then surprised everyone in November 2015 when he joined the 'rising intolerance in India' debate by saying, 'Bihar [election] results proved majority Hindus still believe in harmony.'[22] This was ostensibly perceived as directed at Prime Minister Modi. Most people ignored his comment but BJP leader Subramanian Swamy hit out at the Dalai Lama for these remarks.[23] 'India has a long tradition of peace and amity,' said Swamy. 'The people of Bihar in the recent Assembly polls have proved that a large section of the Hindu community still believes in peace and amity.'

The jibe was not without context. Three years later, in August 2018, the Dalai Lama triggered a fresh storm when he said that India and Pakistan would have remained one country had Jinnah become the first prime minister in place of Jawaharlal Nehru. He said that Mahatma Gandhi actually wanted to make Muhammad Ali Jinnah the prime minister of India, but that Jawaharlal Nehru refused. He thought Nehru was 'a little bit self-centred'[24] although he was a very experienced person.

The Dalai Lama was surely pandering to the ruling BJP government, which is not known to be charitable towards Nehru. But his comment of Nehru being 'self-centred' evoked a negative response from all corners, especially from the Congress Party. Surely, it was an unintended comment from the Dalai Lama's side. However, considering that it was Nehru who had permitted and personally received him when he came into exile in India, the Dalai Lama's utterances could be considered shocking.[25] Clearly, the Dalai Lama's presence in India as a guest is no longer a provisional arrangement, and he is now a factor in India's domestic as well as external policy concerns.

Hope and despair

A glimmer of hope was raised when Xi Jinping came to power in 2013. The Dalai Lama had reasons to embrace a sense of optimism, for he hoped that his past association with the president's father, Xi Zhongxun, coupled with the president's fascination for Tibetan culture and Buddhist members in his family, would enable a gentle embrace. A pilgrimage tour to the Wutai Shan in Shanxi province gained fresh currency. In fact, many concluded a propitious condition for a settlement had been arrived at.

Quite the reverse, a new hardening of policy was illustrated in 2015: during the fiftieth anniversary of the Tibet Autonomous Region, the Sixth TWF and the White Paper on Tibet gave no indications of Xi changing tack on Tibet. In fact, after he came to power, countering the Dalai Lama's influence became the 'highest priority' of its activities in Tibet.[26] Moreover, after the Nineteenth Party Congress held in November 2017, Xi Jinping gave more power to the United Front Work Department (UFWD) in a more resolute manner.[27]

In a high-level meeting on Tibet security policy convened by China's top politburo, President Xi Jinping said that the CPC would pick 'the next Dalai Lama, period! If things do not go well, we are ready to take corrective action.'[28]

Soon after, China issued a White Paper on Tibet in 2015. *China Daily* on 6 September 2015 claimed that Tibet is 'now in its golden age' and cited numerous statistics of achievements.[29]

But the *Global Times* on 8 September 2015 launched a stinging attack on the Dalai Lama, saying he was a 'cruel ruler in exile', a 'cheater' whose 'imaginary Tibet', perhaps the 'world's longest lie', does not exist.[30] The Western forces that 'plotted' a Nobel Prize for him always wanted the Tibetans to remain as 'aborigines', therefore rejecting modernity in Tibet as 'destruction'. The 'lie will disappear' once China takes the centre stage, the media believed.[31]

Unfortunately, the clock is ticking for the Dalai Lama. To be sure, he has a plan, and so does China. But for now, the two seem to be playing the game of patience and biding their time. China, it seems, would wait for the Fourteenth Dalai Lama to pass away and perhaps seek his reincarnation in China according to its plan.

The Dalai Lama has disavowed a violent course of action, but patience would be fraying among his followers. Exploring their disruptive potential is a possibility, and this could start with the succession crisis when grief among believers takes a frenzied turn. Many Tibetans like to forewarn China that it will regret not settling matters with this Dalai Lama.

A sentiment of this sort is also prevalent among many Chinese who doubt Beijing's current policy would bring long-lasting stability, and, therefore, favour a settlement now. In fact, in a game of manoeuvring, the Dalai Lama is seemingly galvanizing support among Chinese Buddhists. But hoping to get political support from them would be a fallacy.

Prospects for the future are indeed bleak. Decades of negotiation remain futile and have not reached anywhere, and the Dalai Lama seems to be left with no cards to bargain with Beijing.

Clearly, Chinese leaders remain unyielding as they still nurture a deep anger against the Tibetan leader and hold him responsible for denting the legitimacy of China's global rise. Any further conciliatory posture by him can hardly be a smart move, considering Beijing has withstood the worst.

There have been no official talks between China and the Dalai Lama's representatives since 2010. However, the two sides still maintain some sort of back-channel communication following India's recent decision to sideline the Tibet issue. In November 2017, the Dalai Lama appeared to have sent Samdhong Rinpoche on a discreet visit to Kunming. Samdhong's visit must have been facilitated by no less than You Quan, the head of the Chinese government's UFWD that oversees Tibetan affairs. You Quan, who formerly served as party secretary of Fujian, is a close associate of President Xi Jinping. He had earlier successfully dealt with Hong Kong, Macau and Taiwan's business communities.

Clearly, Samdhong's visit formed part of the first five-year plan to engage with China, while Lobsang Sangay's seventeen-day tour to Europe and Canada is meant to sustain the struggle for the next fifty years, if the first plan fails.

In the past, Chinese leaders stymied the Dalai Lama's desire to return to Tibet. But there is a distinct possibility that it may bear fruit this time. Samdhong's clandestine visit didn't bear much fruit, but the last interface between the Dalai Lama and a Chinese representative (official proxy) ostensibly held in Tokyo in November 2018 was possibly quite substantive.

If a thaw were to occur, it would be because of the following reasons. First, Xi, widely known to have a soft spot for Tibet, hitherto kept his own approach close to his chest, fearing resistance from hardliners. Unlike others, he held the view that prospects for solving the Tibet problem would peter out once the present Dalai Lama is no more. Xi now finds himself in a perfect position to resolve the issue as no other Chinese leader could do in the past, for he also stands to gain personally both in political and moral terms to become the most credible leader in China's history.

Second, the Dalai Lama has long hoped that Xi will change tack and has hailed him as a 'realist' and 'open-minded'[32] in contrast to his predecessors. In fact, the Tibetan leader has admitted to having received positive signals from top Chinese officials, especially from the moderate elements, as streams of Han Chinese flocked to meet him during Xi's first term. In May 2017, the party was shocked to find their own party members clandestinely funding the Dalai Lama, undermining the fight against 'separatist' forces.[33]

But, most critically, Tibetans living inside Tibet may have pressured the Dalai Lama to seize the opportunity and resolve differences during Xi's second term before the window for a deal closes a few years from now.

With time running out fast, the Dalai Lama can be anything but hopeful. He has been steadily losing international support in the face of China's rise as a world power. No longer does any country dare to receive the Dalai Lama officially.

Apart from his age, the Tibetan leader faces the challenge of keeping his flock together. For example, the delay in reaching a solution causes anxiety, uncertainty and division among his people. Even inside Tibet, rising frustration and hopelessness have been highlighted by people resorting to self-immolation.

And so, in what must be an embarrassing climb-down for the exiled Tibetan leaders, all they can do now is settle for the cause of 'development', besides hoping that the Chinese will not inflict further repression on the Tibetan people.

Therefore, in a way, we are likely to witness the curtains finally being drawn on Tibet's quest for an independent state. Tim Johnson knew this when he aptly titled his book *Tragedy in Crimson: How the Dalai Lama Conquered the World but Lost the Battle with China*,[34] where he unpacks how Tibetan culture is slowly vanishing and how the 'Free Tibet' movement is being assailed by China's use of its economic power around the globe.

The world can do little to keep up the hopes of the Tibetans. The subtext of the future of the Dalai Lama, as the Americans finally conveyed to him at the National Prayer Breakfast in Washington, was that his significance lay in him being an undisputed spiritual world leader.

By 2017, Botswana president Ian Khama was the only political figure who stood up against China's pressure and invited the Dalai Lama to visit Gaborone for an NGO event scheduled for 17–19 August that year.[35] However, the Dalai Lama had to abort his visit citing physical 'exhaustion'.

Ian Khama, as ex-president, despite advice from the state, travelled to India to participate in an event to mark the sixtieth anniversary of the Tibetan uprising day in March 2019. One doesn't hear too much about the Dalai Lama's high-profile foreign visits any more.

It must be a troubling phase for a man who has achieved phenomenal popularity internationally. His supporters have included Hollywood celebrities like Richard Gere, Paris Hilton, Russell Brand and Sharon Stone, among others. Surely, he has made Tibetan Buddhism famous worldwide. But his vociferously led Tibet campaign reached nowhere. He seemed to understand this reality and sought to settle for autonomy within the Chinese constitution, but Beijing remains blasé and has even stopped talking to his interlocutors since 2010.

At a September 2018 academic presentation at the CTRC, Beijing, I heard the Chinese version of the Tibet issue. Chinese experts on

Tibet said that when Deng Xiaoping was seeking accommodation in Tibet in the 1980s, the Dalai Lama was exploring other options in the West against China. On his part, Tibet expert Xiaobin Wang claimed that the most belligerent attempt at confronting China came from the Dalai Lama immediately after the dramatic collapse of the Soviet Union in 1991. It was the year when George H.W. Bush took a stance against China's repressive religious policy after he became the first-ever US president to receive the Dalai Lama officially at the White House.

The Tibetan spiritual leader was perhaps prompted to believe that the mightiest of empires could be pulled down by the shared power of religion. Whether or not such assessments are accurate, there was no doubt about the Dalai Lama's optimism of a Soviet spin-off effect to either opt for a 'political process' or face 'bloody political struggles' as he also decided to drop the dialogue path.

The US Tibet Policy Act Bill (2001) and the Congressional gold medal to the Dalai Lama (2007) caused riots across the plateau in 2008. Wang insinuated how the West had fostered the Dalai Lama to become a potent force and an icon of resistance against China to wage a psychic war against the communist regime. China's vitriol against the Dalai Lama as an 'evil separatist' never stopped until Xi Jinping came to power in 2013. Even so, the dialogue interrupted in 2010 has never been resumed.

Tibet's history and polity are rooted in China's ritualistic Li order, which can't be changed, Wang asserted. The confusion arose after the British Empire (through eight key conventions between 1876 and 1914) tried to alter Tibet's status from a territory of China to a de facto independent nation. The Dalai Lama's middle-way policy is an attempt at regaining 'suzerainty' status, like 'trying to change the liquid, but not the drug', Wang said.

Averting a geopolitical trap

For India, the question is whether New Delhi has any role to play in this rapidly evolving scene, and if so, what the political parameters of its role would be. There is no sign of anyone having even considered the impact. But to be cautious, any Sino-Tibetan deal would seriously risk undercutting India's position on the boundary dispute with China.

Against this backdrop, Prime Minister Narendra Modi has made a foreign policy course correction after realizing that the strategic tilt towards the United States has not only upset India's geopolitical image but also undermined national interests.

First, it has forced India to walk a diplomatic tightrope between the US, Russia and China. Certainly, the policy of intentional ambiguity in conventional terms can be valuable, but a prolonged play can also lead to uncertainty, for it can be hard to maintain the balance between coherence and ambiguity. It could also obscure potential harm and threats.

Second, relying too much on fickle US policies appears risky. As can be seen on the trade front, President Donald Trump is backing out on his commitments to other friends and allies of the US. And there is a lurking feeling that the US was not forthcoming in articulating clear support for India during the Doklam stand-off.

Third, closer military ties with the US could draw India into a larger political quagmire in terms of attracting the attention of global Islamic terrorist groups which are committed to undermining the interests of the US and its allies wherever possible.

And, lastly, the process could eventually result in the US making a Pakistan (a long-time client state or banana republic) out of India and the attendant loss of standing in the world as a great power.

Among all other challenging issues has been the escalating trade conflict between New Delhi and Washington. China has been scornful of India joining the US bandwagon. Foreign Minister Wang Yi had dismissed the 'Quad' and 'Indo-Pacific' formulations as only 'headline-grabbing' ideas soon to be 'dissipated' like the 'foam on the sea'.[36]

In particular, Prime Minister Modi's keynote speech at the Shangri-La Dialogue in Singapore on 1 June 2018[37] seemed a calibrated move to prevent India from falling into a dangerous geopolitical trap vis-à-vis the US, Russia and China. The subtext of the speech was to reaffirm India's commitment to multipolarity, uphold the principles and values of peace and progress, and fight against 'global dominance'. The world knew that India was a power bloc in itself with nations around the world looking up to New Delhi for guidance and support. Modi's Singapore speech was welcomed by every country including China.

Importantly, Modi avoided making a reference to the 'Quad' in Singapore and instead spoke out strongly against 'protectionism'—an oblique reference to the Trump policy. Although he praised the US 'Indo-Pacific' strategy, he also made it clear that India does not see it 'as a club of limited members [or] as a grouping that seeks to dominate', which strongly implied that India is not seeing it as an alliance system. In fact, when US officials described India as the 'fulcrum' of or 'central' to the US Indo-Pacific strategy, Modi deflected the idea by affirming the centrality of the Association of Southeast Asian Nations (ASEAN).

The prime minister played down the China threat, except for exhorting Beijing to play by the rules, saying an 'Asia of rivalry' would hold all its players back. In contrast to US Defense Secretary James Mattis warning China over maritime 'intimidation', Modi instead talked about seeking closer ties with China and termed 'stable relations' between the two countries as 'an important factor for global peace and progress'.

Modi went a step further and advised other powers to avoid a confrontationist line to prevent 'great power rivalries'. These statements were significant given that they were made about a week ahead of the Shanghai Cooperation Organisation (SCO) summit in Qingdao. At Qingdao, he joined other leaders in committing to the 'Shanghai spirit'—a term coined in 2006 to invert the Cold War–era mentality in international relations.[38]

New Delhi needs to be mindful of the fluid nature of the dynamics in security relationships in the Asia–Pacific. The overwhelming impression that India was stooping to become a regional ally of the US in the new strategic theatre of the 'Indo-Pacific' to counter China has since undergone change.

Through his dexterous diplomacy, Modi has deflated the hype created by certain sections of Indian and American think tanks and media outlets which enjoyed a great sense of vanity and smugness about the strategic importance of India for America in counterbalancing China.

To be clear, there can't be an Asia without China just as there can't be an Asia without India. In fact, most Asian nations, despite their disputes and differences, do not approve of all-round hostility against each other.

Instead, India's fellow Asian societies seemed to have learnt from Nagarjuna's non-dogmatic precept of *madhyamaka* (fundamental verses of the middle way concept) that accepts the nature of reality and 'interdependent co-arising or dependent co-origination' to overcome problems.

Realizing that India can no longer continue with the old habit of remaining a geopolitical bystander in Asia, a nuanced shift in Modi's policy away from the West-led confrontationist approach is a welcome move. What Modi essentially lacked until recently was a wise and level-headed foreign policy adviser.

The Wuhan process

The process of resetting ties between India and China had begun in Wuhan in May 2018. It was successful in terms of establishing mutual trust between the leadership. They jointly planned for future improvement and strengthening of their relationship.

The trend so far suggests that India's ambiguous China policy is driven by two inter-related factors: Tibet and the boundary issue. Possibly, the lack of adroit thinking in the past allowed the Dalai Lama to shape the course of India–China relations.

In contrast, the US always encouraged India to play the Tibet card against China, but Washington fully recognized the nature of the Dalai Lama card and prudently used him to gain greater leverage in Beijing. For example, President Obama had once refused to meet the Dalai Lama officially, ostensibly aiming to gain a stronger position to offer a mediator's role between China and the Dalai Lama.

But under the Modi government, India too seemed to have learnt from the Western propensity to deal with China. The Wuhan talks probably enabled Modi to alter the game of using Tibet for leverage against China, rather than simply getting played by the Dalai Lama's agenda.

Yet, the two countries have moved cautiously to take the Wuhan process forward in the right direction. Possibly it does not represent a change of heart, but only a tactical adjustment, with both sides buying a temporary truce due to the imperatives of their respective external and domestic agendas. Yet, despite the occasional hiccups, Modi's China policy has proved to be the most successful case in his foreign policy initiatives.

The overall atmosphere of suspicion and mistrust will take time to disappear totally and require sustained effort from both sides. To be sure, the quiet diplomacy adopted since the Wuhan process has helped resolve many pending issues, including China's role in blocking India's attempts to list Jaish-e-Mohammed (JeM) terrorist Masood Azhar as a 'global terrorist'. In a huge diplomatic win for India, the UN on 1 May 2019 designated the Pakistan-based JeM chief Azhar as a global terrorist after China lifted its hold on a proposal to blacklist him.[39] The proposal was moved by France, UK and the US in the UNSC's 1267 Al Qaeda Sanctions Committee just days after the deadly Pulwama terror attack carried out by JeM on 14 February 2019. In fact, after Prime Minister Modi held bilateral talks with President Xi Jinping on the sidelines of the SCO Summit in Bishkek, the former noted that strategic communication between the two countries had improved, which helped in resolving the listing of Masood Azhar as a global terrorist, said Foreign Secretary Vijay Gokhale.[40]

There had been close discussions between India and China following the Pulwama attack in which forty CRPF personnel were killed. While the US, UK and France moved a proposal to designate Masood Azhar as a 'global terrorist', China stalled it for the fourth time by putting a technical hold on the resolution. The issue raised national hysteria in India, including calls from various sections to ban the sale of 'made in China' products.

Interestingly, the case of Masood Azhar seems intertwined with India's protest against the China–Pakistan Economic corridor (CPEC), which in a reverse way is linked to the issue of the Dalai Lama.

On Masood Azhar, the subtle nature of China's objection seems tied to the US espousing the case for India in the UNSC, while China seems willing to find a solution as long as the issue at hand is discussed between India and China.

China was given a 23 April 2019 deadline by the US, France and Britain to lift its 'technical hold' on listing Azhar. Earlier, in March, US Secretary of State Mike Pompeo said, 'China abuses more than a million Muslims at home, but on the other [hand] it protects violent Islamic terrorist groups from sanctions at the UN.'[41]

China on 17 April 2019 had said it was not facing any deadline to take a call on designating Masood Azhar as 'global terrorist'. It reiterated that progress was being made to achieve consensus on the issue in the 1267 Resolution of the UNSC through communication with the relevant parties and the matter was moving towards the direction of settlement.

Apparently, China is also seen taking a new position on India's refusal to join the BRI. It said that India's absence at the second BRI forum in April 2019 would not affect their engagement and both countries were preparing for a Wuhan-like summit between their leaders this year. India decided to skip China's BRI meet for the second time in protest against the CPEC that cuts through PoK—a legal part of India.

Quite clearly, India and China seem to have decided not to allow these differences to come in the way of taking bilateral ties to a higher level. Undoubtedly, New Delhi seemed to be handling the BRI issue quite cautiously. Foreign Secretary Gokhale's visit to Beijing a week before the BRI summit was scheduled for 25–27 April 2019. This was clearly meant to convey that India's position was not against China but to protect its own interests vis-à-vis the intricate sovereignty issues that involve Pakistan. However, officially, the foreign secretary's visit was termed as one to hold regular consultations.

India should try and prevent the challenges posed by China from multiplying. One hopes that the new team led by Gokhale is able to navigate engagement with China in good faith and not indulge in tactical ploys. Gokhale may just be trying to nip that agenda in the bud before India–China relations are subverted further. Clearly, another ice-breaking Wuhan-type meet between Modi and Xi is in the offing, possibly in the latter half of 2019.

Politics of rebirth

Seemingly fretful about impending developments, the Dalai Lama finds himself walking a political tightrope by espousing reconciliation between India and China, 'living peacefully by putting the differences aside'.[42] He maintained a hands-off position and tried not to get drawn even into the Doklam stand-off, instead calling for a peaceful solution. One hopes he is successful this time.

Clearly, the Dalai Lama knows well that for China, Tibet means Arunachal Pradesh as well. The Dalai Lama's endorsement of this position, for whatever quid pro quo, would hit at the India–China boundary negotiations on the basis of the McMahon Line.

He knows that the stakes for the future of his institution are considerable in geopolitics: the reason the Dalai Lama often tries to assert his view vis-à-vis even India. The Chinese on their part also understand that the post–Dalai Lama ramifications could risk further instability in Tibet.

In 2011, the Dalai Lama also gave up his political authority in favour of an elected leader among Tibetans living in exile. He smartly separated his political responsibility from his spiritual role. In an interview on his website, he said that 'the Dalai Lama as a temporal ruler is a man-made institution. As long as the people accept the Dalai Lama, they will accept me. But being a monk is something which belongs to me. No one can change that. Deep down inside, I always consider myself a monk, even in my dreams. So naturally I feel myself as more of a religious person.'[43] This has a very subtle and ambiguous meaning because under the Tibetan system, temporal authority cannot be de-linked from spiritual authority. Seemingly, the motive was to forestall any alternative plan by Beijing to appoint a successor after him, and challenge the authority of such an appointment if Beijing does so.

Instead, the Dalai Lama's shrugging off of political responsibility probably made the task easier for the Chinese. The dialogue between him and Beijing stopped in January 2010. Beijing has refused to confer any legitimacy on the *sikyong*, the elected head in exile, by resuming a dialogue process with him. The Chinese made it very clear that their problem is with the Dalai Lama only, and that they do not recognize any institution representing Tibetans outside Tibet.

In exile, the Dalai Lama's experiment with building a democratic system for his people also has its challenges, as differences among various factions impede the very purpose of fighting for independence. Already, the delay for a solution seems to be causing anxiety, confusion and division among Tibetans living in South Asia and elsewhere. The election for the government-in-exile in 2015 witnessed detractors openly contest the wisdom of dropping the demand for *rangzen* (independence), for they also held the adopted umaylam approach responsible for 'killing the Tibetan passion to act'.[44] To be sure, the majority still revere the Dalai Lama, but pent-up frustrations may be surfacing. Many Tibetans privately admit that their official strategy has failed hopelessly with China.

More disquietingly, the Dalai Lama leaves the future of his followers in a state of complete limbo. Uncertainty over what will happen to them in the post–Dalai Lama scenario looms large. Sustaining the 'Free Tibet' campaign aside, the fear of dislocation and possible flaring up of long-simmering tension with their local hosts is gaining momentum.[45] Surely, many Tibetans could be pursuing options in the West, but the majority would have no choice but to opt for Indian citizenship, perhaps against their cherished wish to return home.

In addition, holding the religious flock together seems to have become another challenge. Numerous sects are engulfed in sectarian, ideological and leadership rifts that undermine the Dalai Lama's authority.[46] Schisms and differences within and among sects could not be without instigation by the Chinese.

Within Tibet, the unresolved issue seemed to have caused emotional and psychological distress among Tibetan people. China accused the Dalai Lama of orchestrating self-immolation incidents inside Tibet, a charge that Beijing has not been able to substantiate. According to the ICT, a total of 155 Tibetans have immolated themselves between 2009 and 2018.[47]

Given the Dalai Lama's age, the question of his succession worries all stakeholders. But after abdicating his political power in 2011, the Dalai Lama has not stuck to any particular stand regarding the succession issue. Although he has reiterated more than once that the traditional practice of identifying a young Tibetan boy as his reincarnation would no longer make sense in present times.

However, the Dalai Lama has made numerous and conflicting statements such as he will not be reborn at all, he will only reincarnate in a free country, the reincarnate might be female, he could 'emanate' in someone else during his own lifetime, twisted as 'madhey tulku' (mid-emanation or birth before demise), and so on.[48] But he has firmly assured that his successor will be found outside Tibet.

In fact, in an ominous way, the Dalai Lama in 2014 threatened to terminate the over-400-year-old spiritual lineage of his position, saying that Tibetans no longer required the authority of the Dalai Lama and it would be a shame if a 'weak' person succeeded him.[49]

In September 2015, he made an unseemly remark that a woman could be the next Dalai Lama, and that she would have to be 'very attractive'. otherwise she would be 'not much use'.[50] The statement sparked outrage the world over, with several people expressing shock to hear such a 'retrograde opinion' coming from a man of compassion.[51] But in 2019, the Dalai Lama stood up for his earlier comment. In an interview to the BBC on 27 June 2019, the Dalai Lama again stirred up a controversy on the issue while saying that if his successor was female, she should be attractive. 'If a female Dalai Lama comes, then [she] should be more attractive, if not people would prefer not to see that face.'[52]

Surely, his offensive remark on how women are judged or taken seriously based on their physical appearance drew negative reactions on social media. In the same interview, the Dalai Lama also claimed that US President Donald Trump lacked moral responsibility. But more seriously, the Dalai Lama said in a question–answer session: 'If the present situation regarding Tibet remains the same, I will be born outside Tibet away from the control of the Chinese authorities. This is logical. The very purpose of a reincarnation is to continue the unfinished work of the previous incarnation. Thus, if the Tibetan situation still remains unsolved it is logical I will be born in exile to continue my unfinished work. Of course, the Chinese will still choose their own Dalai Lama and we Tibetans will choose our own according to tradition. It will be similar to the present situation of the Panchen Lama. There is a Chinese-appointed Panchen Lama and there is the Panchen Lama chosen by me. One is paraded to serve its master's purposes and the other is the Panchen Lama accepted in the hearts of all the Tibetans.'[53]

China, of course, disagrees with the Dalai Lama's future plans. In 2015, Beijing quickly rebuked the Dalai Lama's threat of terminating his succession, calling it 'profaning' Buddhism—a sign of 'disrespect' and 'betrayal' of the old Tibetan tradition. China said it is not up to him to decide, just as he did not decide when he was born. CPC officials said that the 'Dalai Lama was losing influence while insisting he is betraying his religion by saying he will not reincarnate at his death'.[54]

To be sure, China is gearing up to pick the next Dalai Lama as per its norms supposedly established during the Ch'ing period.

I recall that during my trip to Tibet in 2018, talking about the Dalai Lama and the Karmapa wasn't off limits. However, I didn't make any direct mention of the situation in Tibet for it was also awkward to ask probing questions. Local Tibetologists were conspicuously restrained in their remarks on the prospect of the Dalai Lama's return to Tibet or about his next reincarnation. Quite a few Tibetans said that the situation inside Tibet is quite complex. But they said the Karmapa was most welcome to return as he is one of the living Buddhas recognized by the central government.

Tibetan officials explained to me that the reincarnation of a 'living Buddha' is a unique inheritance system and follows an integrated religious ritual and historical convention and China's laws and regulations. They said there exists a 300-year-old traditional and institutional procedure laid down to select a Dalai Lama, and China cannot deviate from those rituals that were followed even for the appointment of the current Dalai Lama in 1940 by the Chiang Kai-Shek government. No foreign country will be allowed to interfere in identifying the Fifteenth Dalai Lama, they emphasized. Local Tibetan officials revealed a figure of 358 'living Buddhas' currently registered under the national-level Management Regulation of Tibetan Buddhist Monasteries.

Clearly, in case of a dispute, there will be two claimants to the position after his death: one selected by the Dalai Lama's office and another by the Chinese government. To be sure, the exiles would reject any Beijing-chosen candidate, and it needs to be seen which candidate gets more international legitimacy.

The issue of succession can become explosive within the Tibetan community. Even if the exiled Tibetans decide to find the next Dalai Lama, there would be an internal crisis that would start within the immediate gestation period—normally the immediate five years to locate and authenticate the reincarnate. Creating the Regency Council would not be without controversy, given the problems with Beijing, besides deep divides among major Tibetan sects, the feudal elite, clans and coteries that impact the process.

The critical issue remains whether the Gelug sect will be able to retain its decisive role in the Dalai Lama's selection process. The conflict would intensify if there are two claimants to the post. Moreover, the conflict could arise as to where the memorial stupa of the Fourteenth Dalai Lama would be built—in India or in Tibet?

There are no easy answers but there is much risk of fallout, including for India. It is hard to figure whether the Dalai Lama's ambiguous and inconsistent position is directed against China or an expression of his unhappiness over a lack of unity amongst his clergy.

A blueprint already exists on the next reincarnation spelled out by the Dalai Lama himself in 2011. But the CTA has been advocating a view that the reincarnation of the Dalai Lama should be decided by the various heads of major Tibetan Buddhist sects. The CTA dared China to interfere in the religious practices of Tibetan Buddhism.

The CTA tried to hold the Thirteenth Religious Conference of the Schools of Tibetan Buddhism and Bon Tradition from 29 November to 1 December 2018 to decide on the future of the institution of the Dalai Lama. But on 24 November, it suddenly deferred the meet indefinitely on the grounds that the supreme head of the Nyingma sect, Kathok Getse Rinpoche, had passed away at the time in Nepal. Kathok Getse's presence would have been important but it was the absence of the Karmapa that derailed the CTA's plans. The Karmapa's failure to return to India exposed the rifts among Tibetans. The other factions, such as the head of the Drukpa Kagyu sect, anyway showed scant interest for CTA's game plan.

Meanwhile, major Tibetan lamas successfully built their own persona among their foreign supporters. For them to accept a central authority, especially a contested one, would remain a problem. Such a scenario is also inevitable after the Dalai Lama's abdication of political power. No doubt China will exploit all these factors to its advantage.

Beijing is clearly building its case to find its own Dalai Lama. The Chinese emphasize that they will follow the set rituals, conventions and China's laws and regulations to decide the next successor, and any interference by anybody or any foreign country will not be accepted.

They have a mechanism under Order No. 5 in place to regulate the reincarnation process, but the complexity involved in refreshing the dead soul, steeped in centuries of Tantric tradition, plus the rhetoric around it, could also make China's task difficult. However, it seems that the CPC has been holding 'closed-door' meetings to discuss the issue.

In 2016, Xi Jinping has ordered to pick the next Dalai Lama and 'take corrective action' if things do not go well.[55]

Beijing is likely to repeat the procedure it followed at the time of installing the Eleventh Panchen Lama in November 1995. A Tibetan official told me in Garzi, 'We don't care if another one is found outside Tibet.'

However, the critical part is whether Beijing will be able to get the Karmapa to return to Tibet and make him, along with the Panchen Lama, Gyaltsen Norbu, jointly authenticate the reincarnation of the Dalai Lama inside Tibet. And here, Beijing would bet on the Karmapa for legitimacy because his institution is nearly three centuries older than the Dalai Lama's. Of course, this would cause a politico-sectarian rift.

China has already expressed opposition to a US Senate resolution on the reincarnation of the next Dalai Lama, saying it amounts to interference in China's internal affairs.[56] In April 2018, the US Senate passed a resolution which claimed that 'the responsibility for identifying a future Fifteenth Dalai Lama only rests with officials of the Fourteenth Dalai Lama's private office, and any interference from the Chinese government is invalid'.

The issue could cause sufficient diplomatic complications for the countries that would support the candidate selected by exiled supporters. In the past, the international community barely showed concern when a similar power struggle played out with the reincarnation of the Panchen Lama in the 1990s. The Dalai Lama's chosen candidate hasn't been seen in two decades, but barring the United States, no other country has affectively made much noise about his disappearance.

As such, the Dalai Lama's successor will be determined in large measure by a combination of China's political, diplomatic and economic prowess. Beijing will deploy everything in its arsenal to get global endorsement for its chosen Dalai Lama. Practising Vajrayana states like Bhutan, Mongolia and even India are unlikely to directly interfere in the selection process.

The Chinese are certainly aware of the need to have India on their side if the issue is to be solved in their favour. Probably, the Wuhan process was about that. Seemingly, China's State Council is already talking to the officials and Buddhist clergy of Mongolia to come to an understanding on the issue. The rest of the Buddhist world does not matter. Any country willing to endorse a candidate born outside Tibet would risk their ties with China, said one Tibetologist.

Saboteurs?

One thing is clear—the Tibet lobby has a track record of ensnaring India in its murky agenda, often at the cost of India's strategic interests. In that sense, India–China ties are driven more by the interests of Tibetan exiles than by India's national interest.

Here, the CTA's 2018 'Thank You India' campaign was possibly yet another cynical ploy to draw India into the exiles' next big agenda: the reincarnation process of the Dalai Lama. Since 2018, the CTA has been building a case that the search for the Dalai Lama's reincarnation is India's problem as well. They have been talking about roping in the Mongolian clergy too.

Not surprisingly, the Dalai Lama launched his most powerful missile in this regard yet in March 2019, when he said he expected his reincarnation to be discovered in India this time around. In a statement in March 2019, the Dalai Lama said, 'In future, in case you see two Dalai Lamas come, one from here, in a free country, one is chosen by Chinese, and then nobody will trust, nobody will respect [the one chosen by China]. So that's an additional problem for the Chinese. It's possible, it can happen.'[57]

Quite clearly, the Dalai Lama has been preparing for such an eventuality for some time now while raising his profile and influence in the Indian Himalayas, especially Arunachal Pradesh and Ladakh. He would prefer Tawang to be his next birthplace for reasons of history and because it is considered South Tibet. However, it could become controversial because China too claims the area to be part of Tibet. His second option would be to be born in a place like Ladakh.

Beijing has reacted strongly to recent remarks by the Dalai Lama that his successor may come from India. Beijing, of course, insists on following the old rule and would do anything to prevent the Dalai Lama deciding the future of his status, and this will be the most dangerous game in the Himalayas that could last for another century. Such a move could rile India's ties with China permanently, with no end in sight.

This would strike at the heart of the future course of India–China relations. In fact, the entire process of normalization of ties between India and China could still be sabotaged by the Dalai Lama with support from the Americans, should they be so inclined.

India neither has any precedence of selecting a Dalai Lama, nor is the institution rooted in Indian history and polity. A rebirth in India, absurd as it might sound in the twenty-first century, would come with high strategic and geopolitical costs and long-term implications. It is like the raja of Kamarupa taking his rebirth in China for political reasons.

One of the risks involved is that the place of the Dalai Lama's birth invariably gets linked to the Tibetan mythical/historical area of influence, like in the case of the Sixth Dalai Lama. The Tibetans and Chinese make the assertion that Tawang is the birthplace of the Sixth Dalai Lama and its monastery an integral part of the Gelug theocratic institution; hence, they can never be parted.

Beijing, in its last move on the chessboard, should be advised to allow the Dalai Lama to return to Tibet or China proper as a spiritual leader, provided he is also allowed to have a say in choosing his successor.

14

How Tibet Overshadows India's Himalayan Frontiers

As analysed before, Tibet was critical for British India to mitigate any potential direct threats from and confrontations with adversarial powers such as Russia and China. To counter them, it devised 'buffer zones', 'inner and outer' territory concepts, employed 'forward policies' and built strategic forts often termed as glacis. Primarily, these policies evolved to protect its mercantile interests. It was also done to ensure that the countries are not engaged in a zero-sum game.

Similarly, the Russians also created a 'sphere of influence' in Eastern Europe, Central Asia and the Far East. Despite its decline in the aftermath of the dissolution of the USSR, Russia under Putin is trying to protect its 'near-abroad' in order to retain its great power status.

The Chinese, on the other hand, have been practising the Li concept that primarily functions on a ritualistic tributary system of the 'core' controlling the 'peripheries' through economic, trade and cultural relationships. This imperial-era idea seems to still shape strategic thinking in present-day China in terms of both gaining additional territory and market access outside the country.

Not surprisingly, unlike other nations which tend to play a straight game of chess to defeat the adversary on a single battleground, the Chinese are used to playing a slower build-up game on multiple battlefronts to inflict progressive losses upon its adversary—explained in the 'go' game.

The only counter to Sun Tzu's 'salami-slicing' strategy was found by the Mongols. A Mongol Khan once reminded the Chinese that a 'small, sharp razor' could tonsure millions of hairs on the scalp at once. Of course, it was said in the context of Mongolian demographic deficiency vis-à-vis China.

The Chinese 'go' game involves taking less risks but also incremental steps while working on the enemy's weaknesses to ensure complete victory. This recipe for winning war is being employed in the ongoing dispute in the maritime domain: in the South China Sea. On land, the slow invasion tactic has been the hallmark of Chinese success in Inner Mongolia, Siberia, Xinjiang and the Tibetan plateau.

In the 1960s, Chinese leaders made a nuanced assertion of Bhutan, Ladakh and Sikkim always being subject to Tibet and thus to the great 'Chinese motherland'. Since the military stand-off in 1962, the Himalayan perimeter between India and China is being defined under the mutually agreed-upon LAC mechanism. But China has not yet accepted the McMahon Line drawn by the British as the boundary between the two countries.

While China has been building infrastructure and military capability along the LAC, it has allowed limited engagement with India on trans-border issues, pilgrimage visits and exchange of hydro data. Similarly, boundary negotiations have been carried out through diplomatic channels but the issue is allowed to remain in a state of stalemate—leaving the matter open-ended.

China's thinking in many ways is indicative of how they eventually hope to change the Himalayan configuration to their advantage. In fact, the Chinese may have been thinking about playing the reverse strategic depth policy by leveraging the critical interplay between Buddhism and the Himalayas for a long time.

After consolidating its hold over Tibet in the 1960s, China seemingly worked on the canvas of the southern Himalayas, what it called South Tibet. Unlike India, China never viewed the Himalayan ranges as a barrier but a bridge to create additional spheres of influence. Here, Beijing probably took its cue from the Qing Dynasty—using Tibetan Lamaism as a useful vehicle for enlarging the empire.

China, in a masterstroke strategy, allowed the Dalai Lama to flee in 1959 to settle down in the southern Himalayas. Many conspiracy theories are afloat about his escape, including a CIA plot. It was a setback but Mao certainly had something else in mind. The Chinese believe in converting challenges into opportunities.

Chinese glacis?

Following the departure of the Dalai Lama and his coterie, China not only let all major Tibetan sectarian heads get away but perhaps also coordinated the exodus of their reincarnates as well. The arrival of fresh lamas continues unabated even today.

Make no mistake, Tibetan forays in India have never been oriented towards fighting a freedom struggle. Instead, they have been part of a cultural movement to bring about trans-boundary transformation in the garb of countering socialist transformation by China. As believed by many, to view the Chinese as ideological (communist) would be a misnomer. They are at best nationalists, an orientation that is imbedded in their history. Therefore, viewing politics from the prism of Chinese communism versus Tibetan Buddhism would be a failure even from an academic point of view. The Dalai Lama has said on many occasions that there is commonality between communism and Buddhism— both believe in equality and justice. For instance, at a gathering at the Indian Institute of Management Ahmedabad (IIM-A) in 2008, he said: 'I am a Marxist monk, a Buddhist Marxist. I belong to the Marxist camp, because unlike capitalism, Marxism is more ethical. Marxism, as an ideology, takes care of the welfare of its employees and believes in distribution of wealth among the people of the state.'[1]

There are certainly essential spatial differences between the Tibetan and Chinese cultures and even between Tibetan Buddhism and Chinese Buddhism, but at the same time, the creation of the Dalai Lama's institution in the seventeenth century is directly associated with China's imperial expansion and influence.

In fact, the Tibetans have for centuries admired Chinese culture, thrived on Chinese money and used the Chinese imperial military to subjugate others' territories, including the kingdoms of the Himalayas. For centuries, they have had a history of power and territory grabbing. As mentioned before, the Tibetan feudatory character is described by Owen Lattimore as having served as agents of one or another alien overlord. Undoubtedly, the medieval-era Tibetan feudatory Ganden Phodrang regime that long served as a front of imperial court ultimately failed Tibet and its people. Let there be no mistake, the traditional spirit of Sino-Tibetan convivial relations would have continued had the CIA not plotted the Dalai Lama's escape from Tibet.

The supporters of this feudatory system, over 1,00,000 exiles, continue to cause quarrels and remain detrimental to Tibetan, Indian and Chinese national interests. They are, in the garb of resistance against Chinese rule, indulging in the same imperial-style territorial expansion while using the very same Gelugpa ideology vis-à-vis the indigenous Himalayan Buddhist tradition. The idea seems to ultimately establish the supremacy of the Gelug politico-theocratic structure: a replica of Ganden Phodrang in the Himalayas which will have a very dangerous portent for India's national security.

It started with the Western world romanticizing Tibet. A plethora of books appeared and were sold on the grandeur of mystic Tibetan Buddhism, which was found to be appealing and even exotic. Yet, the myth of Shangri-La and its profundity grossly overshadowed the reality of Himalayan complexities and intricacies and the urgency of its political and social situation. The ground reality is that China had been in complete control of Tibet and now it is speedily gaining influence in the Himalayas.

Yet, over the decades, powerful exiled Tibetan masters have set up parallel institutional networks sprinkled across India. A clear trend in the source of funding for building such mega-religious infrastructure along the southern Himalayas is quite visible. Clearly, a particular force has been controlling the trends of Lamaism, not just in Tibet but in the Indian Himalayan region as well.

In the last decade, the Chinese seemed to have further refined the policy. China's official outfits, such as the State Administration for Religious Affairs (SARA), UFWD and BAC have been investing heavily in building a nexus with expatriate Tibetans.

Through a well-developed modus operandi, officially 'accredited' and trained Han 'monk diplomats' (with past experience of building ties with the Buddhist diaspora across Taiwan, Hong Kong and South East Asia) are deployed to link up with influential Tibetan lamas abroad. These monk diplomats are trained in fundraising, managing charitable works, preaching in dharma centres and building bridges with overseas Chinese.

They had earlier successfully induced influential Buddhist masters of Taiwan such as Zhao Puchu, Hsing Yun, Sheng Yen and others. They also played a prime role in the rapid thawing of cross-strait relations. They were instrumental in getting powerful Taiwanese businessmen to invest in China.

Seemingly, Hsing Yun and Sheng Yen also played key roles in cultivating foreign-based Tibetan monks and leaders. The methodology again involved pouring in funds as donations, ostensibly for religious activities such as building temples and dharma centres.

Clearly, many Tibetans Lamas living in India are said to be listed as 'patriots' or 'approved' for accreditation with the BAC. They are connected with prospective financers and donors among the overseas Chinese in Hong Kong, Taiwan, Singapore, Malaysia, Australia and other countries where the lamas travel in order to raise funds.

The Chinese may have already won over influential lamas who are seen making frequent visits to Tibet, where they maintain a hold over their institutions and followers. Besides, there is a growing trend towards a 'very subtle and complex religious doctrinal merging process of the Han and Tibetan Schools'.[2] Many canny Han clerics and laity are seen flocking to the Tibetan lamas. Clearly, the objective is to inculcate spiritual devotion as a means to gain Tibetan loyalty towards the 'Chinese motherland'. The scheme, at the functional level, includes promoting the spirit of respecting each other's hierarchy, harmonizing monastic rituals and traditions, finding common ground with equivalent Buddhist deities, promoting devotional prayer music, and so on and so forth.

This harmonizing process between the two Buddhist traditions would have ensured a steady flow of donations to build religious assets in India. Yet, there is another trend of setting up many 'Sino-compatible' Buddhist centres to 'bless' Tibetan communities worldwide.

All in all, the Chinese seem to have accurately diagnosed the Tibetan problem and are now applying the very same Tibetan devotional potential they had undermined during the excesses of the Cultural Revolution.

The Tibetans, wittingly or unwittingly, have been able to bring into their fold the entire region of the Himalayas falling south of Tibet through their control over vital monastic resources and institutions of Tibetan cultural connectivity—this can be considered a great service to China!

Beyond the military significance, China's Himalayan strategy is linked to its domestic concerns, economic interests, untapped natural resources and managing domestic dissent. The 'go' principle therefore would present China with a much-coveted strategic advantage. Here, once the Chinese succeed in projecting the Tibetan Lamaist power from afar, it becomes easier for Beijing to find innocent passages, connectivity routes and transport of goods across the Himalayas under its BRI projects—all under the shadowy influence of Lamaism/ Buddhism.

India's missteps

The Pentagon's warning that China is building up troops along the border is something the Indian military feels confident of dealing with effectively. But the more critical issue is how to counter China's countless asymmetric warfare moves in the Himalayas.

For most Indian Mandarins, the game remains unfathomable. Instead, trusting Indians have excitedly facilitated every move made by the Chinese. They have rejoiced in receiving and harbouring a stream of influential Tibetan lamas who they thought would be useful assets for India, without realizing that the Chinese had quietly launched asymmetric warfare vis-à-vis India. Indian policies perfectly suited Beijing. The idea was to employ Sun Tzu's dictum: 'The supreme art of war is to subdue the enemy without fighting.'[3]

Since then, the Indian state has done everything possible, like spend hundreds of crores of rupees annually, for Tibetan rehabilitation and welfare programmes. This is in addition to the financial assistance the cause receives directly from the US and elsewhere. Most importantly, India was made to feel proud of supporting the Tibetans without realizing that the Chinese were directly ensnaring it in a game plan in which the ultimate victory is with China.

Indian policy seemed to have failed on the ground of its inability to strictly follow British policies. As stated earlier, first, British India defined its identifications in the north-western Himalayas for the strategic consideration of containing Russian threats towards India.

Second, setting frontiers in the eastern Himalayas was driven by the need for securing the lower land in Assam for mercantile interests: tea plantation and rice cultivation. Here, the British avoided exerting control over areas that were wasteful and irrelevant for revenue gains. While qualifying those lines, the British were careful not to confront a situation of diminishing returns.

Third, the boundary lines (Inner/Outer and McMahon Lines) in the Himalayas were conceived as against the Tibetan territorial claims. In fact, soon after the British left in 1947, the Tibetan authorities in Lhasa officially asked India to return the alleged (lost) territories of Tibet that virtually claimed the entire Indian Himalayan region.[4]

All in all, British India pursued a national boundary based on objective reality, devoid of any illusionary line that simply wasn't there. However, in the aftermath of British rule, policymaking in India lost subtlety, became lacking in perceptivity and above all the ability to judge spatial patterns and taxonomic distinctness on the ground. While independent India continued to follow the British-drawn 'colonial' boundary line, in reality, policymakers may have grossly negated the inherent basis on which the frontiers were identified by the British, howsoever colonial in scheme they may have been.

Sixty years down the line, India seems to have gained little. Instead, the country now finds itself worryingly and helplessly entangled in a Tibetan quagmire with serious implications for the stability of its frontier region. It may have got trapped in a policy of opacity—the exact opposite of what British strategists had avoided falling into. And this pertained to the so-called 'Tibet card', so obliquely played, detrimental to India's own interest.

The most galling aspect is the absence of a counter-strategy for reversing the game. The system lacks comprehension and understanding, let alone the wherewithal to counter China's asymmetric warfare. It also does not have the kind of scholarship that is needed to understand the depth of Buddhist political disposition. With the exception of a few such as Rahul Sanskrityayan, Raghu Vira, Lokesh Chandra and Ram Rahul, scholarly naivety in understanding the finer nuances may have done more harm than good for getting clarity.

Western scholarship has rather obscured Himalayan geopolitics. Several books have brought to light the grandeur of the Buddhist Himalayas, mostly by tapping into various aspects of Tibetan Buddhism that were found to be appealing and even exotic, especially to Western audiences, in the second half of the twentieth century.

In fact, the influence of the Dalai Lama and his efforts at drawing attention to the Tibetan political cause, combined with the power of publicity in the West, ensured that the Himalayas were projected as a kind of cultural and geopolitical exotica to the outside world.

Tibetan Buddhism even became the subject of pop and rock songs in the 1960s and 1970s. Novels like *Lost Horizon* by James Hilton inspired many myths, such as the one about the legendary Shambhala—a sort of Shangri-La located in the Himalayas. It is also noteworthy that the myth-making process ran parallel to China's massive efforts at transforming the economy and infrastructure on the Tibetan plateau.

Yet, the myth of Shambhala and its profundity had grossly overshadowed the reality of Himalayan geopolitics. For example, the British strategists played the 'Great Game' within the context of consolidating its hold while limiting if not undercutting the Himalayan proximities towards China-controlled Tibet.

Tibetans unsure of future

Tibet has historically remained either as an independent entity or within the zone of Chinese power. Since the seventeenth century, they served as instruments for the expansion of the Qing Empire. Frequently, Tibetans sought Mongol and Manchu support to threaten and subjugate the kingdoms of the Himalayas.

In the last century, the British found it hard to deal with Tibetans, who would tend to hide behind the facade of Chinese imperial authority. Moreover, the Tibetan irredentist claim over pockets of the Himalayas, including Tawang, continued even after the Dalai Lama took political shelter in India in 1959.

On the Tibetan side, even today, no one is clear what they want. The Dalai Lama dropped the original rangzen (independence) demand long back. The detractors in his own community, such as Lukar Jam, hold the Dalai Lama's preferred doctrinal path of umaylam responsible for 'killing the Tibetan passion to act'.[5]

Looking back, the Tibetan executive authority was traditionally run by the Kashag or House of Order under successive Dalai Lamas or regents. The Kashag was run by *kalon*s or ministers who dealt with all administrative, judicial and political matters.

In 1959, the exiled Tibetans under the leadership of the Dalai Lama established the CTA. The Dalai Lama remained as the head of state, and executive powers were vested upon the Kashag, consisting of three lay and two monk officials functioning as kalons. Prior to 2001, the Dalai Lama nominated three names for each kalon post, and the assembly selected one each. The selected kalons then elected the executive head, called the kalon tripa.

In 2001, the charter was amended to facilitate the direct election of the kalon tripa by the people. Samdhong Rinpoche was elected as the first kalon tripa who nominated other kalons with the approval of the Tibetan Parliament-in-exile.[6]

In 2011, the kalon tripa was subordinated to the Dalai Lama. But soon the Dalai Lama gave up his political authority and also said that his 400-year-old spiritual lineage might be terminated since it was no longer required. The Dalai Lama announced that his political authority would be transferred to the newly elected kalon tripa, Lobsang Sangay, while he remained as spiritual leader and figurehead of the CTA.

However, in accordance to the amendments made in 2012, the nomenclature of kalon tripa was changed to sikyong, meaning 'political leader',[7] who was directly elected by the exiled Tibetan populace. The sikyong, in turn, headed the seven-member Kashag of the CTA. Interestingly, Lobsang Sangay is called the president of the CTA.[8]

In the changed context, the transfer of power to the sikyong remains a far cry from the Dalai Lama—lacking both spiritual and political validity as well as international legitimacy as long as China's pressure continues. In a way, this may have dealt a serious blow to the very cause for which Tibetans fled their homeland almost six decades ago. It is not clear what the Dalai Lama wants, but a sense of hopelessness, confusion, anxiety and even division among his followers is palpable.

In effect, neither a sikyong nor a successor of the Dalai Lama will be able to free Tibet from China. The existing umaylam approach very much suits China to fulfil its wish to create South Tibet, and this is what the successor of the Dalai Lama would wish to continue with. Beijing may have already arranged that alternative.

Where then does India's position stand? Can India allow a Tibetan government-in-exile without the Dalai Lama? Will India allow for the recognition of his reincarnation in India? Will India deal with a Tibetan leader chosen by the Dalai Lama? Or will India also compete with China to decide the next Dalai Lama? These are some difficult questions that India will be confronted with.

India will have no say in deciding the next Dalai Lama. Although it has a small population of practising Vajrayana Buddhists, they are not a force to reckon with as Indian Buddhists do not have even a sangha (council) to take a call on such matters.

Clearly, Beijing would deploy all its political and economic prowess to get global endorsement for its chosen Dalai Lama. The other two practising Vajrayana States like Bhutan and Mongolia are unlikely to directly interfere in the selection process of the Fifteenth Dalai Lama.

There is no visible sign of any sense of direction for the future. The Tibetans may have an opportunity to seek a fresh course altogether in the post–Dalai Lama scenario, but the key issue is who will anchor the new movement.

The answer perhaps lies in the future trajectory of the Indo-US relationship but that also presents quite a challenge. Surely, the Americans are sufficiently invested in the issue of Tibet and the Dalai Lama. The original American motive may have been to defeat communist China through Tibetan Buddhism. That has obviously not worked.

A double-edged sword for India

For all practical purposes, Tibet's problems seem to have become India's problems, which does not portend well unless India has thought up a contingency plan. Undoubtedly, India has invested a lot in Tibet and that cannot be allowed to go waste. Thousands of powerful lamas and leaders have been sheltered and nurtured in India. However, the pattern of these people settling down in the southern Himalayan ranges and building mega infrastructure with dubious funds from outside the country cannot be allowed to continue endlessly.

The Tibet issue obliviously acts like a double-edged sword for parties playing the Himalayan game. It is time for New Delhi to play the reverse game and seek its own glacis in Tibet rather than let China realize its game plan in the Himalayas. It should be worthwhile for India to find a via media with the Chinese to organize the dignified and safe return of the Tibetans. India's interests would be served if the influential Tibetan lamas were to return to their respective places in Tibet and serve India: the land of their supreme masters Lord Buddha, Padmasambhava, Nagarjuna, Dipankar Acharya, Shantarakshita and many others. Clearly, the challenge for India is to convert its current strategic liability into a long-term strategic asset.

More importantly, India's response would be determined by how it is able to play its own Himalayan frontier game to ensure that Nepal and Bhutan do not become Chinese allies in this 'game of thrones'.

The keystone that drives the main connection with India for the Himalayan people, including those of Bhutan, Sikkim and Nepal, is their deep devotion to *gyagar* (the holy land India)—the fidelity embedded into the Himalayan ethos by the wisdom of eighth-century Indian leader and philosopher Padmasambhava.

Largely, this piousness today seems to be restricted to one side, but the people, including the Bhutanese, have so far diligently stayed true to their religio-cultural links with India. Sadly, on the Indian side, that sense of historical responsibility and cultural affinity seems to have been lost forever.

On their part, the Himalayan states of Bhutan, Nepal and even Sikkim are deeply conscious of the underlying historical tension over sectarian dominance. This is the reason why Bhutan and Nepal chose to stay away from Tibet-related politics, though they were openly encouraged by India in conjunction with the US.

The Dalai Lama is never invited to visit Bhutan—the only Vajrayana nation apart from Mongolia. The fear factor of China cannot be the only explanation; it is the sectarian factor of Gelug assertion over the Nyingma/Kagyu traditions that underpinned Himalayan geopolitics.[9] Same is the case with Nepal, which refuses to get sucked into Tibetan politics.

While Bhutan and Nepal have ably guarded their interests, India has failed to fully grasp the underlying mix of ethnic and sectarian dynamics that underscore Himalayan politics. Barring a few, Indian policymakers, in their fervent desire to irk the Chinese, often overlook the sensitivities of countries like Bhutan. The sort of reckless policies pursued over the years by India may have served to confuse several issues, including the status of Arunachal Pradesh, which will eventually conflict with India's own interests.

It is paradoxical how the Dalai Lama, whose predecessor conquered and ruled Mon-Tawang (an integral part of India) from 1681 to 1951, is being hailed by the Indian state as a bulwark against China. Similarly, India may have muddled its own case by excessively encouraging a Tibetanization trend in the western Himalayas. The developments in Ladakh seem to be assuming a dangerous proportion, which is going to bounce back on India sooner than later. In fact, the Indian state, in a relatively short time span, has systematically ruined what the British had strategically achieved in the Himalayas.

With the annexation of Tibet by the Chinese in the 1950s, India had genuine cause for concern, especially when it lost the British-designed 'outer' strategic buffer. New Delhi at first followed a pragmatic policy of not challenging China's sovereignty over Tibet, but after the launch of American covert operations to bring the Dalai Lama to India in 1959, the situation took a different turn for India. The geopolitics of the Himalayas has become more obscure ever since the mantle of India's Tibet–China policy fell into the hands of the Americans.

There is no doubt that the Tibet issue and the presence of Tibetans have long overshadowed the Indian Himalayan region. Inevitably, this seems to have served to further blur the Indian frontier outlook. Not only has India lost its 'outer' strategic buffer but it has also risked as a result its own 'inner' strategic buffer: Ladakh, Sikkim, Arunachal and even Nepal and Bhutan. There are already direct and visible pointers of the Chinese beginning to harness Tibetan resources for steering the Himalayan game in their favour.

At the popular level, especially among the informed circle, the move to play the Dalai Lama card wasn't seen to be normal behaviour on the part of the government. In fact, many were baffled by the China–India stand-off over the Dalai Lama amid improving ties.

Yet, it was not clear whether New Delhi actually has a Tibet policy or it was deliberately playing with the Dalai Lama to counter Chinese aggressiveness. Or was it a way to finally let out the long-festering anger towards China for pinpricking it on a number of occasions?

Quite possibly, it may have been done under some special circumstance. Clearly, it was meant to bring the Tibet issue to the table when President Trump had just taken over in the US. But the decision to allow the Dalai Lama's Tawang card may have crippled New Delhi's strategic vision. The matter was diffused and the anger did not extend beyond a verbal outburst, though months later the tension in the Himalayas erupted in the form of Doklam. Clearly, the soft power of Lamaist linkages, reincarnation, social and ethnic bonds and cross-border economic interests could become crucial elements of the superpower influence of China.

In the changing Tibetan sectarian context, when the Kagyu order (that has remained confined to the Himalayan borderlands since the seventeenth century) is once again assuming prominence, India's approach in favour of abandoning the Kagyu leaders including the Karmapa seems illogical.

This factor would also have an impact on Indo-Bhutan ties. Let us not forget, Bhutan could also potentially hold a key to influencing the situation because it shares ethnic, religious, cultural and historic ties with Tibet. By having Bhutan on its side, China could easily moderate the politics of Lamaism.

The central issue would be the asymmetrical nature of Bhutan's cultural relationship with China vis-à-vis India. This will have implications for the geopolitical balancing game in the Himalayas. The disquieting part is that Beijing may have already succeeded in expanding its cultural presence all along the Indian Himalayas. At least in Bhutan, the state has a law enacted for regulating the reincarnation of tulku lamas, their rights and their role in the country. In India, no such law exists, which makes the country vulnerable to external manipulation. Lamaism's rebirth politics may already be infringing on key aspects of Indian polity and national security.

The government needs to pull itself out of its seeming confusion and ambiguity on Tibet or the Himalayan region will slide irretrievably into chaos. China is in no hurry to settle either the border disputes with India or the problem of Tibet itself. From its perspective, there is nothing to be resolved in Tibet.

15

Rekindling Himalayan Buddhism

India's worst fears might become reality, with China rapidly infusing a plan for Buddhist globalization using its financial, political and market clout. Not surprisingly, President Xi Jinping is not just asserting territorial claims in the South China Sea and expanding connectivity under the One Belt, One Road (OBOR) initiative, but also embarking on the path of making China a world leader in Buddhism.

Interestingly, Xi had started building partnerships between party and religion when he was only twenty-nine years old and serving as a bureaucrat in the provinces. The story began when he encountered Shi Youming, a Buddhist monk who was restoring ruined temples in Zhengding county in Hebei province.

Xi was probably also influenced by his father, Xi Zhongxun, who in 1980 had warned the CPC in his 11,000-word report, 'Document 19',[1] against banning religious activity, suggesting it would alienate too many people. In fact, one of Xi's signature lines is said to have been, 'If the people have faith, the nation has hope, and the country has strength.'[2]

Interestingly, Xi helped rebuild several famous temples, but strangely ordered the pulling off of 1500 crosses from church steeples when he was the chief of Zhejiang province during 2002–07. Clearly, he was not as partial to religions deemed foreign, like Christianity and Islam, as he was to Buddhism.

Using faith to legitimize rule is not new. Many see Xi's policy as akin to Vladimir Putin's spiritual feat of adopting orthodoxy, which gives him a strong moral legitimacy to be the leader of the Slavic world.

This is despite Article 14 of Russia's constitution that declares the country 'a secular state'.

Nobody knows whether Xi is a practitioner himself, but he did firmly start efforts to put Chinese Buddhism on the global stage in 2005. Seemingly, at the domestic level, Xi is turning to religion not just to bolster his hold on power but also to save the CPC from dwindling.

He certainly sees Buddhism as a useful way of arresting flagging moral values and to prevent the middle class from crumbling under the weight of a deepening social crisis and an economic downturn. Its rapidly ageing population caused the country to abandon Mao's one-child policy in 2015. More importantly, Xi intends to infuse moral ethics among party officials—deemed necessary to bring further economic reforms or risk stagnation.

Under Xi, Buddhism seems to have already made a strong comeback. Economic affluence seems to be steering the people's quest for spirituality. For instance, millions of Chinese seeking their *yin guo* (karma) connections with the Buddha Amitabha has become a new trend.

The yin guo is having a strong secular resonance; from students to businessmen, ordinary Chinese are beginning to link their existential happiness to the interdependent nature of karmic fruition.

According to the Chinese master Jingzong, China's intent to realize its economic and political destiny would pale in comparison to the urge amongst millions to accomplish their spiritual fortunes. He cannot visualize a future that has China without Buddhism.[3]

Clearly, China is finding a new template for re-imaging the nation along the lines of the imperial Chinese state. With humanistic Buddhist values diffusing into society, China is likely to resemble in future the kind of practice of Buddhism one witnesses in Thailand and other Buddhist countries today. To be sure, it is having consequences for the rest of Asia, where 97 per cent of the world's Buddhist population lives and where Buddhism defines its core values.

Taking a cue from its imperial-era practice, China could even be using the very powerful Tibetan cultural connectivity to expand influence across the Indian Himalayan belt, Mongolia and Russia. Becoming a guardian of Buddhism is helping Xi successfully promote China as an acceptable world power with a soft image. Buddhist globalization is also helping Beijing push its economic projects.

It is now getting embedded into China's latest OBOR initiative, which is nothing but the 'political geography of Buddhism' or the geopolitics of Buddhism at play. Nepal is proposing to link OBOR with the Buddha's birthplace, Lumbini. Pakistan is reviving the 'Gandhara trail' to link Lahore, Taxila and Peshawar. Taxila relics are sent to Sri Lanka for public exposition during the Vesak month.

If Sri Lankan monks visit Taxila to celebrate Buddha Purnima, top Bhutanese monks visit the Saidu Sharif monastery in the Swat Valley (birthplace of Guru Padmasambhava). Surely, China's edging in on its cultural space worries India and makes it see China as a geopolitical threat.

India's lack of a credible institution

Soon after coming to power, Prime Minister Narendra Modi prudently decided to emphasize India's rich tradition of Buddhism in a soft-power approach to Asian geopolitics. Apart from countries like Nepal, Bhutan, Japan, Sri Lanka, South Korea, Mongolia and others, he struck a direct chord with China to revive India–China ties. He visited China's ancient temples in Xi'an and made an offering in front of the massive golden statues of the Buddha amidst monks chanting sutras.

Moreover, the Modi government undertook several diplomatic measures, mainly organizing Buddhist cultural festivals and gathering Buddhist leaders and experts from Asian countries to attend conferences, conventions and shows. But these efforts showed no mark of desired progress on the ground.

The reasons could be many, but India's lack of a credible institution for espousing Buddhism or a traditional sangha order has led to the recurring failure of Indian cultural diplomacy in this regard.

In the past, India nurtured the institution of the sangha, or 'assemblage', which epitomized the idyllic order (*arya sangha*)— followed traditionally by ordained monks and nuns (or the monastic community known as *bhikkhu sangha* and *bhikkhuni sangha*). The higher form is called the arya sangha (noble sangha).

The sangha stood for selflessness or freedom from existential dilemmas; it claimed no moral authority but set a path for individuals and communities to attain higher virtues, impelling them to form a common vision and concord. The nature of the sangha allowed communities to adapt to changing times. This powerful concept spread from India to find roots far and wide.

The mistake often made in India is that Buddhism is thought of as an alien or rival religion, forgetting that the watchwords 'Buddha, dharma, sangha' or the *tri-ratna* (three jewels) still define the underlying spiritual and moral foundations of Asian societies.

Buddhism underpins core Asian values. 98 per cent of Buddhist followers live in the Asia–Pacific region. Fourteen Asian countries are more than 50 per cent Buddhist in their populations, seven of which have over 90 per cent of their populations practising Buddhism.

In fact, the powerful Indian sangha concept not only intersects deeply with the social, political and economic contexts of many Asian nations, but also anchors their nationalist assertion. In modern times, Buddhism powerfully spurs the Asian quest for modernity, spirituality, democratic values and economic prosperity.

It is no surprise that even China, after a gap of several decades, is now fervently taking to the 'three-fold refuge'—appropriating sangha ideals to try and arrest the fraying of its moral and social fabric. The CPC is fully aware of how its middle-class population is affected by the economic slowdown and could crumble under the weight of deepening social problems. Sustaining people's modern consumerist living and avoiding the risk of triggering friction between poor farmers and the affluent state elite, which could even potentially affect the CPC's lifespan, is the biggest worry.

It is ironic that India no longer has the fuel for spinning its own dharma wheel, leave aside replenishing that of others. Instead, China's version of Buddhism is already having immense consequences for the Asian landscape.

China's economic rise has certainly boosted its people's quest for spirituality. In fact, after having failed to project Confucianism as an ideal alternative guide for ethical standards, the Chinese state began patronizing Buddhism as an important social and spiritual movement, realizing that it would also make China more acceptable to the world outside.

The world didn't realize how and when China injected new life into the hitherto moribund BAC, established in 1953. The BAC's activities have grown phenomenally both within China and outside.

Within China, the number of people who believe in Buddhism seems to have risen at an astonishing rate. As told to this author in July 2017 by the prominent Chinese scholar Hu Shisheng, the total number of people professing a combination of Buddhism and Taoism in China would be almost one billion. In fact, for the Chinese, the Buddha is not just a teacher but is considered a God, to be worshipped by those seeking salvation.

It is the external dimension of Buddhism that the Chinese are keenly promoting. They are already translating their economic weight into spiritual might—aggressively projecting China as the chief patron of Buddhism on a global scale. In fact, Beijing is doing everything possible to build psychological links with the people of other nations through Buddhism.

Not only has the BAC deepened links with overseas Chinese Buddhists, but it has also done so with other Asian Buddhist nations. With the idea of setting up Confucius centres the world over being abandoned, China seems to be using Buddhism as the latest tool to project the country's softer image and its 'peaceful rise' on the global stage.

Never has China projected Buddhism globally like this before. After 1949, China held the World Buddhist Forum for the first time in 2006. The forum, held four times since, draws thousands of monks from across the world. China now plans to build Lingshan city as the Vatican for Buddhism.

Almost every prominent Buddhist institution in the world seems to have fallen into the BAC's fold. The most prominent, the World Buddhist Sangha Council founded in Sri Lanka in 1966, is run directly by Chinese teachers.

Similarly, the prestigious WFB, founded in Sri Lanka in 1955 by twenty-five nations (headquartered in Bangkok), is currently headed by Masters Hsing Yun and Yi Chen of China and Taiwan. China also hosted the annual general conference of the WFB in 2014 in the city of Baoji that drew global Buddhist leaders.

China's outreach programme extends to cover the sanghas of both the Theravada and Mahayana traditions in Sri Lanka, Thailand, Laos, Cambodia, Myanmar, Korea, Mongolia and other countries. Chinese Buddhists make generous donations to deepen institutional ties through funding Buddhist projects and assisting educational systems, such as the *daham pasala* education system in Sri Lanka. The Chinese Mahayana institutions devote funding to reviving new bhikkhu and bhikkhuni sanghas across Asia.

It is another irony that Buddhist globalization and diplomacy, originally practised by Indian emperors such as Ashoka and Kanishka, are now being employed by the Chinese in their soft-power game. Beijing has started helping friendly countries repair, renovate, resurrect and even build new Buddhist institutions. It garners support in favour of friendly countries to hold major international events such as the UN Vesak Day.

What does this mean for India?

One shouldn't lose sight of the strategic dimension of Buddhism. China sees a great advantage in employing Buddhism alongside its hard-power pursuits, especially to seek political and economic leverage in the context of China's latest OBOR initiative in Asia.

For quite a few years now, China has been conducting 'Buddha relic diplomacy' to improve ties and win important economic and infrastructure projects, such as in Myanmar, Sri Lanka and elsewhere. In Nepal, the BAC tried to invest $3 billion to develop Lumbini as a Buddhist Mecca or mass pilgrimage destination.

In the north, the Chinese are reaching out to rebuild monasteries in Mongolia that were destroyed during the Stalinist era. Beijing is also trying to replay the Ching-era legacy of directly patronizing Mongolian Buddhism. A visit by China's Panchen Lama to Mongolia planned for 2017 did not materialize. Interestingly, the tussle continues over controlling a moribund Soviet-era outfit, the Asian Buddhist Conference of Peace (ABCP), which enjoys UN recognition.

During Prime Minister Modi's visit to Ulaanbaatar, the Mongolian side asked him to help India revive the ABCP. India has seemingly sponsored Mongolia at the Eleventh General Assembly of the ABCP held in Ulaanbaatar on 21–23 June 2019, with delegates from Cambodia, India, Nepal, Russia, South Korea, Sri Lanka and Vietnam, but excluding China.[4]

The politics here is that the Mongolian Buddhist clergy may have at least a notional or symbolic say while selecting the next Dalai Lama. Therefore, the event is linked to the Dalai Lama's succession issue. Interestingly, a Tibetan delegation led by the Venerable Thupten Ngodup, the Nechung Kuten, with representatives from all major Buddhist traditions, were denied visas by Mongolian authorities, thus preventing them from attending the ABCP meet in Ulaanbaatar.[5]

Beijing may also have taken a cue from the Qing Dynasty's (1644–1911) strategic practice of using Tibetan Buddhism as a useful vehicle for enlarging its sphere of influence and projecting its power from afar. In fact, the very powerful theology of Tibetan Buddhism is among the list of weapons that the Chinese seem to have considered best suited to employ even in the Indian Himalayan belt. This may already have achieved some results, starting with control over vital Indian monastic resources and institutions through the shadow influence of Tibetan cultural connectivity. In any case, China always considered the Himalayan region its playground.

To be sure, all these moves have an impact on other nations' political and economic security. China's ability to edge in on India's cultural influence has geopolitical benefits for Beijing.

Modi was quick to gauge how Buddhism could play an attractive role for India in a globalizing marketplace. He certainly pegged the Buddhist connection at the centre of his cultural diplomacy with key Asian countries. He took up the legacy of resurrecting the glory of the ancient Nalanda University left by his predecessor, Manmohan Singh. Unfortunately, Buddhism is being used as yet another front for the rivalry between India and China.

However, there are also systems operating in India that prefer to employ Buddhism for meeting narrow interests, such as using the 'Tibet card' to offset China's influence. Already, the objective of Modi's diplomatic initiatives may have been hijacked by vested interests. Such a myopic approach has always damaged India's ability to manoeuvre in the outside world and worked against the growth of India's own Buddhist legacy.

Instead, India's responsibility should have been to build its own Buddhist profile and employ it for advancing its interests and making sure that China does not gain primacy in Asian Buddhism.

Seeking a rivalry with China over Buddhism is even more unnecessary. Instead, the challenge should be to reach out to the swelling number of Buddhists in China, like Modi did by reaching out to a new generation of Chinese through Weibo microblogging on Buddha Jayanti in 2015. It should make India happy to see China culturally transforming from within and lead to imagining the impact of such a change on India's future ties with China and Asia at large.

More importantly, India needs to take immediate steps to restore millennia-old tourist Buddhist heritage sites lying in ruins. They are directly linked to the spiritual destinies of millions. By improving infrastructure and connectivity, India could tap into the potential of Asian pilgrims. This could provide lucrative employment to many Indians.

Buddhism is now definitely gaining a strategic dimension and, to be a serious player in the game, India needs more than posturing. Initiatives like fixing events and conferences through NGO-style outfits that enjoy neither the spirituality nor the depth of Buddhist scholarship will end in failure. For India to seriously reaffirm its central role, it must facilitate its own Buddhist sangha to emerge in strength.

Creating a powerful council has never been easy, given the fractious nature of monastic communities within the Indian Theravada and Mahayana traditions. The Maha Bodhi Society of India, established in 1891 by Anagarika Dhammapala of Sri Lanka, ostensibly for the resuscitation of Theravada traditions, remains fractured. The All India Bhikkhu Sangha, All India Bhikkhu Maha Sangha and other splintered groups carry no weight on the world stage.

Similarly, India's diverse Mahayana traditions are rife with sectarianism. The foray of Tibetan religious leaders into India may have caused serious disarray among the Indian Mahayana community and affected the growth of the Buddhist leadership in India. It is rather ironic that Buddhanet's World Buddhist Directory does not list a single Indian among the world masters in any of the major Buddhist lineages—Theravada, Mahayana, Zen or Tibetan Vajrayana. It reflects the sorry state of Buddhism in the region where Siddhartha Gautama attained enlightenment.

It is difficult to visualize the creation of a pan-Indian sangha comprising both Theravada and Mahayana traditions, so there is a strong case for creating a Mahayana Buddhist Sangha in India on a priority basis. It is needed not only for handling the complexities of Buddhism-related affairs at the domestic level, but also for anchoring India's soft-power projection at the global level.

This council can be carved out of Himalayan Buddhism and other institutions sprinkled all over the country. There are over 100 big and small Mahayana Buddhist monasteries and centres in the country, with over 12,000 monks and nuns.

Instead of wasting resources on needless activities, the Government of India under its own aegis should draw up a plan to set up a sangha, with the president or prime minister heading the council. It is only through the powerful institution of the sangha order that India would be able to reconnect with the Buddhist world and retain its leadership role.

In order to meet the above challenges, as also to maximally harness India's Buddhist assets, it is important that the government takes the initiative for setting up the Indian Mahayana Sangha Council on a priority basis. While establishing the Indian sangha it should keep in mind the importance of major Indian Mahayana institutions including major Buddhist heads, leaders and scholars. The critical institutions include:

- Tsona Gontse Rinpoche (TGR): It needs to be noted that the most popular lama of Arunachal Pradesh, Rev. Jetsun Tenzin Jampal Wangchuk, popularly known as the Thirteenth Tsona Gontse Rinpoche or T.G. Rinpoche, passed away on 16 May 2014 under mysterious circumstances[6] in New Delhi. T.G. Rinpoche was a high lama of the Gelugpa sect of Himalayan Buddhism who founded the Gontse Gaden Rabgyeling monastery in Tawang.

  Tsona Rinpoche's main monastery is located in Tibet, north of the McMahon Line, but he lived amongst his Monpa people in Tawang region. He remained a strong Indian nationalist and actively served his people and the country both in his spiritual as well as political capacity. Rinpoche held important positions in the Arunachal Pradesh government and contributed towards the development of the state.

  He was a great philanthropist and worked for the poor. He made persistent endeavours towards the preservation and promotion of Buddhism in India. He was the first-ever

Buddhist representative from the Himalayan region to attend the Millennium UN World Peace Summit at the United Nations Assembly Hall.

Tsona Rinpoche's demise has been a loss for the Monpa people of Tawang and for the nation. Immediate steps are required to find his reincarnation within the Monyul in India. The Chinese would be too happy to find his reincarnation inside Tibet so that Beijing could use him as another formidable card to stake claim over Tawang.

- Lama Stagsang Respa (SR): The great Stagsang Respa is the head lama of Ladakh's biggest monastery, the Hemis. He lives in Lhasa and has not returned to India in a long time. Stagsang Lama is nearing eighty and is unlikely to return to Ladakh in the future.

- Kushok Bakula Rinpoche (KBR): The previous Bakula Rinpoche—the long-time MP from Ladakh and former Indian ambassador to Mongolia—played a critical role in mainstreaming the sensitive region of Ladakh with the nation. He passed away in 2003, and his present incarnation is around ten years old. It is important that the new KBR is brought up in the right educational environment in India.

16

Time for a New Tibet Story

In September 2018, China invited me—a long-time sceptic of the country's policies—to visit Tibet. The four-day trip to the Ganzi Tibetan Autonomous Prefecture organized by China's foreign ministry was probably meant to influence perception, and to ensure China's 'Tibet story' reaches the world outside.

The full-time security detail never prevented us from walking out of the hotel to talk to ordinary Tibetans, despite our tightly packed itineraries. The chalked-out routine was more of a leisure trip, with exciting sightseeing tours to visit religious sites, herdsmen dwellings, schools, hospitals, scenic spots, sample Tibetan delicacies, et al.

The official briefs, as opaque as Chinese Internet firewalls, talked mainly about the state's achievements in Tibet. But there was scope of some affable smoke passing through: a lone lama of the Bon sect present at a meeting smiled when I gifted him a packet of Indian sandalwood incense sticks.

There wasn't much scope for entirely disagreeing with the 'achievements'. Ganzi (thrice the size of Punjab) had proven its economic vitality. There wasn't any case of poverty. The Government Work Report (2017) showed the Ganzi Prefecture's GDP at 26.1 billion yuan ($3.74 billion), its fixed assets at 46 billion yuan, and its per capita income at $4250 (urban) and $1500 (rural).[1] The middle-class population drew its income from hydropower, geothermal, solar, mining, tourism, forestry, sandstone, etc.

Ganzi alone produced hydropower of 2,60,000 KW. The mining industry had 3.45 million tonnes of output worth 10 billion yuan.

The area has the world's largest methyl card lithium ore deposits (proven reserves of 18,87,700 tons and potential reserves of 3 million tonnes in an area of 35.96 square kilometres around Kangding, Yajiang and Daofu).[2] Ganzi plans to create a 'China lithium capital' under the ecological mining frame.

Its agro-products, mostly vegetables, are directly supplied to Hong Kong, and the region has a thriving and popular Sino-Tibetan pharmaceutical industry. I saw one in Daofu county.

One could feel the churn in Tibet—ethnic Chinese-owned shops are everywhere and the Tibetans are moving in every direction, buying properties in Chengdu and other cities. I got the sense that Tibetan esotericism was gradually failing against China's commercial reasoning.

Ganzi officials say the 'Holy G' brand brings in billions—of dollars—in revenue. Han tourists flock to enjoy the breathtaking landscapes and the stunning engineering marvels of the tunnels dug through those mountains. It took just three hours to reach Khanding from Chengdu, almost 400 kilometres away. But the traffic on the Sichuan–Tibet Highway was heavy. The planned Sichuan–Tibet Railway will reduce travel time to Lhasa from forty-eight to thirteen hours.

My wish to visit Khanding's Jili monastery couldn't be realized, but on the way upwards one day, I got a chance to see the ancient Lhagang monastery of the Sakya sect. In Daofu, the 300-year-old Gathar Shangbaling monastery where the Seventh Dalai Lama spent seven years from 1728 to 1735 was a sight to behold. The head monk pointed out to me the birthplace of the Eleventh Dalai Lama, Khedrup Gyatso (1708), located a little away from Gathar. The house in which Gyatso was born is being rebuilt now, said the monk.

Even in the Song'an monastery in Danba county, built in the seventeenth century, I stumbled upon some preferential treatment. The lama in-charge from Amdo stopped all foreign tourists but me from entering the Palden-Lhama (Kali Devi) temple. Could it have been my accent in Tibetan that warmed the lama to me, I wondered, since I was told by some locals that my spoken Tibetan was closer to the Amdo dialect.

Whatever it was, I cherish the moment. I had thought before my trip that Tibetans would be generally excited to meet an Indian Buddhist. But I got a somewhat mild response. I had even brought some sacred items from Tibetan shops in Delhi, including *chin-labs* (blessed items) of high lamas, to gift to people in Tibet as I had heard they really liked the holy objects available in India. But nobody seemed too impressed.

Political whispers

I felt that whenever I spoke Tibetan with locals, the officials listened with keen ears. The Tibetans I met were very discreet in making political comments. A lama in the town of Xiede told me that President Xi Jinping was referred to as 'lingxiu'—a wise man. 'People in general are very respectful towards Xi,' he said.

My ears caught some criticism of the Dalai Lama too. When I discreetly asked someone why they weren't inviting the Dalai Lama to return home, the reply was, 'Why should we invite him? He left the country by himself.' In the past, the Chinese have said that all doors are open 'if he gives up the call for independence'. This line is not repeated now. Instead, one official said, 'Any prospect of his return would be resisted by the power elite network; people are more interested in better living than risking uncertainty.'

Obviously, China still suspects the Dalai Lama of harbouring the intention to split Tibet from China. It is wary of his 'disruptive potentials'. It is not ready to risk the chaos ensuing upon his arrival. 'Tibet is an outlying region and its vulnerabilities could be exploited by anti-China forces,' noted an official in Khanding.

Yet I felt that the Dalai Lama is still revered as a god-king by the people although this question was met with polite reticence by local officials. No radical policy change is visible, though nobody I spoke to in Ganzi or Beijing thought reconciliation was coming anytime soon. After decades of vilification of the Dalai Lama, the CPC seemed to have very little room left to bring about a change in public opinion. At the same time, more and more ordinary Chinese seemed to be drawn towards Tibetan Buddhism, which could be judged from the high number of Han pilgrims visiting Tibetan monasteries.

I wasn't entirely certain about my takeaways from the trip. I was certainly amazed by the area's development and natural beauty, but a bit of self-censorship in observation was needed to neither highlight nor undermine China's successes in Tibet. Of course, one has to be careful to not hurt Tibetan sentiments back home by narrating China's 'Tibet story'.

The rhetoric apart, I felt neither any sense of exuberance among the Tibetans nor any sense of nervousness among the Chinese.

On the downside, despite China's high development achievements, some unsettling elements could be felt. The situation concealed as much as it revealed. I could understand the Tibetan obsession for an epistemological- and metaphysical-driven life, but failed to figure out why, as practitioners of the most erudite Buddhist philosophy like the Indians, Japanese, Koreans, Chinese and others, they had failed to adopt the transformative changes.

Perhaps Tibetan thinking is out of sync, perpetuated mostly by its old-fashioned leaders. Clearly, the challenge before young Tibetan masters is not just using Buddhism as a bridge but also recognizing the hard geopolitical reality of employing Buddhism to find common ground and bringing about transformative change in Tibet.

After all, Asian societies have succeeded in spurring an enduring socio-economic change this way.

There certainly wasn't any case of poverty in Tibet but the people's anger against cultural deprivation or interference in religious affairs could be addressed through certain modernizing methods and governance reforms. In fact, addressing the issue of governance, especially economic and cultural concerns, could become one of the initial steps to ease tensions and promote peace-building efforts.

The path ahead

Time is running out for the Dalai Lama. The CTA too has been pleading of late for strengthening efforts to make the return of the Dalai Lama to Potala Palace in Lhasa a reality.[3]

There have been some recent speculations about the Dalai Lama soon returning to Tibet at least to visit the Wutai Shan Mountain in Shanxi, which is sacred to the Bodhisattva Manjushri—the symbolic centre of Tibetan, Mongolian and Manchu unity.

According to former RA&W officer Jayadeva Ranade, Beijing is making a strategic overture to get the Dalai Lama to return home.[4] He speculates this against the backdrop of mounting pressure from the

US on tariffs, growing dissatisfaction with Xi Jinping inside China, apprehension in the CPC about US plans to stir up trouble in Tibet, and finally the rumours circulating in China about the Dalai Lama's health. There is no direct visible indication of Beijing inviting the Dalai Lama to visit China anytime soon. Surely, there is a back-door channel open between the Dalai Lama and Beijing.

But the Dalai Lama's key backer, the United States, under President Trump did not appear inclined to embrace the Tibet issue as he refused to meet the Tibetan leader and instead proposed zero aid in 2018 to the Tibetans, reversing the decades-old American policy of appointing a special coordinator for Tibet, required under the Tibetan Policy Act of 2002.

However, President Trump did sign in December 2018 into law the Reciprocal Access to Tibet Act of 2018 which requires the State Department to punish Chinese officials who bar American officials, journalists and other citizens from going freely to Tibetan areas in China.[5]

The US ambassador to China, Terry Branstad, also insisted on a trip to Tibet in May 2019. He criticized Beijing for interfering in religious freedom and also insisted that China hold talks with the Dalai Lama.[6]

The State Department did submit to Congress its Tibet Negotiations Report in May 2019, highlighting steps taken by the Trump administration in 2018–19,[7] but the report contained nothing substantive except for reiterating the usual oft-repeated concerns about human rights violations and destruction of Tibetan cultural heritage.[8]

Interestingly, President Trump never raised Tibet during his four summit meetings with President Xi Jinping. Rex Tillerson and Mike Pompeo, who succeeded Tillerson as Secretary of State in 2018, have also barely raised the issue with their Chinese counterparts. Although in June 2018, Pompeo did tell the Congress that he would publicly ask China to engage in direct dialogue with representatives of the Dalai Lama, without preconditions.[9]

Ironically, in July 2019, when the US State Department held its Second Annual Ministerial to Advance Religious Freedom,[10] the focus was more on the suppression of Uyghur rights in Xinjiang than on the Tibetans in Tibet.

Pompeo called the mass incarcerations of Uyghurs the 'worst human rights crises' and 'the stain of the century',[11] while Vice-President Mike Pence described the internment camps there were meant for 'round-the-clock brainwashing' to strangle and 'stamp out the Muslim faith.'[12]

Earlier, Nancy Pelosi, speaker of the House of Representatives, had warned that the US risked losing its moral authority[13] if it didn't hold China accountable for its violations of the Uyghurs' rights and called for sanctions against Xinjiang's party secretary, Chen Quanguo, under the Global Magnitsky Act.

President Trump[14] did hold an unscheduled meeting at the event with twenty-seven survivors of religious persecution from sixteen nations. But the focus was again more on Jewher Tohti, the daughter of jailed Uyghur professor Ilham Tohti who told Trump to 'not let the potential monetary gains from trade negotiations silence your country'.

Trump's other meetings included those with a Rohingya Muslim, Christians from North Korea, Myanmar and Vietnam, ethnic Uyghur and Kazakh Muslims, Tibetan Buddhists, Catholics, Protestants and a Falun Gong practitioner, among others.

Notably, when Tibetan activist Nyima Lhamo was pleading with Trump to help the Dalai Lama return to Tibet, he had a perfunctory reply: 'Please say hello!' Perhaps he meant to say hello to the Dalai Lama who had recently called out Trump for 'lacking moral principle'.[15]

Clearly, Tibet no longer seems to be a priority, and Trump's rivalry with China on trade is not necessarily benefiting the Dalai Lama.

Strangely, the United States, which was solely responsible for inducing the Dalai Lama to disavow the Tibetan agreement with China and planned for his flight into exile, has now reached the stage of effectively abandoning it. In fact, the entire Tibetan saga had started with the US Secretary of State Dean Acheson approving of a verbal message transmitted to the Tibetans in August 1951 that the best way the Dalai Lama could serve his people and country was by evading Communist control at the earliest opportunity and by denouncing the agreement with communist China after he reached safe asylum.

It was the then American ambassador in New Delhi, Loy W. Henderson, who on 17 September 1951 conveyed to the Dalai Lama the US readiness to assist him in fleeing on the condition of his public disavowal of the Seventeen-Point Agreement, concluded under duress between his representatives and the Chinese government, signed in May 1951. The Dalai Lama disavowed the agreement after he fled Lhasa in 1959.

Sixty years down the line, there is nothing much in the way of the Dalai Lama proving his achievements in altering the political status of China except his becoming a global icon. At the age of eighty-four, he seems to have been caught in a tight spot. The Trump administration seems disinterested in the Tibetan issue. But it is also true that the Dalai Lama still has friends in the Congress willing to back him, which means the Dalai Lama has to wait for someone like Mike Pence to win the next election.

He has expressed his wish to return home but the Chinese are not responding to his call. But surely he is shrewd enough to sustain his struggle.

While sensing the changes on the global front, a week after Trump's November 2017 China visit, the Dalai Lama abruptly selected two personal emissaries (for an indefinite period) to represent him in all global engagements. He has cited increasing physical fatigue, but the decision to appoint two emissaries was probably meant to send a calibrated signal to China.

Meanwhile, the CTA has been working on a new plan—the Five-Fifty vision—that envisages a five-year strategy for returning to dialogue with China, but also preparing for a fifty-year struggle if needed, along the lines of the 'hope for the best and prepare for the worst' proverb.[16] The Five-Fifty strategy reaffirmed his middle way approach as a realistic political means of realizing the dual aim of his early return to Tibet and fulfilling the aspirations of the Tibetan people.

Clearly, Samdhong's visit forms part of the first five-year plan to engage with China, while Lobsang Sangay has been visiting the US and Western countries with a view to sustain the struggle for the next fifty years, if the first plan fails.

Will the talks succeed now? In the past, Chinese leaders have stymied the Dalai Lama's desire to return to Tibet. But there is a distinct possibility that it may bear fruit this time.

Long back in 1933, the previous Dalai Lama feared that the Tibetan political system would soon disappear without a trace. No sooner did the

Indian consul in Lhasa, Sumal Sinha, note that the Tibetan political elite were making fortunes by collaborating with the Chinese, and the Dalai Lama's authority had 'lost all its generals'.

As for India, the Tibet issue no longer seems to be a crucial sticking point in its relationship with China. India's position has changed considerably under the Modi government. In recent years, New Delhi has been looking for other options to deal with China to safeguard its national interest. India has responded to China's sensitivities with considerable savoir-faire—curtailing activities of the Dalai Lama's government-in-exile.

No wonder then, the ruling BJP's general secretary, Ram Madhav, while speaking at the event to mark the sixtieth year of the Dalai Lama in exile, expressed the hope that the Dalai Lama 'would be able to find a solution to the Tibetan issue through peaceful and democratic means that will facilitate an honourable return to his homeland'.[17] That actually sounded like a farewell speech for the Dalai Lama.

China is unlikely to seek any third-party mediation in Tibet; certainly not from the West, when its role is diminishing in the face of China's rising influence. The UN is also not going to play a role. However, in the changed context, the Russia–India–China (RIC) axis is emerging as an alternative dialogue mechanism for trust-building.

New Delhi's leveraging power with Beijing will go up if it is able to play the Xinjiang card positively—perhaps the time has arrived now to think in this direction. Quite clearly, China does require India's support, even if the issue is to be resolved in its favour. The Wuhan process was probably just about that, and hopefully it will succeed!

New Delhi will do better if it is able to channel its own resources and institutions like the International Buddhist Confederation (IBC) or the ABCP in this direction rather than misleading the Tibetans in the guise of containing China. The Chinese, on their part, need to undertake governance reforms in order to remove Tibetan anger and ease tensions over economic and cultural deprivation.

The overwhelming impression I got during my last visit to Tibet in 2018 was that the Chinese have a high level of self-confidence on Tibet. Most Chinese do not carry reservations about India's intentions vis-à-vis Tibet, but they do remain apprehensive of US policy aimed at dismembering China.

My visit has also given rise to the idea that India should consider the possibility of normalizing ties now that the ice with China is broken. China should allow India to resume its traditional trade and cultural ties with Tibet, including reopening an Indian consulate in Lhasa. Equally vital is to find ways to send high Tibetan lamas back to Tibet if the fruits of the investments made by India in them for such a long time are to be reaped fully.

But one thing is clear: the Tibet lobby in the West has a track record of ensnaring India in its murky agenda, often at the cost of India's national interests.

On his part, the Dalai Lama has lately been giving interview after interview, which indicates his growing anxiety. Recently, he said the Tibet issue is no longer the struggle for political independence. This was probably meant to please China and simultaneously and indirectly pressurize India. To build further pressure on China, he has threatened to decide his next birth and also hinted at taking a rebirth in India this time around.

Beijing, of course, insists on following the old rule and would do anything to prevent the Dalai Lama deciding the future of his status, and this will be the most important game that could last for another century.

But having played this game for too long, India seems to have failed to grasp the dynamic interplay between sectarian affiliation and power politics, between the Tibetan plateau and the political landscape that is the Indian Himalayas. As mentioned earlier, understanding the Tibetan polity in India requires much more than bureaucratic bean-counting!

All in all, even on the Karmapa issue, the policy New Delhi follows is as per Dharamshala's interest without adequately appreciating that it might destabilize the Himalayas, particularly Sikkim, where it could take a geopolitical undertone. It also undermines the sentiments of the rest of the Indian Himalayan people whose faith and traditions are rooted in the Kagyu and Nyingma lineages. Surely, if not careful, India's topsy-turvy Tibet policy is going to bounce back eventually with heavy implications for its defence in the Himalayas—traditionally India's natural frontiers. We saw only a glimpse of it during the Doklam crisis.

Clearly, whatever the government is doing with the Tibetan issue, mindfully or otherwise, without telescopic big-picture thinking, would make many of these look meaningless—it will only end up destabilizing the Himalayas and complicating India–China relations further. In any case, the days of India playing any sort of great game in Tibet seem over.

Clearly then, India has so far either had no independent Tibet policy of its own or been highly dependent on Western assessments, or New Delhi had weighed heavily in the Dalai Lama's thinking. Instead of relying on knowledge rooted in Indian experiences, especially on the statecraft carefully evolved during the British period, India's policy objective for the Himalayas and Tibet is subservience to US policy goals. The time has come to change that.

Notes

Preface

1. 'Himalayan Communities Better Placed to Preserve Buddhism: Dalai Lama', 17 May 2009, https://www.dalailama.com/news/2009/himalayan-communities-better-placed-to-preserve-buddhism-dalai-lama
2. https://mhrd.gov.in/ctsa (accessed 12 January 2018).

Chapter 1

1. Bimalendu Mohanty, 'Odisha's Contribution to Buddhism Written in Golden Letters', *Pioneer*, 14 May 2014. Also read Umakanta Mishra and Subrata Kumar Acharya, 'Buddhist and Saiva Acaryas (Preceptors) in Newly Discovered Inscriptions of Early Medieval Odisha, India', *Pratna Samiksha, A Journal of Archaeology* 7 (2016, accessed 20 March 2019).
2. Umakanta Mishra, 'Searching for the Lotus Pond of Dhanakosha of Guru Rinpoche: An Alternative Approach from the Archaeology of Buddhism in Odisha', in *Padmasambhava of Uddiyana: Odisha*, ed. Bimalendu Mohanty (Bhubaneswar, 2012), pp. 13–33, https://www.academia.edu/10135499/Searching_for_the_lotus_pond_of_Dhanakosha_of_Guru_Rinpoche_Padmasambhava_An_Alternative_approach_from_the_Archaeology_of_Buddhism_in_Odisha (accessed 6 June 2019). Also read 'Teachings on Lamrim Chenmo' by the Dalai

Lama, Lehigh University, Pennsylvania, USA, https://www.lamayeshe. com/article/teachings-lamrim-chenmo (accessed 7 June 2017).

3. Ram Rahul, *Central Asia: An Outline History* (Concept Publishing Company, 1997), p. 34.

4. John Powers, *Introduction to Tibetan Buddhism* (Snow Lion, 2007), p. 476.

5. Min Bahadur Shakya, 'Buddhism in the Himalaya, Its Expansion and the Present-day Aspects', paper presented on the occasion of UNESCO's integral study of the silk roads: Roads of Dialogue Lumbini Development Trust /Nepal National Commission for UNESCO Buddhist Route Expedition, Nepal, 21–30 September 1995, https:// en.unesco.org/silkroad/sites/silkroad/files/knowledge-bank-article/ buddhism_in_the_himalaya_1.pdf (accessed 6 November 2018).

6. David N. Gellner, 'On the So-Called Schools of Nepalese Buddhism', and Todd L. Lewis, 'Mahayana Vratas in Newar Buddhism', *Journal of the International Association of Buddhist Studies* 12.1 (1989). The importance of Indian Buddhist history has been discussed by Lienhard in 'The Survival of Indian Buddhism in a Himalayan Kingdom'. Similarly, Sylvain Levi in a paper, '*Le Nepal*', discussed the survival of Sanskrit Buddhism in the Kathmandu Valley.

7. Acharya Tsultsem Gyatso, 'A Short Biography of Four Tibetan Lamas and Their Activities in Sikkim', trans. Saul Mullard and Tsewang Paljor, *Bulletin of Tibetology* 49 (2005): 57.

8. Ibid, http://himalaya.socanth.cam.ac.uk/collections/journals/bot/pdf/ bot_2005_02_03.pdf (accessed 7 March 2018).

9. 'List of Sikkim Monasteries', Ecclesiastical Affairs Department, Government of Sikkim. Monasteries in Sikkim, Gangtok, Sikkim, India: National Informatics Center/Tashiling Secretariat.

10. John Ardussi, 'Formation of the State of Bhutan (Bruggzhung) in the 17th Century and Its Tibetan Antecedents', *Journal of Bhutan Studies* 11 (2004).

11. G.N. Mehra, *Bhutan: Land of the Peaceful Dragon* (Delhi: Vikas Publishing House, 1974).

12. Online encyclopaedia of the leaders of nations and territories, WorldStatesmen.org at http://www.worldstatesmen.org/Bhutan.html (accessed 13 December 2013).

13. S. Dutta Choudhury, ed., *Gazetteer of India, Arunachal Pradesh, East Kameng, West Kameng and Tawang District*, Government of Arunachal

Pradesh, Shillong, 1996. Also read Kazuharu Mizuno, Lobsang Tenpa, 'Himalayan nature and Tibetan Buddhist culture in Arunachal Pradesh, India: A study of Monpa', *Springer* (2015): 8–9.

14. L.A. Wadell, *The Buddhism of Tibet, or Lamaism* (Cambridge, 1959), p. 385.

15. 'After 400 years the Gyalwang Karmapa Returns to Arunachal Pradesh', 30 July 2018, https://kagyuoffice.org/karmapa

16. Ibid.

17. The three settlement areas of Tsosum comprised of Shar, Shru and Lhau.

18. T.S. Murty, 'Early History of the Mon-Tawang', in *Himalaya Frontier in Historical Perspective*, ed., N.R. Ray (Calcutta: Institute of Historical Studies, 1986), pp. 41–67; cited by Stuart Blackburn, 'Memories of Migration: Notes on Legends and Beads in Arunachal Pradesh, India', https://www.soas.ac.uk/tribaltransitions/publications/file32489.pdf (accessed 2 March 2019).

19. Tsewang Dorji, 'Tibetan Narrative on Tawang: A Historical Approach', *Phayul*, 13 October 2017.

20. L.A. Wadell, *The Buddhism of Tibet, or Lamaism* (Cambridge, 1959), p. 385.

21. The institution of the Dalai Lama as a religious and political order formally came into existence after the supreme head lama of the Drepung monastery in Lhasa. Ngawang Lobsang Gyatso was conferred with the title of Dalai Lama in 1642 by the Mongol ruler Ghurshi Khan (1582–1655). The institution of the Ganden Phodrang government established since then received continued patronage of the Mongol rulers and thereafter the Manchu Qing emperors. The relations between the Manchus, Tibetans and Mongols under the Qing Empire was stitched around the Gelug order based on the *chö-yön* (priest–patron) relationship. The system lasted until the Manchu Empire collapsed in 1911.

22. G.N. Mehra, *Bhutan: Land of the Peaceful Dragon* (Delhi: Vikas Publishing House, 1974).

23. Niranjan Sarkar, 'Tawang Monastery', Directorate of Research, Government of Arunachal Pradesh, 1981.

24. T.S. Murty, 'Early Mon and the Foundation of Tawang Monastery', in *Himalayan Frontiers in Historical Perspective* (Calcutta: Institute of Historical Studies, 1986).

25. 'Article 33, Factual Records of Qing Dynasty 163, fourth month of the thirty-third years of the reign of Emperor Kangxi', as quoted by Chen Qingying, *The Reincarnation System of the Dalai Lama* (China Intercontinental Press, 2014).
26. Rick Fields, 'Footsteps in the Snow: The Life Story and Love Poems of the Sixth Dalai Lama', *Tricycle*, spring 1994, https://tricycle.org/magazine/footsteps-snow (accessed 3 January 2019).
27. HH the Sixth Dalai Lama, 'Some Poems of the Sixth Dalai Lama', *Where Tibetans Write*, 26 December 2007, http://tibetwrites.in/index.html%3F_HH-the-VI-Dalai-Lama_.html (accessed 7 July 2018).
28. Chen Qingying, *The Reincarnation System of the Dalai Lama* (China Intercontinental Press, 2014).
29. 'Memorials from Frontier Pacification General 7, p. 7, on travel to Tibet on the twenty-second day of the fourth month of the fifty-ninth year of Emperor Kangxi's reign', as quoted by Chen Qingying, *The Reincarnation System of the Dalai Lama* (China Intercontinental Press, 2014).
30. Tsangyang Gyatso and Paul Williams, 'Songs of Love, Poems of Sadness: The Erotic Verse of the Sixth Dalai Lama', Dalai Lama VI Tshans-dbyans-rgya-mtsho (I.B.Tauris, 2004), https://www.cse.iitk.ac.in/users/amit/books/gyatso-2004-songs-of-love.html (accessed 6 October 2018), also at HH the VI Dalai Lama, 'Some Poems of the Sixth Dalai Lama', *Where Tibetans Write*, 26 December 2007, http://tibetwrites.in/index.html%3F_HH-the-VI-Dalai-Lama_.html (accessed 7 July 2018).
31. Chen Qingying, *The Reincarnation System of the Dalai Lama* (China Intercontinental Press, 2014), p. 85.
32. 'Tibet Opens Museum to Commemorate 6th Dalai Lama', 5 May 2017, http://in.china-embassy.org/eng/xzjx/t1459268.htm (accessed 5 May 2017).
33. Tibet and Manchu, 'An Assessment of Tibet–Manchu Relations in Five Phases of Historical Development', Department of Information and International Relations, Central Tibetan Administration, Gangchen Kyishong Dharamsala, 2001.
34. Michael Aris, *Hidden Treasures & Secret Lives: A Study of Pemalingpa (1450–1521) and the Sixth Dalai Lama (1683-1706)* (Routledge, 1989).
35. Tsewang Dorji, 'Tibetan Narrative on Tawang: A Historical Approach', *Phayul*, 13 October 2017.

36. Barbara O'Brien, 'Padmasambhava, the Precious Guru of Tibetan Buddhism', 28 February 2019, https://www.thoughtco.com/padmasambhava-450201
37. A.H. Francke, *A History of Western Tibet* (1907).
38. Read the biography of Orgyenpa Rinchen Pel in *Treasury of Lives*, https://treasuryoflives.org/biographies/view/Orgyenpa-Rinchen-Pel/2733 (accessed 3 December 2019).
39. Luciano Petech, *The Kingdom of Ladakh: c. 950–1842 A.D* (Roma: IsMEO, 1977), pp. 171–72.
40. Ibid.
41. Johan Elverskog, *Buddhism and Islam on the Silk Road* (University of Pennsylvania Press), p. 223.
42. Yonten Dargye, Per Sørensen and Gyönpo Tshering, *Play of the Omniscient: Life and Works of Jamgön Ngawang Gyaltshen, an Eminent 17th–18th Century Drukpa Master* (Thimphu: National Library & Archives of Bhutan, 2008).
43. The Tibetan version of the peace treaty between Ladakh and Tibet at Tingmosgang (1684) is reproduced from M.C. van Walt van Praag's 'Status of Tibet: History, Rights and Prospects in International Law', http://www.tibetjustice.org/materials/treaties/treaties2.html (accessed 4 July 2018).

'The Drukpa (red sect) Omniscient Lama, named My-pham-wang-po, who in his former incarnations had always been the patron Lama of the kings of Ladakh, from generation to generation, was sent from Lhasa to Tashis-gang, to arrange the conditions of a treaty of peace-for the Ladak king could never refuse to abide by the decision of the Omniscient One. It was agreed as follows:

1. The boundaries fixed, in the beginning, when king Skyed-Ida-ngeema-gon gave a kingdom to each of his three sons, shall still be maintained.
2. Only Ladakhis shall be permitted to enter into Ngarees-khor-sum wool trade.
3. No person from Ladakh, except the royal trader of the Ladakh Court, shall be permitted to enter Rudok.
4. A royal trader shall be sent by the Deywa Zhung (i.e. the Grand Lama of Lhasa), from Lhasa to Ladakh, once a year, with 200 horse-loads of tea.
5. A 'Lo-chhak' shall be sent every third year from Leh to Lhasa with presents. As regards the quality and value of presents brought for all ordinary Lamas, the matter is of no consequence, but to the Labrang Chhakdzot shall be given the following articles, viz:

(a) Gold dust: the weight of 1 zho 10 times
(b) Saffron: the weight of 1 srang (or thoorsrang) 10 times
(c) Yarkhand cotton cloths: six pieces
(d) Thin cotton cloth: one piece.

The members of the Lapchak Mission shall be provided with provisions, free of cost, during their stay at Lhasa, and for the journey they shall be similarly provided with 200 baggage animals, twenty-five riding ponies, and ten servants. For the uninhabited portion of the journey, tents will be supplied for the use of the mission.

6. The country of Ngaress-khor-sum shall be given to the Omniscient Drukpa Lama, Mee-pham-wang-po, and in lieu thereof the Deywa Zhung will give to the Ladakhi king three other districts (in Great Tibet).

7. The revenue of the Ngarees-khor-sum shall be set aside for the purpose of defraying the cost of sacrificial lamps, and of religious ceremonies to be performed at Lhasa.

8. But the king of Ladakh reserves to himself the village (or district?) of Monthser (Minsar) in Ngaress-khor-sum, that he may be independent there; and he sets aside its revenue for the purpose of meeting the expenses involved in keeping up the sacrificial lights at Kang-ree (Kailash), and the holy lakes of Manasarwar and Rakas Tal.

With reference to the first clause of the treaty, it may be explained that, roughly speaking, king Skyed-Ida-ngeema-gon gave the following territories to his sons:

a. To the eldest son: the countries now known as Ladakh and Purig extending from Hanley on the east to the Zojila Pass on the west, and including Rudok and the Gogpo gold district

b. To the second son: Googey, Poorang and certain other small districts

c. To the third son: Zangskar, Spiti and certain other small districts.

44. In conversation with Dr Smanla in Leh, 2019.

45. Shawaripa,   https://www.palpung.org/english/mahamudra/refugetreemaster/default.asp?thepagename=05_shawaripa (accessed 17 January 2019); also at http://www.chinabuddhismencyclopedia.com/en/index.php/Shawaripa (accessed 17 January 2019).

46. http://ladakh.drukpa.com

47. https://kagyuoffice.org/kagyu-lineage

Chapter 2

1. P.K. Bhattacharya, *Aspect of Cultural History of Sikkim* (Calcutta: K.P. Bagchi & Co., 1984), p. 11.

2. Online encyclopaedia of the leaders of nations and territories, WorldStatesmen.org, http://www.worldstatesmen.org/Bhutan.html (accessed 13 December 2013).

3. Rongthong Kunley Dorji, another spiritual lama and a close associate of Shabdrung, wrote in his article 'My Understanding of Shabdrung' in *Bhutan Today*, 20 July 2014, http://www.bhutandnc.com/aprilmay03_3.htm

4. Sunanda K. Datta, 'From Frothy Romance to Ecstasy', review of *Chronicles of Love and Death: My Years with the Lost Spiritual King of Bhutan*, by Norma Levine, *Telegraph*, 29 April 2011.

5. The Shabdrung was quoted in the *Himalayan Times* as saying, 'I myself am living a life of an exile in India for three decades now despite my wishes, and as such, am virtually helpless at this stage', http://www.bhutandnc.com/aprilmay03_3.htm (accessed 15 April 2014).

6. *Telegraph*, 'Rinpoche Murder Theory Dismissed', 14 April 2003 (accessed 2 June 2018). For more details read 'My Understanding of Shabdrung, by Rongthong Kunley Dorji, https://www.bhutandnc.com/aprilmay03_3.htm (accessed 9 July 2018).

7. Ibid.

8. http://www.chinabuddhismencyclopedia.com/en/index.php/Shabdrung (accessed 9 March 2019).

9. Dhurba Rizal, *The Royal Semi-Authoritarian Democracy of Bhutan* (Lexington Books, 2015), p. 102.

10. Ibid.

11. Indrakari, 'Is New Shabdrung Threat to Bhutanese Royals?' *IPA Journal*, 26 September 2012, http://ipajournal.com/2012/09/26/is-new-shabdrung-threat-to-bhutanese-royals (accessed 11 March 2014).

12. Kuensel Online, 'National Assembly of Bhutan Finalises Rules on Recognition of Trulkus and Lamas', 23 November 2005, https://www.buddhistchannel.tv/index.php?id=40,1977,0,0,1,0#.XQ4NtYgzbIU (accessed 10 June 2019).

13. Dorji Lopon (principal assistant of the Je Khenpo in charge of religious teachings) headed the high-level committee (set up in August 2005). It included Drabi Lopon (master of literary studies) of the Zhung Dratshang,

the Zhung Kalyon, the eminent Ningma lama, Lam Kinzang Wangdi, Sungtruel Rinpoche (speech incarnation Terton Pema Lingpa), Dasho Sigay Dorji of the Royal Advisory Council, home secretary, Dasho Penden Wangchuk, and secretary, dratshang Lhenstshog, Dasho Sangay Wangchug.

14. The verification committee had found that Pema's supporters manipulated a recognition letter from the Karmapa, Ugyen Trinley Dorje, who later realized that he had been forced into issuing the letter and hence withdrew the recognition. The committee quoted from Ugyen Trinley Dorje's letter—since the child and his propagators had indulged in unethical and immoral practices by using the Karmapa's name, he revoked his first letter of recognition.

15. Kuensel Online, 'National Assembly of Bhutan Finalises Rules on Recognition of Trulkus and Lamas', 23 November 2005.

16. In early 2007, the home ministry of Bhutan via the Incarnation Committee, Bhutan Ministry of Culture, ordered the Shabdrung's detention. Buddhist Channel, 'Respected Buddhist teacher under house arrest in Bhutan, 3 February 2007, http://www.buddhistchannel.tv/index.php?id=40,3674,0,0,1,0

17. Indrakari, 'Is New Shabdrung Threat To Bhutanese Royals?' *IPA Journal*, 26 September 2012, http://ipajournal.com/2012/09/26/is-new-shabdrung-threat-to-bhutanese-royals (accessed 11 March 2014).

18. Interview with Pema Tenzin, who attended the Seventh South Asia Conference at IDSA, New Delhi, 30–31 October 2013.

19. Quoted by Sandhya Jain, 'Pema Namgyel Unseen Since 2007', http://www.vijayvaani.com/ArticleDisplay.aspx?aid=2831 (accessed 30 January 2018).

20. S. Dutta Choudhury, ed., *Gazetteer of India, Arunachal Pradesh, East Kameng, West Kameng and Tawang District* (Government of Arunachal Pradesh, Shillong, 1996).

21. The report is quoted by Bertil Litner, *China's India War: Collision Course on the Roof of the World* (New Delhi: Oxford University Press, 2018), p. 112, and also by Lobsang Tenpa.

22. Dawa Norbu, *China's Tibet Policy* (Routledge, 2012), p. 155.

23. Lobsang Tenpa, 'The Centenary of the McMahon Line (1914–2014) and the status of Monyul until 1951–2', *Tibet Journal*, Autumn–Winter 39.2 (2014): 57.

24. Tsering Shakya, *The Dragon in the Land of Snows: A History of Modern Tibet Since 1947* (New York: Columbia University Press, 1999), p. 279.
25. Ibid.
26. The last Tibetan administrator of Tawang was Thubstan Chospel who handed over the charge to Assam Rifles Major R. Khating in 1951. Lobsang Tenpa quotes from L.N. Chakravarty, *Secret: Notes on Indo-Tibetan Relations from: 1772-1951 (with Special References to the McMahon Line)* (1953), describing Thubstan Chospel as a very cunning person and a major thorn in the Tawang administration.
27. Lobsang Tenpa, 'The Centenary of the McMahon Line (1914–2014) and the Status of Monyul until 1951–2', *Tibet Journal*, Autumn-Winter 39.2 (2014): 63.
28. S. Dutta Choudhury, ed., *Gazetteer of India, Arunachal Pradesh, East Kameng, West Kameng and Tawang District* (Government of Arunachal Pradesh, Shillong, 1996).
29. Jian Liang, 'Tawang's History Affirms China's Sovereignty', *Global Times*, 13 April 2017, http://www.globaltimes.cn/content/1042333.shtml
30. S. Dutta Choudhury, ed., *Gazetteer of India, Arunachal Pradesh, East Kameng, West Kameng and Tawang District* (Government of Arunachal Pradesh, Shillong, 1996).
31. Sir Roter Reid, *History of the Frontier Areas Bordering on Assam* (Delhi, Reprinted 1983), p. 294, as also quoted in the *Gazetteer of Arunachal Pradesh*.
32. Alastair Lamb, *The McMahon Line: A Study in the Relations between India, China and Tibet, 1904 to 1914*, two volumes (London: Routledge and Kegan Paul, 1966).
33. Jian Liang, 'Tawang's History Affirms China's Sovereignty', *Global Times*, 13 April 2017.
34. Neville Maxwell, *India's China War* (Anchor Books, 1972), pp. 50–51.
35. Very little is written about Major Ralengnao Khating (1912–90) who was one of the greatest India heroes. He joined the British Indian army in 1941 and served in the Hyderabad and Assam regiments. Later, Major Khating served as cabinet minister in the Manipur maharaja's government. He rejoined the Indian army and served in the Assam Rifles and took the task of liberating the Tawang tract from Tibetan control in 1951. For his excellent service to the nation, Major Khating was absorbed into the newly formed Indian Frontier Administrative Service (IFAS) in 1957. He was awarded the Padma Shri in 1957.

While he served in the IFAS, Major Khating served as the first deputy commissioner of Mokokchung district of Naga Hills, NEFA's chief security commissioner (1962–67), Nagaland's chief secretary (1967–72) and the first Indian ambassador (1972–75) to Burma. The IFAS was created in 1956 and disbanded in 1974 to be merged with the Indian Administrative Service.

36. Bertil Litner, *China's India War: Collision Course on the Roof of the World* (New Delhi: Oxford University Press, 2018), p. 112.

37. S. Dutta Choudhury, ed., *Gazetteer of India, Arunachal Pradesh, East Kameng, West Kameng and Tawang District* (Government of Arunachal Pradesh, Shillong, 1996).

38. Sir Roter Reid, *History of the Frontier Areas Bordering on Assam* (Delhi, reprinted 1983), p. 288, as also quoted in the *Gazetteer of Arunachal Pradesh*.

39. Randeep Ramesh, 'Last Vestige of Old Tibetan Culture Clings on in Remote Indian State', *Guardian*, 20 November 2006, https://www.theguardian.com/world/2006/nov/20/india.china

40. Some reports suggest that Dirang Dzong was used as a prison by the British during the Second World War.

41. A Monpa political activist, Gumbo, told this author so in 2018.

Chapter 3

1. Robert Stanley, 'The Nineteenth-Century Mapping of the Himalaya by the Pundits', https://open.conted.ox.ac.uk/sites/open.conted.ox.ac.uk/files/resources/Create%20Document/12_Stanley_pp113_119%20corrected.pdf; also read Rasoul Sorkhabi, 'The Great Game of Mapping the Himalaya', *Himalayan Journal* 65 (2009), https://www.himalayanclub.org/hj/65/3/the-great-game-of-mapping-the-himalaya (accessed 8 July 2018).

2. Peter Hopkirk, *The Great Game* (London: Barnes & Noble, 1992).

3. Premen Addy, *Tibet on the Imperial Chessboard* (New Delhi: Academic Publishers, 1984), p. 59.

4. Sir Charles Bell, *Tibet Past and Present* (London, 1968), p. 247.

5. Peter Hopkirk, *The Great Game: On Secret Service in High Asia*.

6. Treasury of Lives, 'The Thirteenth Dalai Lama, Tubten Gyatso', https://treasuryoflives.org/biographies/view/Thirteenth-Dalai-Lama-Tubten-Gyatso/3307

7. Alex McKay, 'The British Invasion of Tibet, 1903–04', *Inner Asia* 14.1, Special Issue: The Younghusband 'Mission' to Tibet (2012), pp. 5–25, https://www.jstor.org/stable/24572145; also read the Project Gutenberg ebook of *India and Tibet*, Francis Younghusband, https://www.gutenberg.org/files/48996/48996-h/48996-h.htm (accessed 8 June 2018).

8. Tsering Shakya, 'The Thirteenth Dalai Lama, Tubten Gyatso', https://info-buddhism.com/13th_Dalai_Lama_Tubten_Gyatso_Tsering_Shakya.html (accessed 23 May 2019); also see https://www.tsemrinpoche.com/tsem-tulku-rinpoche/great-lamas-masters/the-thirteenth-dalai-lama-tubten-gyatso.html (accessed 1 June 2019).

9. Phurbu Thinley, 'Tibet–Mongolia Treaty of 1913, a Proof of Tibet's Independence', *Phayul*, 11 December 2008.

10. Elliot Sperling and Muthiah Alagappa, 'The Tibet–China Conflict: History and Polemics', *East-West Center Policy Studies* 7, East-West Center, Hawaii, US, 2004.

11. Department of Information and International Relations, 'Tibet and Manchu: An Assessment of Tibet–Manchu Relations in Five Phases of Historical Development', Central Tibetan Administration, 2008.

12. Chen Qingying, *The Reincarnation System for the Dalai Lama* (China Intercontinental Press, 2014).

13. 'Buddhism is a Science of the Mind: Dalai Lama', https://www.dalailama.com/news/2006/buddhism-is-a-science-of-the-mind-dalai-lama (accessed 3 July 2018); 'Buddhist Science Book In Process Of Finalising: Tibetan Scholars', http://www.thetibetpost.com/en/more/peace-art/3653-buddhist-science-book-in-process-of-finalising-tibetan-scholars (accessed 7 July 2018).

14. Jeremy Hayward and Francisco Varela, eds, *Gentle Bridges: Conversations with the Dalai Lama on the Sciences of Mind* (Shambhala, 2001). For more details read the review by William Kowinski, 'The Science of Tibetan Buddhism: Neuroscientists, Physicists Have Questions, the Dalai Lama #answers', 14 April 2001, https://www.sfgate.com/books/article/The-science-of-Tibetan-Buddhism-2768142.php (accessed 8 July 2018).

15. Sarat Chandra Das, *Journey to Lhasa and Central Tibet* (New Delhi: Manjushri Publishing House, 1970).

16. Dawa Norbu, 'The Europeanization of Sino-Tibetan Relations, 1775–1907: The Genesis of Chinese "Suzerainty" and Tibetan

"Autonomy"', *Tibet Journal* 15.4 (1990): 30, www.jstor.org/stable/43300374; also read Bruce Elleman, Stephen Kotkin and Clive Schofield, *Beijing's Power and China's Borders: Twenty Neighbors in Asia* (Routledge, 2014), p. 206.

17. 'Tibetan and Nepalese Conflict', earlier available on the official website of the Nepal army, now removed.

18. Tricycle, 'Introduction of Drawing Lots from a Golden Urn System', https://tricycle.org/trikedaily/treasury-lives-controversy-golden-urn (accessed 20 January 2019), http://eng.tibet.cn/eng/index/Archive/201903/t20190306_6518871.html (accessed 30 June 2019).

19. Dawa Norbu, 'Imperialism and Inner Asia: How British India and Imperial China redefined the Status of Tibet (1775–1907)', paper presented at national seminar on Ethnicity Politics and Development in Central Asia, 16–17 February 1990, JNU, New Delhi, p. 12.

20. Patrick French, quoted from the Oriental Office Collection, British Library, L/P&S/11/208.

21. Dawa Norbu, 'Chinese Strategic Thinking on Tibet and the Himalayan region', *Strategic Analysis* 32.4, July 2008, p. 692.

22. Dawa Norbu, 'The Europeanization of Sino-Tibetan Relations, 1775–1907: The Genesis of Chinese "Suzerainty" and Tibetan "Autonomy"', *Tibet Journal* 15.4 (1990): 28–74, www.jstor.org/stable/43300374

23. Thubten Samphel, 'Geopolitical Importance of Tibet', CTA, 13 September 2012.

24. Read Patrick Booz, 'To Control Tibet, First Pacify Kham': Trade Routes and 'Official Routes' (Guandao) in Easternmost Kham, Pennsylvania State University, at https://cross-currents.berkeley.edu/sites/default/files/e-journal/articles/booz_0.pdf (accessed 7 June 2018).

25. Treasury of Lives, 'The Thirteenth Dalai Lama', https://treasuryoflives.org/biographies/view/Thirteenth-Dalai-Lama-Tubten-Gyatso/3307 (accessed 8 June 2018).

26. Tsering Shakya, 'Bhutan Can Solve Its Border Problem with China—If India Lets It', *This Week in Asia*, 22 July 2017, https://www.scmp.com/week-asia/geopolitics/article/2103601/bhutan-can-solve-its-border-problem-china-if-india-lets-it

27. Treasury of Lives, 'The Thirteenth Dalai Lama', https://treasuryoflives.org/biographies/view/Thirteenth-Dalai-Lama-Tubten-Gyatso/3307 (accessed 7 June 2018).

28. Melvyn C. Goldstein, 'Religious Conflict in the Traditional Tibetan Estate',   http://case.edu/affil/tibet/booksAndPapers/conflict.html (accessed 7 June 2018).

29. Owen Lattimore, 'Inner Asian Frontiers of China', p. 227, https://faculty.washington.edu/stevehar/Lattimore.pdf as quoted by Patrick French, *Tibet, Tibet: A Personal History of a Lost Land* (UK: Penguin, 2011); also see Warren W. Smith, 'China's Policy on Tibetan Autonomy', East-West Center Working Paper No. 2, 2004.

30. Warren W. Smith (Jr), *Tibetan Nation: A History of Tibetan Nationalism and Sino-Tibetan Relations* (Boulder, CO: Westview Press, 1996), p. 162.

31. Melvyn C. Goldstein, with the help of Gelek Rimpoche, *A History of Modern Tibet, 1913–1951: The Demise of the Lamaist State* (Munshiram Manoharlal Publishers [1993], University of California [1991]), p. 830.

32. Eckart Klein, 'Tibet's Status under International Law', *Tibet-Forum* 2 (1995).

33. Ibid, p. 232.

34. Tsering Shakya, 'The Thirteenth Dalai Lama', Tibetan Buddhism in the West, https://info-buddhism.com/13th_Dalai_Lama_Tubten_Gyatso_Tsering_Shakya.html (accessed 9 June 2018).

35. Ibid.

Chapter 4

1. Alice Albinia, *Empires of the Indus: The Story of a River* (John Murray, 2008), p. 288).

2. https://www.mea.gov.in/in-focus-article.htm?23520/ Encyclopedia+of+IndiaChina+Cultural+Contacts   (accessed   3 September 2018).

3. The use of Indian troops in the Opium Wars apart, the burning of the Summer Palace in Beijing and their deployment as policemen in cities like Shanghai and Hong Kong had created a negative folklore imagery of Indians as bogeymen of the West.

4. Zhitian Luo, 'The Rise of Materialism: A Trend in Twentieth-century Chinese Culture', *Inheritance within Rupture*, https://doi.org/10.1163/9789004287662_011, https://brill.com/view/book/edcoll/9789004287662/B9789004287662_011.xml?crawler=true (accessed 13 March 2019).

5. Sarvepalli Gopal, ed., *Selected Works of Jawaharlal Nehru,* Volume 8, (New Delhi: Orient Longman 1976), p. 709. Also quoted by Madhavi Thampi, *India and China in the Colonial World* (Taylor & Francis, 2017).
6. https://epdf.tips/nehru-routledge-historical-biographies.html (accessed 20 March 2018.
7. Sarvepalli Gopal, 'Jawaharlal Nehru: Europe 1926–1927', *Indian Literature* 48.1 (219) (January–February 2004): 61–74, https://www.jstor.org/stable/23341426 (accessed 28 January 2019).
8. Ibid.
9. 'The History of Sino-Indian Relations and the Border Dispute between the Two Countries', http://new.resurgentindia.org/the-history-of-sino-indian-relations-and-the-border-dispute-between-the-two-countries-5 (accessed 20 June 2018).
10. The text of the Seventeen-Point Plan for the Peaceful Liberation of Tibet (1951) is available at http://www.tibetjustice.org/materials/china/china3.html. By signing the 1951 agreement, the Tibetans lost control of their treaty-making power to China and by implication India lost even the legal trading agencies in Tibet.
11. 'Thirty years of India–China relations (1947–79)', *China Report* 15.3 (May–June 1979): 142.
12. Jia Liang, 'Tawang's History Affirms China's Sovereignty', *Global Times,* 13 April 2017, http://www.globaltimes.cn/content/1042333.shtml
13. http://www.mea.gov.in/Uploads/PublicationDocs/191_panchsheel.pdf (accessed 9 July 2018).
14. Quoted by R.N. Ravi, '60 Years on: Unforgiving Legacy of the Panchsheel Agreement', https://www.rediff.com/news/column/60-years-on-unforgiving-legacy-of-the-panchsheel-agreement/20140429.htm (accessed 3 July 2018), Also read Claude Arpi, *Born in Sin: The Panchsheel Agreement* (New Delhi: Mittal Publications, 2004).
15. Claude Arpi, 'The Famous Five That Broke India's Back', *Pioneer,* 24 April 2014.
16. https://www.mea.gov.in/bilateral-documents.htm?dtl/7807/Agreement+on+Trade+and+Intercourse+with+Tibet+Region (accessed 29 June 2018).
17. Stuart Reynolds Schram, 'Mao Zedong: Chinese Leader', 22 December 2018, https://www.britannica.com/biography/Mao-Zedong
18. Ibid.

19. Neville Maxwell, 'Settlements and Disputes: China's Approach to Territorial Issues', *Economic and Political Weekly* 41.36 (9–15 September 2006): 3873–81.

20. English translation of *li* is 'propriety' and some Chinese scholars explains its meaning in the Five Constant Virtues (五常 wu chang: 仁 ren, benevolence; 义 yi, righteousness; 礼 li, propriety; 智 zhi, wisdom; and 信 xin, fidelity). Read Xue Li and Cheng Zhangxi, 'What Might a Chinese World Order Look Like? Using the Ancient Concept of Li to Understand a Chinese Order', 13 April 2018.

21. Alice Albinia, *Empires of the Indus: The Story of a River* (John Murray, 2008), p. 288.

22. D. Devahuti, *Harsha: A Political Study* (Oxford University Press, 1983). The book has the entire *stotra* of Harsha, transcribed by Fatien in the tenth century and preserved in China.

23. Heilbrunn Timeline of Art History, 'Cosmic Buddhas in the Himalayas', https://www.metmuseum.org/toah/hd/cbud/hd_cbud.htm (accessed 7 December 2018).

24. Read Tang Chung, 'Himalaya Calling: The Origins of India and China', *World Century*, 2015.

25. Joe Thomas Karackattu, 'India–China Border Dispute: Boundary-Making and Shaping of Material Realities from the Mid-nineteenth to Mid-twentieth Century', *Journal of the Royal Asiatic Society of Great Britain & Ireland*, 24 July 2017.

26. Note given by the MEA, New Delhi, to the Embassy of China in India on 5 January 1962 with reference to the Indian mission in Lhasa and the trade agencies in Gartok, Yatung and Gyantse, 'Notes, Memoranda and Letters Exchanged and Agreements Signed between the Governments of India and China', White Paper VI, December 1961–July 1962.

27. Nehru gave a report on the Indian trade agency buildings in Gyantse in the Lok Sabha on 6 August 1959. *Selected Works of Jawaharlal Nehru* 2.51, 1–31 August 1959.

28. http://shodhganga.inflibnet.ac.in/bitstream/10603/86843/11/11_chapter%202.pdf (accessed 9 June 2018).

29. See 6 August 1959, Lok Sabha Debates, Vol. XXXII, cols 930–34 and also see the *Selected Works of Jawaharlal Nehru* 2.51, 1–31 August 1959. Also see 6 August 1959, Lok Sabha Debates, Vol. XXXII, cols 930–34.

30. http://shodhganga.inflibnet.ac.in/bitstream/10603/86843/11/11_chapter%202.pdf (accessed 9 June 2018).

31. See note, the ambassador of India to China (G. Parthasarathi) to the Chinese Foreign Office, 25 July 1959; Government of India, Ministry of External Affairs, 'Notes, Memoranda and Letters Exchanged and Agreements Signed between the Governments of India and China, 1954–1959', White Paper (New Delhi, 1959), pp. 92–95.

32. http://shodhganga.inflibnet.ac.in/bitstream/10603/86843/11/11_chapter%202.pdf

33. 'Thirty Years of India–China Relations', *China Report*, p. 45.

34. As quoted by Neville Maxwell, 'Sino-Indian border dispute reconsidered', *Economic and Political Weekly* 34.15 (10–16 April 1999), pp. 905–18.

35. Daljit Sen Adel, *China and Her Neighbours* (New Delhi: Deep & Deep, 1984), pp. 22–23, http://shodhganga.inflibnet.ac.in/bitstream/10603/86843/11/11_chapter%202.pdf

36. Ibid.

37. Ibid.

38. Ibid, p. 13.

39. 'Premier Chou En-lai's Letter to Prime Minister Nehru (8 September 1959)', https://digitalarchive.wilsoncenter.org/document/175958.pdf?v=bfc618a2773b51fbbe159096697b640a (accessed 4 March 2018).

40. Letter from the prime minister of India to the prime minister of China, New Delhi, 22 March 1959, http://www.archieve.claudearpi.net/maintenance/uploaded_pics/SW47.pdf; also read Karunakar Gupta, 'Hidden History of the Sino-Indian Frontier: II: 1954–1959', *Economic and Political Weekly* 9.19 (11 May 1974): 765–69.

41. Robert J. McMahon, 'Food As a Diplomatic Weapon: The India Wheat Loan of 1951', *Pacific Historical Review* 56.3 (August 1987): 349–77, https://www.jstor.org/stable/3638663 (accessed 28 January 2019).

42. 'Sino-Indian War 1962: Causes and Consequences', http://shodhganga.inflibnet.ac.in/bitstream/10603/86843/11/11_chapter%202.pdf (accessed 9 April 2018).

43. P.C. Chakravarti, *India–China Relations* (Calcutta, 1961), p. 93, http://shodhganga.inflibnet.ac.in/bitstream/10603/63962/9/09_chapter%205.pdf

44. To cite a few, read Jack Anderson, *The Anderson Papers* (New York: Random House, 1973); Thomas Powers and Richard Helms, *The Man Who Kept the Secrets* (Knopf, 1979); Kenneth Conboy and James Morrison, *The CIA's Secret War in Tibet* (University Press of Kansas, 2002).

45. Tsering Shakya, *The Dragon in the Land of Snows* (Penguin, 2000), p. 207.

46. Lok Sabha Debates, Vol. 28, 1959, cols 9274–76.

Chapter 5

1. 'Indo-China relations from Cold War to Détente', *China Report*, Sage Journals (May–June 1976): p. 59.

2. Sarvepalli Gopal, *Jawaharlal Nehru: A Biography*, Volume 2 (Oxford, 1984), p. 138.

3. Jawaharlal Nehru, *India's Foreign Policy: Selected Speeches, 1946–47* (New Delhi: Publication Division, Ministry of Information and Broadcasting, Government of India, 1961), p. 435.

4. Bhabani Sen Gupta, *The Fulcrum of Asia* (New York: St Martin Press, 1970), p. 105.

5. Benjamin Zachariah, *Nehru* (London: Routledge, 2004), https://epdf.tips/nehru-routledge-historical-biographies.html   (accessed   2 September 2018).

6. Ibid, p. 206. Also read Joel Whitney's article 'How the CIA Sponsored Indian Magazine that Engaged the Country's Best Writers', Wire, 15 March 2017.

7. S. Gopal, *Jawaharlal Nehru: A Biography, Vol. 3* (Jonathan Cape, 1984), p. 122.

8. Benjamin Zachariah, *Nehru*, p. 235.

9. Tan Chung, ed., *Across the Himalayan Gap: An Indian Quest for Understanding China* (1998), http://ignca.gov.in/eBooks/India_world_ks_41.pdf (accessed 30 May 2019).

10. B.N. Mullik, *My Years with Nehru: The Chinese Betrayal* (Bombay, New York: Allied Publishers, 1971).

11. Lok Sabha Debates, Vol. 27,1959, cols 6683.

12. Ibid, Vol. 28, 1959 cols 7707–78.

13. Ibid, p. 171.

14. Ramachandra Guha, 'Jawaharlal Nehru and China: A Study In Failure?', https://www.harvard-yenching.org/sites/harvard-yenching.org/files/featurefiles/Ramachandra%20Guha_Jawaharlal%20Nehru%20and%20China.pdf (accessed 30 December 2018).

15. Benjamin Zachariah, *Nehru*.

16. Ramachandra Guha, 'Jawaharlal Nehru and China: A Study In Failure?', https://www.harvard-yenching.org/sites/harvard-yenching.org/files/featurefiles/Ramachandra%20Guha_Jawaharlal%20Nehru%20and%20China.pdf (accessed 30 December 2018).

17. V. Longer, *The Defence and Foreign Policies of India* (New Delhi, 1988), p. 85.

18. Benjamin Zachariah, *Nehru*, p. 244.

19. 'On the Tibetan Uprisings, 1959: The Policy & the Parliamentary Responses', https://shodhganga.inflibnet.ac.in/bitstream/10603/63962/9/09_chapter%205.pdf (accessed 4 January 2019). Also read Chanakya Sen, ed., *Tibet Disappears: A Documentary History of Tibet's International Status* (New Delhi: Asia Publishing House, 1960), https://archive.org/stream/in.ernet.dli.2015.136485/2015.136485.Tibet-Disappears_djvu.txt (accessed 7 July 2018).

20. P.C. Chakravarti, *India's China Policy* (Bloomington: Indiana University Press, 1962), p. 91.

21. Ibid, p. 98.

22. As quoted by Ranjit Kalha, 'There Is No Tibet Card for India to Play. Here's Why', Wire, 13 January 2017.

23. Lok Sabha Debates, Vol. 30, 1959, cols 13,499–502.

24. Lok Sabha Debates, Vol. 31, 1959, cols 15,925–35.

25. http://shodhganga.inflibnet.ac.in/bitstream/10603/63962/9/09_chapter%205.pdf (accessed 30 July 2018).

26. Chanakya Sen, ed., *Asia: Tibet Disappears* (Mumbai: Asia Publishing House, 1960).

27. General Assembly official records, 1959, Session 14, Plenary Meeting 834, pp. 519–21.

28. Ram Rahul was a professor of Himalayan studies at the School of International Studies at JNU and he claimed that he had advised Nehru on the issue. He was admittedly never consulted by the government in 1959 after the Dalai Lama landed up in India for the second time.

29. CIA Staff Study, 'The Sino-Indian Border Dispute', Section 3: 1961–62, Reference Title: POLO XVI, 5 May 1964, p. 6; declassified with redactions in May 2007.

30. Conversation with former foreign secretary of India, Shivshankar Menon.

31. Chanakya Sen, *Asia: Tibet Disappears*, p. 201.

32. Melvyn C. Goldstein, *A History of Modern Tibet, Volume 2: The Calm Before the Storm: 1951–1955* (University of California Press, 2007), p. 228.

33. Ibid, p. 232.

34. Note given by the Chinese Foreign Office to the Indian counsellor in Peking, 23 June 1959, 'Notes, Memoranda and Letters Exchanged and Agreements Signed between the Governments of India and China, 1954–1959, White Paper 1', Extracts (1959), MEA, Government of India, http://www.claudearpi.net/wp-content/uploads/2016/12/White_Paper1_1959new.pdf (accessed 20 January 2019).

35. Quoted by Ramachandra Guha, *Patriots and Partisans* (UK: Penguin, 2016).

36. Quoted in Neville Maxwell, *India's China War*, p. 250.

37. The operation, code-named ST CIRCUS, was one of the CIA's longest-running projects since 1957 until 1969. It was a cover name for the training of Tibetan guerillas on the island of Saipan, and at Camp Hale in Colorado.

38. CIA/RSS DD/I Staff Study, 'The Sino-Indian Border Dispute', Section 3: 1961–62', Reference Title POLO XVI, 5 May 1964, p. 6; declassified with redactions in May 2007, at https://www.cia.gov/library/readingroom/docs/polo-09.pdf (accessed 21 December 2015).

39. Benjamin Zachariah, *Nehru*.

40. Quoted by Hemen Ray, 'Sino-Soviet Conflict Over India: An Analysis of the Causes of Conflict Between Moscow and Beijing Over India Since 1949', Abhinav Publications, 1986, p. 12.

41. Joe F. Leeker, *Missions to Tibet*, https://www.utdallas.edu/library/specialcollections/hac/cataam/Leeker/history/Tibet.pdf (accessed 4 May 2019).

42. Quoted by Praful Bidwai, 'The Panic of 1962', *Frontline*, 17 December 2010.

43. Benjamin Zachariah, *Nehru*.

44. Jack Anderson, *The Anderson Papers* (New York: Random House, 1973).
45. Thomas Powers, *The Man Who Kept the Secrets* (Knopf, 1979).
46. James Morrison, *The CIA's Secret War in Tibet* (University Press of Kansas, 2002).
47. 'Register of the Bruce Walker papers', https://oac.cdlib.org/findaid/ ark:/13030/kt067nd9sk (accessed 4 January 2019).
48. Mikel Dunham, *Buddha's Warriors: The Story of the CIA-Backed Tibetan Freedom Fighters, the Chinese Invasion, and the Ultimate Fall of Tibet* (Tarcher Perigee, 2004).
49. https://www.utdallas.edu/library/specialcollections/hac/cataam/ Leeker/history/Tibet.pdf (accessed 4 May 2019).
50. Joe F. Leeker, https://www.utdallas.edu/library/specialcollections/hac/ cataam/Leeker/history/Tibet.pdf (accessed 4 May 2019).
51. Livemint, 'The Nanda Devi Mystery', 18 April 2015, https://www. livemint.com/Leisure/3QfYqLadggrbnrn41H0mAJ/The-Nanda-Devi-mystery.html (accessed 8 January 2019). Also read *Economic Times*, 'James Bond in the Himalayas: The Buried Secret of Nanda Devi', 10 August 2018, https://economictimes.indiatimes.com/news/ defence/james-bond-in-the-himalayas-the-buried-secret-of-nanda-devi/articleshow/65350186.cms?from=mdr (accessed 6 August 2019).
52. James Morrison, *The CIA's Secret War in Tibet*, p. 174.
53. CIA Staff Study, 'The Sino-Indian border dispute', Section 3: 1961–62, Reference Title: POLO XVI, 5 May 1964, p. 6; declassified with redactions in May 2007, https://www.cia.gov/library/readingroom/ docs/polo-09.pdf (accessed 21 December 2015).

Chapter 6

1. John Garver, 'The Unresolved Sino-Indian Border Dispute: An Interpretation', *China Report* 47.2 (2011): 99.
2. 'Cultural Roots of Arunachal Pradesh', Government of India, https://blog. mygov.in/cultural-roots-of-arunachal-pradesh (accessed 2 March 2019).
3. Malinithan Temple, https://www.indianmirror.com/temples/ malinithan-temple.html (accessed 4 May 2018).
4. 'Bhismaknagar', Government of Arunachal Pradesh, https://web. archive.org/web/20170611120146/http://arunachalpradesh.gov.in/ bnagar.htm (accessed 23 February 2019).

5. Sumit Ganguly and William R. Thompson, *Asian Rivalries: Conflict, Escalation, and Limitations on Two-Level Games* (Stanford, California: Stanford Security Series, 2011), p. 101.

6. S. Dutta Choudhury. *Gazetteer of India, Arunachal Pradesh, East Kameng, West Kameng and Tawang District*, 1996.

7. Zhang Han, 'Buddhism encouraged to serve BRI', *Global Times*, 17 October 2018.

8. John Garver, *Protracted Contest: Sino-Indian Rivalry* (New Delhi, Oxford University Press, 2001).

9. Minerals and mining, 23 June 2014, http://www.tibetnature.net/en/minerals-mining (accessed 3 June 2018).

10. The vice director of the China Geological Survey Bureau announced preliminary estimates of 30 to 40 million tonnes of copper, 40 million tonnes of lead and zinc and billions of tonnes of iron. Xinhua, 'Huge Mineral Resources Found on Qinghai-Tibet Plateau', 13 February 2007, http://www.chinadaily.com.cn/bizchina/2007-02/13/content_833286.htm.

11. Ibid.

12. PTI, 'Now, China Finds $100bn Mineral Deposits in Tibet', 6 December 2010.

13. Multinational Monitor, 'The Scorched Earth: China's Assault on Tibet's Environment', https://multinationalmonitor.org/hyper/issues/1992/10/mm1092_08.html (accessed 5 October 2018).

14. 'Tibet: A Human Development and Environment Report, 2007', https://tibet.net//wp-content/uploads/2011/08/TibetAHuman DevelopmentAndEnviromentReport.pdf (accessed 8 September 2018).

15. *Hindustan Times*, 'Dalai Lama Calls for Protection of Tibet's Environment', 20 October 2015, https://www.hindustantimes.com/punjab/dalai-lama-calls-for-protection-of-tibet-s-environment/story-XdYiDOyNYrrpKJdQM8ETaP.html (accessed 20 October 2018). Also read Dechen Palmo, 'The World's Third Pole is Melting', https://tibet.net/2019/03/the-worlds-third-pole-is-melting (accessed 5 October 2018).

Chapter 7

1. G. Deshingkar, 'India–China Relations: The Nehru Years', *China Report*, Sage Journals, 1 May 1991.

2. Claude Arpi, 'The Indian Village in Tibet', Rediff, 13 February 2018, https://www.rediff.com/news/special/the-indian-village-in-tibet/20180213.htm (accessed 9 March 2018).

3. 'Notes, Memoranda and Letters Exchanged and Agreements Signed between the Governments of India and China', White Paper II (September–November 1959), MEA, p. 57.

4. 'The History of Sino-Indian Relations and the Border Dispute between the Two Countries', http://new.resurgentindia.org/the-history-of-sino-indian-relations-and-the-border-dispute-between-the-two-countries-5 (accessed 2 January 2019).

5. http://shodhganga.inflibnet.ac.in/bitstream/10603/28609/7/07_chapter%201.pdf (accessed 20 January 2019).

6. 'Seventeen-point Plan for the Peaceful Liberation of Tibet', 1951, http://www.tibetjustice.org/materials/china/china3.html (accessed 9 June 2019).

7. 'Sino-Indian Trade Agreement over Tibetan Border', 1954, http://www.tibetjustice.org/materials/china/china4.html (accessed 2 June 2019).

8. 'The fruits of the forum will be borne by younger generation of the Tibetan people in future: Former kalon tripa Professor Samdhong Rinpoche at Five-Fifty Forum', https://tibet.net/2017/10/the-fruits-of-the-forum-will-be-borne-by-younger-generation-of-the-tibetan-people-in-future-former-kalon-tripa-prof-samdhong-rinpoche-at-five-fifty-forum (accessed 21 January 2019).

9. Bertil Lintner, 'Did the Dalai Lama Prefer Exile in Myanmar to India?', Asia Times, 15 July 2017, https://www.tibetsun.com/features/2017/07/15/did-the-dalai-lama-prefer-exile-in-myanmar-to-india; also read Bertil Lintner, China's India War: Collision Course on the Roof of the World (Oxford University Press, 25 January 2018).

10. Melvyn C. Goldstein, A History of Modern Tibet, Volume 2: The Calm Before the Storm: 1951–1955 (University of California Press, 2007), p. 232.

11. Times of India, 'Tawang is part of India: Dalai Lama', 4 June 2008, http://timesofindia.indiatimes.com/articleshow/3097568.cms?&utm_source=contentofinterest&utm_medium=text&utm_campaign=cppst (retrieved 30 August 2018).

12. PTI, 'Arunachal "Inseparable Part" of India: Tibetan PM', 6 December 2006.

13. Nilova Roy Chaudhury, 'China Lays Claim to Arunachal', Hindustan Times, 19 November 2006.

14. Foreign ministry spokesperson Lu Kang's regular press conference on 12 April 2017, http://is.china-embassy.org/eng/fyrth/t1453181. htm

15. View expressed with the author at the China Tibetology Research Center (CTRC) in Beijing, September 2018.

16. Tsewang Dorji, 'Tibetan Narrative on Tawang: A Historical Approach', *Phayul*, 13 October 2017.

17. Tashi Phuntsok, 'How Could India Expect to Have the McMahon Line without Recognizing Tibet As an Occupied Territory?', *Phayul*, 27 November 2006, http://www.phayul.com/news/article. aspx?id=14892&t=1

18. Lobsang Tenpa, 'The Centenary of the McMahon Line (1914–2014) and the Status of Monyul until 1951–2', *Tibet Journal*, Autumn–Winter 39.2 (2014).

19. Nayanjyoti Medhi, 'Dalai Lama Not to Appoint Tawang Monastery Abbot', 24 May 2016, https://inshorts.com/en/news/dalai-lama-not-to-appoint-tawang-monastery-abbot-1464092845693

20. Sangeeta Barooah Pisharoty, 'The Chinese Response Isn't the Only Reason the Dalai Lama's Visit to Tawang Is Significant', Wire, 4 April 2017.

21. Jarpum Gamlin, 'Beneath the Fissures', *The Hindu BusinessLine*, 20 May 2016, https://www.thehindubusinessline.com/blink/know/beneath-the-fissures/article8621329.ece

22. http://arunachal24.in/tawang-dalai-lama-inaugurates-dorjee-khandu-memorial-museum (accessed 23 March 2018).

23. https://www.dalailama.com/news/2017/empowerment-and-visits-to-ugyen-ling-the-dorje-khandu-memorial-museum (accessed 23 March 2018).

24. http://www.phayul.com/news/article.aspx?id=38353&t=1 (accessed 23 November 2018).

25. Ashish Chakravarti, '1947 to 2009, Claim to Tawang Is Shed: A Twist in a Future Tale', *Telegraph*, 9 November 2009, https://www.telegraphindia.com/india/1947-to-2009-claim-to-tawang-is-shed-a-twist-in-a-future-tale/cid/573979 (accessed 10 July 2018).

26. *South China Morning Post*, 'Mongolia Pledges to Halt Visits by the Dalai Lama', https://www.scmp.com/news/china/diplomacy-defence/article/2056498/mongolia-pledges-halt-visits-dalai-lama (accessed 23 July 2018).

Chapter 8

1. Shivshankar Menon, *Choices: Inside the Making of India's Foreign Policy* (New Delhi: Penguin Books, 1985).
2. Ibid.
3. Dai Bingguo's statement as reported by *Financial Express*, 3 March 2017.
4. PTI, 'Concession on Tawang Can Resolve India–China Border Dispute, Says Former Chinese Diplomat', 3 March 2017.
5. M.K. Narayanan, 'Cross Signals Across the Himalayas', *The Hindu*, 15 April 2017.
6. Ibid.
7. International Campaign for Tibet, 'Chinese Policy and Dalai Lama's Birthplace', 2014, https://savetibet.org/chinese-policy-and-the-dalai-lamas-birthplaces/#2 (accessed 7 July 2018).
8. Ibid.
9. Reuters, 'China Opposes India Hosting Dalai Lama in Arunachal Pradesh', https://in.reuters.com/article/china-india-dalailama-idINKB N1721E9 (accessed 4 July 2018).
10. Roland L. Higgins, 'The Tributary System', http://www.olemiss. edu/courses/pol337/tributar.pdf (accessed 24 June 2014); see Garver, *The Unresolved Sino-Indian Border Dispute*, p. 103. Norbu, *Chinese Strategic Thinking on Tibet and the Himalayan Region*, p. 692. Wang, quoted in Topygal, 'Charting the Tibet Issue in the Sino-Indian Border Dispute'.
11. *The Hindu*, 'Arunachal Pradesh Not Part of India, says Beijing', 26 July 2003.
12. P. Stobdan, 'Never Trust China', *Outlook*, November 27, 2006; Rediff, 'Arunachal Pradesh is our territory: Chinese envoy', https:// www.rediff.com/news/2006/nov/14china.htm (accessed 23 December 2018).
13. Wire, 'India Need Not Worry about China's Bluster on Tawang and the Dalai Lama', 9 April 2017, https://thewire.in/diplomacy/122468 (accessed 3 January 2018).
14. https://www.ibcworld.org
15. http://www.phayul.com/news/article.aspx?id=38353&t=1 (accessed 8 June 2018).
16. *Financial Express*, 'Australian Cricket Team Meets Dalai Lama in Dharamshala; Has India Snubbed China?', 24 March 2017,

https://www.financialexpress.com/sports/by-getting-australia-to-play-in-dharamshala-is-india-snubbing-its-nose-at-china/600896

17. *Times of India*, 'Dalai Lama and Tibet: India's Leverage against China', 3 April 2017.

18. Claude Arpi, 'On Dalai Lama, India Stops Being Defensive', 15 December 2016.

19. *The Hindu*, 'China Slams India over Invite to Dalai Lama at Rashtrapati Bhavan', 16 December 2016.

20. NDTV, 'China Says Delhi "Insisted" on Dalai Lama at Rashtrapati Bhavan', 16 December 2016.

21. *India Today*, 'China Tells India to "Not Complicate" Border Issue after Karmapa Visit, 5 December 2016.

22. http://www.phayul.com/news/article.aspx?id=38353&t=1 (accessed 7 July 2018).

23. http://www.tibetanreview.net/mongolia-welcomes-dalai-lama-despite-strong-chinese-objections (accessed 2 March 2018); also read Associated Press, 'Dalai Lama Preaches in Mongolia, Risking China Fury', 20 November 2016, https://www.apnews.com/0900814ceeb74674ba1998265dc18686 (accessed 2 March 2018).

24. *Hindustan Times*, 'China Angry at Dalai Lama's Nalanda Visit, Says Move Could Disrupt Ties with India', 21 March 2017.

25. Jaishankar had visited Beijing in February 2017 and met Yang Jiechi, chief negotiator on the border, Foreign Minister Wang Yi and Executive Vice Foreign Minister Zhang Yesui.

26. While in Assam, the Dalai Lama recalled how he escaped from Tibet way back in 1959 and was received by Indian officials on the border in the Kameng sector, but he didn't refer to how a contingent of Assam Rifles evicted Tibetan troops from Tawang in the 1930s. But, in what turned out to be a damp squib, a warning coming from a faction of ULFA led by Paresh Barua asked the Dalai Lama not to make any remarks against China during his visit to the region.

27. Pratul Sharma, 'No Political Motive behind Dalai Lama's Visit to Arunachal, Says India', 9 March 2017.

28. *Financial Times*, 'China Accuses India of Using Dalai Lama against It', https://www.ft.com/content/7c6a121c-1a8d-11e7-bcac-6d03d06 7f81f (accessed 3 April 2018).

29. *Indian Express*, 'Dalai Lama's Arunachal Visit: China Said No to Foreign Ministers' Meet in Delhi', 5 May 2017.

30. Liu Jianxi, 'New Delhi Using Dalai As Diplomatic Tool Harms Sino-Indian Ties', *Global Times*, 5 April 2017.

31. Firstpost, 'Dalai Lama in Arunachal Pradesh: How the Happy Warrior Has Consistently Taken on China', 5 April 2017 , https://www.firstpost.com/world/dalai-lama-in-arunachal-pradesh-how-the-happy-warrior-has-consistently-taken-on-china-3368630.html

32. Foreign ministry spokesperson's regular press conference, 17 April 2017, http://durban.chineseconsulate.org/eng/fyrth/t1454241.htm (accessed 4 June 2018).

33. Jyoti Malhotra, 'Chinese Media Is Right, Modi's Stand on Dalai Lama Is Big Change', NDTV, 5 April 2017.

34. M.K. Narayanan, 'Cross Signals Across the Himalayas', *The Hindu*, 14 April 2017.

35. Jyoti Malhotra, 'Chinese Media Is Right, Modi's Stand On Dalai Lama Is Big Change', NDTV, 5 April 2017

36. Jaideep Mazumdar, 'Dalai Lama's Current Arunachal Tour Marks Burial Of '62 Ghost', Swarajya, https://swarajyamag.com/politics/dalai-lamas-current-arunachal-tour-marks-burial-of-62-ghost (accessed 4 March 2018).

37. *Times of India*, 'Dalai Lama Wraps Tawang Visits, Promises to Attend *Kalachakra* Ritual Next January', 11 April 2017, https://timesofindia.indiatimes.com/india/dalai-lama-wraps-tawang-visits-promises-to-attend-kalachakra-ritual-next-january/articleshowprint/58131303.cms

38. P. Stobdan, 'Is India Playing the Tibet Card?', *India Today*, 16 December 2016.

39. Told to this author by a member of the Mongolian delegation at the international Buddhist conference on 'The Relevance of Buddhism in the 21st Century' at Nalanda in March 2017.

40. Reuters, 'Mongolia Says Dalai Lama Won't Be Invited Again', 22 December 2016.

41. Zolzaya Erdenebileg, 'China–Mongolia Relations: Challenges and Opportunities', China Briefing, 6 January 2017. Also read P. Stobdan, 'Is India Playing the Tibet Card?', *India Today*, 16 December 2016.

42. *Times of India*, 'India Responds to Mongolia's SOS on Chinese Sanctions', 9 December 2016.

43. *Hindustan Times,* 'Chinese Media Says Mongolia's Call to India for Help "Politically Harebrained"', 9 December 2016.

44. Indrani Bagchi, 'India to Help Mongolia, Staying Away from Its Spat with China', *Times of India*, 8 December 2016.

45. NDTV, 'Endless Trouble For India If China–Nepal Project Opposed: Chinese State Media', 12 December 2016.

46. Ibid.

47. *Times of India*, 'China Launches New Cargo Service Linking Tibet with Nepal', 10 December 2016.

48. Tom Lantos, 'Tibet: The Washington Perspective', *Cultural Survival*, March 1988, https://www.culturalsurvival.org/publications/cultural-survival-quarterly/tibet-washington-perspective

49. John Avedon, *In Exile from the Land of Snows* (Vintage; reprint edition 2015).

50. http://news.xinhuanet.com/english/2009-10/20/content_12282061.htm; *Indian Express*, 'China Opposes Dalai Lama's Visit to Arunachal', 20 October 2009.

51. http://news.rediff.com/report/2009/oct/21/why-indo-china-rivalry-may-spin-out-of-control.htm, 21 October 2009.

52. 'Dalai Lama Can Visit Arunachal: Krishna', 18 September 2009, http://theasiandefence.blogspot.com/2009_09_01_archive.html

53. *Times of India*, 'Day before PM–Wen Meet, Rao Says No Curbs on Dalai', 24 October 2009.

54. Ibid.

55. At the press conference following the Seventh India–ASEAN and Fourth East Asia Summit in Hua Hin (Thailand) the PM said the 'Dalai Lama Is Our Honoured Guest'. Read *Outlook*, 25 October 2009.

56. Subramanian Swamy, 'Sino-Indian Relations through the Tibet Prism', *Frontline*, 15 September 2000.

57. The Dalai Lama has been articulating the phrase for a long time in the context of India–Tibet relations.

58. The Dalai Lama and his prime minister, Samdhong Rinpoche, have started making statements since 2006 that Tawang is part of India.

59. http://tibetreport.wordpress.com/page/2, 19 November 2009

60. *Wall Street Journal*, 'India Shows the World How to Stand Firm with China', 28 October 2009.

61. Ibid.

62. China Tibet Online, 'Claiming "Fear in Tibet", Dalai Lama Tells Lies Again', 6 November 2009, http://chinatibet.people.com.cn/6806275.html; also see Agencies, 'Chinese Official Media Slams Dalai Lama as a "Liar"', 6 November 2009.

63. Prem Shankar Jha, 'It's a Dim Sum Game', *Hindustan Times*, 20 October 2009.

64. *Hindustan Times*, 'Tawang Is Part of India: Dalai Lama', 4 June 2008.

65. AFP, 'Dalai Lama Draws Huge Crowds on Visit Slammed by China', 9 November 2009.

66. PTI, 'Dalai Lama Surprised over China's Claim to Tawang', 8 November 2009.

67. *Times of India*, 'Centre Curbs Dalai Lama, Tells Media to Leave Tawang', 12 November 2009.

68. *Hindustan Times*, 'India on the Wrong Track, Says Chinese Scholar', 10 November 2009.

69. *People's Daily*, 'India Covets Dalai Lama's Visit', 9 November 2009; Times Now, 'After Dalai Lama's Rebuke, China Breathes Fire', 9 November 2009.

70. As quoted in *Times of India*, 'Dalai Visit a Betrayal: China', 15 September 2009.

71. *Outlook*, 'Dalai Lama's Tawang Visit his Own Initiative: Tharoor', 9 November 2009.

72. AFP, 'US Supports Dalai Lama Visit to Indian State: Report', 7 November 2009.

73. *Hindustan Times*, 'Dalai Lama Damaging Ties with India: China', 3 November 2009.

74. The MEA denied him permission, reportedly under pressure from China. Read *Hindustan Times*, 'Sino–India Hotspot Tawang on Dalai Lama Radar Again', 9 September 2009.

75. *Week*, 'Dalai Lama Feels His Next Reincarnation Could Be from India', 19 March 2019.

76. *Global Times*, 'Standardization of Terms Aimed At Reaffirming Sovereignty: Experts', 18 April 2017.

77. PTI, 'China Defends Its Decision, Says It Has Lawful Right to Standardise Names in Arunachal', 21 April 2017.

78. *Hindustan Times*, 'China Has No Right to Rename Our Cities, Arunachal Part of India: Naidu', 24 April 2017.

79. Wire, 'ULFA Faction Warns Dalai Lama against Making Anti-China Comments on Upcoming Visit', 29 March 2017.

80. NDTV, 'Pak Journalist Compares Dalai Lama with Masood Azhar, Slammed on Twitter', 14 March 2019.

81. Mary-Anne Toy, 'Dalai Lama a Terrorist: China', *Sydney Morning Herald*, 3 April 2008.

Chapter 9

1. B. Raman, 'The Karmapa Controversy', *Outlook*, 1 February 2011; also read Rahul Tripathi, 'Govt Set to Lift Travel Restriction on the 17th Karmapa', *Indian Express*, 24 May 2017, https://indianexpress.com/article/india/govt-set-to-lift-travel-restrictions-on-17th-karmapa-4670688 (accessed 3 November 2018).

2. 'The Gyalwang Karmapa Expresses His Birthday Wish—To Visit His Homeland', https://kagyuoffice.org/the-gyalwang-karmapa-expresses-his-birthday-wish-to-visit-his-homeland (accessed 4 January 2019).

3. Naresh Kumar Sharma, 'Raid at Karmapa Monastery over Benami Land Deal', *Times of India*, 28 January 2011, https://timesofindia.indiatimes.com/india/Raid-at-Karmapa-monastery-over-benami-land-deal/articleshow/7376096.cms

4. P. Stobdan, 'The Flight of the Karmapa is Further Proof That India Has No Tibet Card', Wire, 7 August 2018.

5. 'The Karmapa Speaks of His Plans: An Interview with Radio Free Asia', Offices of Radio Free Asia, Washington, D.C., 30 July 2018; also see https://kagyuoffice.org/the-karmapa-speaks-of-his-plans-an-interview-with-radio-free-asia (accessed 9 July 2018).

6. The message has been removed since from the Kagyu's official website (http://kagyuoffice.org) and Facebook account (https://www.facebook.com/karmapa) but it is available on YouTube, https://www.youtube.com/watch?v=AdI4DMRFkm4 (accessed 2 January 2019).

7. 'Karmapa Has Something Special and Personal to Share with You . . .', https://www.karmapa.org/special-news (accessed 6 October 2018).

8. Asia News, 'The Karmapa Lama Issued Passport of Dominica', 11 February 2018, http://www.asianews.it/news-en/The-Karmapa-Lama-issued-passport-of-Dominica-45369.html (accessed 20 December 2018).

9. P. Stobdan, '2 Karmapas Are Uniting and It's Time for India to Deal with It in a Mature Way', Quint, 10 December 2018.

10. Joint Statement of His Holiness Ogyen Trinley Dorje and His Holiness Trinley Thaye Dorje, https://kagyuoffice.org/joint-statement-of-his-holiness-ogyen-trinley-dorje-and-his-holiness-trinley-thaye-dorje (accessed 2 January 2019).

11. https://www.facebook.com/pg/Gyalwang.Drukpa/posts/?ref=page_internal (accessed 11 October 2018).

12. Lobsang Wangyal, 'India Still Hasn't Issued Visa to Karmapa to Attend Conference', *Tibet Sun*, 11 September 2018, https://www.tibetsun.

com/news/2018/11/09/india-still-hasnt-issued-visa-to-karmapa-to-attend-conference (accessed 9 March 2019).

13. https://www.youtube.com/watch?v=T45aMxg6w4Q&feature=youtu.be (accessed 9 March 2019).

14. Wire, 'Asked the Indian Government for a Visa Last Year, Says Karmapa in New Video', 23 January 2019 (accessed 6 March 2019).

15. Wire, 'Despite Grievances, India Said to Be Willing to Grant Visa to Karmapa Claimant Dorje', 27 December 2018 (accessed 1 March 2019).

16. Ibid.

17. *The Hindu*, 'Cloud over Key Tibetan Meet As Delhi Stalls Karmapa's Return', 8 December 2018.

18. *Times of India*, 'Dorje No Longer Recognised by Indian Govt As 17th Karmapa', 28 December 2018, https://timesofindia.indiatimes.com/india/dorje-no-longer-recognised-by-indian-govt-as-17th-karmapa/articleshowprint/67279793.cms 2/3

19. 'The Measures for the Administration of the Reincarnation of Living Buddhism in Tibetan Buddhism' was adopted by the State Council for Religious Affairs on 13 July 2007 and came into effect on 1 September 2007, http://www.gov.cn/gongbao/content/2008/content_923053.htm (accessed 3 May 2019).

20. http://www.xinhuanet.com/english/2018-04/28/c_137142349.htm (accessed 3 May 2019).

21. 'The Gyalwang Karmapa Expresses His Birthday Wish—To Visit His Homeland', https://kagyuoffice.org/the-gyalwang-karmapa-expresses-his-birthday-wish-to-visit-his-homeland (accessed 4 January 2019).

22. Swati Chawla, 'India & China Find Another Doklam-like Controversy in 17th Karmapa', Quint, 7 January 2019, https://www.thequint.com/voices/opinion/india-china-seventeenth-karmapa-visa-controversy-doklam (accessed 6 May 2019).

Chapter 10

1. Peter Schwieger, *The Dalai Lama and the Emperor of China: A Political History of the Tibetan Institution of Reincarnation* (Columbia University Press, March 2015).

2. Thubten Jigme Norbu and Colin Turnbull, *Tibet: Its History, Religion and People* (Penguin Books, 1987, reprint), p. 272.

3. L.L. Mehrotra, 'India's Tibet Policy', Tibetan Parliamentary and Policy Research Centre, New Delhi, 1997, p. 15.

4. Warren W. Smith, *China's Tibet? Autonomy or Assimilation* (Rowman & Littlefield, 2009), p. 48.

5. Ibid.

6. https://www.dalailama.com/office/the-dalai-lama-trust (accessed 8 July 2018).

7. http://siddharthaschool.org (accessed 8 July 2018).

8. https://www.dalailama.com/news/2016/visiting-the-villages-of-saboo-and-stok (accessed 9 July 2018).

9. https://www.dalailama.com/news/2009/hh-the-dalai-lama-visits-jamyang-school (accessed 9 July 2018).

10. http://www.wiseoldsayings.com/authors/george-orwell-quotes (accessed 24 January 2019).

11. 'Teachings', https://www.dalailama.com/teachings (accessed 7 June 2018).

12. 'Tibetans Are Not Anti-Chinese, His Holiness Tells Chinese Reporters', 16 April 2008, https://www.dalailama.com/news/2008/tibetans-are-not-anti-chinese-his-holiness-tells-chinese-reporters (accessed 7 June 2018).

13. '[Géopolitique] Buddhist soft power, Chinese-style', 23 June 2014, https://www.market.ch/fr/blogs/details/article/geopolitique-buddhist-soft-power-chinese-style.html

14. *New Indian Express*, 'Hush! Tibet Government in Exile Plays Footsie With China', 1 May 2016.

15. Quoted by K. Wariko, *Himalayan Frontiers of India: Historical, Geo-Political and Strategic Perspectives* (Routledge, 2019), p. xi.

Chapter 11

1. 'China Through a Lens', http://www.china.org.cn/english/features/67817.htm (accessed 3 March 2019).

2. 'Water Security for India: The External Dynamics', *IDSA Task Force Report* (2010): 44, http://www.tibet.net/en/pdf/diirpub/environment/4/chap-2.pdf

3. Ibid.

4. Indrani Bagchi, 'China's River Plan Worries India', *Times of India*, 23 October 2006; *Financial Times*, 'Opening the Sluice-Gates of Controversy', 8 November 2006.

5. Arthur Thomas, 'Diverting the Brahmaputra—Start of the Water Wars?', OnLine Opinion, http://www.onlineopinion.com.au/view.asp?article=7310&page=0

6. *Indian Express*, 'Brahmaputra Dams: Govt Was Alerted, Didn't Move', 17 October 2009.
7. Xhau Wei, 'Divided Waters in China', Chinadialogue, 2011, https://www.chinadialogue.net/article/4539-Divided-waters-in-China (accessed 6 March 2018).
8. Cited by Jesper Svensson, 'Managing the Rise of a Hydro-Hegemon in Asia China's Strategic Interests in the Yarlung-Tsangpo River', IDSA Occasional Paper No. 23, April 2012, p. 23.
9. Claude Arpi, 'Water War in South Asia? Brahmaputra: Dam and Diversion', *South Asia Politic*, October 2003.
10. Read more about the project from the site of the Bureau of South-to-North Water Transfer Planning and Design Ministry of Water, http://www.mwr.gov.cn/english1/20040827/39304.asp
11. Emma Young, 'China Approves Colossal River Diversion Plan', NewScientist.com, 26 November 2002.
12. Scott Moore, 'Issue Brief: Water Resource Issues, Policy and Politics in China', The Brookings Institution, 12 February 2013 (accessed 23 October 2018).
13. Kevin Holden Platt, 'China Diverting Major River to "Water" Beijing Olympics, *National Geographic* News, 28 February 2008.
14. Jessica Williams, 'The International Implications of China's Water Policies', E-International Relations, 15 February 2013 (accessed 15 December 2018).
15. The Tsangpo gorge is eight times steeper and three times larger than the Colorado in the Grand Canyon. It makes a dramatic U-turn towards India at the Great Bend. It descends 3000 metres in just 200 kilometres, thus making it the greatest hydropower potential in the world. It has a generating capacity of 67,000 MW.
16. Brahma Chellaney, 'China–India Clash over Chinese Claims to Tibetan Water', *Asia-Pacific Journal*, 3 July 2017.
17. Quoted by Jonathan Holslag, 'Assessing the Sino-Indian Water Dispute', *Journal of International Affairs* 64.2, Sino-Indian Relations (Spring–Summer 2011): 19–35, https://www.jstor.org/stable/24385532
18. Claude Arpi, 'Diverting the Brahmaputra, Declaration of War?', Rediff, 23 October 2003.
19. *Scientific American*, '"Peaceful" Nuclear Explosions', June 1996, http://www.sciamdigital.com/index.cfm?fa=Products.ViewIssuePreview&ARTICLEID_ CHAR=2D0B01AD-FC0F-45C4-B084-0A8DC1C060E

20. Read more on this subject from Claude Arpi, 'The Feasability of Diverting the Brahmaputra', 17 March 2014, http://claudearpi. blogspot.com/2014/02/the-feasibility-of-diverting-brahmaputra.html

21. *Times of India*, 'China Conducted 3–4 Nuclear Blasts in Tibet in 2005 to Divert Brahmaputra', 29 August 2013.

22. Water is adding to China's conflict with the Tibetans. The Dalai Lama has been deploring China's water plans.

23. Elizabeth McDougal, 'Drakngak Lingpa's Pilgrimage Guides and the Progressive Opening of the Hidden Land of Pemakö', https:// www.academia.edu/25285911/Drakngak_Lingpas_Pilgrimage_ Guides_and_the_Progressive_Opening_of_the_Hidden_Land_of_ Pemak%C3%B6 (accessed 6 March 2019).

24. Stephen Chen, 'Chinese Engineers Plan 1,000km Tunnel to Make Xinjiang Desert Bloom', *South China Morning Post*, 29 October, 2017.

25. *Economic Times*, 'China Denies Report of Tunnel Plan to Divert Brahmaputra River'//economictimes.indiatimes.com/ articleshow/61357594.cms?from=mdr&utm_source= contentofinterest&utm_medium=text&utm_campaign=cppst (accessed 9 July 2018).

26. Peter Zeitler, Anne Meltzer, Brian Zurek, Lucy Brown, Noah Finnegan, Bernard Hallet, Page Chamberlain, William Kidd and Peter Koons, 'Surface-Tectonic Coupling At the Namche Barwa–Gyala Peri Massif and Geologic Hazards Associated with a Proposed Dam on the Yarlung-Tsangpo River in SE Tibet', *Himalayan Journal of Sciences*, http://www.nepjol.info/index.php/HJS/article/view/1348/1328

27. 'The abstract of the study of surface-tectonic coupling at the Namche Barwa–Gyala Peri massif and geologic hazards associated with a proposed dam on the Yarlung–Tsangpo River in SE Tibet presented at the Twenty-third Himalayan–Karakoram–Tibet Workshop held in 2008 in India summed up by stating that any dam placed there would be at high risk due to pronounced seismic hazards and focused deformation.' Peter Zeitler, Anne Meltzer, Brian Zurek, Lucy Brown, Noah Finnegan, B. Hallet, Page Chamberlain, William Kidd, P. Koons, *Himalayan Journal of Sciences* 5.7 (September 2008).

28. 'Fresh water flow is decreasing . . . upland diversion of water impacting on agriculture due to desertification', according to Quamrul Islam, former chairman of the Global Water Partnership, South Asia. Sarah Stewart, 'Asian Rivers Being Choked by Detritus of Breakneck

Development', AFP, 22 February 2007, http://www.spacedaily.com/reports/Asian_Rivers_Being_Choked_By_Detritus_Of_Breakneck_Development_999.html (accessed 5 June 2017).

29. Central Water Commission, http://cwc.gov.in/water-info#3 (accessed 5 June 2017).

30. *Pioneer News Service*, 'Raging Sutlej threatens Kinnaur', 28 June 2005.

31. The character of silt in the Sutlej has changed and is causing problems for the Nathpa Jhakri Project in Himachal Pradesh.

32. In 2002, India and China signed an MoU for sharing hydrological information on the Yaluzangbo-Brahmaputra River. The Chinese side is providing hydrological information (water level, discharge and rainfall) in respect of three stations, namely, Nugesha, Yangcun and Nuxia, located on Yaluzangbo/Brahmaputra, from 1 June to 15 October every year. The data is utilized in the formulation of flood forecasts by the Central Water Commission. A similar agreement for hydrological data on Sutlej (Langqen Zangbo) was signed in 2005, http://wrmin.nic.in/printsearchdetail1.asp?skey=china&lid=372 (accessed 9 June 2017)

33. 'Memorandum of Understanding between the Ministry of Water Resources, the Republic of India and the Ministry of Water Resources, the People's Republic of China on Strengthening Cooperation on Trans-border Rivers', Indian Ministry of External Affairs, 23 October 2013.

34. *Times of India*, 'Chinese Assurance on Trans-Border Rivers', 15 January 2008.

35. Experts and environmentalists felt Bangladesh would turn into a desert if the water flow of Brahmaputra was diverted. Read 'China plans to divert Brahmaputra waters', 8 May 2007, http://www.bangladeshnews.com.bd/2007/05/08/china-plans-to-divert-brahmaputra-waters

36. *Times of India*, 'Finally, Pranab Calls China a Challenge', 5 November 2008.

37. Ibid.

38. Ma Danning, 'A Lifeline to Tibet's Medog County', *China Daily*, 21 October 2014, 'Medog was the last county in China to have a road. Highway construction to Medog had begun in 2008. Medog (lotus flower) is located on the southern slope of the Namjagbarwa Peak. Monba and Luoba living in Medog are akin to Cona Monba in Arunachal. Nyingchi's seven counties are Nyingchi, Mainling, Gongbo'gyamda, Medog, Bome, Zaya and Nang.'

39. Amitava Mukherjee, 'China and India: River Wars in the Himalayas', *Geopolitical Monitor*, April 2014 (accessed 16 June 2018).

40. See Q. No. 52: Dam on Brahmaputra by China, Rajya Sabha, 3 December 2015 (accessed 17 January 2019).

41. Q. No. 2520: Dam on Brahmaputra by China, Lok Sabha, 26 December 2018.

42. *Hindustan Times*, 'China Begins Sharing Crucial Brahmaputra Data', 17 May 2018; also see PTI, 'India, China Sign Two MoUs on Sharing of Brahmaputra River Data and Supply of Non-Basmati Rice', 9 June 2018.

43. 'Water resources and the Sino-Indian strategic partnership', 45 China Rights Forum No. 1, 2006, https://www.hrichina.org/sites/default/files/PDFs/CRF.1.2006/CRF-2006-1_Water.pdf (accessed 5 March 2019).

44. Rediff, 'Arunachal Pradesh Is Our Territory: Chinese Envoy', 14 November 2006, https://www.rediff.com/news/2006/nov/14china.htm (accessed 23 December 2018).

45. Navin Singh Khadka, 'China and India Water "Dispute" after Border Stand-off', BBC World Service, 18 September 2017.

46. Anil Sasi, 'As Clearances Turn Into Hurdles, Brahmaputra Edge Lost to China', *Indian Express*, 21 October 2015 (accessed 20 June 2018).

47. Sonali Mittra, 'The Brahmaputra Conundrum', *Indian Express*, 4 December 2017.

48. According to Joseph W. Dellapenna, there is an international agreement that 'only riparian nations—nations across which, or along which, a river flows—have any legal right, apart from an agreement, to use the water of a river'. *UNESCO Courier*, 'Custom-Built Solutions for International Disputes', as quoted by Roman Kupchinsky. 'World: Water Could Become Major Catalyst for Conflict', 16 September 2005, https://www.rferl.org/a/1061446.html

49. Beth Walker, 'India and China Ignore UN Watercourses Convention', *China Dialogue*, 18 August 2014 (accessed 30 January 2019).

50. 'China Admits to Brahmaputra Project', 22 April 2010, http://www.2point6billion.com/news/2010/04/22/china-confirms-brahmaputra-river-projects-5423.html

51. Gareth Evans, http://www.crisisgroup.org/home/index.cfm?id=5648&l=1

52. Claude Arpi, 'Diverting the Indus River to Xinjing: A Pilot Project', 13 December 2014, https://fnvaworld.org/portfolio-item/diverting-the-indus-river-to-xinjiang-a-pilot-project

53. Claude Arpi, 'Diverting the Indus . . . or the Yarlung Tsangpo to Xinjiang', *Indian Defence Review*, 11 August 2017, http://www.indiandefencereview.com/diverting-the-indus-or-the-yarlung-tsangpo-to-xinjiang

54. K.P. Nayar, 'Water Weapons Cuts Both Ways: China Factor in Indus Card', *Telegraph*, 24 September 2016.

55. P. Wester, A. Mishra, A. Mukherji and A.B. Shrestha, eds, *The Hindu Kush Himalaya Assessment: Mountains, Climate Change, Sustainability and People*, Springer, 2019.

56. Geoffrey Dabelko, 'Talking Water and Opportunities for Environmental Peacemaking', *Circle of Blue/WaterNews*, 8 May 2008, http://www.circleofblue.org/waternews/world/africa/geoffrey-dableko-talking-water-and-opportunities-for-environmental-peacemaking; also read *Guardian Weekly*, 'Dam the consequences', 6 April 2007.

57. Kevin Holden Platt, 'A Competition for Water', *Bangkok Post*, 18 March 2008.

58. Gareth Evans, 'Conflict Potential in a World of Climate Change', Address to Bucerius Summer School on Global Governance 2008, Berlin, 29 August 2008, http://www.crisisgroup.org/home/index.cfm?id=5648&l=1; also read Jannik Boesen and Helle Munk Ravnborg, 'From Water Wars to Water Riots? Lessons from Trans-boundary Water Management', Proceedings of the International Conference, December 2003, DISS Copenhagen, published as DISS Working Paper 2004/6.

59. *Forbes*, 'Environmental Protests Expose Weakness in China's Leadership', 22 June 2015; also read Charlton Lewis, 'China's Great Dam Boom: A Major Assault on Its Rivers', https://e360.yale.edu/features/chinas_great_dam_boom_an_assault_on_its_river_systems (accessed 10 January 2019).

60. P. Stobdan, 'As the Brahmaputra Bends', *Indian Express*, 17 April 2013, http://archive.indianexpress.com/news/as-the-brahmaputra-bends/1104650

Chapter 12

1. http://himalaya.socanth.cam.ac.uk/collections/journals/jbs/pdf/JBS_26_01.pdf (accessed 9 July 2018).

2. https://www.thestatesman.com/opinion/little-bhutan-in-tibet-1500238963.html (accessed 3 September 2018).

3. https://www.dailypioneer.com/2016/columnists/one-country-which-has-not-been-nice.html (accessed 23 October 2018).

4. Claude Arpi, *Born in Sin: The Panchsheel Agreement: The Sacrifice of Tibet* (Mittal Publications, 2014), p. 96.

5. Ibid.

6. India's positions since 1959 are vividly reflected in the 'Notes, Memoranda and Letters Exchanged and Agreements Signed between the Governments of India and China (White Paper IV for the period between September 1959–March 1960)', published by the Government of India, http://www.claudearpi.net/white-papers-on-china (accessed 5 April 2018).

7. http://www.claudearpi.net/the-sino-indian-boundary-issue (accessed 6 July 2018).

8. Note given by the Ministry of Foreign Affairs, Peking, to the Embassy of India in China, 2 November 1961, 'Notes, Memoranda and Letters Exchanged and Agreements Signed between the Governments of India and China, November 1961–July 1962', White Paper No.VI, Ministry of External Affairs, Government of India.

9. http://himalaya.socanth.cam.ac.uk/collections/journals/jbs/pdf/JBS_26_01.pdf (accessed 9 July 2018).

Chapter 13

1. Official spokesperson's response to a query regarding a recent media report on the government's position on His Holiness the Dalai Lama, 2 March 2018, https://www.mea.gov.in/media-briefings.htm?dtl/29532/Official+Spokespersons+response+to+a+query+regarding+a+recent+media+report+on+the+Governments+position+on+His+Holiness+the+Dalai+Lama (accessed 7 May 2018).

2. Wire, 'As Dalai Lama Event is Shifted From Delhi, Modi's New Line on Tibet Remains a Puzzle', 6 March 2018, https://thewire.in/diplomacy/experts-unravel-the-puzzle-of-indian-govts-circular-on-distancing-from-dalai-lama-event

3. P. Stobdan, 'The Modi Government Must Realise the Folly of India Playing the "Tibet Card"', Wire, 30 March 2018.

4. https://www.bbc.com/news/world-asia-china-43361276 (11 March 2018).

5. *Hindustan Times*, 'Past Is Past: Dalai Lama Says Tibet Wants to Stay with China, Wants Development', 23 November 2017.

6. Manogya Lolwal, 'From "My Friend China" to "Attractive" Female Dalai Lama: What 14th Dalai Lama Said in Tawang', *India Today*, 8 April 2017.

7. Indiatimes, 'Tibet Wants "Meaningful Autonomy", Not Independence from China, Says Dalai Lama', https://www.indiatimes.com/news/india/tibet-wants-meaningful-autonomy-not-independence-from-china-says-dalai-lama-275005.html (accessed 7 May 2018).

8. PTI, 'Trump Regime Proposes Zero Aid to Tibetans in 2018', 26 May 2017.

9. VOA, 'Citing Fatigue, Dalai Lama Appoints Personal Emissaries, 17 November 2017.

10. *Chicago Tribune*, 'Dalai Lama Laments NYC's Tragedy', 19 September 2003.

11. https://www.cbsnews.com/news/dalai-lama-at-mayo-clinic-for-evaluation (accessed 8 July 2018).

12. https://www.postbulletin.com/news/local/report-dalai-lama-in-good-health/article_f5d797fb-0535-50b7-96f4-ff689af0cbb4.html (accessed 5 July 2018).

13. *Independent*, 'Prince Upsets Chinese with "Appalling Waxworks" Jibe', https://www.independent.co.uk/news/uk/politics/prince-upsets-chinese-with-appalling-waxworks-jibe-326844.html (accessed 23 December 2018).

14. 'Dignitaries Met 2011–Present', https://www.dalailama.com/the-dalai-lama/events-and-awards/dignitaries-met

15. Christian Science Monitor, 'At White House, the Dalai Lama Sidesteps Trash', 19 February 2010.

16. K.P. Nayar, 'Photo-op Gets China's Goat: Tibetan "Debut" at Modi Swearing-in', *Telegraph*, 8 June 2014.

17. Indrani Bagchi, 'Tibetan Leader at Modi's Swearing-in Irks China', *Times of India*, 5 June 2015, http://timesofindia.indiatimes.com/articleshow/36080500.cms?utm_source=contentofinterest&utm_medium=text&utm_campaign=cppst

18. Jyoti Malhotra, 'The Dalai Lama Is Making Overtures to Beijing Even As China Seems to Be Hardening Its Stand', *India Today*, 2 July 2015,

https://www.indiatoday.in/magazine/cover-story/story/20150713-dalai-lama-narendra-modi-beijing-china-india-820022-2015-07-02

19. https://thewire.in/diplomacy/lobsang-sangey-not-invited-modi-swearing-in (accessed 2 June 2019).

20. C. Raja Mohan, 'Chinese Takeaway: Modi's Buddhism', *Indian Express*, 3 December 2017.

21. *India Today*, 'The Dalai Lama Is Making Overtures to Beijing Even As China Seems to Be Hardening Its Stand', 3 July 2015.

22. PTI, 'Bihar Results Show Majority of Hindus Still Believe in Peace: Dalai Lama', 15 November 2015.

23. *DNA*, 'Subramanian Swamy Hits Out at Dalai Lama for His "Majority of Hindus Believe in Peace" Comment', 15 November 2015.

24. NDTV, 'Partition Wouldn't Happen If Nehru Had Not Been Self-Centered: Dalai Lama', 8 August 2018.

25. P.K. Vasudeva, 'Dalai Lama Forgets Nehru's Efforts', *Tribune*, 24 August 2018, https://www.tribuneindia.com/news/comment/dalai-lama-forgets-nehru-s-efforts/641748.html (accessed 9 October 2018).

26. 'First, we must deepen the struggle against the Dalai Lama clique, make it the highest priority in carrying out our ethnic affairs, and the long-term mission of strengthening ethnic unity,' Tibet party secretary Wu Yingjie said in a speech. See https://www.scmp.com/news/china/policies-politics/article/2023969/china-says-countering-dalai-lama-influence-top-ethnic (accessed 9 May 2018).

27. 'Tibet, the 19th Party Congress and UFWD', https://tibet.net/2017/11/tibet-the-19th-party-congress-and-chinas-united-front-work (accessed 5 June 2018).

28. 'China's Communist Party Will Pick the Next Dalai Lama, Period!', http://www.asianews.it/news-en/China%E2%80%99s-Communist-Party-will-pick-the-%E2%80%9Cnext-Dalai-Lama,-period!%E2%80%9D-34948.html (accessed 9 July 2017).

29. *China Daily*, 'China Issues White Paper on Tibet', 6 September 2015, http://usa.chinadaily.com.cn/china/2015-09/06/content_21796167.htm (accessed 6 June 2017).

30. Reuters, 'China Marks Tibet Anniversary with Rallying Cry against Dalai Lama', 8 September 2015.

31. *Global Times*, 'Real Tibet Can't Be Concealed by Dalai's Lies', http://www.globaltimes.cn/content/941137.shtml (accessed 8 July 2017).

32. Annie Gowen, 'Possible Thaw between China and Dalai Lama on Tibet', *Sydney Morning Herald*, 3 October 2014.

33. Livemint, 'China's Communist Party Officials Funding the Dalai Lama: Report', 2 May 2017, also at https://www.tibetworlds.com/2017/10/28/tenzin-dhonden-the-corrupt-emissary-of-dalai-lama (accessed 4 June 2018).

34. Tim Johnson, *Tragedy in Crimson: How the Dalai Lama Conquered the World but Lost the Battle with China* (Bold Type Books, 2011).

35. Richard Moleofe, 'The Dalai Lama Dilemma for Botswana', 11 March 2019, http://www.sundaystandard.info/dalai-lama-dilemma-botswana

36. *Times of India*, 'Quad Move Will Dissipate Like Sea Foam: China', 8 March 2018.

37. 'Text of Prime Minister's Keynote Address at Shangri La Dialogue', Press Information Bureau, Government of India, Prime Minister's Office, 1 June 2018.

38. http://www.xinhuanet.com/english/2017-06/09/c_136352245.htm (accessed 9 September 2018).

39. PTI, 'UN Lists JeM Chief Masood Azhar As Global Terrorist after China Lifts Hold', 2 May 2019.

40. https://www.aninews.in/videos/world/improved-strategic-communication-china-helped-listing-masood-azhar-mea (accessed 13 June 2019).

41. *India Today*, 'US Calls Out China's Hypocrisy of Protecting Masood Azhar and Detaining Country's Muslims', 28 March 2019.

42. http://www.tibetanjournal.com/without-choice-india-china-live-side-side-dalai-lama (accessed 21 January 2018).

43. https://www.dalailama.com/the-dalai-lama/biography-and-daily-life/questions-answers (accessed 2 June 2019).

44. A vocal Tibetan refugee, Lukar Jam, said during the 2015 election, stirring up quite a controversy, 'I have separated the spiritual and political Dalai Lama and criticize only his political policies', https://www.dailysignal.com/2015/10/29/why-the-legacy-of-tibets-cold-war-freedom-fighters-still-matters (accessed 4 September 2017).

45. Mila Rangzen, 'Is Dharamshala Safe for Tibetans?' *Tibet Telegraph*, 12 June 2014, http://www.tibettelegraph.com/2014/06/is-dharamshala-safe-for-tibetans.html

46. Younten Phuntsok, 'We Are Losing Our Ground: Tibetan Struggle', 16 June 2015, https://victimofred.wordpress.com/tag/karmapa

47. 'Self-immolations by Tibetans', 10 December 2018, https://www.savetibet.org/resources/fact-sheets/self-immolations-by-tibetans

48. Evan Osnos, 'The Next Incarnation', *New Yorker*, 27 September 2010.

49. Science Times, 'China Aide Says Dalai Lama Asserting Reincarnation May End with Him Is "Blasphemy"', 16 March 2015, http://www.sciencetimes.com/articles/4273/20150316/tibetan-government-on-dalai-lamas-desire-not-to-reincarnate-its-not-his-decision.htm

50. *Daily Mail*, 'Dalai Lama Says He Could Be Succeeded by a Woman . . . but Only If She Is Pretty', 23 September 2015, https://www.dailymail.co.uk/news/article-3246510/Dalai-Lama-says-succeeded-woman-PRETTY.html

51. 'Dalai Lama's comments demonstrate sexist beauty standards', http://dailyorange.com/2015/09/gala-dalai-lamas-comments-demonstrate-sexist-beauty-standards (accessed 29 December 2017).

52. https://www.huffingtonpost.in/entry/dalai-lama-on-female-successor_in_5d15ddfee4b07f6ca57b9b14?ncid=other_facebook_eucluwzme5k&fbclid=IwAR36KALLV0M0kdQ_fEY78SsRYA_hmxM5BpkVDHl0FnVlJzfPpG66qUSmq-w (accessed 28 June 2019).

53. https://www.dalailama.com/the-dalai-lama/biography-and-daily-life/questions-answers (accessed 23 March 2019).

54. *Ecumenical News*, 'China Aide Says Dalai Lama Asserting Reincarnation May End with Him Is Blasphemy', 12 March 2015, https://www.ecumenicalnews.com/article/china-aide-says-dalai-lama-asserting-reincarnation-may-end-with-him-is-blasphemy/28655.htm

55. *Hindustan Times*, 'China Signals Policy Shift on Dalai Lama', 5 April 2016.

56. Xinhua, 'China Opposes US Resolution on Tibet Issue', 28 April 2018.

57. https://www.business-standard.com/article/news-ians/china-not-to-recognise-dalai-lama-s-indian-successor-119031900561_1.html (accessed 19 March 2019).

Chapter 14

1. https://www.buddhistchannel.tv/index.php?id=42,5778,0,0,1,0#.XRYz0OgzbIU (accessed 28 July 2017).

2. '[Géopolitique] Buddhist soft power, Chinese-style', https://www. market.ch/de/mitteilung/details/article/geopolitique-buddhist-soft-power-chinese-style.html (accessed 8 August 2017).

3. https://www.forbes.com/sites/ericjackson/2014/05/23/sun-tzus-33-best-pieces-of-leadership-advice/#2a1b97095e5e (accessed 9 August 2017).

4. P. Stobdan, 'The Modi Government Must Realise the Folly of India Playing the "Tibet Card", Wire, 30 March 2018.

5. https://www.newsweek.com/tibetan-exiles-heartened-chinese-economy-389129 (accessed 4 September 2017).

6. 'The Charter of Tibetans in-Exile, the Constitution of Tibet', http://www.servat.unibe.ch/icl/t100000_.html (accessed 3 March 2018).

7. Tibetan Review, 'Kalon Tripa to Be Now Referred to as Sikyong', 22 September 2012.

8. 'President of CTA', https://tibet.net/tag/president-of-cta (accessed 5 June 2018).

9. Thierry Mathou, 'Bhutan-China Relations: Towards a New Step in Himalayan Politics', Bhutan Studies 20 (2004): 388–411, http://www.bhutanstudies.org.bt/publicationFiles/ConferenceProceedings/SpiderAndPiglet/19-Spdr&Pglt.pdf (accessed 15 January 2014).

Chapter 15

1. Ian Johnson, 'What a Buddhist Monk Taught Xi Jinping', New York Times, 24 March 2017.

2. Ibid.

3. Teahouse, 'The Buddha's Guiding Hand in the Chinese Dream', https://teahouse.buddhistdoor.net/the-buddhas-guiding-hand-in-the-chinese-dream (accessed 10 August 2017).

4. Lyudmila Klasanova, 'Asian Buddhist Conference for Peace Marks 50th Anniversary in Mongolia', Buddhistdoor Global, 24 June 2019.

5. 'CTA's Religious and Cultural Department barred from attending the ABCP 2019', https://tibet.net/2019/06/bending-to-chinas-pressure-mongolia-bars-ctas-religion-and-culture-minister-from-attending-the-asian-buddhist-conference-for-peace-2019 (accessed 23 June 2019).

6. *Times of India*, 'Tsona Rinpoche Found Dead by Hanging in Delhi', 19 May 2014; Jarpum Gamlin, 'Beneath the Fissures', *The Hindu BusinessLine*, https://www.thehindubusinessline.com/blink/know/beneath-the-fissures/article8621329.ece (accessed 7 June 2018).

Chapter 16

1. 'Government Work Report, the Second People's Congress of the 12th National Congress of Ganzi Tibetan Autonomous Prefecture, 2018', China Ganzi Portal, 10 January 2018, www.gzz.gov.cn (accessed 23 December 2018).
2. Ibid.
3. *Guardian*, 'PM-in-exile Urges Tibetans to Make Dalai Lama's Return "a reality"', 1 April 2018.
4. *Tribune*, 'An Invitation to Dalai Lama', 25 June 2019.
5. https://www.nytimes.com/2018/12/21/world/asia/trump-china-tibet.html (accessed 4 June 2019).
6. Reuters, 'U.S. Ambassador Urges China to Talk to the Dalai Lama', 26 May 2019.
7. https://secureservercdn.net/198.71.233.163/4vo.170.myftpupload.com/wp-content/uploads/2019/06/Tibet-Negotiations-Report-2019-5302019.pdf (accessed 7 July 2019).
8. International Campaign for Tibet, 'Trump Administration Second Tibet Negotiation Report Shows Concern for Human Rights but Lack of Initiatives to Encourage China to Negotiate with Dalai Lama', 19 June 2019.
9. *Tibetan Review*, 'Secretary of State Pompeo assures comprehensive address of Tibetan issues with Chinese leadership', 10 June 2018.
10. https://www.state.gov/2019-ministerial-to-advance-religious-freedom (18 July 2019).
11. *Guardian*, 'China's Uighur Policy Is Human Rights "Stain of the Century": Pompeo', 19 July 2019
12. https://www.state.gov/remarks-by-vice-president-pence-at-the-2nd-annual-religious-freedom-ministerial (18 July 2019).
13. Diplomat, 'Pelosi: US Risks Losing Moral Authority with Silence on Xinjiang', 17 July 2019.

14. 'Trump Meets Survivors of Religious Persecution, Jailed Uyghur Professor Ilham Tohti's Daughter', https://www.rfa.org/english/news/uyghur/trump-07182019172306.html (18 July 2019).

15. https://www.businesstimes.com.sg/life-culture/dalai-lama-says-trump-lacks-moral-principle (18 June 2019).

16. https://tibet.net/2017/10/three-day-five-fifty-forum-concludes-with-pledges-to-revitalise-the-tibetan-movement (8 July 2018).

17. *Hindustan Times*, 'BJP Leaders Attend Dalai Lama's Dharamsala Event, Tibetan Leader in Exile Takes on China', 31 March 2018.